The Culting of America

First Edition
Printed in the United States of America

Creative Director: Saeah Wood
Editorial Director: Amy Reed
Editorial: Rukshani Lye, Matthew Hoover, Christa Evans
Design: Ivica Jandrijević
Cover Illustration: Elizabeth Evey
Author Photos: Jeku Arce (Daniella Mestyanek Young) and Brian Relph (Amy Reed)

Portions of this book originally appeared on author Daniella Mestyanek Young's
social media accounts, including Threads (@daniellamyoung_), Instagram
(@daniellamyoung_), YouTube (@KnittingCultLady), TikTok (@knitting.cult.lady),
and various now-inactive TikTok accounts. These posts have been revised, expanded,
and adapted for inclusion in this edition.

This book is based on research, interviews, and the authors' personal analysis. Some
names and identifying details have been changed. While care has been taken to
ensure accuracy, this work reflects the authors' interpretation and is not intended to
defame or harm any individual or organization. The content is for informational and
educational purposes only. The authors and publisher assume no responsibility for
how the material is used.

Library of Congress Control Number: 2025914874

Hardcover ISBN: 978-1-955671-82-8
Paperback ISBN: 978-1-955671-83-5
E-book ISBN: 978-1-955671-84-2
Audiobook ISBN: 978-1-955671-85-9

OTTERPINE

otterpine.com
Asheville, NC

The Culting of America

What Makes a Cult and Why We Love Them

Daniella Mestyanek Young

AND AMY REED

OTTERPINE

For our daughters

Contents

Prologue

You're probably in a cult, you just don't know it yet.

Don't believe me? See if you recognize one of the world's most notorious and widespread sex cults, with members spanning the entire socioeconomic spectrum.

Followers flocked to a charismatic leader. He radically changed American culture, and maybe even the world.[1] He was edgy, rebellious, and said exactly what the youth of America were thinking at the time. His revelations were sexual and pushed the boundaries of American culture. Men worshiped him with their money, women with their bodies.

Survivors of his cult—a few of them teenagers when they joined— initially arrived with bright eyes and visions of grandeur.[2] Little by little, they began to feel trapped, caught in a world they hadn't signed up for—filled with high commune walls, isolation, and constant surveillance. These young women were often paraded in public, luring in the money and bodies of others with their sexuality.

They had fallen down the proverbial rabbit hole into a world where none of the normal rules applied.[3] To the outside observer, they lived glamorously, while internally they sublimated themselves in order to play their parts, allowing their emotions to be deadened and suppressed, and their bodies and labor to be exploited.

Even years after their leader's death, the cult rakes in millions from followers of the Playboy brand.[4]

How *did* so many come to believe that Hugh Hefner was changing the world for the better?

* * *

This description wasn't Jim Jones, the Branch Davidians, NXIVM, or the Children of God. The Playboy Organization, more or less accepted by mainstream society, isn't the far-away, sinister, and strange world we think of when we hear the word *cult*. How could an organization so well-known actually be something a cult scholar like me could compare to a sex cult?

I was born and raised in the Children of God, a sex cult known as one of the most notorious religious sects in the world.[5] It's what most people would call a "real cult." As a survivor, a scholar, and someone who has already written one book about life behind the walls of the cult, I find a stunning number of parallels between the life I survived and what is woven throughout the reports of the survivors of life at the Playboy Mansion.

After surviving fifteen years in isolation under religious extremists, I escaped to America and threw myself into education. I became an intelligence officer in the US Army—another kind of total institution. Later I studied terrorists for my job, then earned my master's in organizational psychology at Harvard during the pandemic, just as the world slipped into its own strange, cultlike isolation.

Across all these worlds, I saw the same patterns repeat: the pull toward group control, the high cost of leaving, and the sacred assumptions that keep members tethered. Watching the pandemic unfold, I was fascinated but not surprised to see isolation do what it always does: push us into increasingly polarized mindsets, so disconnected from our fellow Americans that it sometimes feels like we no longer share the same reality.

In *The Culting of America*, I explore ten core aspects of group dynamics that I have developed to define what makes a cult. I talk about how the dynamics are used in cults and extreme groups to achieve coercive control, but also how they show up in socially accepted "cults" (like the US Army) and where we find that same behavior in groups we don't call cults—the groups we are all in. Through meticulous research and interviews with sociologists, psychologists, cult experts, and survivors, I make the case that if we look at our regular groups for signs of cultiness, we have to acknowledge that harmful group behavior exists on a spectrum, not a binary—and it is present in even some of our best "good" groups.

The truth is, many of the dynamics that scholars have used to rely on as markers of extreme groups have become strikingly common as primary features of many of America's mainstream groups today. I see cultlike behavior everywhere, in so many groups, and it's been increasing in intensity at a frightening pace. When I put it all together—everything I've studied, everything I've experienced as a cult survivor—I can't help but feel that we are living through the culting of America. And my guess is that you feel it on some level too.

I've spent my life attempting to understand cults, which I've learned is inseparable from understanding human nature, human needs, group psychology, and culture. Braided through the story of my life are truths I've come to know—that human beings will do almost anything to be accepted by a group, that we all search for belonging and purpose more than anything else in life, and that, at the end of the day, extremism is harder to recognize than any of us think.

As humans, we are programmed to look for connection, community, purpose, and an ideology to adhere to—these things give meaning to our lives. You are undoubtedly a member of many groups: families, companies, clubs, churches, political affiliations, communities, nations. You probably also have things you believe in with all your heart, ideas you will defend with passion against anyone who challenges them. But what if the very things that make you feel safest are also the ones trapping you the most? When does conviction turn into an us-versus-them mentality? When does loyalty turn into loss of autonomy?

This book will attempt to answer these questions and more, and ultimately leave you with the biggest question of all: *What cults am I in?*

Introduction

Good Cult/Bad Cult

I t's one of the most well-known groups in the world, recognized for both its pageantry and its violent missions, and many bodies have stacked up in its name. It uses tools of programming and influence like enforced isolation, chanting, appearance and attitude control, and a unique vocabulary with specialized internal significance to reinforce internal culture. This group is not shy about its design to break you down in order to build you back up. It demands strict obedience, requiring members to swear a binding oath of unquestioning loyalty to the Constitution and to obey lawful orders—violations of which may lead to imprisonment or, in extreme wartime cases, death. Never does it relent in its continual, exhaustive expectations of its members.

But it also provides unique learning resources and money for education, has one of the most robust healthcare plans of any American organization, and offers a generous retirement plan. The group is commonly used as a social elevator for people who would otherwise live in poverty. It provides members with an unparalleled camaraderie, sense of belonging, and the satisfaction of pursuing a clear objective alongside driven, like-minded people. The majority of former members—even those who have been required to kill in devotion to the mission, have been forced to invade another nation under false pretenses, or have had to bomb civilians—say they are proud to be veterans of the United States Army.[1]

* * *

What makes a group a cult? And who decides? There are lots of lists and they don't all agree. As both a cult survivor and a scholar of cults and extreme groups, I feel none of the current definitions are exactly right. I think what is sometimes lost in translation is that it isn't a simple binary question that can be easily answered with a check yes or no. A cult *seems* easy to define from the outside. We've probably all seen a quick listicle of "how to tell if you are in a cult." Most Americans, with the specter of Jonestown, Waco, and Charles Manson in our recent history, truly feel we know what makes a cult. But the only thing that cult scholars can agree on is that what makes a cult has many hidden layers and is anything but easy to define.

The group I grew up in, the Children of God, is a capital-C Cult. Nobody would argue that a group guilty of using religious prostitution to gain money and followers, and which eventually became known for the extreme labor trafficking and sexual abuse of its children, was a very bad cult. Everybody outside the cult I have ever spoken to accepts this, and most of them believe that they would never fall for anything like it. Most people, it seems, think of extremism as a line in the sand, where you stand on one side or the other. But what I learned from my time studying the border of Afghanistan and Pakistan as an intelligence officer in an Army combat aviation battalion is that even when a boundary looks clear on a map or from a safe distance, there's just not a sharp line when you're hovering right over it. In fact, crossing that line is incredibly easy to do, especially when you are surrounded by others who look and think just like you, sharing your utter dedication to the mission at hand.

We Americans love the idea of the binary: black-and-white thinking,[*] good versus evil, our destiny manifest, and something we can be as

---

[*] In this book, we talk a lot about binary thinking—the all-or-nothing, good-versus-evil, us-versus-them mentality that cults and high-control groups thrive on. Historically, this kind of rigid mindset has been casually referred to as "black-and-white thinking." But as Rebecca Slue (aka the White Woman Whisperer, who is herself Black and white) pointed out to me, that phrase is deeply problematic. When we casually link *black* with bad and *white* with good—even metaphorically—we're reinforcing harmful associations

sure of as the "fact" that we are number one. Since the publication of my memoir *Uncultured*, in which I unapologetically compared the US Army to a cult, I'm often asked if the Army might be a "good cult." We need the idea of a good cult because we cannot bear the cognitive dissonance of admitting that one of our oldest, largest, and proudest organizations—one we all help fund with our tax dollars—might also be a high-control and high-demand institution where group behavior can, and does, trend toxic. If we look closely enough, we might notice that an army, while it may be beloved, is a *total institution*[*] whose job is to program individuals to conduct violence on behalf of the state. We might notice, in fact, that when a military unit goes away to training or war, they are by definition going in for a cultic experience.

As much as we love our binaries, we Americans also love our blinders. We turn to patriotism rather than acknowledge these parallels and apply what experts have learned about extreme groups. We don't ensure that the leaders we put at the top aren't narcissists behind all that charisma that earns them stellar evaluations. We certainly don't train soldiers on how to determine when the logic is breaking down. If the Army *is* a "good cult," what does it owe its members in return for the exploitation of their labor and the sublimation of self that will, by definition, be required for mission success? What are we failing to see behind the veil of conviction that we are the "good guys?"

---

long embedded in our culture. This language isn't just outdated; it's alienating and painful. And if we're going to challenge culty systems of control, we have to start by examining even the metaphors we take for granted. So we are leaving *black-and-white thinking* behind. Throughout this book, we'll use words like *binary*, *either/or*, *all-or-nothing*, *dualistic*, and *polarized thinking*. Instead of *gray*, we'll talk about *nuanced*, *spectrum-based*, and *complex thinking*. Because, as you'll read more about in chapter 6, the words we use matter. And we're not here to reinforce old metaphors that served oppressive systems.

[*] A term coined by sociologist Erving Goffman, a total institution is defined as "a place of residence and work where a large number of like-situated individuals cut off from the wider society for an appreciable period of time together lead an enclosed formally-administered round of life" (Goffman, *Asylums*). More on this in chapter 4.

From my experience as an intelligence officer at war, I know we don't keep the "good guys" safe by exclusively studying other good guys, or by assuming that bad things will never happen to us. We do it by learning as much as we can about the enemy. By studying the tactics of our culture's most extreme and dangerous groups, we can learn how to keep ourselves, and our groups, safe. But this also requires the willingness to accept that the "good" groups we're in may already share some of those toxic traits, and we may already have lost some of ourselves to make way for group identity to take over.

When I first started to tell my story and share the things I was gleaning from my studies that led to this book, I was met with primarily two responses: people musing that the Children of God was an "obviously evil cult," and proud Americans stating that the "US Army is a wonderful organization." From my lived experience with both, I knew it wasn't that easy to boil down at all. As often as people laugh at my habit of drawing parallels between the cult and the Army, they also rush to assure me, and I think themselves, that there are obvious differences between a reviled sex cult and the revered US Army—and I agree. It's only when I try to define the exact difference between those two groups in the precise, scholarly, and research-based language that we use to categorize organizational dynamics, that it becomes significantly more complex to define what those differences are. People say to me that the US Army simply cannot be a cult because we "have to have an Army, and we'll always have war." So I'm stuck wondering if one of the major factors in whether we choose to call something a cult is how socially acceptable—or simply necessary—we find that group to be. We can more easily overlook red flags the more used to something we are, or the more we think we need it.

But what if "cult" isn't a yes-or-no label at all? What if it's a sliding scale—and we are all somewhere on it? For this book, I propose we set the binary aside, and reject the idea of an "obviously evil cult" or a "wonderful organization," because real life just never divides that cleanly. Instead, we'll look at all our groups through the lens of what I call "the cultiness spectrum" in order to find the parallels in toxic behavior that might be hiding in plain sight—even in our most beloved groups.

I believe a cult is both a list of qualities a group possesses and also a journey that the group and its members go on. These two cannot be easily extricated from each other. To help us assess where groups fall on the cultiness spectrum, I propose a ten-part framework, which gives a nod to both the qualities and the journey.

A cult is a group that:

1. has a defined, charismatic leader
2. requires a shared "sacred assumption"
3. pursues a transcendent mission so big it justifies sacrifice
4. demands continual sublimation of individuality
5. limits members' access to outsiders
6. creates a private vernacular
7. programs an us-versus-them mentality
8. exploits members' labor
9. enforces high exit costs
10. justifies extreme behavior as their endgame nears

At a certain tipping point in the cult journey, with the aid of inflexible group norms and strong systems, the leader practices nearly complete, and often coercive, control over its members. The "endgame" can include acts of violence, even on a mass scale, which the cult members continue to justify in pursuit of the transcendent mission. And it all makes sense to them, one step at a time. As long as the sacred assumption holds, anything is justifiable.

If your group has all ten of these features dialed up to extreme, congratulations, you are in a cult! And you probably have some strong feelings about that. For most of us, our recognition will be more subtle. You likely recognize some aspects of some of these qualities in some of your groups, and that's not necessarily a reason to panic. Most of these features are not fundamentally harmful on their own—after all, Martin Luther King Jr. was a charismatic leader; high school football teams have an us-versus-them mentality; our most esteemed charities operate with a transcendent mission; and your friend's *Dungeons & Dragons* group certainly has its own vernacular. The key is where these features fall on the spectrum of cultiness, how they operate in combination with the others, and ultimately, what harm they cause to yourself and others.

By breaking these ten cult-making features into individual parts of group behavior, we'll be able to isolate and spot them in our regular groups, without all the fear wrapped up in the question *Is this a cult?* We'll discover how these features tie directly to programming, influence, power, and control, and understand how they are weaponized in society's "obvious" cults, like the one I came from, but also in socially accepted cults, like the US Army. And we'll learn enough about these parts of coercive and controlling group dynamics to be able to see them in our own "good" and "normal" organizations, when perhaps only one or two dynamics are becoming problematic, long before it all gets out of hand and you have to call in someone like me to put a name on it—and long before you lose too much of yourself in the process.

To understand how cults show up in everyday life, we need to expand our mental map. When most people hear the word *cult*, they picture a doomsday commune in the desert, matching robes, isolation, and a charismatic leader with apocalyptic promises. And they're not wrong. Those "commune cults" are real, and some of the most harmful groups in history fit that mold. I grew up in one. But that's not the only way coercive control works. It's not even the most common way anymore.

In writing this book, I wanted to expand our collective imagination of what a cult can be. Commune cults are just one corner of the map. In my life and research, I've encountered at least three other kinds of cults that are just as real, just as damaging, and far more common than most people realize.

The 1:1 Cult. The abusive relationship that operates like its own totalitarian regime. One person calls the shots, controlling everything from what their partner wears to who they talk to, what they believe, and how they see the world. It doesn't always look like abuse—it can look like love, devotion, or protection. But if you've ever known someone who seemed to vanish into a relationship, whose light got dimmer instead of brighter, chances are you've seen a 1:1 cult in action. As they say in Alcoholics Anonymous, "It only takes two people to have a meeting"; well, the same is true for cults.

The Single-Family Cult. Not all cults need a congregation. Sometimes it's one household. One parent—usually a father, sometimes a mother—sets themselves up as the voice of God, the law of the land, the center of gravity. Their children grow up in an echo chamber of fear and control, often under the guise of religion, culture, or simply "how we do things in this house." When those kids try to leave, they face the same identity crises, exit costs, and lingering trauma as anyone fleeing a commune.

The Internet Cult. The fastest-growing category, and the hardest to spot. It doesn't have walls or uniforms. Instead it lives in group chats, TikToks, YouTube channels, and subreddit threads. These groups offer belonging, purpose, and identity. They speak in code, shut out dissenters, and often revolve around a single charismatic content creator or ideology. And like all cults, they promise transformation—but only if you buy in, follow the rules, and cut ties with anyone who doesn't get it.

Each of these groups can include all ten cult features I outline in this book—charismatic leadership, sacred assumptions, transcendent missions, the whole coercive package—just on a different scale. They don't need compounds or matching outfits. They only need your trust, your loyalty, and your willingness to surrender autonomy in exchange for certainty and belonging.

That's why this book exists: not just to help us spot the obvious cults, but to shine a light on the ones we live inside every day—the ones we join not with a bang, but with a slow, quiet nod of agreement. Cults aren't always far away and bizarre. Sometimes they're intimate. Sometimes they're inherited. And sometimes they're just one click away.

Understanding that requires both lived experience and a careful, outside perspective—which is why this book, while told in my voice, is the product of collaboration. It reflects a truly joint effort with my co-writer, Amy Reed. Our relationship began with my memoir *Uncultured* and has evolved over the years into a deeply creative and intellectual partnership. While this book remains personal and grounded in my point of view, every chapter and idea has been shaped through countless conversations, drafts, and redrafts with Amy. It wouldn't exist without the unique strengths we each brought to the table— Amy's writing craft and analytical nuance, and my obsessive research and firsthand experience. I am also immensely grateful to my talent manager, Lizy Freudmann , who contributed the essay "How America Was Born—and Learned It Was Special" in chapter 7, and to my friend and colleague Rebecca Slue (aka the White Woman Whisperer), who contributed the essay "From Groups to Community: A Shift from Performance to Presence" in chapter 11. I am still learning what community means, but I know I have found it in writing.

As Amy and I explored the inner workings of cults and control, we kept returning to one urgent question: Why are so many people vulnerable to high-control systems right now? One clue comes from President Obama's 2017 farewell address to the nation, in which he warned us of the dangers of isolation and the silos that our world, upended by technology and globalization, has put us into:

> For too many of us, it's become safer to retreat into our own bubbles, whether in our neighborhoods or on college campuses, or places of worship, or especially our social media feeds, surrounded by people who look like us and share the same political outlook and never challenge our assumptions. The rise

of naked partisanship, and increasing economic and regional stratification, the splintering of our media into a channel for every taste—all this makes this great sorting seem natural, even inevitable. And increasingly, we become so secure in our bubbles that we start accepting only information, whether it's true or not, that fits our opinions, instead of basing our opinions on the evidence that is out there.[2]

These words are eerily prescient, given the presidency and epidemic that followed, both of which exacerbated the isolation and extremism Obama identified. Although many people were shocked by these cultural shifts, some of us witnessed what seemed like the natural progression of tendencies already entrenched in the collective American psyche. We are—and always have been, since those first religious extremists, the Pilgrims, set foot on American soil—a nation defined by the distrust of institutions, a persecution complex, and stubborn self-righteousness. In many ways, cults are the most American thing there is.

Author's Note

Content Notice

This book explores cults and other high-control environments, including the emotional, psychological, and sometimes physical harm they can inflict. If you are a survivor of such an experience, please know that some of the content may be triggering or emotionally activating.

While this book and its accompanying workbook, *Unculture Yourself*, draw from research, lived experience, and the insights of others who have walked similar paths, neither is a substitute for professional help. Everyone's healing journey is different, and it's important to have support from professionals trained in the specific dynamics of cultic and high-control trauma.

If you're seeking guidance, a valuable resource is the International Cultic Studies Association (icsahome.org), which offers information and referrals for survivors, families, and professionals.

Please take care of yourself as you read. Step away when you need to. You are not alone.

On Perspective, Privilege, and the Limits of Lived Experience

I am a white woman raised in a global sex cult, trained by the US military, and educated at Harvard. These three institutions—despite their differences—share an affinity for hierarchy, mythmaking, and charismatic control. Each one taught me something about power, and about the ways people are trained to follow it. That training lives in my body, and it shapes the lens through which I view the world.

But as much as I've tried to expand my lens—to learn from the stories of others, to challenge the boundaries of what I was taught to see—I know it still has edges. I write this book as a cult survivor, a researcher, and a woman navigating systems that were never built for our full humanity. But I also write it from a place of whiteness, of access, of being granted the benefit of the doubt in rooms and systems where others are not.

Whiteness has been my shield and my sword. It opened doors that should never have been closed to begin with. It softened the edges of my rebellion and made my critiques easier for mainstream America to swallow. It also, for a long time, let me believe I was the exception—that I could walk through these systems and stay intact, that I could win the game without questioning who the game was built for.

We also need to state that the field of cult studies itself has long been shaped by white Western academics—people who, consciously or not, framed the definitions and thresholds of "extremism" through their own cultural lenses. That legacy has skewed which groups are studied, which abuses are taken seriously, and which voices get believed. And we are still reckoning with the reality that many of the tools used to analyze coercion and control were built inside the same institutions that have exercised it.

I now know better. And I know that knowing better isn't the same thing as doing better.

So while this book examines cults and high-control systems with as much rigor, honesty, and lived experience as I can bring, it is not the final word. It can't be. This is not a universal survivor story. It is not an exhaustive account of how cults harm people across lines of race, gender, class, ability, or faith. There are stories I cannot tell, and patterns I cannot see—not because they aren't there, but because my perspective is incomplete.

My co-writer, Amy Reed, also brings her own set of limitations in perspective—different from mine, but present nonetheless. As a queer woman and the granddaughter of a Filipino immigrant farmer, born to a biracial mother on one side and a white, rural, working-class lineage on the other, her experience stretches beyond whiteness and heteronormativity in ways mine does not. At the same time, her worldview is shaped by a liberal, middle-class upbringing, femme presentation, and often being read as white. Together, we've done our best to include a broad range of voices, but we recognize that even our most intentional efforts have boundaries. We are deeply grateful to Rebecca Slue—known professionally as the White Woman Whisperer—for her guidance and for lending her voice to close this book with the grace and gravity it calls for. Her words offer more than reflection; they serve as a companion—deepening the conversation around whiteness, complicity, and what it might mean to choose another way forward.

And while writing this book, we have added another level of perspective—yours. So many of you helped me stress-test these ideas as I was developing them, offering your personal stories of the cults you survived and the nuanced systems of behavior control you encountered in families, fandoms, companies, churches, and more. You revealed patterns I never could have seen on my own. This book is stronger, more honest, and more expansive because of you. Thank you.

I hope this book offers language and clarity for those seeking to understand their own group experiences. I hope it disrupts some of our most sacred assumptions. But I also hope it invites you to seek out the voices this book cannot contain—to learn from Black, Indigenous, disabled, queer, and global survivors whose insights stretch far beyond my own. Because if we are going to dismantle the systems that control and divide us, we need all of us. And we need to start by listening.

—Daniella

Chapter 1 (Part I)

Charismatic Leadership: A Hitler and a Churchill...

Two kids from communes found themselves in a New York City elevator one day, striking up a conversation that sparked an unexpected connection. That chance encounter would eventually lead Adam (from a Kibbutz in Israel) and Miguel (from a "five-mother collective" commune in Oregon) to build an organization together, taking the good from the communal experiences of their youth and eschewing the bad.[1] Like any kids who grew up in a communal setting, Adam and Miguel understood the intensity of the connection between the members, a kind of funky communal-living math that added up to the whole being greater than each individual could hope to be on their own. They dreamed they could harness the power of community to change the way people worked, and eventually lived and studied. They were doing more than starting a business—they were going to change the world.

What could go wrong? Early followers and investors seemed to believe that nothing could. The organization grew at a breakneck pace, recruiting young people from all over the world who were willing to dedicate themselves to a punishing work pace in the interest of the missionized message of change. And the package came complete with the messianic figure—Adam, the more charismatic of the two founders—who had become the peddler of the big dream.[2] As he ramped up the transcendental messaging, investors and customers flocked to bring his vision into a reality.

But at some point, the focus on "we" became a focus on "me," as Adam became the savior who was going to deliver everyone their wildest dreams. And though the red flags had been there from the start, when the growth was too rapid and the promises too vague, most folks threw caution to the wind in their desire to believe in him.

* * *

From the beginning, the story of WeWork reads like a cult—complete with a navel-gazing focus on the charismatic leader, a grandiose vision, and intelligent individuals who should have seen the signs. They should have questioned Neumann receiving nearly $6 million in WeWork shares for transferring the rights to the trademark "We," should have balked at having real estate he owned leased back to the company, really should have dug deeper when he made his wife (who also happened to be Gwyneth Paltrow's cousin) the one to legally choose his business successor, and certainly should have sounded the alarm when he began to show the characteristics of an authoritarian and unstable leader.[3]

Instead, they just saw Adam—larger than life, handsome, the genius bringing it all together. And because he was unlike anyone else—an incredible salesman, tall and commanding, and with the ability to inspire anyone—they were willing to believe that he could deliver results nobody else could. By the time Adam was selling "me" instead of "we," the process of deification had already begun. Today there's no way to discuss the astronomical rise and inevitable plummet of WeWork without using the word *cult*. What started as a true desire to harness the power of community quickly morphed into a $47-billion, real-world lesson on the power of charisma and the delusion of crowds.

The Essence of Charisma

Over and over in American history, we've been privy to the meteoric rise, often followed by catastrophic fall, of a charismatic leader—a term itself that should call to mind as many negative as positive examples. Still, for as long as many of us can remember, scholars of leadership and management have focused on charisma as a desirable quality in a leader, something to be studied and emulated. Certainly we can think of leaders, people like JFK and MLK, CEOs like Bill Gates and Steve Jobs, any number of nationally recognized football coaches or pop stars or megachurch preachers, maybe even your own yoga teacher or the queen bee of your daughter's middle-school clique, who can all be described with the ethereal moniker "charismatic."

Meanwhile, on the other side of the charisma coin, research from 2021 suggests that psychopathic traits are up to twelve times more common among corporate leaders than in the general population—which is probably unsurprising to anyone who's held a corporate job.[4] It's the same as prison numbers, and I'd be willing to bet my Army career that if we polled military officer ranks, we'd find similarly high numbers associated with that vocation. The reality is, a lot of the traits common to antisocial and narcissistic personality disorders—charisma, persuasiveness, confidence—are widely considered effective leadership qualities in today's America. In a commentary, Professor Simon Croom, part of the 2021 study's research team, tells us that "psychopaths can often be very successful for this reason, especially if they are high-functioning ones who are able to avoid detection over the long term."[5]

I grew up walking around the cult commune of my childhood quoting the words of David Berg—the random white dude who convinced tens of thousands of people* that he was the prophet of God

---

* According to The Family International website, "over 35,000 people have at some point devoted themselves to Christian service with the Family International" and current membership is "over 1,400 members in nearly 80 countries" (https://www. thefamilyinternational.org/en/about/membership, accessed July 20, 2025). With cults, it's nearly impossible to know real numbers because they often inflate or deflate numbers for their own purposes.

for the end of days—and it didn't feel much different than marching around Kandahar Airfield as an intelligence officer quoting General Petraeus in 2011, or the way everyone walked around Microsoft's campus quoting CEO Satya Nadella when I worked there in 2016. So why did we become so obsessed with charisma? What happened to leaders who were simply great administrators? What happened to focusing on systems and rational thought, to paying attention to numbers and data, rather than how we can tweak facts to fit the messaging our charismatic leader wishes them to fit?

We live in a society that loves to deify individual humans for one reason or another—artistic ability, political savvy, sports wins, or because they were in a movie we all watched. Tom Hanks spoke at my master's graduation—which, of course, I've mythologized ever since—and you better believe I'll be crowing about that until the day I die. As we look at recent American history, however, we can see that as our world has gotten louder and louder, we've turned more and more of our interest and attention toward these charismatic leaders and the ideas they enthrall us with. I understand it well, as I'm an adult woman fully in the cult of Taylor Swift (self-described as Swifties, in case you've been living under a rock). This shift away from rational thought, reason, and systematic inquiry—those Enlightenment-era values that modern Western societies have so prided themselves on—and toward awe-inspiring leaders and their messages actually fits quite well with what we know about charisma, charismatic leaders and, well, cults.

So what are these charismatic qualities, and how do we understand them as something we can explain, break down, and measure? According to *Psychology Today*, charismatic traits include things like "confidence, exuberance, optimism, expressive body language, and a passionate voice."[6] We tend to look at extroverted people, or those who are comfortable speaking often and with assertiveness, as charismatic people. Experts say charisma is not a personality trait, and that people can become more charismatic through working on it—in fact, much of modern corporate leadership coaching is based on that idea. But they also say you can't necessarily "perform" charisma. However, as someone who grew up at the feet of cult leaders who were doing so with every breath, I have always felt that I learned how to, and in fact can, perform charisma.

The leadership traits considered "charismatic" are certainly in high demand on the job market today. Even leaders at regular companies and organizations understand that having charismatic qualities will help them go far—and many pay hefty amounts to be trained on cultivating such traits. These leaders study things like presentation, speaking style, hand gestures, and eye contact, all of which will help them more effectively *influence* people. An article on Inc.com, an online magazine for private businesses—including startups, which, it's worth noting, can be more than a little culty—tells its readers that "anyone can become more charming and engaging over time, all it takes is a little practice." The article gives us seven ways to increase our charisma, all psychologist approved. These tips tell us to:

1.   Start showing more expression in your face.
2.   Listen actively to what people are saying.
3.   Practice reading other people's emotions.
4.   Share stories and anecdotes.
5.   Ask rhetorical questions to encourage engagement.
6.   Set high goals, and express confidence that you can achieve them.
7.   Use words that people can relate to.[7]

As I read this list, my mind goes back to the leaders I've worked under in the military, and to people like WeWork's Adam Newman, and to the cult leaders who raised me. They all did these things.

Sociologist Max Weber, one of the founding fathers of sociology in the early 1900s (and who therefore has somewhat of his own cult following), gave us the term "charismatic authority." The term itself has decidedly religious origins, where outstanding qualities are seen as a "gift of Grace," a kind of divine endorsement that gives the leader his authority.[8] This went hand in hand, of course, with the "divine right of kings." Weber generalized the idea for everyday use, and in the 2020s the concept of charismatic leaders is applied broadly to politicians, military leaders, celebrities, CEOs, and many others.

Weber defined the difference between power and authority by telling us that power relies on force or coercion, while authority depends on subordinates recognizing and accepting the legitimacy of their leaders' commands. Charismatic authority tends to endure the longest because the leader is viewed as flawless, making opposition to them feel like a betrayal of the entire system.[9] Charismatic rule is often seen in authoritarian states, dictatorships, autocracies, and theocracies—the kind of governing we thought we left behind during the Enlightenment.[10]

Max Weber viewed disenchantment as a consequence of the modern world's shift toward rationalization and secularization, suggesting that charisma emerged to fill the void left by the fading belief in magic. He wrote that *charisma* was a word "applied to a certain quality of an individual personality by virtue of which he is considered extraordinary and treated as endowed with supernatural, superhuman, or at least specifically exceptional powers or qualities. These are such as are not accessible to the ordinary person, but are regarded as of divine origin or exemplary."[11] Notice all that religious-sounding language? The charismatic leader brought back some of that sense of divine magic, but at a cost. One of the three types of domination described by Weber, in which the governed are willingly compliant, is charismatic leadership.

It's no coincidence that cults appear to be having a moment of resurgence right now, and not just the obvious ones—everything from the health and wellness industry, to startups, to apps we can all download on our phone are displaying a startling level of culty tendencies. Cults tend to arise in direct response to times of social turmoil, and the early part of the twenty-first century has indeed been confusing and overwhelming for most of us. Amanda Montell, author of *Cultish: The Language of Fanaticism* and host of the popular podcast *Sounds Like a Cult*, says that American unrest (with a corresponding lack of top-down social systems that other developed nations enjoy—also known as "socialism" by those in the cult of late-stage capitalism)

> was also responsible for the rise of cultish movements throughout
> the 1960s and '70s, when the Vietnam War, the civil rights
> movement, and both Kennedy assassinations knocked US
> citizens unsteady. At the time, spiritual practice was spiking,
> but the overt reign of Protestantism was declining, so new
> movements arose to quench that cultural thirst. These included
> everything from Christian offshoots like Jews for Jesus and the
> Children of God to Eastern derived fellowships like 3HO and
> Shambhala Buddhism to pagan groups like the Covenant of the
> Goddess and the Church of Aphrodite, to sci-fi-esque ones like
> Scientology and Heaven's Gate. Some scholars now refer to this
> as the Fourth Great Awakening.[12]

We find throughout history that charismatic leaders appear in greater numbers during times of social turbulence. According to sociologist Thomas Robbins, the responding groups that arise are "composed of people who are fearful of the future, who hope that by placing their faith in some charismatic leader they will eradicate the past and protect their lives against unknown and unseen dangers."[13] We saw this all too well when wellness grifters edged their way into the mainstream during the chaos of the COVID epidemic. If Dr. Fauci and Big Pharma couldn't cure COVID fast enough, maybe the guy talking about Ivermectin could, or that pretty lady on Instagram who says all you need to do is clear your chakras (and buy her tinctures) to avoid getting sick. When we are scared, when the world feels uncertain, and when there are no easy answers, we are more likely to look to whoever is most persuasive in convincing us they have the solution to our problems. There's a reason the world produced both a Hitler and a Churchill at the same time, and that they were able to rally whole nations—their own and others—around them.

As you can see, an investigation into the history of the concept of charismatic leadership doesn't take long to end up at cult leaders and murderous dictators. Once when I was discussing my own life stories, a psychologist told me that we study the extremes to understand everyone else. This is true for all kinds of groups and leaders: We can learn as much from the extremely "bad" ones as we can from those we think of as extremely "good" or successful. But during my graduate studies I noticed that every time we talked about the great qualities of leaders, we would quietly mention the dark triad of leadership—Machiavellianism, psychopathy, and narcissism—and every time, without fail, the professor promised that we would come back around to discuss them. We never did.

What I realized is that when we talked about leadership, we framed *effective* leadership as inherently *positive*—so we studied examples of what most people would consider to be history's most exemplary leaders. If someone meets our definition of a "good leader," we don't spend a lot of time examining the darker sides of the very same qualities that got them there. History's charismatic leaders, both good and evil, are two sides of the same coin. And they often share an alarming number of the same "effective" leadership traits.

Building on Weber's theories, Dr. Rakesh Khurana wrote *Searching for a Corporate Savior: The Irrational Quest for Charismatic CEOs*, where he examines how corporate culture elevates leaders to near-mythic status—essentially bringing spiritual or sacred ideals into the secular world of business. Khurana suggests that while charismatic leadership reaches its apotheosis in religious cults, it is very present in everyday corporate life, in slightly less extreme ways. He argues that the ascendance of charismatic leadership in corporate life reflects a return to an older, more volatile form of authority—one that lacks the stability of institutional rule. As I read Khurana's book, I was comforted to know I'm not the only one who is concerned about the parallels between cult leaders I've known and charismatic leaders I've served under—and all the motivation, influence, power, and control techniques I've seen them use. Khurana builds on Weber's position that charisma and rationality are incompatible, further suggesting that Western societies have traditionally shifted from charismatic leadership to governance based on formal rules.[14] After the devastation caused by Hitler and Mussolini, Americans became deeply wary of leaders who rely too heavily on personal magnetism. One of the key democratic achievements, Khurana notes, is our ability to distinguish the person from the position they hold. One of the best ways I've heard this separation explained is that in America, your surgeon can be religious and still respected—until he tries to not operate on you because God told him so.

So what happened in the '80s and '90s for us skeptical, rationally minded Americans to begin to shift, in both business and politics, toward giving all credit to, and hanging all our hopes on, charismatic leaders? When we gave Lee Iacocca credit for "single-handedly" saving Chrysler, we tended to forget about the government bailout, political landscape, and a multitude of other contributing factors. When we focused on Bill Gates as an individual genius who built an empire, we told ourselves, and the world, a certain story about leadership—the one where the leader was central.

I think it's because of what we can call a kind of *apocalypse*—the abrupt end of the industrial age and the cataclysmic shift into the information age, a change that began in the late '80s and shook the world so hard that it left not a single business untouched. A 2002 *Harvard Magazine* review of Khurana's book tells us that "the trend toward charisma may have started when the idea took root that if a firm was doing poorly or well, it was because of the CEO...The image of a CEO changed from being a capable administrator to a *leader*—a motivating, flamboyant leader."[15] Business and politics were quick to respond to this narrative. It was easy to discard the dirty language of making money and instead embrace that of mission, vision, values, and purpose.

The charismatic leader soon took on a whole new quality in the world of tech, with the rise of Steve Jobs being the most famous example (perhaps now rivaled by the more overt cult leader Elon Musk). Venture capital paid attention and fell in line, and the turn of the twenty-first century delivered countless stories of unicorn companies brought to greatness by one or two charismatic guys, and once in a while, a woman. Simultaneously, we experienced the ascension of the charismatic leader in politics, culminating with American presidential wins on both sides of the aisle by men who oozed inexplicable charisma, albeit very different from one another—Barack Obama and Donald Trump. It can be argued that neither candidate was qualified for the job of the most powerful man in the world, but both rode to stunning victories nevertheless, amid so many millions commenting on their "likeability" and counting on them to "save America."

The success of the charismatic leader approach in tech and politics over the past thirty years has led to many businesses becoming more insular and siloed, and ever more enthralled by and beholden to the single leader at the top. And then came the stories of the survivors— former employees of companies like Zappos, WeWork, LuLaRoe, and Twitter who have described how insidious the creep of power and control was. Both the fervent commitment and the deplorable actions usually reserved in our minds for folks in cults are becoming more common in our everyday companies. Just look at any tech startup in Silicon Valley, where employees commonly work sixty-plus hours per week without complaint, following a single genius at the top with unwavering loyalty and obedience—and plied with free beer on tap, built-in community, and the promise that their product will somehow save the world. Every startup manual (or TikTok video) coaches young people (usually white men) on how to ramp up their charisma and give their employees a sense of life-or-death purpose in order to better motivate them to dedicate their time, labor, and brain power—and often money or earning potential elsewhere—to the company "mission."

With the growth of the internet, we've also seen the rise of the "thought leader" and "influencer," ever more popular with the debut of each new social media platform. The cultivation of a "personal brand," in today's lingo, includes some element of shaping one's naturally occurring personality traits into a charismatic persona. The social media platforms we all use seem to have been built to be inherently culty, where it is all too easy to tune out anyone whose views don't align with yours, where members are labeled "followers," and where leaders are rewarded by the algorithm gods for collecting more followers. Social media has given a platform to people with no medical or scientific education who can claim to be health experts and spread wild, sometimes harmful ideas, and sell their products—like Anthony William, aka "Medical Medium," self-proclaimed chronic illness expert and celery juice evangelist with no formal medical training, whose authority on health comes from the medical advice bestowed upon him by angels, and who is seemingly legitimized by his millions of Instagram followers and endorsements by people like the queen of alternative wellness herself, Gwyneth Paltrow (remember her cousin Rebekah Neumann, wife of WeWork founder Adam Neumann?).[16] People with no discernable talents, skills, or sometimes any actual product besides themselves can become the biggest social media leaders of all, and all because of their charisma (think of, say, the entire Kardashian family). This form of fame is so ubiquitous that more than half of kids aged twelve to fifteen now say their top career choice is social media influencer—more than those who aspire to traditional careers like doctor, teacher, lawyer, or athlete.[17]

Commitment to these business, political, or cultural gods has only intensified as the world has increased in noise and confusion pulling us in every direction, and with once-in-a-lifetime emergencies becoming our daily norm. In the early 2000s, when I walked out of a separatist cult my grandfather had joined in the '70s, it was much rarer to meet an American like me, someone who had been cut off by their family and friends because of their refusal to adhere to one leader, guru, or totalitarian way of life. Now it seems like many of us have that story—whatever side of the equation we are on.

The Road to Deification

Jim Jones started as a Christian pastor who grew his Northern California congregation with progressive messages of inclusivity and love, but eventually the Peoples Temple became pointedly non-Christian, with a focus on Jones as the ultimate head—their god and messiah, if you will. And he worked hard to become so. In his youth, Jones worked to develop the persuasive and charismatic skills he first encountered in Christian denominations such as Pentecostalism—abilities that would later serve him in leading a cult.[18] He honed these skills and, as Amanda Montell describes in *Cultish*, "boasting the intonation and passion of a Baptist preacher, the complex theorizings of an Aristotelian philosopher, the folksy wit of a countryside fabler, and the ferocious zeal of a demented tyrant," he became "a linguistic chameleon who possessed a monster arsenal of shrewd rhetorical strategies, which he wielded to attract and condition followers of all stripes."[19] Once he found his place as a preacher, Jones turned to advocating racial equality, something that, as a white man in the tumultuous 1960s, made him stand out. Being a racially conscious white pastor became his unique value proposition, and he convinced hundreds of Black Americans to join his congregation, helping build a church that was integrated to a level unheard of at the time.[20]

Over the next few years, Jones proved himself to be a master of the cult leader's playbook, finding ways to increasingly isolate his followers and build their righteous, persecuted, paranoid, and apocalyptic group identity. As he gained more and more control, Jones eventually renounced religion altogether, claiming that it had always been his plan to use religion to make Marxism appear more palatable. His followers, trained not to question him, didn't blink—and they no longer needed religion because Jim Jones had successfully replaced God in their hearts and minds. Jones had long feared government intervention in his church, a paranoia likely intensified by a persecution complex. When press allegations eventually prompted an investigation, he and the group fled California for Guyana. By the time he'd coaxed them into geographic isolation, where he had complete access to exploit their labor, he'd also turned himself into the venerable messiah of the Peoples Temple.

Whatever he said would now be taken as divine mandate by his followers, who were, according to the journalist Tim Reiterman,* "decent, hardworking, socially conscious people, some highly educated," who "wanted to help their fellow man and serve God, not

---

* Reiterman was present on the Jonestown airfield during the attack that killed Congressman Leo Ryan and three others.

embrace a self-proclaimed deity on earth."[21] But it was too late, and the process of Jones's deification was complete—they would follow their messiah anywhere, even as far as repeatedly rehearsing the act of "revolutionary suicide" in preparation for their coming apocalypse. The writer Shiva Naipaul argues that the Peoples Temple was at heart a fundamentalist religious project "obsessed with sin and images of apocalyptic destruction, authoritarian in its innermost impulses, instinctively thinking in terms of the saved and the damned." The result, Naipaul writes, "was neither racial justice nor socialism but a messianic parody of both."[22] Nearly 1,000 dead in a mass murder/suicide was the ultimate result of one man's deification.

The process of becoming a charismatic leader—which can be understood in its most extreme form by studying cult leaders like Jones—includes an element of deification, or how the leader makes themselves appear to be godlike: infallible, all-powerful, and all-knowing—even in secular vocations such as business or war. Kings of old relied on the power of deification to confer authority outright, speaking of the divine right of kings, while the pharaohs of ancient Egypt named themselves directly as god-rulers. Pick up any modern book on leadership and you'll likely find a discussion of the power of myth when it comes to leadership, of holding oneself a bit separate and above while crafting a singular story of the superhero leader who arrives to save the day. And doesn't that sound just a little bit like Weber's concept of charismatic authority infusing magic back into our workaday lives?

One aspect of deification has to do with "being saved," even in secular form. If a religious leader—or army general, or startup CEO, or wellness influencer—is riding in on a white horse to save us from hell, or terrorists, or the toxic byproducts and existential disappointments of the modern age, then we can put our faith in them, ultimately unburdening ourselves of both the responsibility of having to take action and the discomfort of uncertainty. In chaotic times, their sureness and clear picture of the path forward are a relief, even if what we're moving toward is a kind of apocalypse—at least we know what to expect. Culty leaders thrive on this kind of teleological thinking, that is, approaching the future as though the outcome is already decided, whether in our religions, culture, work, or political viewpoint (we'll talk more about teleology in chapter 10).

In *Leaders: Myth and Reality*, General Stanley McChrystal (commander of all coalition forces deployed to Afghanistan to fight the war on terror) says that although leaders are the subject of much scrutiny, "too many of us, seduced by the mythology of what good leadership looks like, miss the reality. We intuitively know that leadership is critical to success in the modern world, but we don't really understand what that leadership consists of."[23] So we use storytelling to build our myths of the singular, heroic leader at the center of the story, the Chosen One who is endowed with special talents and traits not shared by mere mortal men. This sounds an awful lot like the Great Man theory popularized in the 1800s, which asserts that those in power are entitled to lead because of the traits they've been born with, and that history is nothing more than a collection of biographies of great and powerful men. No modern historian or sociologist worth their salt would take such a theory seriously, and yet the myth endures, encouraging people to follow and, as McChrystal says, "emulate painted idols rather than real people."[24]

Anyone who was either transfixed by Adam Neumann's performance at a WeWork company offsite or who was brought to God by the early impassioned sermons of Jim Jones could tell you that "being in the presence of an effective leader often feels akin to the pull of beautiful music or a rousing speech...We are inspired by the charismatic leader, even when we can't put a finger on why."[25] An important part of this particular magic of charisma is the power of holding oneself as someone a bit separate, which creates an element of mysticism and mystery that cannot be explained, and further emphasizes to followers that the world is full of uncertainty but the leader alone has the answers. Even the US military swears by their policies that forbid officers from fraternizing with the soldiers under their command, because heaven forbid you are seen as a human and they begin to question your orders and authority when things go bang.[26]

Because we've failed to understand why charismatic leadership often produces its magic effect, we tend to focus on the outward traits that we feel make a "good leader"—extroversion, personableness, confidence— which causes us to ignore the deification process as these leaders turn themselves into mini-gods in their own companies, military units, churches, startups, nonprofits, and fandoms. Because we don't fully grasp why the myth of the charismatic leader endures, we select, train, and assess leaders in ways that seem flawed or insufficient. From this decade, we have cases like FTX, Twitter, and Theranos, companies who seem to "have fallen victim to an all too popular belief that 'superhero' leadership trumps boring management," according to *Harvard Business Review*.[27] And General McChrystal tells us that "leadership is often more about the symbolism, meaning and future potential leaders hold for their system, and less about the results they produce."[28] In this, Adam Neumann shone brilliantly. He took the concept of a single word—*we*—and infused it with so much meaning, symbolism, and future potential that people simply failed to notice that the results were far from what had been promised, and that nothing was adding up.

It can be argued that our attitude toward the charismatic leader has come nearly full circle to be religious once again. This worshipful, unquestioning relationship to leadership is culturally ingrained in those of us raised in the Western, Judeo-Christian world, which itself has been defined by millennia of hierarchical, patriarchal spiritual traditions. If you look outside business, politics, and religion to the lower-stakes world of pop culture, you even see this holy/royal tendency in our seemingly harmless female-centric cultural icons: "Saint" Dolly Parton, "Queen" Bey (Beyoncé), not to mention the influential Taylor Swift fandom who rarely questions her, fiercely defends her online, and quickly mobilizes against perceived threats—whether or not she weighs in. Americans love to worship, whether it's a pop music star who makes them feel empowered and understood, a CEO who will lead them to abundance, a religious leader who will teach them how to be righteous and give them a ticket to heaven, or a politician who will help them take their country back.

According to Max Weber, authority can only be exercised when followers recognize and accept it.[29] And just like in ancient times when seasons of disaster sent people rushing back to their gods, today's social turmoil drives us to demand guidance from charismatic leaders in our organizations and groups. The actual process of deification, becoming godlike to a group of followers, hasn't changed. Charismatic leaders, who love to think of themselves as unique, actually set predictable enough patterns that they appear "to have all attended the same Messiah school," according to renowned cult expert Dr. Janja Lalich.[30]

It all starts innocently enough, usually with a big idea to change the world, though if we look back to cult leaders' childhoods, there are usually signs that should have been concerning. Jim Jones had always been manipulative, deceitful, and willing to do whatever it took to make people follow him, while David Berg of the Children of God was over-controlled and abused by his parents and was already a sexual deviant at a young age.* Elizabeth Holmes, the CEO of Theranos and an "emotionally withdrawn child of a once-illustrious family being driven by a jealous mother who wanted her daughter to make a name for herself,"[31] declared to her father (a vice president at Enron!) at the age of nine that all she "really want[ed] out of life [was] to discover something new, something that mankind didn't know was possible to do."[32] Adam Neumann's parents split early, leading to a turbulent childhood during which he lived in thirteen places before moving to the US at twenty-two.[33] Life on a kibbutz as a teen, however, stood out as a positive experience thanks to the close bonds he formed there. In retrospect, it's perhaps unsurprising that a kid whose early life was so fractured grew up to found a company that wanted to change the world with the "power of community." Cult expert Dr. Steven Hassan† once

---

* It is worth noting that Berg disclosed being molested as a child by his nanny—an incident that led his mother to fire the woman but also to shame him. This in no way excuses his later behavior, but it does provide important context for his fixation on deviant sexuality (Kent, "Lustful Prophet," 146–49).

† I am hesitant to cite Hassan in this book and have gone back and forth about doing so. Long considered the world's leading expert on cults, he was someone I looked up to as

told me that he thinks all cult leaders grew up in cults, that is to say situations of complete coercive control and culty dynamics. While we'll probably never be able to confirm that, it is an intriguing concept.

I'm not saying, of course, that any of these things mean the child in question was predetermined to grow up to be a cult leader. Plenty of children have divorced parents, are ambitious from a young age, or move around a lot. But cult leaders are often people with significant experiences in childhood that forced them to develop skills of manipulation, turning them into somewhat of an ingénue of charisma, who desires to recreate those manipulative patterns. It's not always a bad thing—if they don't make bad choices. Jim Jones, for instance, initially built a reputation by accomplishing what investigative journalist and Jones biographer Jeff Guinn called "absolutely magnificent things." In a *Vice* interview, Guinn explained:

> If Jim Jones had been hit by a car and killed somewhere toward the end of the 1950s, he'd be remembered today as one of the great leaders in the early civil rights movement, and he would have earned that reputation. That makes what happened to him even sadder and actually more tragic. He had the ability to do great things, and instead he used his talent for provocation, for manipulation, and as a result, he's remembered today as a terrible person. Frankly he earned that.[34]

It is a pattern we see often: Charismatic leaders use their unique talents to build something that most people would agree is good, but at some point in their accumulation of power, a kind of switch gets

---

both a scholar and survivor for years. In recent years, however, Hassan has aligned himself with the cult of transphobia—publicly defending and championing transphobe author J. K. Rowling, and questioning the validity of transgender identity, though, strangely, he still calls himself a trans rights activist on his website. I include his research here because I believe that much of his earlier work remains valid and useful, and is foundational in the field of cult studies. Ironically, Hassan's shift into culty thinking seems to prove his own theories: People who have been in cults are statistically more vulnerable to getting caught in new ones.

flipped, and they begin to weaponize the control they hold over their followers. In Jones's case, years of amphetamine and barbiturate abuse were certainly exacerbating, but more than anything, he had become intoxicated by his own power.[35] Just as nobody ever knowingly joins a cult, few people set out to actually start one, I would argue. The problem is that these leaders inevitably drink their own Kool-Aid— being deified by their followers gives them increasing proof that they are God, and they start to believe it.

This desire to acquire followers often becomes apparent in the early adulthood of the charismatic leader on the road to deification, punctuated with a series of attempts—and failures—to build themselves something, anything, with a following. David Berg was nothing but a "failed Pentecostal preacher and wildly successful alcoholic" before finding his calling by saving lost souls searching for meaning among the hippies gathering in California, according to Lauren Hough, a fellow survivor of the Children of God and author of *Leaving Isn't the Hardest Thing*.[36] Adam Neumann experimented with multiple product ideas, launched a company that failed before finding his initial success with GreenDesk, and later exploded onto the entrepreneurial scene with WeWork. Elizabeth Holmes had mediocre grades before she got into Stanford through a back door, but ultimately dropped out anyway. She only got investment for Theranos because of strings her father could pull, and an overreliance on her charisma and famous ancestors.[37] Keith Raniere was involved in starting a myriad of companies before finding "success" with NXIVM. Their stories all ring with a familiar note: These individuals needed to build something. What it was wasn't important, as long as it came with followers.

Once they've built something, these charismatic leaders set their unique talents to code-switching in order to become something to one segment of their followers and something else to another, which Jones was known to be an expert at. Code-switching is an important tool in the arsenal of the aspiring cult leader, as it allows them to speak "in several tongues at once...appealing to different but overlapping audiences" according to Derek Beres, Matthew Remski, and Julian

Walker of the hit podcast *Conspirituality* and book *Conspirituality: How New Age Conspiracy Theories Became a Health Threat.*[38] It also has the benefit of keeping their followers off-balance, never knowing what will happen next. We can see this easily in the rantings of cult leaders (who usually show a fondness for having themselves recorded, so no "pearls of wisdom" might slip away). But we can also see it in the famously mercurial temperament of Steve Jobs; or in Donald Trump's habit of nicknaming political opponents and allies alike; or even in a Bikram hot yoga teacher training, where students are yelled at, insulted, and forced to keep going to the point of fainting or vomiting—which then makes the little nuggets of approval feel like a sacred blessing.[39] Hot-and-cold behavior is often accompanied by threats of "if you don't like it, you're free to leave anytime," a loaded phrase intended to remind you of the exit costs you incur by disagreeing on any point with the guy at the top (more on exit costs in chapter 9).

Aspiring cult leaders often become politically or socially active, which helps attract passionate and intelligent followers who are willing to work hard for change and are seeking a transcendent mission (more on this in chapter 3), such as save the world before the end of days (David Berg), unlock your ultimate potential (Keith Raniere), transform medical science (Elizabeth Holmes), become the first nation to ever win a counterinsurgency fight (General David Petraeus), or "elevate the world's consciousness"[40] (Rebekah Neumann and countless New Age and alt-health influencers). This grandiose mission can be weaponized to transform the worldviews of their followers, bringing them under a shared *sacred assumption* (more on this in chapter 2), which is usually centered around the absolute superiority of the leader or the group.

As we've touched on in this chapter, mythology is extremely important to authoritarian or charismatic forms of leadership—the leader derives much of their power from the mythology that surrounds them and justifies their authority in the first place. In cults, this mythology, a focus on the founder's image and story (often accompanied by everyone celebrating the leader's birthday), and the group's origin story all contribute to the process of deification. The past failings of the leader can be included in this story: David Berg struggled until God called him to be a prophet, Adam Neumann had his string of big ideas, and Keith Raniere told fantastical stories about what conspired to keep success from his grasp prior to NXIVM. The cult leader knows he must address his earlier failure, so he writes it into his mythology: *I just hadn't found the right thing (or God hadn't yet found me ready), and then after a sufficient number of trials and tribulations, I was chosen and saved.* Cult leaders are usually the cult's original salvation story, their example serving as a promise to their followers.

With deification well underway, the cult leader turns their attention to blurring the line between themself and any God figure they may have initially claimed to be speaking for. In the Children of God, David Berg said his revelations and the words in the Bible were of equal importance, while David Koresh told his followers he was the Messiah come anew. Sarah Edmonson, one of the whistleblowers of NXIVM, tells us in her book *Scarred: The True Story of How I Escaped NXIVM, the Cult that Bound My Life* that Keith Raniere's teachings "were making us...disciples. He wanted us to worship him."[41] Raniere bragged to his followers that he'd even had people killed for his beliefs. Meanwhile, at a campaign rally in early 2016, Donald Trump declared his godlike status to Americans when he bragged that he could shoot a man on 5th Avenue and his followers would still vote for him. *The New York Times*, in its review of *The Cult of We: WeWork, Adam Neumann, and the Great Startup Delusion*—the definitive insider account of WeWork— called Adam Neumann "a startup demagogue who aspired to be a demigod, but got hamstrung by his ego and greed."[42] The leader may also claim some actual godlike powers—like Jim Jones staging miracle healings, various New Age "channelers" talking with the Universal Spirit (or sometimes aliens) or accessing the cosmic library of the Akashic records, or Elizabeth Holmes perpetuating tales of medical miracles from her cunningly fake technology.

The final step for these leaders in achieving demigod status is usually a ruthless culling of their formerly dedicated followers and the organization's leaders. Jim Jones surrounded himself with only yes-men and

-women, to the point that he was never criticized and constantly told how brilliant and wonderful he was. Keith Raniere moved people around in the NXIVM organization and threatened to demote people down his "stripe path" if they questioned him.[43] David Berg was so dedicated to constantly replacing leaders to keep them off balance that his targets included his own wife and four children and many of the people who'd started the organization with him. Elizabeth Holmes testified that she owned 51 percent of Theranos and could fire CEO Ramesh Balwani at any time,[44] which in practice included "employees who questioned [Theranos] technology, its quality control or its ethics."[45] Rebekah Neumann is said to have fired a mechanic for WeWork's Gulfstream jet within minutes of meeting him because she didn't like his energy. This wasn't a one-time thing. "When her husband needed to thin out the ranks, Rebekah would allegedly walk through the WeWork offices looking for anyone giving off bad energy."[46] And everyone has heard way too much about Donald Trump's penchant for firing people.

With their authority now nearly complete, and with nobody left who might dare to question them, these men's (and occasionally women's) paths to greatness predictably include isolating their followers, demanding more of their labor, demonizing formal education, discouraging followers from going to anyone but the leader themself for advice, and failing to delineate the edges of their own education or expertise (as true experts will do). They impose themselves further in their followers' lives: giving reading advice or banning certain types of books, giving medical advice or forbidding traditional medical care, as well as giving exercise advice, sexual advice, or other forms of "life coaching." Their aim is to convince their followers that the leader alone holds all the answers, while portraying the outside world as not only misguided but beneath them. Such controlling behavior may sound extreme, but look no further than your average evangelical Christian community and see how much power the pastor has over the everyday choices of his congregants.

And the reality is, being devoted to a guru or messiah figure without the ability to critically question is not just foolish but incredibly dangerous. As Thomas Robbins notes in the *Encyclopedia of Religion and Society*, when followers justify their leader's unpredictable behavior (a pattern known as the "deification of idiosyncrasy"), and when there are no institutional checks on that power, it creates conditions where extreme or even violent actions can occur.[47] Scholars like Roy Wallis and Steve Bruce, who write about the volatility of charismatic authority, say that this type of authority creates conditions that allow for sexual misconduct and violence, as seen in groups like the Peoples Temple, Synanon, and the Children of God. Charismatic leadership, they suggest, can open the door for leaders to act on their more destructive or harmful impulses.[48]

Charisma is so powerful that it can be impervious to rationality. In a review of Rakesh Khurana's book *Searching for a Corporate Savior*, Craig Lambert writes that "charismatic authority is a precarious, profoundly vulnerable thing, as history has repeatedly proved," and that

> allegiance to charismatic leaders is in fact antithetical to an open society. The atavistic corporate quest for charismatic CEOs, with its deference to the personality and vision of a particular individual, comes bundled with risks of abuse, misconduct, and incompetence. The results are now spread before us, and their name is not Legion, but Enron.[49]

As enamored by hero and superhero narratives as we are, it is far too easy for individuals to be deified in our society—from the online yoga teacher who claims a certain pose can heal your trauma, to the brilliant but erratic CEO of the startup you work for, to that Tony Robbins seminar your cousin won't stop talking about, to the man who your aunt is still convinced the 2020 presidential election was stolen from. I like the words of Dr. Janja Lalich—a brilliant sociologist who once fell for her own political guru-turned-cult-leader, who in an interview warns us: "There are no gurus."[50]

Chapter 1 (Part II)

...And His Skinny White Woman

The guru usually isn't doing it alone. Time and again, when an American cult has come to public attention—often because it's crossed some very clear lines and has victims or bodies to show for it— we find, very near the cult leader, a skinny white woman pulling some of the strings. When NXIVM was all over national news in 2017–2018 and it came to light that Allison Mack was one of Keith Raniere's lieutenants who helped with his schemes to groom and sexually abuse women, I was heartbroken (not sweet Chloe from *Smallville*!), but also intrigued. Why her? Why, in culty groups, did there seem to be so many women like her—thin, white, overly dedicated to the leader, with more access to him and more privileges than most of the other members? Outliers exist, as they always do, but the few exceptions only underscore how dominant the pattern is.

My own childhood had been very much marked by our leader's death, when his Skinny White Woman (SWW) took over as the anointed leader of the cult. When the news could speak of nothing other than Jeffrey Epstein and his teenage sex-trafficking ring, there she was again, the SWW in the body of Ghislaine Maxwell. I saw her everywhere—in the matriarchs of the Duggar family, in the woman at the center of OneTaste, Hollywood's infamous orgasm cult—and I started to notice the pattern in so many American culty groups, going all the way back to the beginning of the country. What was it about the Skinny White Woman that made her necessary to the success of the cult leader and his establishment of coercive control?

I knew instinctively that both her whiteness and her skinniness were important. I could think of countless aunties who fit this description in the communes of my childhood: always close to the highest leaders, plugged deeply into the organizational structure, bullying other women and girls about their behavior, including their weight. These women at the top were always white, even though we lived in countries where most people were not white. Their significance didn't hit me until a fellow survivor of the Children of God, who is a woman of color, commented on one of my Facebook posts: "What, do cult leaders not like voluptuous women or something?" In that joke, the truth revealed itself. Of course it had nothing to do with the woman being voluptuous or not. It was the whiteness that mattered—that was exactly the point!

I took to TikTok, eager to explain my eureka moment and to see if anyone thought it had merit. I explained that the cult leader, whether a man or a woman, often has a Skinny White Woman dedicated to them and playing a very important role in the cult. One of her many jobs is to whitewash the sins of the leader, to both members and outer society. Her power comes from the white-supremacist (and patriarchal, and Christian) concept of the pure, chaste, white woman. Her very presence acts as a civilizing agent in a way we've seen white women play throughout history. In regular organizations as well, women (often white, often skinny) are let into the leadership in order to whitewash what could be perceived as the sins of the organization.[1]

With this realization, I also saw that I had played that role in the US Army—thinking I was fighting hard for the equality of women in the military, but in reality maybe being more of a shield against critical complaint: How can the US Army possibly be a toxic place for women if Captain Daniella Mestyanek has been so successful there, doing the things they usually only let the boys do? In my memoir I tried to tell a more nuanced story—that I was broken by playing a game never designed for me to win, all the while trying not to bleed to death from the shards of the glass ceiling I was helping shatter. I stopped playing the role of the SWW, stopped being the perfect, proud, woman veteran who would never say a critical word. I was not afraid of calling out the Army colonels and generals—and the cult uncles—for their bad behavior. By letting it all come out, I had let it—and myself—get ugly, which goes against everything the SWW is supposed to do.

On social media my musings about the Skinny White Woman concept went viral, with hundreds, then hundreds of thousands, of people liking, saving, and commenting on my posts. It turns out that I'm not the only one who's noticed her, both in cults and in countless forms of our regular organizations. In *Cultish*, Amanda Montell noted the pattern of power abuse, with "an older man at the top, and by his side, a clique of fair-skinned, twenty- and thirtysomething women who acquiesce to exchanging their whiteness and sexuality for a few more grains of power."[2]

Artist and anti-racism educator Amanda K Gross names this dynamic "Mistress Syndrome" in her book *White Women Get Ready: How Healing Post-Traumatic Mistress Syndrome Leads to Anti-Racist Change*—and she doesn't pull any punches. In her words, "The Mistress is not simply an accessory to white supremacy; she is its loyal lieutenant, actively maintaining the master's house for her own comfort."[3] Gross explains that white women have historically secured their survival and limited power not by dismantling oppressive systems, but by upholding them, smoothing their brutal edges with a smile, and protecting the very men who built them. She describes the Mistress as someone who weaponizes her whiteness and performative vulnerability: She shields patriarchal and racist power structures from scrutiny, but also brutalizes people who threaten the status quo. It's a pattern that stretches from the blood-soaked cotton fields of the American South to the sterile cubicles of today's corporate cults. Mistress Syndrome captures exactly the role the Skinny White Woman plays—she is not a victim, not an innocent bystander.*

* Gross's concept of the Mistress (my Skinny White Woman) allows for both intentional and unintentional participation in oppressive systems. The lens I've applied here emphasizes agency.

She is the system's secret weapon, bought off with scraps of proximity to power, in exchange for her loyalty and silence. And make no mistake: Loyalty is a choice. Choosing to protect the master's house while others burn outside is still choosing the master's house. "As more than one Black woman in my life has confided to me," Gross writes, "If white women would get their act together, oppression wouldn't stand a chance."[4]

Even when a woman seems to be in power, such as CEO of a major corporation, or even your #girlboss neighbor who's making bank with her work-from-home scheme, she is still propping up a system ruled by men. The authors of *Feminism for the 99%: A Manifesto* tell us that this kind of "executive feminism" enables the forces supporting global capital to portray themselves as "progressive" while maintaining the status quo.[5] The SWW softens the cruel image of capitalism with her perceived sensitivity and nurturing nature. In *The Trouble with White Women: A Counterhistory of Feminism*, Kyla Schuller writes, "When shed by the CEO, white women's tears become a commodity, an asset, and a safeguard—proof that capitalism can have a heart. The emotional feminist CEO secures her own likability and cleanses (or whitewashes) the means of production at the same time, sanctifying runaway profits with the humanity streaming down her face."[6]

Through social media conversations and my own research into intersectional feminism, the image of the SWW began to take form—she's the Allison Mack to NXIVM's Keith Raniere, the Ghislaine Maxwell to Jeffrey Epstein, the Melania to Donald Trump, the Rebekah Paltrow to Adam Neumann, and any number of evangelical pastors' wives. She is thin, because in our culture being skinny is ideal and a visual representation of self-sacrifice (more in chapter 4 on how cult leaders weaponize this desire to be thin). She is at once both a role model and proof that the ideal is achievable.[7] For those outside the cult, she serves as an attraction, or a distraction. In short, she is exactly who you want by your side if you *are* sex-trafficking children, as Ghislaine Maxwell and my own cult leader Karen "Mama Maria" Zerby demonstrated so well.

If you asked the SWW, she would tell you that she has real power. And she truly believes she does. Sarah Edmonson, one of the women who initially reported NXIVM as a cult to *The New York Times*, says, "We didn't know that Keith had created a dangerous psychological hierarchy among us. That he didn't think of us as the principal leaders of his company—that instead, he thought of us as the most devout followers in his cult."[8] While the scope and details in the world of business and politics are different than in cults like NXIVM, the pattern is the same: The civilizing effect the white woman confers by her very existence is ultimately used against her and others by those at the top really pulling the strings. As white women "lean in" and conquer the corner office, Kyla Schuller tells us that their duty is to in fact redeem capitalism itself, "turning cutthroat companies like Google into the kinds of places with pregnancy parking spots." Women in this category, Schuller continues, "ought to master the feminine performance of making everyone else comfortable while subordinating their own needs to those of the company at large. Smiling your way through outlandish sexism plays the long game—by not rocking the boat, the boat can become yours."[9]

Elizabeth Holmes exemplifies a woman who seemed to make the boat her own by transcending gender and making it to the top of the man's world of Silicon Valley. As the charismatic leader of biotech startup Theranos, she created a hypnotic, myth-like origin story of the gifted little girl who was afraid of needles, who lost a beloved uncle to cancer, who now wanted to improve the world by providing faster, better blood tests. In the height of her status as Wall Street golden child, she was "feted as a biomedical version of Steve Jobs or Bill Gates, a wunderkind college dropout who would make blood testing as convenient as the iPhone."[10] Holmes fully embraced the role of a charismatic leader—donning Jobs's signature black turtlenecks, promoting the Theranos device as a revolutionary breakthrough for humanity, and surrounding herself with directors who were more captivated by her persona than equipped to provide meaningful oversight. While not explicitly calling Theranos a cult in his book *Bad Blood: Secrets and Lies in a Silicon Valley Startup*, journalist John Carreyrou describes a scene where "still visibly angry, Elizabeth told the gathered employees that she was building a religion. If there were any among them who didn't believe, they should leave. Sunny [Balwani] put it more bluntly: anyone not prepared to show complete devotion and unmitigated loyalty to the company should 'get the fuck out.'"[11]

But if we look a little closer, we see that Holmes had a double role: Not only was she the charismatic leader of Theranos, she was also, in many ways, acting as her own Skinny White Woman. Investors would admit in hindsight that they overlooked potential red flags because of her looks and connections to famous (and white) ancestors.[12] "She aligned herself with very powerful older men who seemed to succumb to a certain charm. And those powerful men could influence people in the government," Phyllis Gardner, Holmes's former Stanford professor, said in *The Inventor*, an HBO documentary.[13] Essentially, many people trusted—and were duped by—her *because* she was a woman.

Holmes's own image and cultivation of the ideal of the thin, white woman was sharp enough to beat the boys at their own game and functioned as the SWW often does, drawing everyone's attention away from the many red flags. From my own experience in the US Army, fighting hard to play the boys' game and becoming one of the first Army women to be on an integrated deliberate ground combat team, I learned that the woman saddled with the role of breaking glass ceilings (or being the female Steve Jobs) can't recognize how she's being used, in fact, to reinforce the patriarchal and hierarchical systems. A *Rolling Stone* article by E. J. Dickson titled "How 'Lean In' Feminism Created Elizabeth Holmes and the Toxic Ladyboss" articulates quite well how Holmes's rise and fall encapsulates a core problem of white feminism: "What Holmes failed to realize is that cloaking yourself in feminism only works if you actively advocate for women other than yourself."

On perhaps a smaller scale of the #LadyBoss trend, we've seen the Skinny White Woman transcend the role of sidekick to ostensibly rule the world of New Age alternative wellness. People like Goop matriarch Gwyneth Paltrow and essential-oil-selling moms may seem harmless, but there is an increasingly sinister side to this world in the form of the "tradwife" trend, the "pastel" arm of far-right ideological movements (remember QAnon?), anti-vaxxers, and influencers like self-described "spiritual catalyst" Teal Swan—who has millions of online followers and has stirred controversy with YouTube videos on suicide, including ones that encourage followers to vividly visualize their own deaths. Some of Swan's most devoted followers travel to her retreat center in Costa Rica, paying thousands of dollars for spiritual "healing" programs, with reports that a number of them stay indefinitely, working for free to support her operations.[14]

Primarily online, conspiracy-minded wellness influencers find ways to monetize the suffering of trauma, illness, and parenting children with special needs (vaccines cause autism, you know?), exploiting the legitimate distrust people have of America's capitalistic and misogynist healthcare system, and promising the soulful, nurturing, and intuitive alternative. Women like "holistic psychiatrist" Kelly Brogan and Dr. Christiane Northrup (self-described women's health expert, best-selling author, and guest on *Oprah*) seized upon the vulnerabilities of their followers to promote anti-vaccine conspiracy theories, all while peddling their spiritual coaching and nutritional supplement businesses. The Center for Countering Digital Hate's 2021 report found that, in a sample of content shared on Facebook and Twitter, just twelve anti-vaccine activists were responsible for up to 65 percent of anti-vaccine posts—including those about COVID-19 vaccines. Both Brogan and Northrup made it onto the "Disinformation Dozen" list.[15]

When I looked deeper into the concept of Skinny White Women, it stood out to me that there are three subtypes of the SWW trope that we see played out in our culture.

First up, you have the vacuous, pretty sidekick, whose job it is to make the leader's message palatable, sexy, and alluring. She is sweet and nice and nonconfrontational (in the case of many pastors' wives, Michelle Duggar, Alison Mack and all those NXIVM girls, and Ghislane Maxwell), serving to soften the hard edges of her man.

Sometimes she is just beautiful and voiceless arm candy, like Melania Trump, her mere presence "proving" the masculinity and virility of her man. Sometimes she even speaks and has a voice of her own, like Trump's former press secretary Kellyanne Conway (and, at the time of writing, his current press secretary Karoline Leavitt), but even then, she is just toeing the line, serving as spokesperson and interpreter, with no original ideas, and certainly no critical ones, of her own. For the first half of my childhood in the Children of God cult, I watched our prophet's wife, Karen Zerby, play this type of SWW to perfection— until she ultimately stepped into greater power right after his death.

The second type of SWW is the secret controller; she meets the criteria for pretty sidekick but is influencing things behind the scenes. In the book *The Cult of We*, we see Rebekah Neumann, played by Anne Hathaway in the hit miniseries *WeCrashed*, embody this type of SWW to perfection. In the Children of God, those close to the leadership saw Karen Zerby slip into this role as our prophet got closer to death and became more dependent on substances (alcohol for him, amphetamines and barbiturates for Jim Jones a couple decades earlier) to keep him going. In the political era of the 2020s, we've seen Ron DeSantis's wife take this role on too. In a *Politico* article titled "The Casey DeSantis Problem: 'His Greatest Asset and His Greatest Liability,'" she's described as being seen by many as "an absolute superstar of a political spouse, a not so 'secret weapon,' even something like his saving grace—an antidote for her sometimes awkward husband, social in a way that he is not, charismatic in a way that he is not, generally and seemingly at ease in the spotlight in a way that he so often and so evidently is not."[16] Interviews with people on the inside paint a picture of a first lady integral in shaping and driving the governor, seeking power through her proximity to it.

But sometimes the sidekick gets ideas of her own, and sometimes the secret controller decides she wants power of her own, bringing us to the third type of SWW. In the Children of God, Karen Zerby transitioned from the prophet's loyal wife and spokesperson to become his replacement—almost as if she had been planning it all along. On his deathbed, when his death became obvious to him, Berg advised Zerby to never tell the followers of his demise—demonstrating just how perfect she'd become at being him. Ultimately, she disregarded this advice (I know this only because my very young mother was a secretary in the room) because she knew she could seamlessly take over his organization of complete and coercive control and lose almost none of the followers. We could argue she'd become the ultimate SWW, finally gaining what they all think they are working toward—real power—just like #LadyBosses Elizabeth Holmes and Sheryl Sandberg, or perhaps, at the most absurd extreme, fake German heiress Anna Delvey, who created an entire fictional identity to start a business, get rich, and gain status, while swindling investors and Manhattan socialites. When this type of woman does become the boss, she steps over the line of "acceptable" power for a woman in our society to wield. So when they fall—these female cult leaders, toxic CEOs, and criminals—I would argue that society is much more gleeful than if she had been a man, as though she has doubly earned her punishment and shame, as much for stepping outside of the proper role for women and daring to grasp at absolute power, as for whatever crimes she committed while wielding said power.

But sometimes, this third type of Skinny White Woman forgets her place and becomes a problem for the men she supports as her one and only job. Princess Diana comes to mind, a woman who refused to toe the line of the British royal family, tone herself down, or play the role required of her. Tammy Faye Messner (formerly Bakker) ruffled the feathers of her husband Jim Bakker and evangelical powerbroker Jerry Falwell by using her "Praise the Lord" TV ministry to express compassion for gay people and those with AIDS—insisting they deserved love, not condemnation. And of course, there was the #MeToo movement, when women around the world refused to be silent about men's sexual abuses and bad behavior any longer, amplifying the call to action that Tarana Burke, an activist and founder of the original MeToo movement, had started years earlier. In my memoir I write about the ultimate demise of my military career after my once-vaunted status as a "golden child" in my unit, when I stopped being quiet and obedient and pushed back too hard against the system. Mark Ackman, an Army major who was a captain alongside me when it all happened, said it best in a text to our "Lieutenant Mafia" group: "What happened to Daniella is ironic, because usually when the Army realizes that someone is too different for the group, and drums them straight out, it's through their own fuckery. But this time, other people's fuckery brought Daniella into the spotlight, where she was still discovered to be too different to tolerate."

The cult of white supremacy and patriarchy, which we've all been indoctrinated under to some extent, has taught us that it's the job of "good" women to be quiet, skinny, and a light shade of beige, and to not be or say anything that stands out, that draws attention to ourselves, that makes us, in any way, unique. Here, my own experience as a Skinny White Woman stands in interesting parallel to my experience as a US Army soldier, where a common Army saying told us that all you have to do to be successful is to be in the right place, at the right time, in the right uniform—and never volunteer for anything (more on uniforms and appearance policing in chapter 4). The message is as familiar as it is striking: Be calm, quiet, well-behaved, ready for anything—and don't stand out. I would argue that a similar message is conveyed in most every school, church, and workplace in this country. As soon as we start deconstructing our American cult experience, we are able to see that white supremacy, patriarchy, and capitalism are major cultic systems that we've all been indoctrinated by, and those systems have a whole country's worth of Skinny White Women propping them up.

By continuing to toe the line, we fail to critically question the cults and systems we are all in, and our silence is complicit in harming others. White women can no longer just be pretty, quiet sidekicks to the cult of whiteness, only using our voice when it benefits us personally ("Can I speak to your manager?"). As someone commented on one of my TikTok videos, where I actively discuss all the concepts going into this book: "When a white girl is dressed like that, you know she's about to drop some truth." My violently purple bathrobe and the large, beaded, fluorescent-pink tropical parrot earrings hanging from my ears were code that communicated, without me saying a word, *I'm no longer playing their game. Let's tear this thing down.* Only when we all question the sacred assumption of the cult of whiteness—that whiteness itself is sacred—will we be able to wake up from our cults.

Chapter 2

Sacred Assumption: But We Are Saving Lives

This young man was first introduced to the group because it was court-ordered after an arrest. At first, it all felt strange—the chants, the slogans, the group prayers. But there was also a real kindness there, a relief in finding people who didn't judge him, who seemed to *get it* without him needing to explain. He kept coming back, and as the weeks stretched into months, he found his identity shifting. He wasn't just "Michael" anymore; he was "an alcoholic," a label he had to fully embrace to stay sober. He internalized the idea that leaving the group would mean jails, institutions, or death, and he began to see the outside world—the people who drank, the therapists who recommended moderation or harm reduction—as dangerous. Questioning the program wasn't just risky, it was heresy—and a death sentence. What started as a reluctant agreement turned into a sacred assumption that everyone around him shared: Alcoholics Anonymous was his salvation. It was the only path that worked. Walking away from it was unthinkable.

* * *

Despite its emphasis on anonymity, chances are you know someone who regularly attends AA meetings. They're famous for a reason— the program has helped save countless lives. Their model is simple but strict: a spiritual path to total abstinence, guided by the 12 steps and peer-led support. There's no central charismatic leader, unless you count the ghosts of their long-dead founders, Bill Wilson and Dr. Bob Smith. Their foundational texts—the "Big Book" (*Alcoholics Anonymous: The Story of How Many Thousands of Men and Women Have Recovered from Alcoholism*) and *Twelve Steps and Twelve Traditions*—are considered gospel, offering spiritually based principles for overcoming alcohol addiction, and guidelines for how members and groups should interact with each other and with society. Though AA chapters vary widely in tone and intensity depending on local culture, a shared ethos prevails: surrender, humility, and the belief that alcoholism is a disease requiring lifelong fellowship to manage. For many members, this translates to the conviction that AA is the only effective path to recovery.

Founded in the 1930s, back when our understanding of the brain was limited, the program has many aspects that aren't backed by research and medical science. Studies do show that AA, despite lacking a scientific origin, is still the most effective path to abstinence we have, better than psychotherapy alone, largely due to its focus on social interaction and mutual support.[1] AA is recommended, sometimes required, by doctors, mental health professionals, courts, and even the military, and its influence dominates addiction treatment facilities. Because the stakes are so high—life and death, really—the program has developed a powerful resistance to critique. It's free, widely available, and there's no denying it has helped many people. But its numbers still aren't great—in *The Sober Truth: Debunking the Bad Science Behind Twelve-Step Programs and the Rehab Industry*, psychiatrist Lance Dodes argues that Alcoholics Anonymous has a long-term success rate of only 5 to 10 percent, based on studies showing low retention and sobriety rates among participants. He criticizes the widespread reliance on AA and 12-step models in addiction treatment despite limited scientific evidence of their effectiveness.[*2] Still, many members remain deeply loyal—sometimes for life—convinced that leaving the program would mean relapse and ruin. My co-writer Amy vividly recalls times at meetings when an old-timer (ignoring the "no crosstalk" rule against commenting on others' shares) responded to a newcomer's concern about brainwashing with a smug line: "Well, sometimes brains need to be washed."

Why Do People Join Cults and Extreme Groups?

Before jumping into the sacred assumption, it's essential to understand why people join cults in the first place, and why they stick around, even when things get abusive or when the red flags are painfully obvious. From the outside, it's easy to think, *That would never be me. Only naive or gullible people fall for that kind of stuff.* But the reality is, no one is totally immune. I mean, one of the Branch Davidians who died during the FBI standoff in Waco was a Harvard-educated lawyer. For a long time, researchers thought it was just stupidity or poverty that drew people into these extreme groups—turns out, it's way more complex than that.

When you dig deeper into why people join these groups, you start to see how cults and terrorism studies overlap in some pretty interesting ways. As an intelligence officer working in counterterrorism during the so-called war on terror, I saw firsthand how terrorist organizations offer recruits a complete transformation—an entirely new worldview and a deep sense of purpose. Once people buy in, they become fiercely loyal and almost cultlike in how they dedicate themselves to the group. You see the same patterns in gangs, too. It's all about finding identity and belonging, and perhaps a feeling of protection, in something larger

---

* It's worth noting that Dodes's claims have drawn criticism for selectively citing data and applying clinical standards to what is fundamentally a peer-support program. Subsequent reviews, including a 2020 Cochrane analysis, suggest AA may be effective for some individuals—particularly those who remain engaged over time—but support his broader call for more evidence-based, individualized treatment options.

than yourself. And it's even more appealing when the world doesn't seem to offer another place where you fit.

The emotional pull of belonging to a group can feel a lot like being in love with your fellow team members—and that pull can be what brings people in to begin with. Clark McCauley and Sophia Moskalenko, in their article from the research journal *Terrorism and Political Violence*, explain that "love often determines who will join [a terrorist group]. The pull of romantic and comradely love can be as strong as politics in moving individuals into an underground group."[3] Expert in persuasion psychology Dr. Robert Cialdini backs this up with his "liking rule"— simply put, people are more likely to say yes to people they like.[4]

Radicalization doesn't happen in a single dramatic moment; it happens over time, one small rationalization at a time. People don't realize they're in a cult until they're deeply entrenched, and most violent extremists don't set out to become terrorists. No one joins a "dangerous cult" or "terrorist cell"—they join something that feels like a solution, a salvation. The slow shift into extremism mirrors how the sacred assumption forms: tiny, almost invisible steps, each one just close enough to normal that you don't notice you've crossed a line.

Financial motivations might play a role for some people joining terrorist groups or gangs, but it's not just about money or a lack of resources. Early on, scholars used the idea of "relative deprivation"— the gap between what people think they deserve and what they actually experience—to explain why some turn to extremism.[5] But then came the student movements of the '60s and '70s, and that theory started to crack. You could see the same kind of thing happening with cults in the '70s, and more recently with everything from justice movements like the Arab Spring and antifa to the rise of homegrown American white-supremacist terrorists like many of those who stormed the US Capitol on January 6, 2021. The people who joined these groups came from all kinds of backgrounds, so it's clear that deprivation isn't the only factor at play here. Something deeper is going on.

As research on cults progressed, scholars realized that the idea of relative deprivation just didn't hold up. What researchers did discover is two key things that most people in extreme groups have in common. The first, and probably the easiest to explain, is the lack of strong social connections. Sociologist Lorne L. Dawson, in his article "The Study of New Religious Movements and the Radicalization of Home-Grown Terrorists: Opening a Dialogue," explains that people with fewer social ties tend to have lower stakes in conforming to societal norms. This makes them more open to joining groups that are in tension or conflict with society. This ties directly to Cialdini's social proof theory, which he discusses in his book *Influence: The Psychology of Persuasion*. "One means we use to determine what is correct is to find out what other people think is correct," he writes.[6] So if someone doesn't have those normal social connections to offer counterbalance, they're more likely to get drawn into extreme beliefs. Cialdini also tells us that "the problem comes when we begin responding to social proof in such a mindless and reflexive fashion that we can be fooled by partial or fake evidence"—which is right where cults want you.

Having more friends or strong social ties can be a protective factor. Leah Remini's memoir *Troublemaker: Surviving Hollywood and Scientology* and her A&E series *Scientology and the Aftermath* provide numerous personal examples of family and friends discouraging involvement in Scientology. One major theme is that loved ones are often the first line of defense—stepping in when someone begins accepting the auditing process or deeper levels of Scientology. In *Misguided: My Jesus Freak Life in a Doomsday Cult*, Perry Bulwer says his lack of strong social ties and guidance led him to drop out of high school in Canada and join the Children of God cult. Among a list of things he describes that could have kept him from making such a momentous decision, he also includes "a public school education emphasizing critical-thinking skills that taught me how to think, not just what to think....[This] would've equipped me to examine and dispute the religious beliefs instilled in me. And a reliable mentor could've helped me with that process, advising me before I made the misguided decision to drop out of society."[7]

This pattern of social isolation is seen across other extreme groups too. Researchers have suggested that violence may be connected to unmet psychological needs, like the need to feel a sense of belonging. Studies focusing on individuals involved in solo acts of terrorism have found that, compared to the general population, they are significantly more likely to experience social isolation or have gone through divorce, separation, or widowhood.[8] This aligns with the significance-quest theory, developed by Arie Kruglanski and colleagues, which, at its core, is about the universal need to matter, and how people pursue that need depends on their sociocultural context.[9] When someone is lacking solid social connections, their need for significance becomes even stronger.

Without close relationships to ground them, a person ends up looking for meaning elsewhere, and that's when radical or even violent movements start to look appealing. These groups offer the promise of purpose, a clear sense of belonging, and a way to feel important again. So someone on this kind of quest might latch onto extreme ideologies or actions in an attempt to feel like they matter. Psychologists and researchers Margaret Singer and Janja Lalich named two conditions that make an individual especially vulnerable to cult recruiting: being depressed, and being in between important affiliations.[10*]

This search for belonging ties directly into the second major factor that scholars highlight in cult recruitment: being a "seeker."[11] Many high-control groups even have recruiters trained to spot and draw in people with these traits. In a general sense, a seeker can be defined as a person who is actively looking for something. In a spiritual context, this often means a search for meaning or a mission of self-discovery. You'll hear words like "authenticity" and "higher purpose" and "alignment" as part of this search. When I took an informal TikTok survey of my 260k+ followers, many of whom are self-described cult survivors, some common things came up in their descriptions of this seeker mentality. Seekers are often looking for things like safety in a sense of community, a clear mission or purpose in life, answers to big existential

* The 2003 edition of *Cults in Our Midst*, which I cite frequently, lists only Margaret Singer as the author. However, the original 1995 edition names both Margaret Thaler Singer and Janja Lalich as co-authors. In this work, I refer to both Singer and Lalich as the authors to acknowledge their joint contribution.

questions, an alternative view of power and authority, or "that thing that functional families have."[12] They're searching for something that feels deeper or more meaningful than what they've found in the mainstream. Sometimes it's also about wanting to feel special or superior, or even trading one addiction or obsession for another. And don't underestimate the power of romantic or comradely love—they're often seeking those emotional connections too. One commenter said, "I was seeking unconditional love." For many seekers, the search is also about finding a place where their grievances about the world are validated. They want a space where their frustrations or disillusionment make sense, where they feel like they belong to a group that understands their pain or confusion. And cults, with their clear narratives and tight-knit communities, are really good at providing that.

Dr. Janja Lalich describes the common stereotype of cult members as "deranged, unstable, weak-minded, or weak-willed. They must be needy lost souls who cannot think for themselves…dysfunctional, mentally ill, or coerced by charismatic but insane leaders." But, she explains, "the confounding behaviors of some cult members occur as a logical conclusion to lives that have been gradually constrained in an increasingly oppressive social structure."[13] It's not about weakness or instability—it's about a slow, methodical process. I like to say that onboarding into either a cult or the US Army takes a solid six months. Each step seems rational enough at the time, even as things slowly get more extreme, until you're increasingly cut off from the outside world and inundated in that group's culture. As Dr. Alexandra Stein reminds us in her book *Terror, Love and Brainwashing*, "The stereotype gets an important fact wrong—these people are not looking to submit to a malevolent authority figure, or to join a cult or a totalist group."[14] Nobody signs up with that goal in mind.

In 1972, out in California, my grandfather had what you could call a rough day. After a bad LSD trip, during which he was convinced he'd met Satan himself, he found himself sitting in a park, head in his hands, trying to recover (because what else do you do after meeting Satan?). And then, right on cue, along came the happy, smiling, guitar-strumming members of the Children of God. They were offering peace, love, and all the easy answers to his complicated questions. So just like that, he took off with them—and he never looked back. He has stayed loyal to the cult to this day, after quickly climbing high in the leadership ranks. Although there is some scholarly disagreement, I know that the seeker path is real—maybe seekers don't know what they are looking for, but they sure do feel like they know when they find it.

While the common image of a joiner is someone actively searching for spiritual or political commitment, Stein explains, this is only one of several pathways into totalist groups. In fact, many individuals enter such groups through other, more prevalent routes—such as being unintentionally drawn in, raised within the group from childhood (as I was), coerced or abducted, or simply by living under a totalitarian regime.[15]

In *Psychology of Terrorism*, Randy Borum credits terrorism expert Martha Crenshaw for pointing out that most terrorists are "pulled in" almost by accident while chasing completely different goals.[16] They might join through a friend or get involved with a front group that seems totally legit at first, only to find themselves deep in a completely different organization. This bait-and-switch tactic is pretty common with cultlike groups, too. Take NXIVM—it cleverly marketed itself as a self-help or personal transformation group, but before long, members found themselves wrapped up in what was really a work (and sex) cult.

Colonel John M. Venhaus gives us a clear breakdown of the different types of seekers he's come across in his work as a psychological operations officer in the US Army. He sorts these individuals into four distinct categories, but at the core, they all share the same drive: They're searching for something that gives their life meaning, looking to define themselves in a deeper way. These four types of seekers represent different paths toward that goal, but they're all essentially trying to fill the same void.

- **The Revenge Seeker** is diffusely frustrated and angry and wants to discharge that frustration or anger toward some person, group, or entity seen as being at fault.

- **The Status Seeker** wants recognition and esteem from others.

- **The Identity Seeker** is compelled by a need to belong and to be a part of something meaningful, wants to define a sense of self through group affiliations.

- **The Thrill Seeker** is attracted to the group because of the prospects for excitement, adventure, and glory.[17]

Seekers come from all kinds of backgrounds and have different reasons for their search. Some are looking for meaning or are frustrated with the current social systems. Others are driven by anger, a desire for revenge, or a passion for social justice, while some are simply trying to escape tough situations at home. Interestingly, these motivations aren't too far off from what drives people to enlist in the US military. Whether they're searching for answers, community, or a sense of purpose, seekers come with an openness to shifting their worldview if they believe they've found the answers they've been looking for. By being open, they may adopt the ideology of a coercive or totalitarian group in disguise, ultimately becoming ensnared under its sacred assumption.

The Worldview Shift...

We all have a worldview—that's part of being human. *Worldview* can be defined as a framework of beliefs, values, and assumptions through which a person interprets and makes sense of the world—and their place in the world. It shapes how we see things, what we believe, and how we act. It helps us connect with other people who share similar perspectives, allowing us to cooperate on a large scale. In fact, creating and sticking to shared myths might have given *Homo sapiens* the evolutionary edge over other animals. In *Sapiens: A Brief History of Humankind*, Dr. Noah Yuval Harari explains that "fiction has enabled us to not merely imagine things, but to do so *collectively*." Our ability to gossip, or to "speak about fictions," is a skill that's crucial for large-scale cooperation among *Homo sapiens*.[18]

Human interactions revolve around the stories we tell and how we convince others to buy into those stories. "The real difference between us and chimpanzees," Harari says, "is the mythical glue that binds together large numbers of individuals, families, and groups."[19] It's this shared belief system, this "mythical glue," that has made us so successful as a species. Without it, we wouldn't be able to organize in the large, complex societies we have today. This glue is powerful, and when people join cults or extreme groups, their worldview begins to shift. They start to adopt the group's shared narratives, which become their new stories, and their new glue. This is the key to how these groups maintain control—by slowly altering someone's belief system until they've completely bought into the sacred assumption the group promotes. Cult leaders know this all too well. Their big goal? Getting you to set aside your personal worldview, even just for a little while, and take on theirs instead.

Randy Borum, one of the pioneers in developing a heuristic model to assist law enforcement officers in better understanding the process of radicalization, highlights that terrorist groups provide their members with not a religion, but a comprehensive worldview.[20] Four types of worldviews emerge consistently in studies on extremism and violence, drawn from concepts explored in political and psychological research by a range of scholars. I posit that the worldviews of most cults and high-control groups would also fit within these categories, which Borum defines in his chapter "The Etiology of Radicalization" in *The Handbook of the Criminology of Terrorism*:

- **Authoritarianism:** A rigid mindset characterized by unquestioning obedience to authority, unwavering adherence to tradition, and deep suspicion of outsiders. This perspective often aligns with anti-democratic and extremist ideologies.

- **Dogmatism:** A closed belief system that revolves around absolute authority, fostering intolerance toward opposing viewpoints and creating barriers to accepting alternative perspectives.

- **Apocalypticism:** The conviction that existing evils will soon be eliminated through a major, divinely ordained event. Adherents typically interpret current world events as fulfilling a predetermined cosmic plan.

- **Fundamentalist mindset:** A polarized worldview defined by deep paranoia, expectation of apocalyptic transformation, unwavering devotion to a singular leader, and the pursuit of complete personal reinvention.[21]

Having a particular worldview doesn't directly lead to radicalization or violent extremism, Borum explains, but it can make someone more susceptible or open to joining extremist groups or engaging in terrorism (or cults, as I suggest), through a variety of pathways. And it's not just the groups themselves that resist easy categorization—our academic fields do too. As Lorne L. Dawson points out, scholars of new religious movements and scholars of terrorism have long worked separately, even though they're studying nearly identical psychological processes. This siloed thinking is a luxury that reality doesn't allow. Extremism doesn't care if you call it spiritual, political, or corporate—regardless of the category, it reshapes your worldview just the same. If we want to better recognize and resist culty behavior, we have to be willing to connect dots across disciplines that have stayed too isolated for too long.

You might notice religious-sounding language like "conversion experience" when we talk about the shift into extremism. But the group doesn't have to be religious in the traditional sense to imbue individuals with a sense of what Dawson refers to as sacralized living. As he explains, people are ultimately searching for—and come to deeply value—a kind of sacred or elevated way of living.[22] Much like monks or other devoted religious figures once admired in society, they long to live with a sense of eternal purpose or meaning—which mainstream culture no longer provides. The ascent of a charismatic leader, essential for cults and terrorist groups to radicalize and carry out significant violence, possesses a pseudo-spiritual essence. This quality taps into the same motivational factors that attract individuals to conventional religions, regardless of whether the group is formally recognized as a religious organization. "Some cults may be part of the new religious landscape," Janja Lalich tells us, "but many more have ideologies that stem from other sources: political, philosophy, nationalism, psychological theories, psychotherapeutic approaches, belief in extraterrestrial life, self-improvement regimens, a charismatic figure, and so on."[23] In short, a cult doesn't have to be religious, but it does give you a worldview, and it does require you to shift your personal worldview until it aligns with theirs.

It's not like flipping a switch—transforming someone's worldview takes time, and it's not as simple as the pop-culture idea of brainwashing. In her book *Bounded Choice: True Believers and Charismatic Cults*, Lalich calls this process resocialization into the cult identity, which she describes as a "willing and willful transformation."[24] What's striking is that this resocialization typically isn't coercive in the obvious sense—it unfolds gradually, subtly reshaping how people understand themselves and the world around them. People may feel a sense of choice is involved, but many don't anticipate how deep the change will go. Whether you're talking about cult members or military recruits, it's less about sheer obedience and more about a slow internalization of the group's values. Lalich emphasizes that even though people claim they willingly chose this path, it doesn't mean they had the full picture from the start.

Lorne Dawson highlights another critical point: Most terrorist organizations, like most cults, don't start out violent. They begin as ideological, political, or religious movements—trying to change the world, not destroy it. Only through the gradual radicalization of both leaders and followers does a more extremist worldview reveal itself.

In the same way, cults don't start by demanding your absolute loyalty or your life. They offer belonging, purpose, and meaning. Only later, after many tiny shifts and justifications, do they engage in this process. Alcoholics Anonymous, with its goal of helping alcoholics stop drinking, changes the alcoholic's value system; the person internalizes principles about how to live their life. While this in itself isn't a bad thing, many of those principles require a person's continued immersion in the group. For example, AA recommends working with a sponsor—a peer mentor that a vulnerable, newly sober alcoholic trusts to guide them through the steps and act as a pseudo-therapist and sobriety coach. The emotional support and practical tools provided by these peers can, when done right, be more effective for long-term sobriety than therapy alone.[25] But sponsors are untrained for any sort of therapeutic role, many certainly carry their own baggage, and they are not supervised by anyone besides their own sponsor, if they have one. In addition to sponsorship, other tools taught by AA assume ongoing membership in, and dependence on, the group. Solutions to cravings or other sticky situations are often "Call your sponsor," "Go to a meeting," "Work the steps," "Talk to another member"—the group itself is the scaffolding required to uphold the value system and principles. People can come to believe that if they leave the group, everything they've worked so hard to build will fall apart.

Similarly, the Children of God cult resocialized tens of thousands of members to abstain from drinking or using drugs, and they were remarkably successful in their efforts. Most stayed sober for forty, even fifty years, until the structure of the organization, and by extension their lives, started to crumble. Once that support system was gone, a lot of members slipped back into old habits—self-medicating and turning to the same vices they had once overcome.

Resocialization into a "total ideology"—whether it's called *brainwashing*, *coercive persuasion*, *thought reform*, or any of the other terms used (even *rehabilitation*, if you want to go that far)—leads to three key behaviors, according to Dr. Alexandra Stein. "First, the follower is glued in anxious dependency to the group,"[26] like how Narcotics Anonymous tells its members that without going to meetings and working the program, their result will inevitably be relapse and "jails, institutions, and death."[27] I got a pretty similar message when leaving both the Children of God and the US Army—some version of "You'll never make it in the outside world." Such messaging keeps people in a state of constant fear, driving them to seek comfort from the very group that instills that fear.

Their anxiety leads to the second behavior Stein mentions, "cognitive collapse, or dissociation, in the mind of the follower."[28] The person starts to believe there's no way out of the threat or situation that the group has made them feel is inevitable, so they begin to operate in a state of constant, or near-constant, dissociation so that they can remain in the group. This dissociation could be the reason for what has been called the "cult glaze" or "Mormon face"—the spaced-out look in the eyes of the Manson Family members, the many Duggar wives and daughters, or current members of The Fellowship, the powerful conservative Christian group that runs the National Prayer Breakfast attended by every US president in modern times.

The third behavior in this resocialization process is that "leadership can now take advantage of this cognitive collapse and interject their own agenda into the cognitive vacuum" that's been created.[29] Once someone is fully immersed, they've adopted a whole new worldview, and the leadership is free to take full advantage of them. Naturally, the new member cuts ties with people in their old life who wouldn't understand or could try to pull them away from the group (more on isolation and entrance costs in later chapters).

This might sound like what people call a "conversion process," but Janja Lalich clarifies that "conversion is the process by which a person develops a new perspective on life...I prefer the term worldview shift to identify the internal change that takes place as a person adopts a new perspective, or worldview, and becomes a practicing adherent."[30] Cults want you to completely shift from whatever beliefs you have until you're fully aligned with their ideology and trapped by what I like to call their sacred assumption.

...Into the Sacred Assumption

I landed on the term *sacred assumption* about fifteen years after I left the cult I grew up in at age fifteen. People kept asking me over and over again, "How could anyone justify things like prostitution and pedophilia as the will of God?"—things my own family and tens of thousands of others accepted in the Children of God. The concept of the sacred assumption explains how even the most intelligent people— like the actresses and well-educated women in NXIVM—could allow themselves to be branded, without anesthesia. It also sheds light on why American soldiers willingly sacrifice their lives rather than let the flag touch the ground. Once your worldview has shifted so completely and you become so entrenched in the group's mentality, you can justify anything under the sacred assumption.

Simply put, the sacred assumption is the one thing you must believe to be a member in good standing—the core, unquestionable belief that serves as the foundation of a high-control group. This assumption is presented as an absolute truth that justifies the group's actions and binds members through a shared worldview. It becomes the lens through which members see everything, making them justify behaviors, rules, and practices they might otherwise question.

In the Children of God, the sacred assumption was that David Berg, a regular, basic white guy and failed preacher from California, was actually the prophet of God. As long as that belief held, members could rationalize any atrocity. In NXIVM, the sacred assumption allowed followers to latch onto whatever supported their belief—such as Keith Raniere's high IQ score—while ignoring the long trail of failures that contradicted it. His followers never questioned it, believing in his supposed genius and the "executive success" program he invented. In the US Army, the sacred assumption is that America is worth dying for. This belief led almost two million of us into Iraq and Afghanistan, following orders to kill, thinking we were deserving of honor. The same kind of thinking led women in NXIVM to hold down their "sisters" as they were branded with Keith Raniere's and Allison Mack's initials. And it's why thousands of adults in the Children of God read the Davidito book—a 762-page manual that normalized pedophilia—and didn't flinch, even when told to do the same to their own children. As long as members of these groups held on to their sacred assumption, they were able to justify anything, all because they couldn't—or wouldn't—ask themselves: *Could we be wrong?*

"A man with a conviction is a hard man to change," are the opening words in Leon Festinger's groundbreaking 1956 book, *When Prophecy Fails*, in which he explores how people respond when events directly contradict their beliefs.[31] A year later, Festinger published *A Theory of Cognitive Dissonance*, which is considered the foundational work on the subject.[32] Back in 1954, Festinger and his colleagues had found a small UFO cult that believed there would be a great flood on December 21 of that year. These social psychologists decided to go undercover and study the cult's members before and after the event. Their hypothesis was that even when the predicted apocalypse didn't happen, the cult wouldn't just dissolve. And they were right. They discovered that many members didn't abandon their belief at all—and, in fact, doubled down on it, working even harder to convert others.

This reaction went completely against what people thought about human rationality: If something you believed in didn't come true, you'd just give it up, right? But instead, these people felt the need to reinforce their belief by trying to get others on board. It's as if recruiting new believers helped lessen the mental discomfort of being wrong. That whole experience led to the coining of the term *cognitive dissonance*—now regarded as one of the biggest breakthroughs in social psychology. Cognitive dissonance explains why people in high-control groups stick to their guns even when faced with hard evidence that they might be wrong. Festinger's work showed us just how powerful that need to avoid being wrong can be—and why, even when the sacred assumption doesn't hold up to reality, people will do anything to keep it intact.

And it's the group that keeps those beliefs going strong. Festinger, discussing how people can believe conflicting things, explained that a single believer is unlikely to hold on to their faith when faced with strong contradictory evidence unless they have social support. An isolated individual would probably struggle to maintain their belief. However, if the person is part of a committed group that reinforces each other's views, the belief is more likely to persist—and the group may even try to convert others or convince outsiders of their perspective.[33]

So basically, people can hold on to even the wildest ideas as long as they've got a group backing them up. Social reinforcement helps them stick to their guns, even when the evidence says otherwise. This explains why, when a cult's prophecy fails or its beliefs are disproven, members lean into their belief even harder. The power of the group dynamic can make people feel like they're part of something bigger, which helps them push away doubts and maintain their faith, no matter how illogical it might seem. And of course, there is quite a heavy dose of sunk cost fallacy here, which we'll talk about more in the chapter on entrance and exit costs.

In cults, with the benefit of hindsight, it's usually easy to spot the sacred assumption that leads to cognitive dissonance. But in other groups, the ones we don't typically think of as cults, that sacred assumption can be as simple as believing our team, our family, or our religion is right—just because it's ours. We want to belong, and we'll convince ourselves that belonging means agreeing. In some way or another, every cult is preaching the message that they are the best and only way to do life (or sobriety, as Alcoholics Anonymous has claimed for nearly a century). Singer and Lalich say that "almost all cults make the claim that their members are 'chosen,' 'select,' or 'special,' while nonmembers are considered lesser beings."[34] It can even be found in cult naming conventions. "Some cults start their names with 'The,' implying that theirs is the only way to be, to think, or to live," they tell us in *Cults in Our Midst: The Continuing Fight Against Their Hidden Menace.* "Examples include The Tru Believers, The Way International, The Walk, The Process, The Foundation, The Body, The Farm, The Assembly."[35]

But it doesn't stop at "just join the group and you'll be special." Stephen Kent, a sociologist and cult expert, tells Amanda Montell in *Cultish* that in many cases, what's being sold isn't a true transformational change, but rather an induction into a system that thrives on power imbalances and people giving over their absolute trust.[36] These systems are built on devotion and hero worship. Whether it's a cult, a workplace, or a family, the results can look eerily similar. You aren't just signing up to be part of something—you're giving yourself over to a belief that becomes untouchable, no matter how shaky its foundation might actually be.

An electric sense of excitement can take over in groups like cults—Heaven's Gate comes to mind—but you can also see it among soldiers. In my memoir, in a chapter titled "Drink the Kool-Aid," I describe the intensity of Army basic training and how it felt like the identity-breaking indoctrination cult scholars talk about. I recall that big moment when we officially became soldiers and how closely it resembled the "graduation" ceremony (i.e., memorial service) of my cult's prophet so many years before:

> The pageantry, the ceremony, the messaging. Standing straight as boards, not daring to move an inch. Singing of freedom, when we were, at this moment, anything but free.

> Despite my feelings of apprehension, I also felt the stirrings of fervor, of dedication, and the sweetly sad idea of death in service of country. I saw commitment and pride overtaking fear and exhaustion in the faces of the trainees around me.[37]

It was a familiar sensation. I remember seeing that same kind of excitement back in 1993 among the uncles and aunties in the Children of God when they believed the apocalypse was just around the corner. As Y2K got closer, it felt like they almost *wanted* the disaster to come, like they craved it, because it would validate the years of dedication and sacrifice they'd put in.

That mix of commitment and excitement can be intoxicating, whether you're in a cult, an army, or any other high-pressure group. But, as I learned, that feeling of fervor can also be a warning—when dedication becomes absolute, it's easy to lose sight of the bigger picture and fall under the influence of the sacred assumption. Lorne Dawson writes, "As one researcher of Islamic terrorist groups in Pakistan points out, 'When I began this project, I could not understand why killers I met seemed spiritually intoxicated. Now, I think I understand. They seem that way because they are.'"[38]

This intoxication can become a kind of addiction, leading to "cult hopping"—moving from one extreme group to another—which happens more often than you'd think. It's exactly what I did when I joined the US Army only a few years after leaving the cult I grew up in. In some ways, the military almost felt too easy, because I was already used to suppressing individuality and sacrificing myself for the group's mission. When a person leaves one cult, they often find themselves seeking that same intensity and sense of mission, purpose, and community elsewhere—only to land in another group that demands the same level of conformity. And when your identity is being defined for you, that's when you're most vulnerable to being radicalized.

As mentioned earlier in this chapter, one of the most significant indicators of someone who might be vulnerable to cults is feeling isolated and disconnected from society. This vulnerability is especially prevalent in addicts and alcoholics, who you'll often hear (in AA meetings) talking about their lifelong search to fill the "God-sized hole" inside themselves (more about the language of cults in chapter 6). Both the craving for relief and the addictive tendencies themselves play a huge role in why people, especially addicts and alcoholics, get sucked into groups like cults. At first, these groups offer a way out of their vices—strict rules, a whole new lifestyle, and, most importantly, a sense of belonging and acceptance. But what starts off feeling helpful and supportive quickly becomes suffocating, completely overshadowing their previous lives. The intensity and control provided by the cult end up matching the intense feelings they used to get from addictive substances. That's where "intensity addiction" comes into play—the need to constantly chase that high—and cults are experts at providing it. High-control, high-demand environments are the perfect substitute for what they used to get from alcohol, drugs, or whatever their vice was.

Groups like the Children of God back in the '60s or Scientology today have been incredibly successful in getting people to quit their previous addictions. But the trade-off is that the cult becomes the new addiction—members get hooked on the control, the mission, and that feeling of superiority that comes with being part of something that promises to "fix" them. Even well-meaning groups like AA, which genuinely aims to help people abstain from alcohol, can sometimes fall into this trap. When all the members of a group have the same interests, it can create a situation of optimal control—making it easier to keep everyone in line because everyone's chasing the same goal.[39] Because there is ostensibly no one "in charge" of AA, it's not so much about leaders exerting control, but the group itself maintaining its ideological bottom line. The group's mission starts to replace the addiction, but that same dynamic of dependence and intensity is still there. It can be argued, of course, that in a "good" and helpful group like AA, the benefits outweigh the drawbacks, and this new dependance on the group is ultimately positive if it keeps the member sober. Many members have found this to be true. But that experience is far from universal.

What consistently benefits the cult is that members willingly embrace their own indoctrination. As Janja Lalich points out, the primary objectives of a cult's system of influence is to get each member to fully identify with the leader and the group. For this to work, members must believe they are in control of their own fate, even as they hand that control over to their leaders. Lalich gives the example of Heaven's Gate, where members were "agents of their own transformation" when they committed mass suicide with a cocktail of alcohol, phenobarbital, and asphyxiation in order to transform themselves into immortal extraterrestrial beings.[40] They knew the change would be tough, but they were committed to it—not because it was forced on them, but because they believed it was their choice. This sense of ownership over the process makes it even harder for them to recognize the manipulation at play.

Once they've fully committed, members become so tightly bound to the group's control that any critique from an outsider is met with immediate defense, often invoking the group's sacred assumption. A passionate AA member might say, "But we are saving lives," sidestepping the group's problems, including its less-than-impressive success rate. Still, belief in the group's lifesaving mission keeps members devoted when faced with contrary evidence. Willingness to embrace the group's doctrine as a personal choice reinforces the group's grip. The member isn't just following orders; they're actively choosing to conform. The illusion of autonomy makes it incredibly difficult to break free, even when the methods clearly aren't working. Members see themselves as the heroes of their own story, which is exactly what a cult or high-control group wants them to believe.

This reveals a deeper, uncomfortable level of the sacred assumption—that even something we can all agree is good and saving lives isn't as clear-cut as it seems. We are asked to assume that saving lives is the ultimate good—but at what cost? What else is lost or harmed along the way? Who is then responsible for any damage those saved lives cause? The Children of God sex cult got tens of thousands of people sober too. Did that automatically make them good? One of those people was a founding member of Fleetwood Mac who would never touch a drug again in his long life—but go ahead and Google the accusations of what Jeremy Spencer went on to do with his "saved" life. The Children of God even had a name for this kind of recruiting: "getting high on Jesus." And then, with those lives they saved, they built the world's most notorious sex cult and devastated the lives of their second-, third-, and fourth-generation members—and nobody saved us.

I've been accused of causing deaths by simply suggesting parallels between AA's tactics and those I experienced growing up in a cult. I want to emphasize that I do not consider AA and the Children of God anywhere near the same level on the culty spectrum, and I do not discount anyone's positive experience in 12-step programs (my co-writer Amy being one), or any group for that matter. But I believe it is possible—necessary, in fact—to ask critical questions of the groups we are part of, especially our most beloved, and most especially those we join when we are at our most vulnerable—exactly when it's hardest to ask those hard questions and advocate for ourselves. Questioning is the only way to ensure a group's continuing integrity and our own autonomy within it. For me, it's a red flag if a group's sacred assumption is used as a shield against scrutiny, deflecting any real conversation about efficacy, methods, or collateral damage. If a group cannot weather criticism, if it cannot engage in healthy debate, is it really a group you want to be a part of?

One of AA's clichés is "Take what works and leave the rest," and I suspect that the most successful members—not only of AA but of all groups—are able to do just that.

Chapter 3

Transcendent Mission: Do It for the Children

Imagine a world where diagnosing cancer and other serious diseases could occur with just a few drops of blood. It was indeed a noble and revolutionary mission that unfolded in Silicon Valley in 2003—one undoubtedly worth investing in and sacrificing for. This mission required a visionary leader to bring it to reality, and an unexpected candidate stepped forward. Instead of sparking doubt and demands for more evidence, her complete lack of qualifications seemed to work in her favor. How could a nineteen-year-old Stanford engineering dropout deceive individuals as renowned as Henry Kissinger, Jim Mattis, and Bill Clinton? The mere audacity of her presence seemed to legitimize the endeavor, winning over investors, board members, employees, and critics alike.

The transcendent mission she offered became the tool she used to captivate them all: to create a "world in which no one ever has to say goodbye too soon."[1] This young woman, who had been studying people from a young age, constructed a powerful imaginary world where countless medical tests could be run with just a few drops of blood and deadly diseases could be diagnosed early and from home. It was a safe bet to assume that almost every prospective employee would have known someone who battled cancer or heart disease, struggled with diabetes, or simply loved a child traumatized by needles. She counted on the fact that anyone interested in working at a cutting-edge medical and technological startup would be easily pulled in and motivated by this mission and the worldview she painted for them.

Relying on secrecy and Silicon Valley's "fake it 'til you make it" culture, the organization fostered a toxic environment where employees were siloed and job security was a daily uncertainty. After a decade with the company, the chief scientist tragically took his own life under the pressure of a deposition.* But even as Elizabeth Holmes's lies caught up with her and the company began to crumble, dedication to the transcendent mission, along with an absence of critical scrutiny, kept investors and employees from seeing the truth until it was too late. Former Secretary of State George Schultz even continued to support the organization and its unproven founder over his own grandson, who was a key whistleblower in exposing the nine-billion-dollar fraud that Theranos had become.[2]

* * *

An overlooked lesson from cults is that they actually get some things right. They offer mission, purpose, motivation, and community—the stuff that CEOs, community organizers, and leaders of all kinds crave.[3] It's usually not the leader's charisma that pulls people in. More often, it's the big, compelling goal that convinces them to dedicate their lives to the cause, even when the rules are restrictive or the situation starts feeling off, or despite the leader's obvious flaws. Followers might question the leader or some of the group's practices, but as long as the mission remains strong, they stay committed. People are wired to seek purpose and meaning, and if a group offers that, they'll stick around for the ride. Janja Lalich highlights that having a transcendent belief system is one of the four essential things someone needs to maintain

---

* Cults and coercive groups are frequently linked to elevated rates of suicide, reflecting the extreme psychological toll they exact (Snow, *Deadly Cults*, 2003).

"bounded control" over others, in addition to systems of control, systems of influence, and a charismatic leader.[4]

A transcendent mission is characterized by its broad, vague, and sometimes elusive qualities—stretching beyond time, space, and sometimes even logic.* The key feature of such a mission is that it's hard to pin down when or if success is truly achieved. Take Theranos, for example. According to their still-live LinkedIn page, "By making actionable information accessible to everyone in the world at the time it matters most, we are working to facilitate the early detection and prevention of disease, and empower people everywhere to live their best possible lives." Inspiring mission, right? But it's so sweeping and abstract that there's no clear way to measure success. When will they have they empowered "people everywhere"? How do you know when that's been accomplished?

This kind of mission contrasts sharply with what corporate America calls SMART goals—specific, measurable, achievable, relevant, and time-bound. Companies may struggle to implement SMART goals effectively, but they at least have a clear structure for what success looks like. A transcendent mission, by design, stays hazy, giving the group or leader room to continuously shift the goalposts, which keeps members striving toward something that feels perpetually out of reach. This ambiguity can keep people locked into a cause, chasing an ideal that's always just beyond their grasp. Consider the phrase "Do it for the children"—a rallying cry heard across a wide spectrum of causes, from the legitimate advocacy work of Save the Children to the QAnon conspiracy theory, which co-opted similar language to lend credibility to unfounded claims about elite child-trafficking rings.[5] In both cases,

_____

* My idea of the transcendent mission has taken shape over years of reflection, inspired and shaped by the work of so many before me. *Bounded Choice* by Janja Lalich helped put words to patterns I'd been sensing for a long time. Eric Hoffer's *The True Believer: Thoughts on the Nature of Mass Movements* captured the deep pull of group identity and belonging. And the work of Margaret Singer and others on cult dynamics gave me a clearer sense of the forces that keep people loyal to high-control groups, even when the warning signs are there.

the emotional appeal is potent, but the goal itself is vague and offers little clarity on what achieving it would actually entail.

The transcendent mission is the glue that holds the group together, something everyone sees as crucial and inherently good. This shared purpose justifies the self-sacrifice and personal compromises that members are expected to make. Cult leaders keep this focus sharp. They demand extraordinary commitments from their followers, who stay dedicated because they believe they're part of something much bigger than themselves. The collective mission is what keeps the group unified and driven.

You see the same phenomenon at Fortune 500 company retreats, at AA conventions, or during a megachurch's Sunday service. In these settings, the mission is glorified, which drives everyone to perform at their peak, relentlessly chasing after the shared goal. The transcendent mission's power inspires extraordinary dedication and achievement, but there's always a cost for the member—and rarely does the group return enough in exchange.

In today's corporate culture, words like *mission* and *values* get tossed around like free snacks in the breakroom—ubiquitous, branded, and often devoid of real substance. In fact, *Merriam-Webster* named *culture* the word of the year in 2014, right around the time corporate America became visibly obsessed with it. But despite a decade of HR slide decks and motivational posters, most companies still struggle to define what a healthy culture actually looks like—it's not superficial perks like pool tables, bean bag chairs, and craft beer on tap. Employees aren't the problem here; in fact, many are genuinely seeking community, purpose, and shared meaning. But corporate branding machines co-opt those desires and promise connection while delivering control.

During graduate school for my master's in organizational psychology, I noticed something surprising: No one really wanted to talk about problematic groups. My classmates and professors seemed to assume that the companies we'd work for would always be "good," even while using cultlike methods to influence their employees. It hit me that the whole discipline of organizational psychology (which is often critiqued for its toxic positivity and lack of diversity) is full of people studying how to manipulate and motivate groups so they can then sell that knowledge to corporate America. A core lesson these organizational psychology experts teach their corporate clients to implement: how to build a shared mission and belief system.

Janja Lalich describes a transcendent belief system as "a system of thought that explains past, present, and future. It is transcendent in the sense that it looks to, indeed predicts, a radical change—either progressive or reactionary—in the social order. It not only holds forth a utopian vision, but also offers the actual means by which to get to the new world."[6] And this is what we observe in what I call the *mission-izing*—or weaponizing the mission—of cults and companies alike: a desire to create radical change, and a path through which to do so— that path being membership in the organization. And once a group believes that its mission, and the group itself, is exclusively virtuous, it opens itself up to risk in ways its members may never see coming.

One particularly powerful draw of cult belief systems is their promise of transcending death or achieving a new and improved life beyond this one. The idea of conquering mortality holds universal appeal (who wouldn't want the chance to live forever, or at least have a shot at a better existence after this one?). It taps into fundamental human fears and desires, giving people a reason to endure the hardships that come with being in a high-control group.[7] This promise becomes a compelling force that cult leaders skillfully use to keep members engaged and willing to sacrifice.

The mission serves as the bait, the initial draw that hooks people in, especially when it's framed as noble or life-changing. For Jim Jones, it was creating a racially integrated community, and for Theranos it was transforming medical diagnosis and reducing pain. On the surface, these missions sound meaningful, admirable. In reality, the leader's true intent is often more about personal gain, power, or control.

Yet the vast majority of cult members genuinely believe they're working toward a higher purpose—whether that's racial harmony or preparing for the apocalypse. Ted Patrick—former community relations consultant to California governor Ronald Reagan in the '70s and a key figure in the era of snatch-and-grab deprogrammings, back when the country was still deciding if it was acceptable to forcibly remove people from groups deemed cults—once described his near-recruitment into the Children of God this way: "With the exception of David Berg (the leader) and a few of his close associates, the people doing the brainwashing in Children of God are themselves true believers."[8] This manipulation, which the group members themselves commit, is often worlds apart from the cult's hidden agenda. It shows just how effective cult leaders are at using noble-sounding causes to draw people in and keep them trapped. It's a stark reminder of how easily a good-sounding mission can be twisted to serve a much more self-serving purpose.

Missionizing in High-Control Religions

The practice of sending young individuals on missions is a deeply ingrained rite of passage in the Mormon Church (the Church of Jesus Christ of Latter-day Saints, or LDS), as well as other Christian sects. Typically undertaken in a member's late teens or early twenties, the mission is presented as the ultimate test of faith, loyalty, and readiness to fully dedicate one's life to the cause. As elementary school-aged children, Mormons are introduced to mission songs that have a distinctly military tone.[9] Songs with structured rhythm and a call to duty are powerful tools for instilling a sense of discipline and purpose in young minds (we'll dive deeper into the impact of chanting in chapter 6). The military metaphors woven throughout these songs and teachings lay the foundation for a hierarchy that emphasizes duty, sacrifice, and unquestioning obedience, from a very early age.

By the time these kids become teenagers, they've absorbed that sense of duty so deeply that when they're called to serve on a mission, they willingly do so with intense commitment. A mission has physical demands—being sent anywhere in the world and covering their own expenses—but also requires emotional and spiritual dedication. These teenagers are often leaving home for the first time, far from the comfort and security of their families, to spend two years spreading the Mormon faith, engaging in community service, and seeking converts. And their mission locations are chosen by the Church, reinforcing the belief that they are following a higher calling, no questions asked.

Before being sent out, young missionaries undergo a rigorous program known as the Missionary Training Center, which lasts anywhere from three to twelve weeks. The training instills discipline, deepens their knowledge of the faith, and sharpens their communication skills, preparing them to serve as soldiers for the cause. The militaristic undertones aren't subtle; the two-year missionary period is sometimes referred to as "the boot camp of Mormon greatness," reflecting how the Church openly embraces the parallel between missionary work and military duty.[10]

Sara, a former Mormon missionary, described her experience to me this way:

> The timing of the mission is part of it. It's right at that transition point into adulthood. For most missionaries, this is the first time they're leaving home to live on their own, and even if it isn't, it's probably the furthest they've been from home. And to have that first independent experience be completely centering Mormon beliefs I think really pushes you to make that a part of your adult identity. I went to the Philippines and learned to speak Tagalog. Most of the vocabulary we learned at first was related to church topics. Though many Filipinos learn some English, most I encountered didn't really speak it much. So literally the only conversations that I could have for the first several months while I learned the language were mostly about Mormonism because that was the limit of my vocabulary. Add on to the fact that we weren't really supposed to talk about anything else, and the church really does become your whole personality. Even as I became more fluent in Tagalog, most conversations were still

about church in some way. So, for the period of the mission at least, the church becomes *the* major thing defining your identity, so even after you go home, you still retain that.

As a woman, I had been taught that a career wasn't as important as preparing to be a wife and mother. When I didn't end up getting married as early as many Mormons do, I felt pressure to go on a mission even though it isn't as strict of a requirement for girls. This was partially family and social pressure, but also because I hadn't really prepared myself mentally to enter a career. Giving my labor to the church allowed me to delay facing that.

And ultimately, the mission is a huge sacrifice. It delayed my college graduation two years. I worked hard to learn a new language, I lived in a foreign country working long hours in all weather. Most importantly, I had to say over and over that the Mormon church was true, and have people know me as someone who said that. The indoctrination of saying something out loud to other people is huge. Nobody wants to be a liar. Nobody wants to waste their time. The sunk costs due to the sacrifice of a mission are huge.[11]

Sara's description mirrors parts of my own childhood in the cult that trafficked me around the world, and it brings up some familiar echoes from US Army basic training too. The mission itself is a form of identity-breaking indoctrination in the Mormon church—a way to get the next generation to fully buy in. Idealistic young Mormons, much like the soldiers who stood beside me at the basic training completion ceremony, see only the sweet allure of the mission. The idea of doing something truly meaningful with their lives pulls them in, even if it means becoming a completely different person and enduring hardships along the way.

One former Mormon missionary who served in Venezuela from 1991 to 1993 shared a story on my old TikTok account that really hits home. She was surprised to find that her visa application said she was in the country for "leadership training." It took her years to realize that the most important person she was being sent to convert wasn't anyone she met there—it was herself.[12] That's the real pull of these missions: You're sold on changing the world, but the truth is, they're changing you.

Focusing on young people for missions occurs across mainstream religions, in programs as seemingly benign as Christian Sunday school, Jewish Hebrew school, Quaker First Day school, and cultural or language schools for various ethnic diasporas. Or there's the Awana Club, a global evangelical children's ministry that kids as young as age two can join. Awana presents itself as a leader in child discipleship, encouraging children to share the Gospel and invite others to the group.[13] At their best, these groups aim to educate children in their family's heritage and traditions, while imparting character-building lessons along the way. But high-control groups beyond the mainstream also know that young people, especially those in their teens and early twenties, are often in a phase of life where they're exploring their identities, values, and beliefs. This makes them more vulnerable to persuasive messaging that promises a sense of purpose, belonging, or empowerment. According to developmental psychologist Erik Erikson, the main and most important developmental tasks for adolescents are to solve the identity versus role-confusion crisis, construct their own unique sense of identity, and find the social environment where they can belong and create meaningful relationships with other people.[14] Extremist ideologies are particularly good at offering that sense of identity and community, which is why they're so effective at recruiting young people.[15] These groups know how to target vulnerabilities, using approaches like online propaganda, peer-to-peer recruitment, and content specifically designed to appeal to youth.[16]

The Children of God cult was notorious for recruiting teenagers as young as thirteen or fourteen, grooming them into the fold. In my Army basic training class, the most common age was seventeen—kids in their junior year of high school, doing pushups with their futures already written in military contracts. They'd go back to finish senior year, their next steps locked in, already molded by the system. My husband was one of those seventeen-year-olds who signed up planning to serve the minimum four years. He ended up serving for twenty before retiring. Corporations also realize the power of getting to people while they're young, eager, and moldable. The idea is simple: Get them early, and you might keep them for life.

And of course, it was Adolf Hitler who famously said, "He who holds the children, holds the future," explaining the creation of the Hitler Youth. This quote has resurfaced in far-right political circles, even used by US Congresswoman Mary Miller in a 2021 speech.[17] It's a chilling reminder that controlling youth narratives can shape the future—and that appealing to young people's need for purpose and identity can be manipulated by any group with a powerful mission, for better or worse.

Evangelical Christians on the American right have been especially strategic in cultivating political engagement among young people. A notable example is Generation Joshua, founded in 2004 by Mike Farris, Mike Smith, and the Home School Legal Defense Association. Inspired by Farris's book *The Joshua Generation*—based on the biblical Joshua who led the Israelites into the Promised Land after Moses's death—the program envisions a new generation of Christian leaders, built around homeschooled teens equipped with civics education and direct political experience. This is more than youth outreach—it's a calculated effort to embed Christian-nationalist ideals into future leadership by fostering early civic involvement. Nearly two decades in, however, cracks in this movement have started to show. Some kids raised within the Joshua Generation are now taking more complicated, independent paths—highlighting the unpredictable outcomes of long-term ideological grooming.[18]

Christian nationalism is playing the long game. By raising up this generation, they're not just influencing the current landscape, they're laying the groundwork for the future. It's a calculated and patient approach, and it's shaping the trajectory of American politics, culture, and governance in ways that will be felt for generations to come.

It's hard to miss the militaristic undertones in the missionizing efforts in certain churches, shaping children to see themselves as soldiers in some imagined "army of God" from birth. I often describe how I felt like I was born a soldier in God's End Time Army. And it's no coincidence that a lot of kids raised with a soldier mentality end up becoming actual soldiers later in life. I made the transition from cult to Army with barely a second thought—nothing the military threw at me was harder than what I'd already lived through.

The path from high-control religious environments to military careers is traveled more commonly than you might think. Within the intelligence community there's an inside joke that CIA stands for Christians in Action because so many missionary kids sign up and thrive there.[19] There's also the joke about how there are so many Mormons in the military that all branches give them a standard underwear exemption so they can keep wearing their Jesus jammies under their uniforms. Steven Mansfield's *The Mormonizing of America* points out that "there is an undeniable link between Mormon religious ideals and the fact that graduates of Brigham Young University are among the most sought after by the FBI, the CIA, the National Security Agency, the Secret Service, and hundreds of graduate schools across the country."[20] It's like the structure, discipline, and sense of mission that high-control religious groups provide are the perfect training ground for future soldiers and government agents.

Missionizing in the Military

One thing that resonates deeply for many of us who've been through both cults and the military is the American military's laser focus on the mission, especially when it mirrors the familiar values we were raised with. That call to duty taps into the part of us that craves a purpose so compelling that we're willing to give everything, even our lives, to serve it. For many of us, that readiness to sacrifice ourselves has been ingrained in us since childhood, growing up in the various "armies of God." So sacrificing ourselves for a cause later in life—whether as soldiers or in more extreme acts of dedication—comes naturally.

Take Aaron Bushnell, for example. He grew up in an apocalyptic Christian community, served in the military, and eventually sacrificed himself in the most extreme way imaginable. In February 2024, Aaron chose self-immolation as his protest—the ultimate sacrifice—when he set himself on fire in front of the Israeli embassy in Washington, DC, screaming "Free Palestine" while wearing Air Force fatigues and standing at the position of attention, a soldier to the end. In 2025, two domestic terror attacks carried out by military veterans on New Year's Day brought renewed attention to an alarming finding from the University of Maryland's 2023 National Consortium for the Study of Terrorism and Responses to Terrorism: "Having a US military background is the single strongest individual-level predictor of whether a subject…is classified as a mass casualty offender"—far outpacing mental health issues, prior criminal history, or social isolation.[21] Researchers found that individuals with military backgrounds were 2.4 times more likely to commit mass-casualty extremist violence compared to those without military experience. Military culture, training, and the challenges of reintegration into civilian life can create unique vulnerabilities for radicalization if left unaddressed.

The missionizing in the US military dates back to World War II, a conflict often remembered as a time of national unity. But the public was significantly divided about entering the war, even after Pearl Harbor. Elizabeth Samet, in *Looking for the Good War: American Amnesia and the Violent Pursuit of Happiness*, highlights how the myth of the "Greatest Generation" overshadows the reality of divided opinions and the military's struggle to motivate soldiers reluctant to use deadly force. The solution wasn't better training but appeals to masculinity, honor, and racialized patriotism, framing soldiers as heroic liberators who were part of something bigger than themselves. This manipulation shaped solders' identities to make the mission seem larger than life—and it persists today.

Military rhetoric often mirrors the tone of religious sermons, invoking a messianic view of soldiers as protectors of America's inherent goodness. Samet captures this perfectly when she says, "Only by the magic alchemy of American exceptionalism can war be made to seem an act of love."[22] In the chaos and trauma of war, creating a myth, a simple narrative to cling to, becomes a natural response, and World War II offered that temptation of myth to every country involved. The narrative of a righteous cause, of being a hero and saving the world, is a powerful tool for rallying people, in the military or in religion. While some causes may certainly be just, leaders can also use the narrative manipulatively to suppress doubt, justify harm, or demand unquestioning loyalty.

Once established, the heroic narrative supported the military's shift toward a missionized approach, motivating soldiers with ideological reasons—like in the war on terror—rather than their duties as soldiers. Vietnam presented a significant challenge to this mindset, as the mission became increasingly hard to justify, leading to an all-time low in military morale. Samet illustrates how World War II profoundly shaped the public's perception of the Vietnam War: "If World War Two seemed like a 'good war,' what did that make the war in Vietnam that most Americans seemed to disagree with?" She quotes Gene La Rocque, a retired rear admiral during the Vietnam era, who reflected, "We see things in terms of [World War II], which in a sense was a good war. But the twisted memory of it encourages the men of my generation to be willing, almost eager, to use military force anywhere in the world."[23] This shift toward ideological justification shows that the "good war" myth of WWII reshaped American military motivations and led to a distorted sense of purpose in conflicts like Vietnam, Korea, Latin America, and repeatedly in the Middle East.

Just like in Vietnam, where defining a clear, winnable mission was problematic, the wars in the Middle East have always been vague in their objectives, yet we clung to the belief that we were there for a righteous cause. 9/11 became our motivational touchstone, a moment we could point to and say, "See? We are fighting for America!" The mission of the US military is "to fight and win America's wars," so we told ourselves that everything we were doing was in service of that mission. We had been conditioned, much like those who had been motivated by the "good war" myth, to see ourselves as soldiers in a battle that was always necessary, even if victory felt elusive. By "we"

I mean America, but I also mean my husband and me, who spent a collective seven years in the Middle East on active duty.*

In today's military, we see an almost religious devotion to the image of the soldier—brave, honorable, sacrificing everything for an unquestionably noble mission: protecting America, a country often perceived (by Americans) as inherently good. Without knowing anything about their actual experiences, we offer up an automatic "thank you for your service" to anyone in uniform, as if the mere act of serving is enough to prove someone's virtue. This echoes cultlike adoration, where the mission is beyond reproach and questioning it feels like blasphemy.

In addition to the allure of honor, soldiers also experience a kind of intensity addiction, much like in any cult, fueled in part by ideological commitment, which keeps us searching for the next mission—the next high—to throw ourselves into. Without that mission, without that cause, we don't know who we are. As Sean Patrick Hughes wrote in *The Washington Post*, "This life is hard to stop living. And the fallen of my generation, more times than not, fell before they had a chance to try. And too many more fell after they left, failing to find the purpose or the drive they once felt at war."[24] That addictive need for intensity and purpose is what many people struggle with once the mission is over. For some, like my younger brother, this void becomes unbearable. He was only thirty when he passed, unable to find that sense of purpose and drive outside of the intense structure that the Army—and before that, the cult—had given him.

Missionizing Extremism

Rising Out of Hatred: The Awakening of a Former White Nationalist by Eli Saslow dives deep into the intense, personal journey of someone who was born and raised in white supremacy. It gives us a raw look at

---

* This background draws on insights from seminal works by thinkers like David Vine, Max Boot, Daniel Immerwahr, and others whose ideas helped shape the foundation of what I'm exploring here.

how an extremist ideology can become a family's mission. The book focuses on Derek Black, the son of Don Black, former grand wizard of the Ku Klux Klan and creator of the white supremacist website Storm-front. Derek was raised to be the "great white hope" for the future of white nationalism, indoctrinated with the belief that it was his mission to help build a "great, white nation."[25]

White nationalism wasn't just a belief for Derek—it was the core of his family's identity and purpose, much like Christianity is for evangelical households. It wasn't a casual ideology, or even an all-encompassing worldview; it was a mission, passed down from his father, deeply woven into their everyday lives. The book lays bare how Derek was groomed from a young age to carry the torch, to be the future of the movement, and to spread their agenda. White supremacy was presented to him as the truth—his family's truth. Derek's story shows us how inherited missions can take root so deeply that they shape every aspect of a person's life, from their worldview to their personal relationships.

One of Derek's most significant contributions to this mission was his role in popularizing terms like "reverse racism" and "white genocide," phrases that have since seeped into broader cultural discussions. These terms were carefully crafted to frame white people as victims and push a narrative that distorted conversations about race and discrimination. By positioning efforts toward equity and inclusion as threats to the privileges of white people, Derek and his father helped shift white-nationalist ideas into the mainstream. They framed their ideology in a way that resonated with a much broader audience, particularly younger people who might not have previously identified with the movement.

The phenomenon of missionizing extends beyond religious groups and cults—it reaches into extreme right-wing ideologies like those upheld by the Proud Boys and other white-nationalist organizations. These groups use their own narratives, like the supposed "coming race war," to keep their followers united under a single cause. Their fabricated threats serve as rallying cries and convince members they need to "save" their race or country. It's about keeping people focused on the mission, willing to make extreme personal sacrifices for the group's agenda.

At a 2008 white-nationalist conference in Memphis, attended by Derek Black and his father, the mission was made unmistakably clear. "Restore white America" wasn't just rhetoric—it was a directive, with the possibility of violence openly acknowledged. This was a call to arms, framing the cause as something worth fighting and even dying for. These kinds of declarations are tools for keeping members deeply engaged and willing to go to extreme lengths for what they believe is a noble mission.

At just nineteen, Derek took the stage as the so-called heir apparent to the white-nationalist movement. The timing was no accident—Barack Obama had just been elected president, an event that sent shockwaves through the movement. Derek's speech was crystal clear: The path forward would require infiltrating politics or co-opting the Republican Party. "The Republican Party has to be either demolished or taken over," he told the crowd.[26] The action plan was not public marches or burning crosses—it was stealth, strategy, and seizing institutional power. The room, filled with longtime white-nationalist figures, didn't need anyone to spell out the endgame. The rhetoric was sharp, the stakes were existential, and the willingness to escalate, if necessary, hung heavy in the air. This was mission setting, cult-style: framing the cause as something righteous enough to die for—and dangerous enough to live for.

Derek Black's story is a textbook example of early indoctrination in a high-control group shaping a person's identity. Derek was immersed in extremist ideology from the start, and conditioned from childhood to devote his life to an idea. By age ten, he had created a "kids' page" for Stormfront, and as a teenager he co-hosted a white-nationalist radio show with his father. He even won a seat on a Florida Republican committee at nineteen, though the party refused to seat him. This trajectory wasn't accidental; it was the result of deliberate grooming to commit his life to a cause.

It's the same formula you see in all high-control groups. The younger you can recruit someone and get them to believe in the mission, the more likely they are to stay deeply devoted, even when the ideology's cracks start to show. Derek eventually renounced white nationalism in his early twenties, after attending New College of Florida and forming relationships outside his ideological bubble, which underscores both the power of early indoctrination and the possibility of change. Their* journey is detailed in their 2024 memoir, *The Klansman's Son: My Journey from White Nationalism to Antiracism.*

The missionizing efforts of far-right ideologies found tangible outcomes in both the 2016 election of Donald Trump and the radicalization that led to the events of January 6, 2021—and Trump's 2024 reelection. The groundwork had been laid years earlier, and by the time Trump began retweeting white supremacists and making inflammatory statements, these mission-driven ideologies from the fringe were clearly shaping national politics. Suddenly, ideas that had once been relegated to the dark corners of the internet and extremist rallies were out in the open, normalized in public discourse. The far-right's mission to "restore white America" found a foothold in mainstream politics, emboldening and mobilizing individuals who had long felt marginalized. For them, Trump's election symbolized a victory, validating years of grassroots organizing and online radicalization.

The culmination of this mission-driven mindset was seen in the January 6 attack on the Capitol. Thousands of people, many of whom had spent years absorbing far-right narratives, stormed the seat of American democracy, believing they were acting in service of a higher cause—protecting their version of America. The radicalization that led to this moment was fueled by the same missionizing tactics used by extremist groups to recruit and indoctrinate followers, now manifesting on a national scale. It is also no surprise that nearly one in five of the people charged in the attack on the US Capitol were military veterans, who had once sworn to protect the Constitution.[27]

---

* R. Derek Black came out as transgender in *The Klansman's Son* and now uses both they/them and she/her pronouns. He/him pronouns have been used in reference to periods of their life when they publicly identified as male.

Missionizing in...Space?

When news broke in 2018 about Donald Trump's plans to found the Space Force, I was literally hopping around my house yelling, "It's culty! It's culty!"—but I couldn't yet explain why.

It wasn't just that the military already had an Air Force division that handled space operations, or that the whole thing sounded like a rejected Marvel plot. It was the symbolism. The branding. The eerie promise baked into the very name: *Space Force*. Something about it screamed cult. And then it hit me: Space is where cults go when Earth stops believing.

And then they made it even better—or worse. They officially named its members "Guardians." Yes, as in *Guardians of the Galaxy*. You can't make this stuff up. We now have a real-life, taxpayer-funded military branch whose service members share a name with the ragtag crew in a Marvel space opera. Not to mention the Space Force logo looks a whole lot like *Star Trek*'s Starfleet symbol.* It sounds like satire, but it's real—and it fits. Because space has always been the final frontier of the transcendent mission.

This isn't a new pattern. Cults love space. Space is the perfect delivery vehicle for transcendence. And I don't just mean literal space—though yes, sometimes they do promise actual spaceships—but also metaphorical space: higher dimensions, new realities, reincarnated bodies, alternate timelines, astral planes. The message is always the same: Your reward isn't here, it's there. Somewhere else. Somewhere better. Just keep going. Just keep giving. Just keep obeying. One more purity test, one more seminar, one more sacrifice—and *then* you'll transcend.

The Children of God cult was obsessed with this idea. Our prophet told us that heaven was a literal city of gold inside the moon, complete

---

* Nerd alert: Amy assures me the resemblance is purely coincidental. Similar delta symbols have appeared in US military insignia since the early 1940s—decades before *Star Trek* launched (Erwin, "U.S. Space Force says its new seal is not a Starfleet knockoff," 2020). Besides, *Starfleet* embodies an optimistic, science-driven, humanitarian worldview—everything the Trump administration stands in contrast to—making it highly unlikely they would intentionally emulate it.

with physical dimensions he claimed to receive in prophecy (definitely a rip-off of Noah's Ark). Because we were so isolated, it took a few years for someone to realize that those dimensions wouldn't actually fit inside the moon. But no problem—those were now metaphorical measurements. The goalposts moved, the space dreams stayed.

Heaven's Gate, of course, made headlines with their Nike-clad exit plan aboard the tail of a comet. Scientology promises the ultimate pay-to-play transcendence: Move up the Bridge to Total Freedom and unlock your true alien self. Even QAnon, that most modern digital cult, traffics in the fantasy of ascension—that after the Storm, the patriots will be vindicated, the evil cabal destroyed, and a purified America will be reborn. It's the rapture, rebranded for Reddit.

These are not just fringe delusions. In America, we have always looked to the stars for salvation. The Mormon faith, arguably the most American religion there is, began with golden plates in the dirt and matured into beliefs about populating other planets in the afterlife. Elon Musk, our modern techno-savior, isn't content to colonize Twitter and the White House—he wants Mars. Even our politics aren't immune. Space Force is ideological cosplay, a flag-planting exercise in Manifest Destiny 2.0, a reminder that, in America, even the afterlife has expansionist goals.

The transcendent mission must always remain just out of reach. It keeps the faithful hooked, the skeptics off-balance, and the leader untouchable. It's not just heaven anymore—it's the multiverse. It's Mars. It's the fifth dimension. And it's coming soon, as long as you don't stop believing—or paying.

Because if the promised land were here, they'd have to deliver. But if it's on another planet, you can keep selling tickets forever.

What About Company Missions?

We've seen how cults, militaries, and extremist groups all rely on keeping their members intensely focused on a mission, demanding extreme commitments along the way. But what happens when these dynamics show up in more unexpected places? Corporations are no strangers to this game. From grocery delivery services to space exploration firms, companies craft sweeping missions that employees are expected to dedicate their lives to. Why? Because it's an easy way to motivate people and, more importantly, it's a handy tool for quelling complaints. The mission can convince employees to prioritize loyalty and self-sacrifice, even when things go south. At the heart of any transcendent mission is the implicit promise that all the labor and sacrifice will eventually be justified, no matter how extreme.

Take Juul, for example. The e-cigarette company's mission-driven façade was masking deeper motivations, as revealed in the 2023 Netflix documentary *Big Vape*. Juul publicly said it helped adults quit smoking, a noble-sounding goal that inspired employees and investors alike. Their actions, however—such as marketing campaigns targeting teens—revealed a different mission: building a cooler cigarette and competing with Big Tobacco. Beneath this lay the founders' unspoken ambition to achieve unicorn status and get rich. Juul exemplifies how lofty missions can disguise self-serving goals.

In *Corporate Cults: The Insidious Lure of the All-Consuming Organization*, Dr. Dave Arnott, a management consultant and professor of business and leadership, lays out a striking view of how corporations balance efficiency and individual value. He tells us that "efficiency is at one end of the continuum and individual value is at the other," making it clear that "what's good for the organization is bad for the individual."[28] He takes it a step further, arguing that corporations often operate as cults, demanding personal sacrifices in exchange for devotion to the company. The sacrifices—time, identity, and personal life—are framed as contributing to a greater good. Companies on *Forbes*'s "Best Places to Work" list often succeed by fostering such devotion, which can come at the cost of individual well-being. Arnott warns that corporations use this devotion not to elevate employees but to perpetuate the organization. Employees become vulnerable to burnout and exploitation when their sense of purpose is tied to the company's success. The real challenge, Arnott says, lies in finding balance. It's up to each individual to figure out how much to give to the company without losing too much of themselves in the process. This constant tension—between contributing enough to be successful at work, and holding on to enough personal space to maintain a sense of self—is the dilemma at the heart of the modern corporate world.

It's easy to get swept up in a compelling corporate mission and put personal concerns for individuality on the back burner, and lose that important balance. "We want to believe we are making a difference in the world and that our work matters," Arnott tells us. "In a survey of 2,285 American workers across 26 fields and a range of pay levels and company sizes, nine in 10 said they would take a cut in their lifetime earnings for more meaningful work. But seeing your job as a higher calling can make you susceptible to being played."[29] At Theranos, for instance, which demanded absolute loyalty to its mission, Elizabeth Holmes's charismatic leadership created a culture where employees sacrificed everything for the vision. Even when doubts arose, Holmes was exceptionally skilled at motivating her staff, inspiring a level of dedication that had employees convinced they were changing the world. Tyler Shultz, who was working closely with malfunctioning devices every day, still found himself reenergized after a simple conversation with Holmes. "You want it to be true so badly," he said, and despite the evidence to the contrary, that's exactly what kept him—and so many others—hooked.[30] This devotion can be seen in traditional cults, where missions mask exploitation for the leader's or organization's benefit.

Arnott's point about devotion speaks to a broader cultural shift—companies are increasingly asking workers for more than just professional dedication. Much like a religious or cultlike organization, these companies cultivate a sense of belonging and purpose, creating environments where employees feel compelled to give more of themselves than they might have intended. When a company mission becomes intertwined with an employee's sense of self-worth or personal identity, it can create a dangerous imbalance. The line between professional commitment and personal devotion blurs, leaving employees vulnerable to burnout, exploitation, or, in extreme cases, a loss of individuality.

Some companies openly embrace this cultlike intensity. In the 1990s, Trilogy Software built its culture on military-style bonding, putting recruits through an intense boot camp to foster loyalty. The goal was to push new recruits to their limits, Trilogy's former VP John Price said, to "create cohesion and bonding at the level the military guys have in a foxhole when they have bullets flying overhead. If you ever study cults, this is how they do it."[31] Trilogy didn't shy away from the comparison. It actively tried to build a culture that mirrored the intensity of a cult environment; early executives even compared building the company to building a cult. While Trilogy grew rapidly during the dot-com boom, it ultimately collapsed, exposing the hollowness behind its hype. As former Trilogy employee Jocelyn Goldfein, who later became Facebook's director of engineering, put it: "Everyone got rich off a company that was basically nothing."[32] This story echoes companies like Theranos and WeWork—businesses that were propped up by charismatic leaders, big promises, and intense internal cultures but eventually crumbled under the weight of their own hype.

Trilogy might not be a household name now, but it played a key role in shaping what we now call "bro culture" in tech—a phenomenon so pervasive it has its own shorthand. It's the frat-house mentality (more about frats in chapter 7) that runs underneath startup offices and billion-dollar firms alike, where competitiveness, bravado, and exclusion are mistaken for innovation. In these spaces, success gets measured by how hard you can push, how loudly you can shout, or how ruthlessly you can outmaneuver the guy next to you—*guy* usually being the operative word. As Emily Chang points out in *Brotopia: Breaking Up the Boys' Club of Silicon Valley*, the discrimination women face in tech isn't always the obvious, headline-grabbing kind; sometimes it's the slow, ambient kind—the thousand tiny ways you're made to feel like you don't belong, don't fit, don't matter. It's an invisible current running just beneath the kombucha taps and the ping-pong tables. And the result isn't just a bad day at work—it's a system where loyalty to the tribe is prized above ethics, equity, or even the mission the company claims to stand for. And tech companies, with their aggressive approach to "building culture," have had an outsized impact on how other industries think about cultivating their own work environments.

In tandem with bro culture is a growing movement among organizations "to extract higher levels of commitment by treating employees as members of the family," according to Dr. Arnott. He goes on to caution, "I get worried about organizations that seem to operate as 'one big happy family,' because that usually means that someone has subordinated individual self-interest to the interest of the group. That's fertile ground for the growth of a corporate cult."[33] When a company asks employees to put the business's needs ahead of their own, especially when it's dressed up as being part of the "family," look out. The company is trying to get people to work harder and sacrifice more without realizing the toll it's taking on them as individuals.

Corporate cults blur the line between professional dedication and personal sacrifice. They use mission-based language and emotional appeals to inspire loyalty, often at the expense of workers' individuality and well-being. They also create environments where employees are exploited under the guise of pursuing a noble cause. Anything that calls itself a "family" often demands more than it gives in return, expecting employees to overwork while being underpaid, and excusing exploitative behavior as loyalty.

We've talked a lot about companies that construct missions for strategic purposes, but what about fields where the mission is built right in? Professions like teaching, healthcare, social work, the military, nonprofits, ministry, and politics are often seen as callings. These careers tend to attract people motivated by purpose rather than profit, where professional school and years of training blur the line between career and identity. The more time, money, and effort you invest in it, the more it feels like who you are.

This idea of a "calling"—work you'd do even without pay—is celebrated by happiness experts as the secret to loving your job and living a fulfilling life. But this passion can also be exploited. When leadership takes advantage of that dedication and the industry itself is designed to demand more than you can give, that sense of purpose can quickly become a tool for burnout and manipulation.

Take teaching, for example: The mission is literally framed as "do it for the kids." Teachers spend their days locked in with students, cut off from the outside world, and are constantly urged to sacrifice for the greater good of raising future leaders. Work-life balance? Forget it. Teachers find themselves working outside of work hours, using their own money for supplies, neglecting their health (let's face it, even finding time for a bathroom break is hard), and pouring their emotional energy into the job—all for the mission. How do you say no when all your obligations are framed as saving the next generation?

Social workers face a similar dynamic. When they ask for a manageable workload or fair pay, they're reminded, "You didn't get into this for the money." Their compassion is exploited until they burn out. Nonprofits operate much the same way. People leaving high-control environments like cults or the military often gravitate toward nonprofits and social work, seeking that same sense of mission and purpose, only to get sucked into another system that demands endless labor for "the cause." It's worth noting that the lowest-paid mission-based jobs— like teaching and elder care—are traditionally held by women. As Ted Patrick points out in *Let Our Children Go!*, nonprofits, much like cults, use inspiring rhetoric to justify relentless sacrifice without offering real rewards. The mission becomes the ultimate excuse for exploitation.

You've seen the pattern by now—it doesn't matter which group, cause, or industry. The mission gets weaponized. Personal boundaries blur. And slowly, the self is sacrificed at the altar of the collective. In the Children of God, they weaponized love. In both Trump administrations, loyalty. Whatever the sacred assumption, under enough pressure and the right culty conditions, it stops being a guiding principle and becomes a tool of control. And once the group convinces you that your worth exists only in service to the mission? That's when the real transformation begins. Because what comes next is always the same: You disappear.

So buckle up, dear reader. The next chapter dives into that elusive magic trick: how to make an identity vanish in plain sight. No wand required. Just a high-control group and a willingness to believe.

Chapter 4

Self-Sacrifice: Give Till It Hurts

How can this organization be called a cult when it's so widely recognized, especially with a slogan like "Doing the Most Good"? Most of us see it as a charitable institution with a mission to help those in need, associated with kindness, giving, and a commitment to service. But behind that image lies a different story, as told by people who consider themselves "survivors" of this well-known nonprofit. The group, founded in 1865 by a man determined to rid England's underclass of what he called the "three As" (alcohol, atheism, and anarchy), views itself quite literally as an army. It's steeped in military traditions, complete with ranks, uniforms, and a strict hierarchical structure. Full membership, requiring complete acceptance of the group's regulations, is called "soldiership." Members wear uniforms as symbols of their dedication to purity and the cause, serving as a constant reminder of the discipline required to adhere to the group's order. The military-style structure goes all up way up; it demands unquestioning obedience to the higher ranks, especially "the General," who has almost total power.[1]

Today, 160 years since its founding, the organization continues with intense focus on religious evangelism, along with controversial practices like burning secular music records, the belief in an imminent apocalypse, extreme homophobia, and racism that's often cloaked in subtlety.[2] Members are expected to dedicate significant time and energy to spreading their faith, frequently at the cost of personal relationships or other pursuits. "This emphasis on evangelism can sometimes feel like coercion, with pressure to conform to rigid doctrines and practices," says one survivor who wished to remain anonymous. Yet most people are unaware of any of this when they drop their spare change into those iconic red Salvation Army buckets during the holidays.

* * *

You'd never guess it from shopping at their thrift stores, but children raised in the Salvation Army don't just grow up attending church—they grow up enlisted.[3] From their earliest memories, service is not optional. Free time is rare; weekends, after-school hours, and summer breaks are swallowed up by mandatory charity events, uniformed appearances, church services, and endless community obligations. Their childhood isn't a time for self-discovery—it's a training ground for loyalty and discipline, wrapped up in the language of faith and sacrifice.

Like military families, Salvation Army officers are routinely reassigned, uprooting entire families with little notice. Children are expected to endure frequent relocations with grace and gratitude. Their schools change, friendships end, identities are rebuilt from scratch over and over again—all under the careful watch of an organization that demands they view these sacrifices as honorable.[4]

Yes, they learn compassion. They learn service. But it's compassion tied to obedience, service wrapped in surveillance. Life is a series of performances for an audience that never stops watching. The result is a hollowing-out of personal freedom and a gradual erasure of self. Casual friendships, curiosity, small rebellions—developmentally necessary things that help kids figure out who they are—are treated as risks to be mitigated or sins to be corrected.

In many ways, it mirrors the experience of military "brats," who also grow up shaped by the grind of relocation, strict discipline, and the constant expectation to represent something bigger than themselves.

But while the military at least acknowledges its demand for sacrifice, the Salvation Army cloaks it in spiritual righteousness. You're supposed to feel chosen and lucky to be giving up your childhood.

Total Institutions

The word *cult* always feels like it should come with an ominous soundtrack. When I say, "I grew up in a cult," people's eyes widen, and some even take a dramatic step away from me, as if I have some kind of communicable disease. It's a loaded word, dripping with intrigue and dread. Most people are sure that *they* could never fall for something like that, and there's definitely something wrong with people who do. Cults, they believe, are for people who are naive, gullible, or desperate. But here's the truth: "Normal" people join total institutions all the time.

Renowned sociologist Erving Goffman defines a total institution as "a place of residence and work where a large number of like-situated individuals, cut off from the wider society for an appreciable period of time, lead an enclosed, formally administered round of life."[5] At first glance, that might sound extreme, but closed systems like these are everywhere: Prisons, juvenile detention centers, convents, work camps, boarding schools, military barracks, mental health facilities, in-patient rehabs, nursing homes—and yes, cults—all fit the definition. Even the staff-served households of wealthy families can qualify under the right circumstances. If *Downton Abbey* counts, then it's safe to say the British royal family fits the bill too.

What's fascinating is that most people scoff at the idea of joining a cult but don't think twice about participating in these other institutions. Children are sent to boarding schools, and "problem" kids are shipped off to religious reform camps. Teenagers enlist in the military, and workers dive headfirst into the grind of tech startups. Sociologist Susie Scott, in her article "Revisiting the Total Institution," even argues that college Greek life is best understood through this lens (more about that in chapter 7). Prisons and psychiatric facilities take in those deemed "unfit" for mainstream society. Adults are called to monastic service or sent to assisted living homes as they age. In every case, lives are shaped by rigid rules, isolation, and an intense focus on the purpose of the institution itself. These environments are not rare. They are, in fact, a way of life. Chances are you know someone who's lived inside one—maybe even you.

"I was afforded many things while I lived in the Playboy Mansion... but never the opportunity for the sort of self-discovery most twenty-somethings enjoy," writes Holly Madison, known best for her role in the reality TV show *Girls Next Door* about life as one of Hugh Hefner's multiple girlfriends, in her book *Down the Rabbit Hole: Curious Adventures and Cautionary Tales of a Former Playboy Bunny.*[6] When a kid ends up in a total institution, they pretty much lose their shot at figuring out who they really are. They're cut off from the world during the exact years when they're supposed to be diving in headfirst, soaking up everything, and testing their limits. Instead of exploring and growing, they get boxed in, their instincts dulled by a system that demands conformity over curiosity. It's like hitting pause on the part of life that's meant to be wide open and messy.

Science supports the idea that the prefrontal cortex, the part of the brain largely responsible for personality, decision making, and social behavior, is not finished forming until around age twenty-five.[7] Developmentally speaking, according to Goffman, adolescence is supposed to be a time for young people to try things and fail, to discover their own skills, and to figure out what they want to do in adulthood. Many societies build this into their culture, but total institutions tend to skip this step, boiling things down to group experiences, "batch living," us-versus-them mentality, and a predetermined and unquestionable mission.[8] The goal of total institutions is twofold: first to systematically break down the identity the individual arrived with, and then to replace it with a new one—a kind of "pseudo-personality."[9]

Sociologists and psychologists are just starting to scratch the surface of what it means to grow up in a closed system built almost entirely on self-sacrifice. I can tell you from experience that it's a childhood that outsiders can barely wrap their heads around, whether you're born into something as extreme as I was or something more socially palatable, like the Salvation Army or Buckingham Palace. In these environments, childhood isn't a time for play or discovery; it's spent becoming the group's version of perfect and making sure your personal needs never interfere with the greater cause. Your needs are secondary—always. The cost? A childhood stripped of spontaneous moments of joy and the freedom to just be a kid. Life is calculated, controlled, and tied to the greater purpose—and you're expected to fall in line without question.

These systems make it clear that blending in is essential for everything to run smoothly. Individuality is suppressed, and personal growth takes a backseat to the group's agenda. Members are isolated from the outside world, forfeiting their freedom but gaining a sense of purpose through dedication to a larger mission. The intense camaraderie in these environments can create deep bonds and emotional highs that are hard to find anywhere else. For many people, sacrificing personal autonomy feels like a fair trade for purpose and connection.

But Margaret Singer warns us that "cults are the antithesis of structures in which full human growth can develop."[10] Your sense of purpose comes at a heavy price: conformity. Individuality is stifled to maintain control. In institutions like prisons, military boot camps, or psychiatric hospitals, every aspect of life is governed by strict rules and routines—your schedule, how you talk to people, your appearance, even when you can use the bathroom. Standing out via thoughts, actions, or looks is discouraged or outright banned to enforce uniformity and suppress dissent.

Total institutions often use emotional manipulation and psychological tricks to exploit people's loneliness, insecurity, and fear to foster dependency. One go-to technique is love-bombing—showering new members with over-the-top attention and affection—to make people feel like they belong right away, like they've finally found the place they've been searching for. But over time love-bombing shifts into something much darker: thought reform. The group starts to break down a person's beliefs and behaviors to fit its ideology. The process starts subtly but escalates into full reprogramming, teaching members to see the group's way as the only way.

One of the biggest ways cults get people to self-sacrifice—often without them realizing it—is by framing everything around "what's good for the group." In the Army, we call it "needs of the Army" whenever personal desires get set aside for the mission. The goal is to mold individuals into a collective that prioritizes loyalty above all else. Little by little, members give up pieces of their identity until the group identity takes over. In high-control groups, identity markers can include precise details like what members wear and eat, and even when and where they work, sleep, and bathe.[11] Sometimes the control extends to what they do with their money, which we'll explore in other chapters.

The Salvation Army is no stranger to managing its members' personal lives. Officers are generally expected to marry within the organization—preferably another officer—or risk seeing their careers quietly disappear, like a soldier who asked too many questions. Love is nice, but loyalty to the mission comes first. Unsanctioned relationships are frowned upon, broken up, or reassigned into oblivion. Families are uprooted like chess pieces on a board.[12] In this tradition, you learn early that if it's a choice between your personal life and the organization's mission, you better pack light.

The system's genius lies in framing all of this as noble devotion, making members believe their self-denial is virtuous. This manipulation reinforces leadership's power, and traps members in a cycle where leaving feels like an unthinkable violation of everything they've been taught to believe. Leaders exploit loyalty, as seen in the Children of God, which demanded members relinquish all possessions under the guise of following Jesus. These initial entrance costs set the stage for exit costs, making it harder to leave (which we'll talk about more in chapter 9).

Everyone who joins the military knows they're signing up to sacrifice something—it's practically the first unwritten rule of service. From the moment service members put on the uniform, their identity is subsumed by duty. Training and camaraderie instill a mission-first mindset, with the ultimate expectation being the willingness to sacrifice your life. It's a lifestyle of prioritizing the mission and the people beside you over your own needs, comfort, and even health and safety. In the Army, limited "sick call" hours and stigmatizing terms like "sick call Ranger" discourage soldiers from seeking care, fostering a macho "suck it up" mindset. And ex-soldiers with unresolved health issues face an even harder transition to civilian life. Self-denial culture extends to military families, where personal needs are secondary and spouses and children learn early that they never come first.[13] "If the Army wanted you to have a spouse, they would have issued you one" is a lovely saying that probably every one of us military spouses has heard.

Sacrificing for a group isn't all bad, of course. It fosters solidarity, cooperation, and shared purpose, which enables efficiency and mutual support. But when exploited, group loyalty harms mental health and personal development. Toxic leaders manipulate loyalty by pushing members into abusive situations in the name of the greater good. In her *Harvard Business Review* article "Loyalty to a Leader Is Overrated, Even Dangerous," Julie Irwin warns that "unethical behavior in organizations almost always is caused by belief in and too much loyalty to a 'great leader' who turns out to be morally compromised." Sacrifice can be a powerful force for good, but it must be balanced with personal autonomy to avoid becoming dangerous.

Under late-stage capitalism, such balance is elusive. Businesses are often prioritizing profit over fairness, underpaying workers, exploiting resources, and widening wealth gaps. Individuality is suppressed for efficiency; conformity is valued over creativity. The emphasis on obedience over autonomy stifles workers' potential, reducing individuals to cogs in the machine.[14] This system of exploitation and subjugation has managed to weave its way into surprising aspects of American daily life, as the following examples illustrate.

The Cult of Parenthood and the Loss of Family

Although family is perhaps humanity's oldest and most revered institution, American culture has found insidious ways to contort parenthood into something disturbingly cultlike. American parenthood—let's be honest, it's usually motherhood—is framed less as a role and more as a total identity, a calling that demands devotion and self-erasure. The cultural script insists that "good mothers" sacrifice everything: their time, their ambitions, their bodies, even basic self-care.* The social demand to be the perfect mom can leave women feeling completely drained, emotionally burned out, and trapped in a cycle of chasing impossible standards.

Add to that the systemic lack of real support systems—whether it's affordable childcare, parental leave, or even just a little grace—and it's no wonder so many moms feel isolated and overwhelmed. It's a relentless balancing act, and the pressure takes a major toll on mental health and well-being. In a *Time* magazine article titled "I Lost Myself to Mother-hood," Katie Gutierrez says we are suffering a maternal mental health crisis as "people with uteri [are] forced to sacrifice themselves for a role the U.S. deems more important than autonomy, more important than ambition, more important than our own actual lives, and yet will not support at any point." By design, capitalism places greater value on the labor that makes the most money, which greatly undervalues the unpaid "women's work" of child-rearing, kin-keeping, emotional labor, and the complex project management involved in running a household. A 2025 study estimates that the value of an American mother's unpaid work is approximately $145,235 per year, marking a 4 percent increase from last year—the high end of professional project managers.[15]

The parallels of American motherhood to cult dynamics are striking. Consider exhaustion, for instance. In cults, followers are deliberately overworked and sleep-deprived to break down resistance. If you're always running on empty, it's hard to think clearly, let alone question what's going on around you. In motherhood, the same dynamic plays

---

* Of course, this is not only an American issue; it is the plight of women all over the world. Some would (rightfully) argue that American women, especially white American women, have it much better than those in places where mothers are expected to endure horrific conditions such as lack of basic rights or medical care. I acknowledge my incredible privilege here.

out: The nonstop demands of parenting, managing a household, and often holding a paid job leave little energy for reflection or resistance. Constant exhaustion chips away at your sense of self, making it harder to hold on to your own thoughts or push back. Eventually, you're stuck in a cycle of dependency, too worn out to figure out how to break free. The demands placed on women—whether as moms, caretakers, partners, or professionals—mean we're often more worn out than men. Naomi Wolf captures it perfectly in her book *The Beauty Myth: How Images of Beauty Are Used Against Women*: "Working women are exhausted; bone-tired in a way their male colleagues may not be able to imagine."[16]

On the flip side of this loss of self to the idealization of parenthood, one of the most heartbreaking aspects of many high-control groups is that they demand the sacrifice of family bonds. Members are pushed—or outright required—to sever ties with loved ones, cutting themselves off from anyone who might challenge the group's control. Singer and Lalich tell us that "in many cults...spouses are forced to separate or parents forced to give up their children as a test of devotion to their leader."[17] Leaders sell these sacrifices as noble, even essential for spiritual growth, manipulating people into believing that abandonment is the price of salvation.

Separating children from their parents to be raised communally is a common practice in fringe religious and cultural movements. Examples include the addiction rehab community Synanon, Osho's Rajneesh movement, Jim Jones's Peoples Temple, the nineteenth-century Oneida commune, and even the early socialist utopias of the Kibbutz movement, though communal child-rearing in kibbutzim largely ended by the late twentieth century.[18] In the Children of God communes I grew up in, we were separated from our parents and made to sleep together in large rooms with bunks stacked three beds high, and permitted to see our parents only one hour a day at most. Parents were told to leave their children behind for the group's mission, and children would be sent away to work for weeks at a time. These "choices" were painted as divine obligations, leaving parents buried in guilt and grief—but their feelings were labeled as selfish or weak. The result? Traumatized children and isolated, dependent members, trapped in the group with nowhere else to go. The Army has its own version of this, separating soldiers from their families for months or years at a time. Duty comes first, even if it means missing birthdays, graduations, and other moments you can't get back. The strain on families is framed as a noble sacrifice, reinforcing loyalty while pulling people further from their personal lives.

Even the so-called American Dream demands significant sacrifices, particularly from parents striving to provide a better future for their children. People uproot their lives, relocate to new cities or countries in search of opportunity, or work grueling hours chasing financial stability. In the process, they miss out on irreplaceable time with their kids. A relentless pursuit of success can eerily mirror the sacrifices demanded by cults and high-control institutions, where devotion to a cause or leader takes precedence over personal relationships. By framing hard work and loyalty to a mission as ultimate virtues, American capitalism normalizes the idea that financial goals and professional achievement should come before emotional bonds, perpetuating a culture where connection and presence are treated as secondary to productivity and material gain.

The Price of Purity

In addition to micromanaging who you can marry and when you're allowed to see your family, cults and controlling groups love to impose "purity requirements"—a shiny term for rules designed to crush individuality into a fine powder. These standards go beyond dictating your moral behavior; they take over your diet, your wardrobe, your friendships, your bedroom, and eventually your thoughts. Obedience serves as both proof of loyalty and a way to distinguish members from outsiders.[19] Want to make a free choice? Sorry, that got sacrificed at the altar of "higher consciousness" somewhere around your third mandatory fast. Purity isn't just a virtue—it's a performance.

And if you slip up, even a little, you've conveniently outed yourself as disloyal, deviant, or demonically possessed. Impossible expectations make it incredibly easy for leaders to spot and punish anyone stepping out of line, while the rest of the group looks on in terror, silently wondering if they'll be next. These rules are essential for your spiritual enlightenment or salvation because they're divinely ordained, leaders say, thereby justifying extreme measures and tightening control even more.[20]

Want to be pure? Stop eating sugar, cut off your parents, renounce all sexual desire, wear that purity ring your dad gave you, wear matching prairie dresses, and think only approved thoughts about The Leader. Easy! Leaders frame these restrictions as divinely ordained—God's will, cosmic law, universal truth, whatever branding works best. And because the stakes are nothing less than eternal damnation (or losing your "high vibration"), there's no limit to how extreme the measures can get.

Dr. Janja Lalich tells us that

> the demand for purity is essentially a black-and-white worldview with the leader as the ultimate moral arbiter. This creates an atmosphere of guilt and shame, where punishment and humiliation are expected. It also sets up an environment wherein members report on one another. Through submission to the guilt-inducing and impossible demand for purity, members lose their moral bearing.[21]

Cults say that their path to purity is the *only* path, which not only isolates members but creates a sense of moral superiority and an us-versus-them mindset. Sociologist Susie Scott's concept of "performative regulation" highlights how members internalize these values when they "submit themselves to the authority of an institution, internalize its values, and enact them through mutual surveillance in an inmate culture." She explains that "power operates horizontally as well as vertically, as members monitor each other's conduct, sanction deviance and evaluate their own progress in relative terms."[22] Your friend, your bunkmate, even your own spouse becomes another set of eyes making sure you never stray from the sacred path. It's basically a surveillance state run by people who once promised you unconditional love.

But purity rules aren't about progress or personal growth, no matter how many wellness influencers slap pastel Instagram quotes over them—they're about reinforcing the group's power and making it harder to leave. They condition members to believe that failure to meet the standards is a failure of their entire identity, ensuring their dependence on the group for validation. Meanwhile, in the ultimate plot twist nobody asked for, the leaders—the ones barking orders about purity—almost never follow their own rules. This double standard reinforces the power imbalance and traps members in cycles of self-blame and devotion. Jim Jones preached celibacy while running his private harem. Keith Raniere demanded monogamy from his followers while collecting branded women. David Berg wrote pages about rejecting worldly corruption while personally embodying every imaginable form of it. American Buddhist leaders like Shambhala's Sakyong Mipham Rinpoche and Ösel Tendzin, Zen teacher Joshu Sasaki, and Noah Levine (to name just a few) were accused of sexual misconduct while teaching their students to do no harm. And then, of course, there's the Catholic Church. Breaking the rules becomes a kind of badge of untouchable authority: *We're so holy, we don't even have to follow our own commandments.*

Now a note about food restrictions and purity. Most people think of adhering to body image standards when it comes to diet and food restrictions (which we'll get to later in this chapter), but controlling people's eating is used as a path to purity both in cults and more mainstream communities. While not yet recognized as an official eating disorder in the *DSM*, orthorexia, which the National Alliance for Eating Disorders describes as "characterized by an extreme focus on 'healthy' eating," is on the rise. People experiencing orthorexia become so obsessed with eating "clean" that their lives are rigid and restrictive, and their fixation on purity often coincides with other lifestyle choices, likely with spiritual packaging. Seemingly benign wellness influencers claim their clean diet plans and green juice cleanses promote spiritual growth and enlightenment, while both veganism and extreme carnivore diets (depending on which sect you're in) position themselves as more natural and spiritually superior. The eating disorder resource for parents More-Love.org notes on its website that the pairing of spirituality and diets is an easy match, as both promote clear rules and rigid expectations with a clear payoff—exactly what cults do.

Perhaps the highest-profile of the countless charismatic alternative wellness leaders with "cult" followings is Anthony William, aka the Medical Medium, who is a best-selling author with over five million Instagram followers and nothing resembling a medical degree; rather, his qualifications include being a self-described clairvoyant who was visited at age four by a spirit that gave him the power to scan bodies for disease by sight. He "prescribes" his followers, many of whom are women dealing with chronic illness, things like a raw vegan diet and celery juice cleanses (and definitely no vaccines!) to cure diseases as serious as cancer. He claims that "negative energy" is often the main culprit for illness, essentially placing the blame on the person if they don't get well. His most devoted followers see themselves as a family, with strong virtual communities on Facebook and Reddit that serve as reinforcing echo chambers for their beliefs. At least one death has been connected with his pseudo-medical advice.[23]

In corporate environments, "professionalism" functions as a form of purity control. Tema Okun and Kenneth Jones note that corporate standards of professionalism are rooted in white-supremacy culture, privileging white norms of appearance, speech, and behavior.[24] These expectations place marginalized individuals, especially Black people, under heightened scrutiny. Much like cult purity rules, professionalism standards exclude those who don't fit the mold, reinforce power imbalances, and create a cycle where individuals must suppress their true selves to survive. Both systems use rigid, often unattainable rules to maintain control and uphold systemic inequality. Professionalism that's tied to dominant white norms is a gatekeeping mechanism— ensuring that people who don't conform face ongoing barriers to inclusion and advancement, or making the rules so tough that some can never fully follow them.

Appearance Control

Cults love using appearance control to break people down and strip away their sense of self. It's one of the first things you notice—whether through literal uniforms, like the black shirts and Nike sneakers of Heaven's Gate, or more subtle group-wide aesthetics, such as the hippie garb of the Twelve Tribes cult (of Yellow Deli fame) or the homogenized "Mormon face." Cults are obsessed with how they appear to the outside world, often putting on an image that seems warm, loving, or united. But the control over how members look and act goes way deeper. As Margaret Singer explains, "If you really want to change people, change their appearance."[25]

In Heaven's Gate, matching outfits symbolized devotion and reinforced the group's extreme beliefs, like their readiness to board an alien spaceship trailing the Hale-Bopp comet. But the uniforms also served to desexualize members, aligning with strict rules of abstinence and discouraging personal relationships that could challenge group loyalty. Similarly, the Fundamentalist Latter-day Saints (FLDS, also known as the polygamist Mormons) impose rigid dress codes, especially for women, who wear pastel, ankle-length prairie dresses with long sleeves and high necklines to promote modesty and conformity. Even the colors are a statement: Red is off-limits because it's supposedly reserved for Jesus when He comes back, and black is avoided since it's tied to Satan. Hair, too, becomes a symbol of obedience—women grow it long, believing they'll need it in heaven for the sacred duty of washing men's feet, and styling it high to reflect their righteousness. The rules keep members visually and mentally tied to the group's ideology.

Other high-control environments, such as the military, prisons, and even some gangs, also use uniforms to erase individuality and enforce hierarchy. Symbols, badges, and color restrictions reflect the group's values, while strict dress codes—like those in the US Army against "looking too faddish"—ensure conformity (like in the Children of God, where we weren't allowed to "look cooler than Jesus"). These rules often disproportionately affect those lower in the hierarchy, who are more likely to be punished for violations than higher-ranking members, revealing the rules as tools of control rather than practical necessity.

Across cults and coercive systems, appearance control consistently targets four key areas: hair, body size, body coverage, and even underwear. By controlling how people look—whether it's in a cult, company, social clique, or an abusive relationship—these groups tighten their grip on how members think and behave, ensuring loyalty and submission.

Hair

Cults enforce hair rules to promote conformity and erase individuality. Whether it's forcing women to wear their hair long, mandating shaved heads, banning dye and styling products, or requiring head coverings or veils, these controls go beyond your appearance—they reshape how you see yourself to fit the group's agenda. As Sylvia Karasu notes in a *Psychology Today* article titled "The Weaponization of Hair: And How It Can Be Used to Oppress, Punish, Seduce, and Rebel," "Hair has been a metaphor for social control and has been used to dehumanize, humiliate, punish, exact conformity, and rebel."

On the very first day of US Army basic training, male recruits are given a mandatory buzz cut—a clear ritual designed to strip away their civilian identity, immerse them in the collective, and convey authority for those in command. But here's the twist: The women recruits don't go through this. Right from the start, hair rules create a divide in a system still dominated by men. For years, the Army required women to wear their hair in tight buns, even though buns were uncomfortable and caused literal headaches and a variety of real medical problems. That bun became a symbol of gender inequality in a place where uniformity was the rule. Thankfully, women can now wear ponytails and braids, though some, like Fox News personality Tucker Carlson, have complained that these "new hairstyles," along with maternity flight suits, are making "a mockery of the U.S. military."[26]

Hair control has a long history as a tool of oppression, weaponized to exert control over marginalized groups. During the Holocaust, Nazis shaved the heads of concentration camp prisoners to degrade and humiliate them. Similarly, French women accused of collaborating with Nazis during WWII had their heads forcibly shaved and were paraded through the streets as public reprimand. Enslaved people in the US were forced to shave their heads as punishment, and Native American children in residential schools had their hair cut to erase their cultural identity and sever ties to their heritage. Even now, many workplaces and schools continue to enforce rigid hair rules, disproportionately affecting people of color under the guise of "professionalism" and "discipline." These policies reflect a legacy of Black hair being deemed to need "taming" to conform to white beauty standards.

Yet hair has also been a powerful site of rebellion and empowerment. The Afro became a symbol of protest during the Black liberation movement, while styles like locs, braids, and cornrows continue to represent racial pride, self-expression, and defiance against oppressive norms. Hair is far from frivolous—it's a marker of identity, a tool of social control, and, when reclaimed, a powerful symbol of resistance. Attempts to regulate it underscore its importance in shaping how people see themselves, how they're perceived, and ultimately how they're allowed to exist in the world. If hair was frivolous, then we wouldn't see the attempt to control it in so many situations of coercive control.

Body Size

Cults place intense emphasis on physical appearance. Members often must maintain specific body types—usually thin, but sometimes muscular or even larger bodies. The cult may impose exercise routines and dieting to further control members' lives. Eating low-calorie diets or fasting will weaken people physically—and increase their dependence on the group, leaving individuals too exhausted to rebel or leave, and much easier to manipulate. Maintaining a specific body type is a public symbol of obedience and loyalty to the cause.

Thinness, in particular, is framed as a moral virtue, equated with discipline, self-control, and spiritual worth. Members are encouraged to embody these traits, because their appearance reflects their devotion. Food rules drain members' mental energy and time, eroding their capacity for independent thought. As Annie Tanasugarn notes in *Psychology Today*, in both high-control groups and high-control romantic relationships, "compliments and intermittent positive reinforcement may be offered for sticking to the schedule, or members may be praised for 'looking good' or 'losing weight,' which can make them second-guess themselves or feel ashamed for questioning whether they're being mistreated." Weight loss becomes a bizarre moral currency, with thinner members often receiving preferential treatment, even from outsiders.

Sarah Edmonson writes in *Scarred* about the women of NXIVM competing to be the skinniest and restricting each other's food intake as a demonstration of purity and devotion. Beyond thinness, restrictive diets bring you closer to spiritual goals, some cult leaders say. While fasting as a spiritual practice has been in use for centuries across countless religions, cults strip fasting of its traditional context and meaning to use it as a tool for control. Food rules also reinforce social isolation; if alcohol or certain foods are banned, members can't easily participate in outside gatherings. In the end, food is weaponized to ensure compliance.

Obsession with body image isn't limited to literal cults, of course. Skinny privilege also seeps into corporate America, where lean bodies are often assumed to be more disciplined, energetic, and better workers. People who don't fit this mold may find themselves overlooked for leadership roles, promotions, or even social interactions. The bias reflects a deeper societal issue where we prioritize appearance over skill, which perpetuates stereotypes and undermines diversity efforts. Dr. Sabrina Strings writes in *Fearing the Black Body: The Racial*

Origins of Fat Phobia that in the US "fatness became stigmatized as both Black and sinful" by the early twentieth century, while thinness was promoted as the ideal for white Protestant women.[27] Body-size biases are about more than just health—they maintain race, class, and gender hierarchies.

The harm caused by American beauty standards and the diet and fashion industries is anything but news, and countless studies have shown social media's contribution to the rise of eating disorders in young people. Various "wellness" influencers use culty ways to make money off their followers' low self-esteem by selling products, classes, and coaching packages. The promise of physical health is paired with New Age spiritual packaging, perverting the idea of holistic wellness to equate beauty and thinness with a more enlightened state. Just look at the top alternative wellness gurus on any social media platform and you'll overwhelmingly see a certain type: women with long, flowing hair; smooth, glowing (white) skin; and a thin, lithe body—and few credentials besides their own appearance and the ability to create aspirational content. These women, and men, sell supplements and other products while promoting intermittent fasting, cleanses, detoxes, and even "purging consulting," the methods of which look a whole lot like rebranded eating disorders. Heath spas offer detox packages where guests pay big bucks to essentially be starved and given laxatives, though there is no medical evidence that these kinds of diets do any good.[28] As mentioned earlier, orthorexia and the obsession with eating "healthy" serves as an often socially acceptable form of eating disorder, disguising the real goal: weight loss, not wellness.

Some cults even take the opposite approach, encouraging larger bodies as a form of control. The leaders of Twin Flames Universe, for example, reportedly promoted weight gain to foster dependency and undermine members' self-esteem. This tactic isolated members from mainstream society, reinforcing the idea that their worth and acceptance could only come from the group. Ultimately, appearance becomes a tool for manipulation, a way to enforce conformity, and a visible reminder of who is in charge.

My husband, who flew military helicopters for fourteen years, jokes that his weight mattered more than his flying skills for his career. The Army takes it so seriously that failing two weigh-ins in a row can lead to discharge. These rules apply to both women and men soldiers, but the prevalence of eating disorders among men may surprise you. Part of a growing trend throughout the Western world, boys and men now make up 33 percent of people diagnosed with an eating disorder.[29] The cultiness of wellness culture has its hooks in men too: "manly" meat-based fad diets like paleo, keto, and the carnivore diet; the biohacking trends in Silicon Valley, the most popular of which is intermittent fasting; competitive gym-bro culture, complete with its own social media influencers; and fitness communities like CrossFit, which seems to always be under fire for being culty. In addition to eating disorders, the incidence of muscle dysphoria (also known as "bigorexia") is also increasing among men, characterized by excessive and compulsive exercise and weight training.[30] Hypermasculinity is at its most dangerous in the online "manosphere"—a network of groups and influencers focused on men's issues but dominated by misogynistic views. Researchers warn that it promotes violence against women and increasingly aligns with far-right political ideologies, amplified by social media algorithms that target teen boys with these messages[31]—along with the promise of a bigger, stronger body.

Body Coverage

Many religious and spiritual cults dictate how their members dress, especially women, masking control with the idea of "modesty." Take the FLDS, who require women to cover their entire bodies as a sign of purity and devotion, framing it as divine protection from the corrupting outside world. But let's be real—these dress codes are designed to separate women from mainstream society, enforce anonymity, and reinforce compliance. As one scholar notes, "Admonitions for women to maintain modest coverage of their bodies are steeped in notions about the inherent eroticism and sensuality of women's bodies that ostensibly distract men from prayer and other religious practice."[32]

This isn't limited to fringe groups. Jehovah's Witnesses, mainstream Mormon communities, and many American churches promote modesty standards rooted in the idea that women's bodies are inherently tempting, which places the burden of moral order on women. If you don't follow these rules, expect a hefty dose of shame and guilt. Globally, modesty norms vary but are often tied to religious beliefs. Some Muslim women wear the hijab by choice, while others in places like Iran or Saudi Arabia are legally compelled to do so. Wearing the hijab can be empowering, but when it's mandated, it becomes another form of control, stripping away personal choice. Some groups manipulate dress codes differently. The Children of God cult promoted nudity, even among children, under the guise of sexual liberation under God, using it to normalize exploitation and abuse, leaving lasting trauma.

Control through clothing isn't only a religious thing. The US military enforces strict uniform rules, some practical, some unnecessary, like banning rolled-up sleeves in the heat (though the Marines do allow this). During the war in Afghanistan, the US was the only country of sixty-six in the coalition that didn't allow soldiers to wear civilian clothes when they were off duty—largely because of ridiculous concerns about women dressing "provocatively." Similarly, school dress codes disproportionately target girls, especially girls of color and LGBTQ students, perpetuate harmful gender roles, and sexualize young women. Laws regulating toplessness, public breastfeeding, and gym attire further highlight systemic control of women's bodies in public spaces.[33]

But here's a story I love: When Mary Barra became CEO of General Motors, she tossed out a 10,000-word dress code and replaced it with two simple words: "Dress appropriately." She trusted her employees to understand what that meant for their roles, creating a more inclusive workplace. It's a powerful reminder that true leadership means empowering, not controlling, others.

Underwear

Let's talk about it—yes, underwear. It's personal, intimate, and surprisingly powerful as a tool for control in high-demand groups. Think about it: If a leader can turn something as basic and private as underwear into a symbol of loyalty and devotion, they've infiltrated the most personal aspects of your life. Historically, underwear has been both private and taboo. Controlling it allows leaders to intrude into followers' lives in deeply invasive ways. In the Children of God, women and girls were forbidden from sleeping in underwear because our leader claimed women were dirty and needed to "air out." This isn't new—society has long stigmatized women's bodies—but cults weaponize these narratives to tighten their control. They frame women as inherently impure and the cult as the only path to cleanliness, which paves the way for abusive practices disguised as spiritual growth.

The Mormon Church's approach to underwear is less overtly abusive but still invasive. The notorious temple garments—typically a two-piece set made from white, lightweight fabrics, which can only be purchased from the church—are required to be worn by initiated members under their clothes as a reminder of sacred promises.[34] In the US military, women must wear supportive bras that don't show lines, with sports bras usually mandatory during training or deployment, and definitely nothing red[35]—even functional garments are a point of scrutiny and control (I think all women vets have a story about a drill sergeant making someone cry because they brought a red bra to basic training).

The darker side of these policies is how they open the door to exploitation. Leaders use dress codes as an excuse for inspections, creating opportunities for abuse and harassment. There are stories of soldiers being pulled into dark corners so that their sergeants can inspect their underwear. Ex-Mormons recount the weird backrubs that Mormons give each other, verifying that sacred underwear is in the right places. These invasions, said to be holding people to high standards, are humiliating reminders of how far control can go. Underwear might seem trivial, but in these contexts, it's a battleground for autonomy and dignity, stripped away one stitch at a time. At the end of the day, if you can convince someone your mission is so important that even their underwear matters, you can probably convince them of just about anything.

Attitude Control

"But Mormons are the happiest people I've ever seen!"

That's the thing about attitude control—it's designed to create a picture-perfect image. In the Mormon Church, children are taught cheerful obedience early, with songs and activities reinforcing positivity and discouraging doubt. In the Children of God, the stakes were even higher. Showing anything less than happiness invited punishment. The constant pressure to appear content silences real emotions and leaves no room or tools for processing sadness, fear, or doubt; mental health struggles remain unaddressed. For high-control groups, forced positivity creates an image of harmony while members bear the emotional costs.[36] "Cult leaders even manipulate people into not having personal preferences," says Robin Stern, a psychoanalyst and co-founder of the Yale Center for Emotional Intelligence. "Some people who grow up in cults don't even know how to recognize their own emotions* because they were told what to feel and [that] certain feelings weren't allowed."[37]

Cults manipulate emotions to maintain control. Rituals, group activities, and charismatic leaders evoke highs like euphoria or belonging, balanced with fear and guilt to enforce compliance. A moving speech might make followers feel chosen; warnings of dire consequences for disobedience keep them in line. This emotional rollercoaster dulls critical thinking and strengthens attachment to the

---

* I had to have not one but two amazing women help me write my memoir *Uncultured*, in part because I was so bad at identifying my own emotions. I remain indebted to them for what I learned from that process.

group, a form of cultic abuse so subtle it can leave victims questioning whether they're being abused at all.[38] In the FLDS, this is epitomized by the "keep sweet" doctrine, which demands cheerful submission—and ties a woman's worth to her compliance, and reinforces patriarchal control.

In the military, recruits are drilled to maintain a "can-do" mindset, enforced through motivational techniques and strict discipline, with peer pressure playing a key role. Although it builds unity and purpose, it suppresses individuality and makes it hard for soldiers to express struggles. In men, this attitude can easily shift into traits of toxic masculinity: emotional suppression, aggression, dominance, hyper-competitiveness, workaholism, self-reliance, and fear of vulnerability, to name a few. Tragically, strict adherence to masculinity has been shown to be associated with more severe PTSD in vets.[39]

Large group awareness trainings like Landmark or Tony Robbins events use emotional control to create intense, transformational experiences. High-energy speeches, group exercises, and emotional sharing stir up euphoria and vulnerability. This emotional intensity breaks down personal barriers and makes participants more open to the group's teachings. The emphasis on positivity and rejection of negativity fosters conformity, leaving little room for critical thought.[40] People who question the group or leader are derided for their negativity, and often publicly humiliated, as in the famous exchange between Tony Robbins and a woman at one of his seminars who confronted him about his dismissive views of the #MeToo movement.[41]

In a similar vein, one major critique of contemporary alternative spiritual movements is their reliance on toxic positivity, as exemplified by the concept of "spiritual bypassing." Coined by psychologist John Welwood in *Toward a Psychology of Awakening*, spiritual bypassing is defined as using "spiritual ideas and practices to sidestep personal, emotional 'unfinished business,' to shore up a shaky sense of self, or to belittle basic needs, feelings, and developmental tasks."[42] In simpler terms, it's avoiding or repressing difficult emotions in favor of focusing on "higher vibrations," manifesting abundance, or embracing the law of attraction—New Age catchphrases that encourage denial rather than growth. This mindset can harm relationships by encouraging people to cut out "toxic" individuals or anyone with "negative energy"—essentially anyone who challenges them—further isolating them from the outside world.

Similarly, Alcoholics Anonymous emphasizes attitudes of acceptance, humility, and gratitude as essential to becoming "happy, joyous, and free." Openly questioning AA's teachings in meetings is often met with disapproval, subtle side-eye, or "helpful" correction by seasoned members afterward. Like many cults and mainstream religious organizations, most AA meetings are centered around member testimony (aka shares), creating a powerful sense of connection, identity, loyalty, and a reinforcement of beliefs—and a social pressure to conform. It's no coincidence that many members lovingly joke that AA stands for "attitude adjustment."

Across religious groups, cults, the military, corporate and nonprofit environments, and self-help and alternative wellness communities, enforced positivity erodes people's autonomy and silences their dissent. Chronically suppressing your emotions can lead to psychological symptoms like anxiety, depression, PTSD, various cognitive impairments, and increased risk of substance abuse, not to mention physical effects like high blood pressure, heart disease, a weakened immune system, and a decreased life expectancy.[43] In other words, the self-sacrifice of suppressing our emotions can literally kill us.

And as if that weren't enough—then comes the isolation.

Chapter 5

Isolation: The No-Contact Order

Thee was a man who lived for the pursuit of happiness. He drew his inspiration from the rave culture mantra of peace, love, unity, and respect (PLUR), a philosophy that fueled his annual pilgrimage to Burning Man, where he found a sense of utopian community that mirrored his idealistic aspirations. In business, his methods were anything but conventional—and he wore that badge with pride. One of the ten core values of his billion-dollar company was, fittingly, "Create fun and a little weirdness." It was indeed a bit weird, a little eccentric, but somehow, it worked. He built multiple successful ventures, eventually selling his e-commerce megastore for a jaw-dropping $1.2 billion. Yet throughout his endeavors—business and beyond—his focus remained on creating, spreading, and "delivering happiness."

After selling his shoe venture to Amazon in 2009, he turned his attention to his next great endeavor—one that would cement his commitment to creating tangible happiness. In 2012 he launched an ambitious $350 million urban renewal project in downtown Las Vegas.[1] He envisioned a thriving hub for entrepreneurs and creatives, built on ideals of connectedness, co-learning, and spontaneous interactions. He called it the Downtown Project, an experiment in community and innovation where people lived in upgraded shipping containers, shared workspaces, and blurred the lines between professional and personal life, all in the name of creativity.

But this constant engagement and relentless collaboration came with a darker side. Pressure to conform, community insularity, and eroded personal boundaries took their toll. Cut off from the outside world and their own support systems, residents and employees faced burnout, isolation, and worsening mental health, while "kept as busy as possible—or at least prevented from spending much of their time alone," according to one account.[2] Tragically, a string of suicides among project members shattered the utopian vision.

When Tony Hsieh died in 2020 under mysterious circumstances, it cast a long shadow over his legacy. Zappos wasn't just about selling shoes, and the Downtown Project wasn't just about urban renewal— they were experiments in happiness. But in the end, they left a haunting question: What's the true cost of chasing utopia?

* * *

Isolation, or sometimes insulation, from the outside world is crucial to high-control environments. Cults frequently push members to disconnect from external relationships and spaces, limiting their interactions in ways that make them more vulnerable to the group's control.[3] Whether it's relocating people to a remote commune, setting up strict rules about who you can talk to, or creating boundaries or demands that make it impossible to keep up with friends and family, the outcome is the same: severing members from their old lives and support systems. Once that's done, the group builds a little bubble where its ideology can thrive, untouched by outside perspectives.

When you're surrounded 24/7 by a group's beliefs, the reinforcement starts to feel like reality, and questioning seems impossible. Margaret Singer explains how this plays out:

> Recruits are brought to camps in the country, weekend retreats, clandestine cult facilities, workshops in the desert, and a host of other places to isolate them from access to their usual social

life. These groups know that physically cutting people off is an effective way to change their behavior and make them more compliant. When you're suddenly removed from everything familiar—your friends, family, job, school—it becomes so much easier to fall in line with the group's expectations.[4]

Physical isolation isn't just a logistical move—it's psychological. Dr. Alexandra Stein tells us that "the combination of fear and isolation is what puts the coercion into coercive persuasion."[5] In an environment where the group's ideas go unchallenged, you're left with no one to remind you who you were before. Janja Lalich says that "after living in an environment where everyone thinks and acts alike, even if you are not as sequestered as those in more restrictive cults, your outlook shrinks and your ability to communicate atrophies."[6] The cult I grew up in was like that—marked by total physical and psychological isolation. We were 10,000 strong, living in communes scattered across the globe, each of us devoting every aspect of our life to the group and severing ties with anyone unwilling to pay the same steep entrance costs we had.

Basic training in the military shares structural similarities with high-control groups. Recruits are cut off from outside influences and immersed in strict routines that reshape identity around collective values. One key feature is the "battle buddy" system (which felt eerily similar to the buddy system I experienced in the Children of God), a mandated pairing of soldiers intended to build mutual support, foster accountability, and prevent isolation—a practice many service members report as positive and even lifesaving, particularly in relation to suicide prevention. Yet while the system encourages camaraderie and safety, it also removes privacy and reinforces internal surveillance. This "isolation together" dynamic fosters deep loyalty that makes soldiers more receptive to indoctrination, and it creates a system where the group polices itself, making sure you stay in line without needing constant top-down enforcement.[7]

The same isolation strategy shows up in the troubled-teen industry—only there, it's dressed up in Patagonia vests and called "tough love." Thousands of American families ship their kids off to these boot camps, wilderness therapy programs, therapeutic boarding schools, and behavior modification facilities that claim to help troubled adolescents with issues like substance abuse, defiance, mental health struggles, or academic failure. Many don't know that the origins of this industry trace back to Synanon, the 1950s drug rehabilitation program that evolved into a full-fledged cult. Synanon's harsh behavior modification tactics later became the blueprint for many troubled-teen programs through offshoots like the North Star Wilderness Camp, the World Wide Association of Specialty Programs, and Straight, Inc.[8] These facilities are often unregulated, many in the middle of nowhere (Utah, we're looking at you), and the first thing staff do is cut off all outside contact—no phone, no internet, no unsupervised conversations. Once inside, kids are told their parents no longer trust them, their friends were bad influences, and any resistance is proof they're in denial and not yet healed.

In facilities like these, as in so many total institutions, isolation *becomes* the treatment. According to Breaking Code Silence, a survivor-led advocacy group, these programs frequently weaponize social deprivation to instill compliance. Survivors have described years of trauma, abuse, and coercion at these facilities—some of which operate entirely without government oversight. Paris Hilton's 2020 documentary *This Is Paris* blew the lid off Provo Canyon School in particular; she detailed the abuse she and other former residents claim to have faced there. This is not therapy. It's indoctrination with a trauma-bonding twist, and like any good cult, they sell it to terrified parents as salvation.

In her book *Terror, Love and Brainwashing*, Dr. Alexandra Stein explains how, like a dysfunctional family, high-control groups create disorganized attachment in their members, further solidifying the control:

> Totalist leaders—either directly or through their organizations—create a relationship of disorganized attachment by isolating people from their prior sources of support and replacing those

with a new and frightening, "safe haven." We know from attachment research that disorganized attachment, which involves
seeking proximity with the frightening attachment figure when
there is no other attachment figure or escape available, causes
a dissociative response. Dissociation separates thinking from
feeling. It dis-integrates the left, logical, verbal, thinking side
of the brain, from the right, emotional, nonverbal side of the
brain. The dissociated person's ability to think clearly about
the relationship is impaired and so they are now in a position to
accept the group's views—its ideology. This ideology is in place
to further bolster the elements of isolation, terror and "love" and
to explain away feelings of fear induced in the follower. Emotionally the dissociated person tends to draw closer to the group as
it is now their only remaining "safe haven."[9]

A group's isolation tactics aren't always obvious. As we'll explore in
the following sections, isolation also involves the emotional and mental
walls that keep people locked into the group's reality. Sometimes these
walls are subtle, reinforced through the group's culture to ensure
everyone toes the line and keeps the status quo intact.

Psychological Isolation

Isolation can happen right inside your own head. You get so insulated
from outside perspectives that the group's worldview becomes your
entire reality. When there's no outside input, leaders can manipulate
you more easily, because you're not hearing anything that might make
you stop and think, *Wait, does this even make sense?*

Cult leaders can isolate people mentally, even when they're physically surrounded by others. They often invoke thought-stopping
clichés. Phrases like "doubt your doubts" or "Satan is testing you" or
"everything happens for a reason" may sound innocent, but they're
designed to shut down critical thinking and remove personal agency.
Little sayings get members to accept whatever the group teaches, so

questioning feels like failure or sin. Leaders don't need to lock you away in some remote place—they just create a mental space where stepping outside the group's teachings feels like stepping into danger. In 12-step programs like AA, for example, members are constantly reminded that "stepping out" literally leads to death. "Over time," Amanda Montell tells us in *Cultish*, this loaded language "acquires a strong emotional charge. When a word or phrase takes on such baggage that its mere mention can spark fear, grief, dread, jubilation, reverence (anything), a leader can exploit it to steer followers' behavior."[10]

The psychological isolation remains even when members are out in the world and socializing with others. The group's all-encompassing influence acts like a filter for their experience. A member might be physically present at a family gathering, but mentally they're still operating within the group's boundaries. They're viewing every conversation and interaction through the lens of the group's teachings, so connecting with others on a real, human level is almost impossible. Everything they see and do is affected by the group's worldview and system of judgment (just ask any AA member if they rate the drinking habits of everyone they encounter). Even though the cult member "will appear as you or I do, and will function well in ordinary tasks," Margaret Singer explains, "the cult lectures and procedures tend to gradually induce members to experience anxiety whenever they critically evaluate the cult."[11] Over time, people learn to avoid critical thinking altogether—especially about the group—because doing so triggers guilt and anxiety. It's a clever, self-policing system that keeps people from even considering dissent.

Social Isolation

Dr. Janja Lalich breaks it down in *Take Back Your Life: Recovering from Cults and Abusive Relationships*: In almost every cult, "over time, members become separated from their past."[12] Loved ones are labeled as negative influences, a threat, or people who "don't get it," and leaders discourage or outright forbid communication with them. Margaret

Singer describes one political cult that had recruits lie to their parents while a leader stood by, coaching them through the call.[13] It's a calcu-lated move, designed not just to sever family ties but to train members to obey irrational orders without question.

But it doesn't stop there. Cults often push members to abandon everything that connects them to their old lives—hobbies, jobs, even the smallest habits that don't align with the group's ideology. Sometimes members are urged to take on new names, symbolizing a full break from their former selves.[14] The deeper someone sinks into this new identity, the harder it becomes to imagine returning to their old life. Every day spent separated from family, friends, and their former sense of self makes the outside world seem more foreign and unreachable. That isolation builds an invisible wall, keeping members trapped.[15]

Social isolation can also occur as a secondary effect of other aspects of the cult's control. For instance, as described in chapter 4, cult members may be subject to appearance and behavior controls that reinforce their otherness in the outside world. Their visible differ-ence makes members feel alienated from anyone outside the group, and deepens their dependency on the cult. What starts as a marker of belonging in the group becomes a source of isolation, reinforcing the idea that no one outside could possibly understand or accept them.

For children especially, strict group rules can also mean missing out on normal experiences, which only adds to the sense of being "other." When kids can't join in on birthday parties, Halloween celebrations, or even simply reciting the Pledge of Allegiance, it makes them stand out in all the worst ways. Think about Jehovah's Witness kids who don't celebrate birthdays, evangelical kids who can't go trick-or-treating, or kids raised on diets, like veganism, who can't eat what their friends are eating. For them, it's not about missing out, it's about being marked as different. That difference can become both a badge of pride and a quiet source of shame. Every "no, you can't" reinforces the feeling of not belonging. When mainstream traditions are treated as the default, the message is "different = excluded." At the same time, exclusion can go both ways—kids from any background may feel judged if others

aren't open to their choices. Promoting mutual respect, not conformity, is key to helping all kids feel accepted, both in school and in the
long term.[16]

Social isolation is taken to the extreme with what I call geographic
abuse, when members are relocated to remote or unfamiliar places,
cutting them off from support systems and making them easier to
control. Without friends, family, or familiar routines, people cling to
anything that offers structure and a feeling of stability. Add in unfamiliar languages or cultural barriers, and it's like throwing a lock on the
door, making escape feel impossible. Jonestown is the most infamous
example, but Jim Jones wasn't doing anything new—history is full of
groups isolating themselves for ideological reasons. Wasn't this just a
modern version of the Puritans heading to America, seeking isolation
for their sacred mission? Same concept, different century. Just look at
any self-described compound or commune and you'll see the same goal
of isolating from the outside world. Seeking a self-sufficient utopia isn't
inherently harmful, but the wrong leadership can easily corrupt it.

Growing up in the Children of God, I experienced geographic abuse
firsthand. We were shipped all over the world, usually to avoid the heat
from law enforcement or bad press, and we had little to no say in where
we lived. When I finally set foot in the US—my own country—I understood why they kept us far away. In San Diego, walking away would
have been easy. But in the middle of Brazil, it was impossible. At ten, I
taught myself Portuguese, realizing that language was power. By twelve,
fluency became my escape plan—if I ever needed to run, I'd at least
have the words to ask for help.

As we explored earlier, both the Mormon Church and the US
Army use geographic displacement as a form of control—isolating
individuals under the guise of service or duty. The result is the same:
disconnection, instability, and a deep sense of rootlessness. But this
isn't unique to cults or the military—geographic isolation is baked
into modern life. Americans are more scattered than ever, chasing jobs,
better housing, and other quality-of-life factors, far from the communities they grew up in. And our ways of connecting have changed.

Remote work and online socializing have eroded real-world connections, making it harder to build friendships, especially in a new place. Without day-to-day physical interactions, we can easily feel untethered and disconnected, which is exacerbated by the information isolation that often comes along with a life lived increasingly online (we'll discuss information isolation soon).

Financial Isolation

High-control groups know exactly what they're doing when they keep members hungry, scared, poor, tired, pregnant, and busy. They're ramping up members' dependency by creating a cycle of exhaustion, stress, and financial strain that makes leaving feel impossible. Economic control plays a massive role here. Financial penalties, debt, and noncompete clauses, for example, can trap members. When you're barely scraping by or drowning in obligations, you're not exactly in a position to pack up and leave.

In the Children of God, as part of "forsaking all" to follow Jesus, members were required to quit their jobs, sell or donate their possessions, and surrender everything they owned to the cult, which would then "distribute to each according to his need." In Scientology's Sea Org, Twelve Tribes communities, and countless failed communes, members also give up everything—freedom, jobs, assets—to live entirely within the group. They donate property, family heirlooms, savings accounts, and most importantly, their labor (more about labor in chapter 8). With no outside income, their survival depends entirely on the group.

Financial control in the workplace often appears as standard business practice, but it can function in ways that restrict employee autonomy. Noncompete clauses, for example, limit where and how workers can use their skills after leaving a job. In 2024 the Federal Trade Commission voted to ban noncompete agreements, calling them exploitative and estimating the change could increase worker earnings by nearly $300 billion per year.[17] However, the FTC's rule was blocked by federal courts, and as of mid-2025, noncompete clauses can still be enforced, depending on state laws and case-by-case circumstances. Unvested stock options are another form of financial tethering. Typically structured to vest over time, stock options encourage employees to remain with a company until a liquidity event, such as an IPO or acquisition, or else risk forfeiting potential earnings.

Multi-level marketing (MLM) schemes similarly use financial control to keep people trapped. MLMs don't just encourage members to quit their jobs; they suggest getting their spouses to quit too. It's eerily similar to the military, where the spouse sometimes ends up even more isolated than the service member, unable to maintain a career because of constant relocations. The bottom line? If someone tells you to "quit your job and come follow me," you should probably run— they're likely trying to rope you into their cult.

Many mainstream religions request tithes, with some Christian denominations requiring 10 percent of each member's income. Mormons must tithe to maintain full membership and be allowed in temples, and Pentecostal and evangelical churches often make tithing a requirement for leadership.[18] The Jehovah's Witnesses rely heavily on financial contributions, requiring members to donate significant portions of their income, along with their time and labor. A 2016 Pew Research survey found that Jehovah's Witnesses rank dead last in household income among American religious groups.[19] Mormon families also pay significant amounts—around $500 monthly—to send their children on missions, adding further financial strain.[20] The LDS Church acknowledges that "financial sacrifice is part of missionary service (see Mark 1:17–18; Alma 15:16). Missionaries and their families have primary responsibility for contributing financially to missionary service. They should make appropriate sacrifices to provide financial support for a mission."[21]

Financial isolation isn't exclusive to cults—it's a widespread problem. According to Pew Research, dissatisfaction with personal finances strongly correlates with loneliness.[22] Financial dependence also keeps people trapped in unhealthy relationships. Many, especially women, remain in unhappy or abusive marriages because they lack the means to leave. It's a sobering reality that just fifty years ago, women in the US couldn't even hold credit cards in their own names. The necessity for the Equal Credit Opportunity Act in 1974—and the determined activism of the women behind it—underscores how control over financial access has long been used to limit people's autonomy. Gaining control of your own finances also means reclaiming agency, stability, and the power to choose your own path.

Today financial control can be seen repackaged online in the "tradwife influencer."[23] Picture pastel-filtered Instagram feeds filled with women baking bread, folding laundry, and waxing poetic about "traditional values." These women glamorize 1950s-style domesticity, complete with perfectly styled aprons and a big helping of nostalgia for the "good old days," pitching financial dependence on a husband as empowerment. The aesthetic may seem harmless, but the message is clear: Give up financial independence and embrace economic reliance. This romanticized version of dependency ignores reality—when marriages collapse, many women are left with nothing. Worse, it downplays that financial control is common in abusive relationships. For women, leaving can feel impossible because the financial fallout of divorce is terrifying. Living on one income (especially if you have little to no work history), covering legal fees, starting over—it's a daunting challenge that can make the idea of staying, even in a harmful situation, seem like the safer bet.

Tia Levings, in her memoir *A Well-Trained Wife: My Escape from Christian Patriarchy*, delves into the mechanisms of financial control within high-control religious environments. She says Christian fundamentalism and the tradwife movement often keep women financially dependent by limiting their access to personal finances, employment, or education, which makes it difficult for them to escape. Levings emphasizes that without financial independence, escaping detrimental situations—be it a controlling relationship, a cultlike environment, or an exploitative workplace—becomes an arduous endeavor.[24]

Patriarchal systems depend partly on unpaid labor and silence to maintain control—especially from women, who are expected to sacrifice their time and energy without recognition or compensation. These dynamics hit women of color the hardest, by compounding existing inequalities like the racial pay gap and limited access to leadership roles. The COVID-19 pandemic made these disparities worse. Women experienced greater job losses and have been slower to recover, largely due to increased caregiving responsibilities and the persistent lack of affordable childcare.[25]

The Isolating Power of Secrets and Shame

"Secrecy is a powerful control mechanism in many areas of group life," Dr. Alexandra Stein explains. "But in the recruitment phase it functions particularly well to establish isolation early on."[26] By presenting secret truths that are accessible only to members, groups create a sense of exclusivity that can feel intoxicating; they also cut off outside perspectives that could challenge their narratives. Secrecy also shields the group from external scrutiny. Members are told that outsiders wouldn't understand or might distort the group's teachings, which reinforces the us-versus-them mentality. Reflecting on her experience in a political cult, Stein notes that "security is the reason given for high levels of secrecy and centralization. Such groups operate on the need-to-know principle." If you've ever worked in the military or held a government job with secret or top-secret clearance, you'll recognize this approach: Limit who gets access to information and ensure that only the inner circle controls the flow.

In cults, new recruits are told not to share what they're learning with outsiders because "they wouldn't get it." This both boosts the recruit's sense of importance and access to outside opinions that could challenge the group's beliefs. As Stein points out, this means "the only people with whom the new recruit can reflect upon their (often unsettling) experience are those already in the group or undergoing the same training." She recalls that secrecy ran through every level of her group, even barring her from discussing organizational matters with her own husband. The enforced silence enabled unchecked abuse and control.

But of course, the secrecy mostly serves to benefit the cult leader. The leader is special, after all, because he has access to secret things. Margaret Singer tells us that

> these determined self-designated gurus seem always to be lurking on the sidelines ready to step in and offer answers to life's problems. They claim they have the only and sure way of life. They induce people to follow them by touting a special mission and special knowledge. The special mission is to preach the contents of a supposedly "secret" learning, which the leaders assert can only be revealed to those who join them.[27]

Secrecy also plays a crucial role in initiation rituals, serving to elevate the transition into membership, making it feel sacred. It can take benign, even sweet and meaningful forms, such as coming-of-age ceremonies in groups like the Girl Scouts or YMCA summer camps, where the secrecy creates a feeling of profundity and magic. In self-help groups like the ManKind Project with its New Warrior Training Adventure weekend, initiates (who pay $500 to $1,000 for the honor) are firmly instructed to never tell anyone what happens (I have it on good authority that the men play drums and run around in the forest naked). Or of course, there are the full-blown cults like Scientology, which has sophisticated levels of membership that reveal new heavily guarded secrets with each step up the ranks, the grand prize being something to do with aliens. In all these groups, being "in" on the secret bestows a sense of specialness and pride on the initiate, further cementing their bond and loyalty to the group and the belief that no one on the outside would understand.

Military and intelligence agencies, especially elite units, operate on strict information compartmentalization, a necessity for security but also effective for fostering toxic environments. Similarly, corporate secrecy shields fraudulent practices. Lauren Rogal notes in "Secrets,

Lies, and Lessons from the Theranos Scandal" that Elizabeth Holmes enforced secrecy through nondisclosure agreements (NDAs) and intimidation, preventing employees from exposing that the company's technology was a sham. Employees were siloed, discouraged from sharing information even internally, to ensure that the central deception remained intact. Zappos, beneath the surface of its celebrated customer service ethos and nontraditional management models, maintained a tightly controlled internal narrative. During the company's transition to holacracy (a self-management system that eliminated traditional hierarchies), employees were discouraged from publicly expressing dissent or uncertainty. Although the change was framed as empowering, employees reported confusion, burnout, and a lack of clarity about roles and accountability. Those who didn't align with the vision were quietly offered severance packages to leave.[28]

Secrecy culture isn't confined to fraudulent or chaotic startups. Rogal points out that NDAs have been used to silence victims in the #MeToo movement, shield corporate misconduct, and suppress political dissent (President Trump required NDAs from employees at the Trump Organization and his presidential campaign[29]). As this book went to press, a recent conference of Jeffrey Epstein's victims revealed secrecy as a common thread—how it was demanded, enforced, and weaponized to keep them silent. Epstein relied on NDAs, sealed records, and the sheer weight of his power, a pattern experts call the "conspiracy of silence," which enables systemic abuse.[30] Companies justify secrecy as protecting trade secrets, but it often functions to prevent transparency and accountability. Keeping employees in the dark about major decisions, financial matters, and pay disparities helps prevent challenges to power structures. Long a staple of corporate legal risk management, NDAs have acquired a dubious reputation for concealing information that would be in the public interest to disseminate.

Enron serves as a prime example. Although "integrity" was carved into marble at its Houston HQ, secrecy enabled its massive fraud. Executives manipulated financial data to hide the truth from employees, investors, and regulators until the entire system collapsed. Pay secrecy is another form of corporate control. Despite existing legal protections for discussing salaries, many workplaces maintain an environment where talking about pay is taboo, which allows wage disparities to persist and keeps workers powerless. Secrecy, it turns out, isn't useful for cover-ups or shady bookkeeping; it's a key component for controlling people, whether in a corporate environment or more overtly oppressive systems. It's what keeps the powerful in power and everyone else guessing.

A close partner to secrecy is shame. Cult leaders, toxic bosses, abusive partners, and narcissistic parents shame their targets to isolate them, make them feel unworthy, and convince them they don't belong. "More intense shame yields a profound sense of isolation due to feeling flawed or even unlovable," Dr. Bernard Golden explains in *Psychology Today*. "It can also foster hyper-vigilance in an effort to avoid exposure of one's perceived flaws or vulnerability to further shaming. As such, it may also be at the core of intense perfectionism." This perfectionism, fueled by shame, drives people to work even harder to please their oppressor, further entrenching the cycle of control.

One of shame's most powerful enforcers is gaslighting—manipulation that makes a person doubt the validity of their own thoughts, feelings, and perceptions. Gaslighting doesn't just distort the truth; it dismantles someone's self-trust and rewrites reality so relentlessly that they stop trusting their own memories and instincts. Cult leaders deny things they said or did, accuse you of misunderstanding, and twist their actions into a higher purpose that you "just can't grasp yet." Push back, and the response is predictable: "You're too sensitive," or "You're not spiritual enough," or "You're crazy." Over time, you stop resisting. Instead you doubt yourself, question your sanity, and convince yourself the problem isn't them—it's you. Shame breeds powerlessness, further cementing their control.

Jim Jones's infamous "catharsis" sessions were emotional eviscerations masquerading as group therapy—confessions turned public beatdowns, which left the confessor shattered and the audience thoroughly warned.[31] Charles Dederich's Synanon called their version "The Game," a brutal, gladiator-style verbal takedown disguised as honesty and self-improvement.[32] NXIVM had similar rituals, where members were confronted by senior figures on stage in front of an audience. As Martha Stout notes, "Sociopaths, people with no intervening sense of obligation based in attachments to others, typically devote their lives to interpersonal games, to 'winning,' to domination for the sake of domination."[33] (Sound like a president we know?)

These "degradation ceremonies" humiliate members, but moreover they erase their personal identity. The goal is to sever the connections that make someone feel grounded so they're left dependent on the group or leader for validation. Stripped of autonomy, individuals become desperate to reclaim even a shred of belonging. Cults rebrand these rituals as "spiritual growth" or "purification," but they're nothing more than mechanisms of control. Hazing in fraternities and the military, public reprimands by religious leaders, and "corrective" meetings in corporate settings all follow the same principle: Humiliate enough, and conformity follows.

At the national level, shaming is wielded like a blunt instrument. Donald Trump built a career on public humiliation—from his iconic "You're fired" on *The Apprentice* to his degrading nicknames like "Crooked Hillary" to personal insults aimed at Ted Cruz's wife. Shaming isn't just his brand, it's his power move. His actions are aimed at more than the targets—they're a warning to everyone watching: Loyalty is rewarded, dissent is punished. Bobby Azarian's *Psychology Today* article titled "Trump Is Gaslighting America Again—Here's How to Fight It" explains how far he's taken it: "Calling Russian intervention in the 2016 presidential election 'fake news' after intelligence agencies have proven it beyond doubt, and claiming to have a record-breaking crowd size at his inauguration, are just two examples that immediately come to mind, although at least a dozen more have been documented." (And that was back in 2018. How many more by now?)

Shame isolates. It silences. And it locks people into a cycle of depen-dence on the very group or leader holding them captive. Whether through physical separation, emotional manipulation, or simply keeping people too busy to think, isolation is the cornerstone of main-taining control. Without any personal autonomy or outside perspec-tives, people will cling tighter to the group for survival.

And we're in an epidemic of isolation. A 2018 Pew Research study revealed that one in ten Americans feels lonely most of the time.[34] Then came the pandemic, which took that already fragile thread of connec-tion and clipped it in two. Our isolation, paired with the increasing siloing of information that we'll explore in the next section, created fertile ground for cults to take an even tighter grasp on America.

Information Isolation

In high-control groups, leaders carefully manage what members see and hear, so that only the group's ideas get reinforced. The Children of God cult had military-style classification on all the doctrine our leader put out. In the US Army, everything is labeled with informa-tion control tags like Unclassified, SECRET, and TOP SECRET to protect against leaks. Mormons fiercely guard what happens inside their temples, Coca-Cola defends its secret formula, and even movies come with ratings to control who gets to see them. And of course there's our current president who, in the first days of his second term, commanded that all federal government websites be scrubbed of content related to climate change science, LGBTQ+ issues, abortion, contraception and STI guidance, and vaccine science, among other things. All of these are different kinds of information control.

Cults have always controlled members' access to information, long before the internet was a thing. Back in the day, it might have looked like banning certain types of books (*Harry Potter* for witchcraft or Darwin's *The Origin of Species* for evolution, in far-right Christian groups), or even all books (have the good guys *ever* turned out to be the ones who banned books?). In recent years, the mainstreaming of far-right ideology has become successful enough to ban books in school districts and libraries across the country.* According to PEN America, "This censorship is being mobilized by conservative groups... and predominantly targets books about race and racism or individuals of color and also books on LGBTQ+ topics as well as those for older readers that have sexual references or discuss sexual violence," and it is happening at a rate not seen since the McCarthy Red Scare era of the 1950s.[35]

One trusty way cult leaders keep information from group members is by teaching them to disbelieve the news or to only believe their biased version of it (and if you are thinking about Donald Trump right now, you are correct). Social media aids information control through its algorithms, feeding people only the content that fits their beliefs. QAnon was a perfect example—people got sucked into their own little digital worlds, completely isolated from reality, and were fed increasingly extreme content. Some people who got deeply involved in QAnon found themselves so immersed in the conspiracy theories and their quest for hidden truths that their real lives started to take a backseat. Glued to their screens, digging through forums, decoding cryptic messages, and watching endless videos that promised to reveal the "truth" about global elites, they'd neglect jobs, miss family events, or withdraw from social activities. Some reported losing touch with loved ones who didn't share their beliefs. Their obsessive engagement led to detachment from the real world, as the line between online conspiracy and everyday reality blurred.

Social media algorithms are designed to keep people hooked, resulting in making the consumer's views more and more radical without them realizing it. Over time, people—on both sides of the political spectrum—see only one side of the story, and getting a bigger picture becomes nearly impossible. With the rise of AI and increasingly

---

* These book bans include two of co-writer Amy's critically-acclaimed young adult novels, *The Nowhere Girls* and *Beautiful*, in school districts in Florida, Iowa, Utah, South Carolina, and Tennessee.

sophisticated algorithms, this kind of isolation is likely going to get worse. "The silos of political groupthink created by social media have turned out to be ideal settings for the germination and dissemination of extremist ideas and alternative realities," Zoe Heller tells us in a *New Yorker* article titled "What Makes a Cult a Cult?" Discussing the phenomenon of QAnon, which scholars struggle to define as a cult via existing frameworks, Heller says that "it's possible that our traditional definitions of what constitutes a cult organization will have to adapt to the Internet age and a new model of crowdsourced cult."

Digital isolation is powerful. Separating people from the truth makes them cling even harder to their group's beliefs. According to a 2021 study on the connection between social media and conspiracy theories during the height of the COVID pandemic, "Once inside a conspiratorial identity bubble, people experience constant reinforcement of their conspiracy beliefs, are encouraged to adopt more extreme beliefs, and are likely to associate core aspects of their self-concept with those beliefs."[36] Basically, when you're constantly surrounded by the same ideas, it becomes really hard to think any other way. Margaret Singer explains that "when cut off from social support, social background, families, familiar surroundings, friends, jobs, schoolmates, and classes"—as most Americans were during COVID lockdown—"and brought into a new environ with a new ambiance, few can resist the pull to fit in"—that new environ being their increasingly passionate online communities.[37] It used to be that cults would almost *have* to physically isolate members, but now we can be just as isolated digitally—often without even realizing it. We're getting trapped in these echo chambers, and soon enough, opposing viewpoints don't even exist to us anymore. We end up in a loop of radical ideas, which isolates us further from reality.

Social media's echo chambers are like escape rooms for the digital age, and the algorithms running our feeds are the ones locking the doors. An article titled "Thinking Outside the Bubble: Addressing Polarization and Disinformation on Social Media" says that platforms like these amplify polarization—not just ideological differences (like debating policy) but something even worse: *affective* polarization. That's when we stop merely disagreeing with people and start actively disliking them just because they're on the "other side." And the scary part? It's all designed to feed us more of what we already believe, reinforce our biases, and keep us stuck in loops of one-sided perspectives. The platforms claim to connect us, but really, they're driving us further apart. Sociologist Jack Goldstone, the article notes, even compares today's political climate to the years leading up to the Civil War—it's that serious.

This "algorithmic radicalization" is so well recognized that it now has its own Wikipedia page. In their attempt to keep us hooked on their platforms, sites like YouTube, Facebook, Instagram, and TikTok are driving users toward progressively more extreme content, essentially preying on the addictive mechanisms of our brain that crave increasing stimulation to get the same rush. Facebook's own research stated as much, according to a slide from an internal presentation: "Our algorithms exploit the human brain's attraction to divisiveness. If left unchecked, Facebook would feed users more and more divisive content in an effort to gain user attention and increase time on the platform."[38] (Did Facebook do anything to remedy this? As of this writing, no. The reasoning being it would negatively affect user engagement and therefore be "anti-growth.") With the help of recommender algorithms that record our interactions, from likes/dislikes and shares to time spent on posts, a mild interest can spiral into extreme beliefs, which are then normalized in a culture full of people who are also at home in front of their screens getting radicalized—convincing, for example, over 77 million people in 2024 that Donald Trump deserved to be president again.

More and more of us are choosing to stay inside comfortable bubbles—whether that's where we live, the schools we attend, the faith communities we belong to, or especially the social media spaces we frequent. We're frequently surrounded by people who look like us, think like us, and rarely challenge our beliefs. As political divisions deepen, and as economic and geographic divides grow wider, and as media becomes increasingly fragmented to cater to every prefer-ence, this siloing starts to feel like the norm—maybe even something unavoidable. And the more we settle into these bubbles, the more we accept only the information that confirms what we already believe, regardless of whether it's actually true.

We are all, to varying extents, participating in the "great sorting" President Obama warned us about in his 2017 farewell address. If left unchecked, these platforms will continue to shape public opinion in ways that prioritize engagement over truth, deepening divisions and making it ever harder to find common ground in a democracy that depends on it.

Chapter 6

Distinguishable Vernacular: The Jargon Jungle

P icture this: A woman stands at the front of the room, eyes locked on her audience. Her voice is calm, just intense enough to make it feel like she's revealing secrets the rest of the world has missed. She talks about "shadow work," "vibrational alignment," "emotional frequency." Spirituality and psychology woven together into something that sounds both mystical and scientific. Heads nod. Tears fall. People lean in. This isn't just a seminar—it's an experience, a revelation. She's selling more than self-improvement; she's offering a key to the universe. And as you listen, you start to wonder: Maybe she really does know something the rest of the world doesn't. Maybe everything you've thought until now is wrong.

Teal Swan, the self-proclaimed spiritual guru whose YouTube sermons and retreats have drawn a fervent following (and whose advice has been linked to more than one suicide),[1] uses words designed to reshape reality. Pain isn't just pain; it's part of your soul's journey. Any doubt is resistance to the truth. Anger and sadness? "Lower vibrations" that need to be cleared. If you're struggling, you haven't elevated yourself enough. And if you question her? That's just your "ego" keeping you trapped. This is not a method—it's a worldview. And the people in that room or on the other side of the screen are rewiring how they see themselves, how they talk about themselves, and adopting a vocabulary only insiders understand. The deeper they go, the harder it is to step outside.[2]

* * *

Swap out Teal Swan for the Medical Medium Anthony William, UFO expert and spiritual teacher Elizabeth April, countless other spiritual influencers, or even former presidential nominee Marianne Williamson. Scroll Instagram and you'll see the same coded language everywhere: energy healing, clean eating, ascension, detox, manifestation, self-care rituals, vibrations, 5D, superfoods, downloads. These words do more than describe—they signal. If you understand them, you belong.

But this world exists at a murky intersection where wellness and spirituality meet conspiracy theories, what some call *conspirituality*. Derek Beres, Matthew Remski, and Julian Walker explain it in their eponymous book:

> As an online religion, conspirituality today is not just a set of ideas that people come to value in their quiet and humble hearts. It is generated and circulated by various churches, revival meetings, and séance sessions in the form of small-group courses and mastermind Zoom meetings.[3]

In this world, "quantum healing" sits comfortably next to "5D consciousness" and conspiracy theories about vaccines. "Awakening" can mean anything from practicing breathwork to believing the government controls our minds with fluoride and chemtrails. Wellness influencers seamlessly pivot from selling organic supplements to whispering about the hidden truths "they" don't want you to know. The deeper people go, the more they feel like they're waking up—while the rest of the world remains blind, programmed, or too low-vibrational to see.

But take a step back, and we have to ask: Isn't this the same formula we saw in chapter 1? The charismatic authority filling the void left when we can't explain the world around us? Because when the world feels overwhelming, when life is uncertain and complex, there's nothing more seductive than someone who can make it *all make sense*—especially if they look good doing it, as many popular alt-spirituality influencers do. The authors of *Conspirituality* describe this phenomenon's rise during the isolation of COVID lockdown: "In a moment of peak cultural anxiety, COVID-contrarian gurus could throw off their brick-and-mortar limitations, re-create themselves on Instagram, and get paid through subscriptions, as they learned how to use the algorithms [and, I would argue, language] of these platforms to spread misinformation."[4] And nothing is more dangerous than someone who convinces you they hold the only key to your transformation.

And that key? It starts with language.

The Power of Language

Research shows that language has a huge effect on the way we think. It can shape even the most fundamental dimensions of human experience like space, time, causality, and relationships to others. Changing a person's language changes their cognition—their way of perceiving, categorizing, and making meaning in the world. Language "appears to be involved in many more aspects of our mental lives than scientists had previously supposed....There may not be a lot of adult human thinking where language does not play a role," according to *Scientific American*.[5]

Language has always been one of humanity's greatest tools—shaping history, controlling narratives, and reinforcing power structures in ways we barely notice. Oliver Wendell Holmes described the power of language poetically when he said, "Language is the blood of the soul into which thoughts run and out of which they grow." But one of my favorite explanations of the power of language comes from Trevor Noah in his amazing memoir *Born a Crime: Stories from a South African Childhood*:

Language brings with it an identity and a culture, or at least the perception of it. A shared language says, "We're the same." A language barrier says, "We're different."...Racism teaches us that we are different because of the color of our skin, but because racism is stupid, it's easily tricked. If you're a racist and you meet someone who doesn't look like you, the fact that he can't speak like you reinforces your racist preconceptions....However, if the person who doesn't look like you speaks like you, your brain short-circuits because your racism program has none of those instructions in the code.[6]

Language gives us a code for understanding the world and our place in it. It has the power to unite people, but it also has immense power to divide—especially when manipulated for that exact purpose.

The fastest way to create identity, loyalty, and exclusivity is to invent a way of speaking that only insiders understand. Every cult, high-control group, and ideological movement develops its own language—that's one of the main building blocks of control. In *Cultish*, Amanda Montell puts it bluntly when she tells us, "Language *is* a leader's charisma."[7] Cults, spiritual movements, and political figures use words to create entire worlds—and when those words are repeated enough, they don't just sound profound. They become truth. Margaret Singer dismantles the illusion that there's anything mystical about how cult leaders manipulate people:

How cult leaders and other clever operators get people to do their bidding seems arcane and mysterious to most persons, but I find there is nothing esoteric about it at all. There are no secret drugs or potions. It is just words and group pressures, put together in packaged forms.[8]

And that's the real genius of it. A charismatic leader's power doesn't come from magic or God—it comes from language.

Amanda Montell explains that cult jargon creates community—but also shuts down critical thinking.[9] Certain phrases act as mental roadblocks that stop members from questioning the group's ideology. Mormonism has "put it on a shelf." If something about the faith doesn't make sense, don't think too hard about it—just set it aside for later. Scientology has "thought-stopping" techniques, where members are trained to immediately counter doubts with approved phrases. MLMs say "winners never quit"—so leaving doesn't mean the system was flawed; it means you failed.

As we learned in chapter 3, Derek Black helped build Stormfront. org, where he normalized "white genocide" and "reverse racism," knowing that if you control the language, you control the way people think. And it worked. Those words spread, warped conversations far beyond their original audience, and made it to the mainstream. Political leaders, religious extremists, and influencers—everyone from Adolf Hitler to Donald Trump to Gwyneth Paltrow—knows that language sells. Trump trademarked the phrase "Make America Great Again," even though Reagan said it first, because he understood what made it work.[10]

History is filled with examples of words alone building entire ideologies. Religious texts shaped civilizations. Political slogans ignited revolutions. Hashtags spawned social movements. Hitler used speeches to manipulate nationalism into something monstrous. And in modern America, Trump, like every good authoritarian, does the same. In an October 13, 2024, interview on the Fox News show *Sunday Morning Futures*, Trump called his political opponents, among other things, the "enemy within." He didn't throw the words around for drama—with this single phrase, he floated the idea of using the military to deal with them on Election Day should things not go his way. In February 2025, he posted these words from Napoleon on his personal X and Truth Social accounts: "He who saves his Country does not violate any Law"—clearly implying he is above the law should it try to curtail his powers by stopping him from doing anything unconstitutional. This isn't just tough talk (or "catnip" for the media, as the White House claimed); it's a deliberate strategy.

Margaret Singer warned us about this decades ago:

Orwell (*1984*) was perhaps the first to note that language, not physical force, is key to manipulating minds. In fact, growing evidence in the behavioral sciences reveals that a smiling Big Brother has greater power to influence an individual's thought and decision-making than does a visibly threatening person.[11]

Amanda Montell adds that Jim Jones understood this better than anyone. His power lay in his words, not his ideas. He could charm and speak people into submission, a talent he'd been honing since childhood.[12] And doesn't that apply to nearly every US president we have recordings of? Every dictator? Every movement leader? Martin Luther King Jr.'s "I Have a Dream" speech changed history not just because of its message, but because of its delivery.

Language shapes realities. It's how people get radicalized, how leaders maintain control, how entire belief systems take hold. The right words, repeated often enough, become truth. At the end of the day, language isn't just a tool. It's power.

Language Shapes Identity and Belief

Every high-demand group—whether a cult, a corporation, or even a fandom—has its own special language. The language helps you feel like part of the "in" crowd. But moreover, the more you use their words, the more your thinking starts shifting too. Your own voice fades, replaced by the group's. Their vocabulary becomes your filter, shaping how you see the world, what you believe, and even what you think is possible. Research indicates that the language we speak can influence our thought processes, a concept known as linguistic relativity. For instance, a study published in *Current Biology* found that bilingual individuals might categorize objects differently depending on the language they are using at the time.[13]

Margaret Singer describes this process as key to cult indoctrination, when "you affirm that you accept and understand the ideology by beginning to talk in the simple catchphrases particular to the groups."[14]

At first you might be repeating phrases without fully understanding them. But the more you speak them, the more they take hold. Amanda Montell tells us, "Speech is the first thing we're willing to change about ourselves...and also the last thing we let go."[15]

This isn't just a cult thing. It happens at every level of culture where language plays a role—in other words, everywhere. Noam Chomsky, in *Manufacturing Consent: The Political Economy of the Mass Media*, explains how mass media uses language to shape public opinion: "The mass media serve as a system for communicating messages and symbols...to inculcate individuals with the values, beliefs, and codes of behavior that will integrate them into the institutional structures of the larger society."[16] Beyond informing us, words can be used to define power and shape belief.

Take corporate jargon. Ever sat through a meeting full of "synergy," "disruptive innovation," and "low-hanging fruit"? Steven Poole, writing for *The Guardian*, calls it what it is: "Bureaucratese is a maddeningly viral kind of Unspeak engineered to deflect blame, complicate simple ideas, obscure problems, and perpetuate power relations."[17] Complex language makes it harder to challenge the system. The tech world takes this further—if you don't know what a startup means by "pivoting to a B2B SaaS model," you're already an outsider. Nonprofits do it too. Terms like "capacity building" and "stakeholder engagement" are meant to create an aura of professionalism but often exclude more than they clarify.

And then there's the military, where acronyms are practically a second language. Sure, shorthand is useful in high-stress situations, but it also serves another function: it reinforces who's in and who's out. *Business Insider* notes that while every US region has its own slang, nothing compares to the military's lexicon, where service members "set themselves apart by speaking in acronyms like 'I was on the FOB when the IDF hit, so I radioed the TOC.'"[18] This language sticks long after people leave the military, reinforcing a bond that's hard to break.

Academia is no different. Scholars use terms like *epistemology* and *positionality* and *inter-rater reliability* as if they're common knowledge.

James Marriott of *The Times* calls university jargon "willfully opaque," a barrier that excludes outsiders while making insiders feel superior.[19] Of course, other groups have their own names for this phenomenon— just ask those who decry "woke academics" and "coastal elites."

Look at any group, good or bad, and you'll probably find specialized language. CrossFit has acronyms like *WOD* (Workout of the Day), *AMRAP* (As Many Rounds as Possible), and *Rx* (As Prescribed). Gaming communities have terms like *nerf*, *buff*, and *noob*. The jargon in the yoga and alternative spirituality worlds is seemingly infinite, with their *chakras*, *prana*, and *vibrations*. Fandoms have their own fanilects: Swifties with their *eras*, *Easter eggs*, and *Swiftmas*; K-Pop fans with their *stans*, *bias*, and *maknae*. AA has the *Big Book*, *HP*, *HALT*, and *90 in 90*, not to mention their countless sayings like *Fake it till you make it*, *It works if you work it*, and *Let go and let God*. Conservative circles have their *woke agenda*, *deep state*, and *RINOs*, while social justice activists have *intersectionality*, *cishet*, and *systemic oppression*. People outside these circles may, at best, have a hard time following their conversations, but at worst, see their language—and ideas—as a threat, purely because they don't understand it.

Specialized language isn't inherently bad. Every group has shorthand, and sometimes it's necessary. But when it's weaponized— when it stops being a tool for understanding and starts being a barrier to entry—that's when it starts looking a lot like a cult. Language can both connect and control. Recognizing how language operates in our own groups—corporate buzzwords we use at work, political slogans we repeat, or jargon we pick up online—gives us the power to question the narratives handed to us.

Because the moment you stop questioning the words you use, someone else starts deciding for you what they mean.

Types of Language Cults Use

The Cult Pitch: *We're Special. They're Not.*

The cult pitch is always the same: *We know something the rest of the world doesn't.* The group offers more than community—it's selling enlightenment, a rare and secret truth that only the chosen few can access. It's intoxicating, powerful, and feeds the ego. Once that belief takes root, you protect it, defend it, and cut off anyone who tries to pull you away. That's how cult leaders reshape reality—convincing followers the outside world is lesser, unworthy, and wrong.

Loaded language reinforces who's in and who's out. As Amanda Montell explains in a *Harper's Bazaar* article titled "Wellness Mommy Bloggers and the Cultish Language They Use":

> What distinguishes a cultish group from, say, a group of energized, enthusiastic people bent on achieving a certain outcome or goal, is the group's employment of certain words and phrases designed to create stark, inalienable binaries between "us" and "them." If you're fluent in a cultish dialect, you are chosen, you are powerful, you are special.[20]

Margaret Singer agrees, saying, "Almost all cults make the claim that their members are 'chosen,' 'select,' or 'special,' while nonmembers are considered lesser beings."[21] Once you buy in, leaving the group means surrendering your place among the enlightened.

The US military sells belonging the same way. The Marine Corps' iconic slogan "The Few. The Proud. The Marines" signals exclusivity. You don't just join; you become. The Army's "Be All That You Can Be" pushed military service as transformation—and it worked (on my husband!).These slogans hammer home the same message: This isn't just a career; it's a calling.

Some of the biggest brands in the world use the same formula. Disney doesn't sell entertainment—it sells "magic." Employees aren't workers; they're "cast members." They don't just do a job; they "create dreams." With its "Think Different" branding, Apple users aren't just consumers—they're visionaries, rebels, creators. Nike's "Just Do It" promises more than athletic gear—it sells a mindset. When you wear Nike products, you're suddenly capable of pushing past limits, overcoming obstacles, and achieving greatness.

Then there are the fitness cults. CrossFit isn't a gym—it's a "box." In addition to their acronyms mentioned earlier, their slogans— "Forging elite fitness" and "The sport of fitness"—separate members from regular gym-goers. SoulCycle isn't a spin class—it's spiritual. Instructors act like gurus, guiding riders toward something deeper than just fitness. The message? This isn't exercise—it's transformation.[22] And of course there are the countless variations of yoga in the US, with their specialized language for poses and breathing techniques—some of which veer smack dab into cult territory (looking at you, Bikram Choudhury and Yogi Bajan).

In AA and other 12-step programs, the exclusivity is built into the foundational literature, with every step framed as a "we" action (e.g., *Step One: We admitted we were powerless over alcohol...*), emphasizing that members are part of something bigger than themselves, and only they are making these choices that will lead them to recovery. The ritualized introductions at every meeting ("I'm ___ and I'm an alcoholic") create a clear distinction between insiders and outsiders, and phrases like "Once an alcoholic, always an alcoholic" reinforce lifelong membership. People not on AA's path of recovery are called "dry drunks," "in active addiction," or "normies," reinforcing the idea that members are different from the rest of the world.

Whether it's the military, CrossFit, Disney, your local yoga studio, or that AA meeting in the church basement, the formula is the same: Not everyone belongs—but if you do, you're part of something rare, elite, and bigger than yourself.

It's intoxicating. It's powerful. And in the wrong hands, it's dangerous.

Familial Language: *We're Not Just a Group—We're Family*

Cults love to blur the lines between community and family, tossing around words like *brother* and *sister* and elevating leaders to Mother or Father. Jim Jones had his followers call him Father (or Dad if extra devoted), which reinforced his role as patriarch, protector, and the one they owed absolute obedience to. Charles Manson did the same, branding his group the Manson Family to establish unquestioned authority.[23]

The word *family* has been normalized in many ways. Yoga studios, sports teams, pop fandoms—even Olive Garden's "When you're here, you're family"—all use it to evoke belonging. Marginalized people often talk about their communities as found family. It's a powerful word with positive connotations—safety, belonging, unconditional love—which makes it that much more tragic when it is weaponized to control and oppress.

When a group starts feeling more like family than your actual family, leaving it stops being an option and starts feeling like betrayal. The more you see your fellow members as siblings and your leader as a parental figure, the easier it is to prioritize their needs, their mission, and their rules over your own. Slowly, your world shrinks. You cancel plans with old friends, avoid conversations that might invite criticism, and before you know it, the only voices left are the ones telling you to stay exactly where you are.

For the Children of God, this wasn't metaphorical—it was literal: They renamed themselves "The Family." We were raised to see cult members as real siblings and our leader as our "Grandpa." Biological families didn't matter. Parents were reassigned, couples repartnered, large families split apart, all to serve the cult's needs. That belief kept us trapped, preventing us from reaching out to anyone who might have shown us the truth. When your concept of family is designed to control you, imagining life beyond it feels impossible.

Cult deprogrammer Ted Patrick describes this manipulation in *Let Our Children Go!*, explaining how cult leaders twist the meaning of love. Using the Unification Church as an example, Patrick says, "God is a God of Love. But [Reverend] Moon doesn't teach you anything except to hate. Hate your mother and father. Hate your brother...But your parents [meaning the "True Parents," Moon and his wife] love you. They would do anything for you."[24] It's a con. Cults flip love into hate, loyalty into blind obedience, and genuine relationships into ones designed to control.

Companies too love to say "we're a family"—usually right before guilt-tripping employees into unpaid overtime. "We're not just coworkers—we're family!" sounds nice, but it often means one thing: exploitation. Blur the line between genuine care and coercion, so employees feel like they owe more than just their labor. After all, you wouldn't let your *family* down, would you?

Amazon's take on the workplace family is just as intense but with an extra dose of corporate survivalism. Jeff Bezos built a company where employees aren't just expected to be dedicated—they're expected to be "obsessed." In a 1998 letter to shareholders, he claimed that he tells his employees to "wake up every morning terrified" of their customers. He has said publicly that he believes work-life balance is a "debilitating" phrase.[25] Long hours, high-stakes performance tracking, and a culture that treats setting boundaries as weakness have created an environment where burnout isn't just common—it's expected. At Tesla, Elon Musk frames the job as a mission requiring "insane hours" and unwavering loyalty, where employees routinely work sixty to eighty hours a week with little job security. Musk urges his employees to go "super hardcore" or "ultra hardcore," parroting the hypermasculinity so common in the tech world.[26] At Chick-fil-A, the family rhetoric comes wrapped in faith and a side of moral obligation: Employees are expected to embody the company's Christian values. At Chick-fil-A, being a *team player* isn't just doing your job well. It's proving you align with the company's belief system. I know firsthand—my first job after the cult was at Chick-fil-A, and it took forever to stop saying, "My pleasure."

In the article "Don't Tell Your Employees They're Family," Will Yakowicz makes a simple but important point: Calling a company a family is a terrible idea. It sets up unrealistic expectations and blurs boundaries in ways that almost always benefit the company, not the employees. A business works best as a *team,* where everyone knows their role, expectations are clear, and performance is measured objectively. Unlike a family, a company isn't built on unconditional love—it's built on results. And results mean tough calls, like letting people go if they're not meeting expectations. That's not how families work.

The next time a company tells you "We're all in this together," it's worth asking "Who actually benefits from that?" Because if history has taught us anything, the beneficiary is probably not you. Real love doesn't demand proof of loyalty. Anytime a high-demand group starts using "family" language, it's a giant red flag. They want your time, your loyalty, your energy—without earning it. And once you start seeing through that, you realize their version of family keeps you stuck, working harder, and questioning less.

Call and Response: The Power of Group Chanting

Repetition and rhythm are very effective at building group identity. Leaders use call-and-response chants like verbal choreography— think "God is good!" in churches, "Four more years!" at rallies, or "No justice, no peace!" at protests. That back-and-forth rhythm pulls people in, amplifies the leader's power, and reinforces group unity.

Science backs this up. Practiced around the world throughout human history, group chanting and singing lowers stress hormones, triggers oxytocin (the "love" or bonding hormone), and can induce mystical experiences.[27] It also enhances social flow.[28] "Flow state," coined by psychologist Mihaly Csikszentmihalyi in 1975, is loosely defined as the optimal psychological state in which a person is completely absorbed in a task, excluding all other thoughts. Social flow involves interdependence with others to achieve this state, fostering a shared sense of purpose and enjoyment. Csikszentmihalyi described it as a state where "the ego falls away"—ideal for creativity.[29] But not so much for critical thinking. Cult leaders exploit this effect—the trance-like rhythm of chanting lowers critical thinking, making people more open to suggestion and craving that euphoric feeling again.

Dr. Janja Lalich places chanting alongside prayer marathons, hypnosis, sleep deprivation, and guided imagery as coercion tactics,[30] while Margaret Singer explains that forced hyperventilation from shouting can induce an altered state.[31] In the Children of God, we had mandatory chants—an adult would walk in and yell, *"It's a Revolution!"* and we had to throw three fingers in the air, Mockingjay-style, and shout back, *"For Jesus!"* over and over.

When you add movement, the impact intensifies. NIH research shows that when people chant and move together, their brain waves literally sync up—a phenomenon called interpersonal synchrony.[32] Social or group flow makes people feel like they're merging into a larger purpose—great for both cohesion and control. In the military, chanting cadences while running or marching does the same, reinforcing discipline and identity. In *Uncultured*, I wrote about how boot camp felt eerily familiar to marching down the hallways of my youth in the cult, singing "Onward Christian Soldiers" during midnight drills. As a soldier, the chant morphed into phrases like "When my right foot hits the ground, all I hear is that killing sound." Same technique, different setting. Whether you're chanting *"Praise Jesus!,"* *"HOORAH!,"* "GO HAWKS!," or *"USA! USA!,"* the goal is the same: Make the message automatic.

Large group awareness trainings like Landmark Forum use the same technique, hyping participants into chanting affirmations like "Live your best life!" and "Say yes to your greatness!" that break down resistance and instill the program's mindset. Megachurches like Hillsong rely on repetitive worship songs to generate emotional highs, blurring spiritual experience with manipulation. Schools do it too—kids recite the Pledge of Allegiance before they're old enough to understand the word *indivisible*.

Sports fans scream team chants in stadiums, locked in a wave of synchronized energy. Even your spin class instructor knows how this works: "*Who's ready to crush it?!*" they yell, and without thinking, the class shouts back, "*We are!*" And suddenly, you're all pedaling a little harder. AA meetings begin and end with everyone saying the Serenity Prayer in unison (or the Lord's Prayer, depending on the regional culture). And don't forget that namaste and om at the end of your yoga class.

The more you say something aloud, the more ingrained it becomes. And that's the trick. When you're caught up in the rhythm, you're *feeling* the words. And once that happens, stopping to question what you're actually agreeing to gets a whole lot harder.

Trance Talk: Hypnotic Speech and Emotional Control

Cult leaders don't just speak—they *perform*. *Trance talk* is a term that gained popularity in the late twentieth century in the pseudoscientific fields of neurolinguistic programming and hypnotherapy.[33] It's a hypnotic, rhythmic style of speech that lulls listeners into an emotionally heightened state, making them more open to suggestion. Jim Jones, like so many evangelical and Pentecostal preachers today, started his sermons slow, his voice calm and repetitive, then built to a fever pitch, whipping his congregation into an emotional frenzy.[34] It wasn't just what he said, but *how* he said it—the pacing, volume shifts, and intensity. By the time he was shouting his words, his followers were feeling them. On the infamous Death Tape—the recording of his speech in Jonestown that convinced hundreds to commit mass suicide—his grip was absolute. A rhetorical analysis of that final speech shows how calculated his manipulation was. He leaned hard on emotion (pathos), painting a world full of enemies and danger. He used ethos—his supposed authority—to position himself as their only protector. And while he occasionally threw in bits of logos, logic wasn't the goal.[35] Jones knew that if he could get his followers to *feel* what he was saying, they wouldn't stop to analyze whether it made sense. And in the end, most of them didn't.

L. Ron Hubbard took a different approach, crafting a hypnotic language of jargon—*engram, auditing, suppressive person*—that made

Scientology feel exclusive. The more complicated it sounded, the more special it felt. If you didn't quite understand, that just meant you had more to learn—like you were working toward unlocking some ultimate, hidden truth. The mystery was the hook. Once you buy into the language, you're already halfway to buying into the belief system. Keith Raniere of NXIVM perfected the rambling philosopher act with lectures that were long-winded, circular, and vague, yet followers believed they contained profound truths.[36] If people didn't understand, they assumed it was their failure, not his.[37] This "word salad" is a common control tactic—keep followers doubting themselves instead of the leader.

Donald Trump too uses repetitive, emotionally charged slogans like "Fake news!" "Witch hunt!" "Lock her up!" More than catchphrases, they're chants, mental shortcuts that simplify complex ideas, bypass critical thinking, and reinforce his version of reality. Like Raniere, his zigzagging speeches rely more on emotional resonance than coherence. You may not be able to explain what Raniere or Trump just said, but you sure know how it made you feel.

Why does trance talk work? It bypasses logic, taps straight into emotion, and makes followers *feel* like they're part of something special, something only *they* truly understand.[38] From religion to politics, the result is the same: unquestioning belief and unwavering loyalty.

Thought-Stopping Clichés: The Phrases That Keep You in Line

Ever noticed how certain phrases shut down conversations before they even start? That's thought-stopping language in action. High-control groups love these verbal shortcuts because they provide easy, comforting answers that keep people from thinking too hard about what's really going on. "Thought-terminating cliché" is a term coined by psychologist Robert Jay Lifton in his 1961 book *Thought Reform and the Psychology of Totalism: A Study of "Brainwashing" in China*. Also known as "semantic stop-signs" and "thought-stoppers," these thought-stopping clichés make complex issues seem clear by replacing discomfort with simple, easy-to-swallow solutions. Over time, they become automatic. Why analyze something critically when the "answer" is already right there in a neat little slogan? It's an effortless way for leaders to maintain control without actually having to engage.

We hear it all the time in politics. "If you're not with us, you're against us" eliminates any room for nuance or discussion (with the added benefit of supporting an us-versus-them mindset). "The market will sort itself out" shuts down any discussion on economic inequalities or regulation. And of course, any information that does not conform to your worldview is "fake news." In the US Army, "Just drink the Kool-Aid" is a go-to phrase for justifying actions everyone knows are ridiculous—but will follow through with anyway.

Mainstream religions have thought-stopping clichés built into them: "God works in mysterious ways" shuts down any questioning of doctrine or suffering, "Just have faith" encourages unquestioning belief, and "Everything happens for a reason" prevents deeper discussion of cause and effect or injustice. A popular saying in American Buddhist circles (and the adjacent self-help worlds that borrow heavily in the form of McMindfulness) is "We choose how we respond to pain," implying that suffering is always a choice, which sounds empowering but ignores the realities of trauma response, mental health issues, and neurodivergence. In the self-help and coaching worlds, thought-stopping clichés disguise scams as success stories. Phrases like "If you can dream it, you can do it," "That's just limiting beliefs," and "You manifest your reality" shift all responsibility—and blame—onto the individual. If you fail, it's not the advice that was flawed; *you* didn't believe or try hard enough. As Unification Church survivor Jen Kiaba explains in a post titled "Toxic Positivity and the Thought-Terminating Cliché," "These techniques suppress critical thinking by quelling cognitive dissonance when encountering contradictory information."

In university Greek life, slogans like "Brotherhood is forever," "This is bigger than you," and "You don't break the bond, you break yourself" elevate loyalty above all else, which makes it harder for members to speak up about hazing, abuse, or anything that might reflect badly on the group. "What happens in the house stays in the house" is more than a rule—it's a silencing mechanism, trapping members in a culture where questioning the system feels like betraying the very thing that gives them belonging. As Hank Nuwer says in the journal article "Greek Letters Don't Justify Cult-Like Hazing of Pledges," "Hazing, like a cult, systematically manipulates and coerces members into compliance."

Thought-stopping clichés are everywhere: "Boys will be boys." "Just trust the process." "Let go and let God." "Stop being a victim." These phrases deflect criticism, discourage doubt, and keep people from questioning the groups they're in and the systems they serve. And the most insidious part? Once they're ingrained, they feel natural— so natural that most people don't realize they're being manipulated.

Blaming Individuals for Systemic Failure

In cults, when things go wrong, the blame never lands on the system, the leader, or the ideology. If you're struggling, it's *you* who isn't trying hard enough, believing deeply enough, or following the rules with enough devotion. The system is never wrong. Cult leaders tell you that without the group's guidance, you're weak, flawed, or sinful, and over time you internalize that message. If you think you're broken, you'll believe you need the group to fix you. That's how they keep you hooked—shame keeps you in line, and self-blame makes sure you never question the system.

In the Children of God, natural emotions—anger, sadness, doubt— were labeled as being "in the dumps with the devil." Feeling tired? That wasn't exhaustion—it was *spiritual weakness*. Questioning something? That wasn't curiosity—it was *rebellion*. You didn't *feel* bad; you *were* bad. And the only way to fix it was to pray harder, obey more, and let the group correct you. Eventually, we started repeating these messages to ourselves. And that was the real trap—once we believed we were broken, we stopped questioning the system that was breaking us.

If you're not achieving the spiritual superpowers Scientology promises, it's not because the teachings are nonsense—it's because you have *counter-intention* or *suppressive tendencies* blocking your progress.[39] You don't question the organization; you pay for another round of auditing, cut negative people out of your life, and dig even deeper. And when that still doesn't work? You must not be *clear* enough—so pay more and keep going.

This kind of blame-shifting also happens in abusive relationships. Manipulators use phrases like "You're too sensitive," "You made me do that," or "If you really loved me, you'd try harder" to make their victims question their own perceptions and feel responsible for the abuser's actions. As *Psychology Today* notes, "Verbal abuse is fueled by an imbalance of power (and a need to control)."[40] The abuser stays in control while the victim spirals into self-doubt, convinced that if they could just be better, the relationship would be fine.

This mindset is baked into American culture. Hustle culture, the capitalist cult that ties self-worth to productivity, uses slogans like "Rise and grind," "No excuses," and, my favorite, "You have the same 24 hours as Beyoncé." These mantras frame overwork as a mindset problem rather than a systemic one, conveniently ignoring that most people don't have Beyoncé's resources or team behind them. (As someone with an awesome team behind me, I can tell you—it makes all the difference.) Hustle culture messaging obscures and implies that if you're struggling, it's not because the system is rigged—you're simply not trying hard enough. Phrases like "Sleep is for the weak" and "No days off" turn burnout into a badge of honor, keeping people trapped in exhaustion while glorifying the very thing that's draining them. (As an aside, I find it telling that many of hustle culture's macho thought-stopping clichés also show up in gym culture.) Conveniently ignoring privilege, nepotism, and sheer luck, this perspective is fueled by the enduring myth of the American Dream and meritocracy, perpetuating a skewed perception of how success is achieved.

Patriarchy runs on the same fuel. From birth, girls are bombarded with messages about how to be thinner, quieter, more accommodating

—but never too much so. They are told what they need to fix to be desirable, valuable, and acceptable. Over time, they internalize those criticisms and repeat them back to themselves without even realizing it. They start believing that they are the problem.

Think about it—when was the last time you heard a man apologize for taking up space in a meeting? Or call himself lazy for needing a break? Women, on the other hand, are taught to second-guess everything, even when they're doing the same work (or more). Research in *Psychology of Women Quarterly* found that women often internalize self-objectification, which leads to lower self-esteem and worse mental health outcomes. Society trains women to measure their worth by how well they meet impossible standards—whether in beauty, behavior, or productivity. Meanwhile, men move through the world without this constant self-policing, free to take up space, to be mediocre, to fail without being told it's their fault for not trying hard enough.

Ironically, the flip side of this systemic bias is also growing, emboldened by the hardline anti-DEI (diversity, equity, and inclusion) policies of the second Trump administration. When certain individuals (let's use entitled white men as a purely hypothetical example) don't land their dream job, some are quick to cry "reverse racism" and blame the system. Both Trump administrations have worked diligently to reframe civil rights protections as applying equally (or, it can be argued, more) to white people and men, casting affirmative action in hiring or college admissions as discriminatory. These shifts have made it easier for white people and men to sue employers and universities under the very laws that were created to protect marginalized communities.[41] In essence, they're weaponizing the hard-won victories of the civil rights movement to claim victimhood for being white men.

At its core, this belief system—the idea that a personal effort and positive attitude are all you need to succeed—convinces people that failure is a personal flaw rather than the result of larger systemic forces. People blame themselves instead of questioning the structures holding them down. The constant push for positivity has created a culture where people feel pressured to stay upbeat, no matter what they're going through. Barbara Ehrenreich points out in her book *Bright-Sided: How the Relentless Promotion of Positive Thinking Has Undermined America* that toxic positivity trains people to feel guilty when things go wrong—like they just didn't think positive enough.

While optimism, grit, and a commitment to working hard have their place, framing failure as a *you* problem instead of a *system* problem prevents people from pushing back against injustice. It's no accident that the people most invested in this mindset are the ones who benefit from keeping everyone else working harder, questioning less, and blaming themselves when they fall short.

Desensitizing and Dehumanizing Language: How Words Normalize Harm

Cults utilize language to make the unthinkable feel normal. One of the most twisted examples in the Children of God was "flirty fishing"—a playful-sounding term that masked the disturbing reality of women being encouraged to use sex to recruit new members. Giving something as extreme as religious prostitution a cute name softened the impact, which made it easier for members to accept, justify, and participate. That's how desensitization works—rebrand something that's uncomfortable, and over time it feels routine instead of horrifying.

Companies, the military, and even sports rely on language to make harm seem acceptable. In corporate settings, phrases like "work hard, play hard" glorify overwork, while describing workers as "human capital" reduces individuals to mere resources. "Lean and mean" makes mass layoffs sound like smart business rather than ruthless cost-cutting. The military similarly distances itself from reality with terms like "collateral damage" to describe civilian deaths. High-stakes sports push a parallel mindset—"leave it all on the field" turns exhaustion or injury into a badge of honor. These phrases blur ethical lines and normalize extreme behavior, making exploitation seem reasonable, even admirable.

Cults and isolated groups also use dehumanizing language to cast outsiders as threats. In Scientology, doubters are labeled "suppressive persons"—people to be shunned and vilified. Evangelical communities use terms like "unbelievers" or "heathens" to frame nonmembers as dangerous influences. Suddenly, a friend or neighbor isn't just someone who doesn't share your beliefs—they're a risk. Historically, missionaries used similar language to justify colonization and forced conversion of Indigenous people, a practice that still persists in some religious circles today.

Politics operates in the same way. Terms like "illegal immigrants" or "invaders" frame refugees and asylum seekers as threats instead of people in crisis. News outlets and politicians describe immigration in terms of "infestations" or "floods," making people seem like an overwhelming, dangerous force rather than individuals seeking safety. Dehumanization goes beyond shaping opinions; it influences policy, justifying harsh treatment, detention, deportation, family separations, and—in the case of Japanese American citizens during WWII—internment. Many people fear we're edging dangerously close to similar territory with today's treatment of immigrants.

This rhetoric permeates culture in both obvious and subtle ways. Calling grown adults "boy" or "girl"—particularly in racialized or gendered contexts—has long been used to demean or diminish people. Labeling women as "hysterical," "emotional," or "crazy" serves to dismiss their concerns. Broadly applying terms like "thugs," "criminals," or "terrorists" to entire groups erases individual identities and feeds fear-driven narratives. Even phrases like "culture war" or "battle for America" frame political differences as existential conflicts rather than debates between people with differing views.

The danger of dehumanizing language is that it erodes empathy. When we label people as less-than—whether it's "enemy combatants" in war or "welfare queens" in political discourse—we find it easier to justify harming them. The us-versus-them mentality deepens divides, so cruelty can seem rational instead of monstrous. Dehumanization is a mental loophole that lets us rationalize harm. It's what fuels racism, sexism, homophobia, war crimes, and genocide.[42]

Recognizing and challenging this kind of language is crucial. When we remove the labels and see people as individuals, we have a harder time justifying their suffering. Dehumanizing words lay the groundwork for real-world violence and oppression. If we want to break these cycles, we have to start by paying attention to the words that keep them going.

Why Do Cults Always Have Comics?

The combination of words and pictures is a powerful tool for propaganda because it engages both the rational and emotional parts of the brain, reinforcing messages more effectively than words or images alone. Images evoke immediate emotional responses—such as fear, anger, pride, or empathy—before the viewer even processes the words. The human brain can identify images seen for as little as thirteen milliseconds—faster than a blink. And when both visual and verbal channels in the brain are activated simultaneously (a phenomenon called dual-coding), our understanding, engagement, and recall increase.[43]

Paired with loaded language, these emotions can be directed toward a specific narrative or agenda. A single phrase may not leave a lasting impression, but when reinforced by a striking image, the message becomes more memorable. Repeated exposure strengthens associations, making ideas feel like common sense rather than constructed rhetoric. Propaganda often reduces complex topics to easily digestible visuals—such as caricatures, symbols, or dramatic photographs—that fit neatly into a preexisting worldview. Words then guide interpretation, ensuring the audience takes away the intended message.

One of the most egregious examples was Joseph Goebbel's Nazi propaganda. Antisemitic slogans were paired with posters depicting Jewish people with exaggerated, grotesque features, portraying them as threats to society and justifying discriminatory policies and violence. Today political memes on social media have perfected this technique, pairing images with short, emotionally charged text that can spread rapidly via algorithms, reinforcing messages without requiring deep engagement. While some memes are harmless entertainment, others play a role in spreading extremist ideology. As Erin Grace of the *Nebraska Examiner* explains:

> Experts are concerned about a subset of memes and the role they play in spreading extremist ideology and potentially radicalizing consumers to violence. By condensing complex, harmful ideologies into simple visuals, these memes can normalize and mainstream dehumanization. Their viral nature and coded messaging make extremist memes more dangerous.[44]

Grace further says that although extremist memes may start in the dark fringes of the internet, they often move into the mainstream, where "when people object, creators and sharers use the cartoonish, comedic nature of memes as plausible deniability: *I was just kidding!*"

Comics don't just explain ideas—they sell them. As Rick Marschall put it in *Drawing Power: A Compendium of Cartoon Advertising*, "Corporations do not spend billions of dollars on advertising unless it works, and works well—programming the patterns of consumer habits. And very often, cartoons and comics have been the bait that has lured the prey, aka, the rest of us suckers."[45] As Dr. Mara Einstein, author of *Hoodwinked: How Marketers Use the Same Tactics As Cults*, a book about how brands use cult tactics, explained to me, "The way brands work is through a combination of symbol and mythology— Disney's castle means magic, BMW is 'the ultimate driving machine,' Apple is 'think different.' The logo is simply the container for meaning-making—a symbol into which ideas can be embedded."[46]

In the Children of God, complicated theology was turned into cartoons—simple, engaging, and easy to remember. My stepfather, in partnership with former Fleetwood Mac guitarist Jeremy Spencer, spent his life drawing cult comics, which we handed out worldwide. These weren't just teaching tools—they were recruiting tools. Rebranding extreme beliefs with playful images softened their impact, making them feel fun and approachable. It's about selling extremism with a smile.

Mainstream religious groups frequently employ this technique. The LDS Church, for example, uses an animated short to explain polygamy's origins in their early theology.[47] Instead of addressing the harm polygamy caused, the cartoon frames it as a righteous, divinely inspired practice—just another part of God's plan. By turning a controversial history into a kid-friendly story, the church ensures young members acccpt it without question.

Chick tracts, created by evangelical artist Jack Chick, are another example. These pocket-sized comics boil Christianity down to dualistic morality tales—literally: *Sin is bad, hell is real, salvation is simple.* Chick tracts work because they don't require deep thinking. They strip away nuance to make complex theological issues feel as obvious as a superhero's fight against evil.[48] Much like cult comics, they sell a worldview in a format that feels familiar and nonthreatening.

The *Become Jehovah's Friend* series, starring two kids named Caleb and Sophia, does the same thing. These bright, friendly cartoons teach Jehovah's Witnesses doctrine through relatable childhood experiences—how to be obedient, why questioning is dangerous, and how to separate from "worldly" people.[49] On the surface, they seem harmless. But for kids raised in the faith, they serve as early indoctrination, reinforcing group values in a way that feels natural and fun. Much like VeggieTales, the cartoons turn theology into entertainment, ensuring kids absorb doctrine before they develop the ability to question it.

Logos. Comics. Cartoons. They're not just about storytelling— they're about control. Because a message that's seen over and over goes beyond informing—it shapes reality. And once you've absorbed that reality, questioning it feels impossible.

Unlearning Cult Language

Breaking free from a high-control group requires more than physically leaving—you also need to rewire your brain. And language is one of the hardest things to shake. As Amanda Montell explains, "Cultish language works so efficiently (and invisibly) to mold our worldview in the shape of the guru's that once it's embedded, it sticks. After you grow your hair out, move back home, delete the app, whatever it is, the special vocabulary is still there."[50]

Ex-Scientologists talk about how strange it feels to think without using words like *suppressive person* or *clear*—terms that once defined their reality. Former Jehovah's Witnesses describe struggling with phrases like *worldly people* or even *the truth* because their group's unique definitions of those words were drilled into them as absolute, unquestionable facts. Even after leaving, the language lingers, making it hard to untangle personal thoughts from the cult's ideology.

Dr. Janja Lalich explains why: "Former members commonly discover that they continue to use group jargon without being aware of it."[51] And those words still carry weight. Encountering them unexpectedly can trigger confusion, anxiety, terror, guilt, or rage, especially for people who grew up in the group. The vocabulary also isolates former members from the outside world. Friends and family don't understand the loaded language, and until you learn new words to replace the old ones, even basic communication can feel like translating your own thoughts while relearning how to speak for yourself.

One of the most important steps in breaking free? Stop using their words. Start calling things what they really are. Cult language distorts reality, like a pair of warped glasses that only let you see their worldview and version of the truth. Taking off the glasses means learning to see clearly again.

In the Children of God, we were told flirty fishing was about spreading God's love. Yet it was systematic sexual exploitation. Reclaiming the correct words removes the cult's spin and lets you process your own truth. Calling things what they are is how you rebuild your sense of self, own your story, and take back your power. Because when you take back the language, you take back *you*.

Chapter 7

Us-Versus-Them Mentality: We Are the Best, Down with All the Rest!

E very fall, they return. Young, eager, and easily molded. They arrive in droves, drawn by promises of belonging, status, and power. To the outside world, it all seems innocent enough—smiling faces, coordinated outfits, a series of strange but seemingly harmless rituals. But beneath the polished surface lies something far older, far darker.

The initiation is brutal. They are broken down, tested, made to prove their devotion through suffering. Some will be publicly humiliated. Others will be pushed to their limits, in both mind and body, in a desperate bid to be deemed worthy. Some will even die in the process. Only the most obedient, the most loyal, will be accepted. And once inside, there is no turning back.

They are expected to give everything—their time, their money, their dignity. They speak in coded language, adhere to rigid hierarchies, and perform ceremonies that outsiders will never fully understand. Parents watch as their children change, their personalities shifting, their priorities warping. The need to belong becomes an obsession, one that drives them to dangerous extremes.

Some will emerge unscathed. Many will not. And every year, the cycle repeats. This is the world of college Greek life.

* * *

Fraternities and sororities have long been embedded in college life, promising lifelong friendships, social prestige, and networking opportunities. But beneath this image of camaraderie and tradition lies a culture built on exclusivity, hierarchy, and an entrenched us-versus-them mindset. The structure of Greek life doesn't just create division—it thrives on it, shaping people's attitudes and interactions both within these organizations and across the broader campus.

The consequences are far-reaching. As *The Atlantic* notes, despite their small numbers on campus, fraternity members have long held an outsized influence in American institutions:

> While only eight and a half percent of American male college students is a member...fraternity men make up 85 percent of U.S. Supreme Court justices since 1910, 63 percent of all U.S. presidential cabinet members since 1900, and, historically, 76 percent of U.S. Senators, 85 percent of Fortune 500 executives, and 71 percent of the men in "Who's Who in America."[1]

Though the Greek system touts itself as a training ground for future leaders, these statistics point to something more troubling: an entrenched system of nepotism that reinforces American power structures.

Greek life is something most of us accept as normal, but the numbers tell a very different story. Studies show that "fraternity men are three times more likely to commit rape than other men on college campuses," a staggering indicator of the dangerous culture of hypermasculinity , entitlement, and unchecked power within these organizations.[2] Conformity to extreme gender norms fuels this dynamic: Fraternities promote dominance and aggression, while sororities often emphasize passivity, appearance, and desirability to men.[3] The result is a system that perpetuates sexism, objectification, and internalized misogyny, shaping how both men and women perceive themselves and each other.

Excessive drinking, especially in fraternity settings where men control the environment, blurs boundaries around consent and increases risks of sexual assault. Sorority women are especially vulnerable. One study found that sorority women at a midsize university reported being sexually assaulted at a rate four times higher than their non-sorority peers.[4] Studies consistently link fraternity membership with rape-supportive attitudes and predatory behavior—which are sustained by traditions, secret rituals, peer reinforcement, and protection from accountability.

Greek organizations foster an us-versus-them mentality through exclusivity, secrecy, and rigid group loyalty. Their selective recruitment process draws a sharp line between insiders and outsiders—those who receive bids are welcomed into a tight-knit circle, and others are dismissed as irrelevant. The exclusivity of this divide is reinforced through hazing rituals that push obedience via silence and submission. Fraternity hazing is indoctrination—a controlled trial by fire meant to prove your worth and build dependence and loyalty among frat brothers. Though hazing is illegal in most states, it's no secret that it continues. Hazing is one of many ways that fraternities mirror cults—exclusivity and suffering are spun into pride, belonging, and unquestioning obedience.[5] Since 1970, at least one hazing-related death has occurred on a US college campus each year,* and 82 percent of those deaths involved alcohol.[6]

Secrecy further fuels this insularity. Hidden rituals and internal codes elevate members above the rest of the campus, promoting the idea that outsiders just wouldn't understand. Even within Greek life, hierarchies persist—prestige varies by chapter, and competition for status fractures even the "in" crowd.[7] Greek organizations also dominate campus social life, controlling access to events and reinforcing

---

* This stat includes hazing in all college groups, not just within the Greek system.

a social order where belonging grants privilege—and exclusion signals inferiority.

These realities have sparked backlash. In 2020, the Abolish Greek Life movement emerged on campuses across America, calling for an end to the misogyny, racism, and homophobia of fraternity and sorority culture. And yet the system endures; large numbers of students continue to pledge each year, and around 750,000 undergraduates registered as members as of early 2025.[8] Some national surveys have even linked participation in Greek life to improved mental health and campus engagement.[9] For many people, these organizations offer friendship, structure, and a sense of belonging—benefits that have been echoed by students across racial and cultural lines.[10]

Greek life can be transformative, for better or worse. That duality is what makes it so deeply rooted, and so difficult to reckon with. The line between camaraderie and coercion can blur quickly. What starts as a tight-knit community sometimes shifts into something more controlling—dictating who you spend time with, what you wear, even how you think. The pressure to conform can be intense, and for those who push back, the social consequences can be isolating.

Which begs the question: Why would anyone choose to be "them" when they could be part of "us"?

Us Versus Them—The Most American Thing There Is

High-control groups thrive on an all-or-nothing mentality, perfectly captured by the phrase "You're either with us or against us." Most famously, President George W. Bush used a version of this in his September 20, 2011, speech following the 9/11 attacks: "You're either with us, or you're with the terrorists." Variations of this sentiment have also been echoed by figures such as Lenin, Mussolini, Trump—and even Jesus Christ.

This binary worldview is everywhere in today's America—political parties, religions, social movements, sports teams, even the brands we swear by. We love sorting the world into winners and losers, the chosen and the outsiders, good and evil. By integrating this human tendency into their members' core belief system, high-control groups weaponize the idea that outsiders are dangerous, ignorant, or just plain wrong. And it works: Loyalty stays strong, and doubts get buried. The tighter the bubble, the harder it is to hear anything that might offer a different perspective—or a way out.

To really get why America is so uniquely vulnerable to the us-versus-them trap, we need to zoom out a little. Humans, by nature, are tribal—it's how we evolved to survive in the wild among much faster and stronger animals, and in a lot of ways, it's what kept us alive. But the US has taken that instinct and twisted it into something singularly American—and extreme. Consider how this country was founded, who did that founding, and the manner in which they did it (by "country," I mean the colonized land of the Indigenous people who were already very much here). The first European settlers planted the seeds of the exceptionalism that have been part of the United States' DNA ever since, a spirit that has grown over the generations, culminating today in what could be seen as the inevitability of Trump's MAGA America and a political ideology rooted in us-versus-them thinking.

In many ways, I am still learning what it means to be American. As I wrote about extensively in my memoir *Uncultured*, I have lived much of my life outside US borders, either in the Mexican and South American communes of my youth, or in Afghanistan during military service. In my many years of schooling, I have taken a measly total of four classes on US history. For these reasons and many more, I thought it would be best to feature the voice of someone who knows a lot more on the topic of America's history than I do: my very smart talent manager, Lizy Freudmann, who happens to have a degree in American civilizations from Brown University, with help from my co-writer, Amy Reed.

How America Was Born—and Learned It Was Special

By Lizy Freudmann
MBA and Master of Global Management

At its core, American culture is built on a paradox—we pride ourselves on being a melting pot, a place where anyone can belong, yet we're constantly sorting ourselves into tribes, often defining ourselves as much by who we exclude as who we include.

When you really dig into it, it's not hard to see the Puritans as America's first cult: Though separated by centuries and circumstance, they were fueled by the same us-versus-them mentality that later drove Jim Jones to lead his followers to Guyana. The Puritans saw themselves as God's chosen people, set apart to create a new, pure society, free from what they perceived to be the moral corruption of the Old World. Disgusted by the English government's failure to uphold their perception of the "right" type of Christianity, they made a choice to separate themselves from the insufficiently devout Anglican church and start fresh in what is now known as Massachusetts. As with Jonestown, the leaders fostered a mindset that made it easy for followers to dismiss, distrust, or outright demonize anyone who wasn't part of their group. They believed they had a divine mission to separate themselves from those who didn't share their strict religious beliefs, because anyone outside their circle was spiritually inferior or even damned.

Although many people use the terms *Puritans* and *Pilgrims* interchangeably, they actually refer to two distinct groups of settlers. It was the Pilgrims who landed on Plymouth Rock in 1620 and feature in the First Thanksgiving story (with all its questionable historical detail). They were, as the myth describes, motivated by religious concerns and persecution. At the time, every British citizen was required to be a member of the Church of England. The Pilgrims had broken away from the church over doctrinal disagreements, which was illegal. The only way to safely live according to their beliefs was to leave, so they first set out for the Dutch Republic, and then left for the New World. The Pilgrims were also known as Separatists, because they separated entirely from the existing church system.

The Puritans, who first started arriving ten years later in 1630, were also unsatisfied with the Church of England but felt that they could observe their faith according to their interpretation without separating from the larger church body headquartered in England. They saw the New World as a great opportunity on two fronts: As a group, the Puritans had some money and saw the opportunity to make more of it on the other side of the ocean; they also believed that by living according to the true church doctrine, they could change the Church of England from within. The term *Puritan* was originally a pejorative, mocking their zeal for moral and ecclesiastical purity. That same zeal fueled some of the nation's darkest moments—one of the most infamous being the Salem witch trials of 1692, where fear and fanaticism led to the deaths of twenty-five accused witches, a tragic outcome of mass hysteria and religious extremism in a tightly controlled community.

The Pilgrims and Puritans, though they differed in some significant ways, largely laid the foundation of core American cultural values and identity. Some of these—like belief in democratically elected government and public education—most everyone can agree are positive. But others are a little murkier. Both groups believed deeply in their moral mission, a sense of divine purpose that helped shape the later doctrine of American exceptionalism: the belief that the United States is uniquely destined to lead or redeem the world. This has had countless ramifications over the years, from the Manifest Destiny that fueled westward expansion and the genocide of Native Americans, to contemporary global policy that assumes "We're #1!" in all things.[11] Also inherited from the Pilgrims and Puritans was their hallmark individualism, which fueled the growth of capitalism, the celebration of entrepreneurs and the self-made man, and at times, an almost pathological devotion to individual rights. And of course, there are the Protestant work ethic and the myth of the American Dream.

The Protestant Work Ethic and the American Dream

Most Americans in 2025 might not distinguish between Pilgrims and Puritans, but they can likely recount the core message: The first European settlers in the New World faced immense hardship, yet survived through hard work (with or without the help of Native Americans), strong community, and a commitment to the greater good, passing down their values of self-sacrifice and perseverance.

The themes of *hard work* and *self-sacrifice* in this origin story are praised as both virtuous and practical, part of the broader ethos of the Protestant work ethic that is deeply ingrained in American identity. This framework defines a "good" life as one centered on diligence, discipline, and frugality.[12] On the surface, this might seem paradoxical—after all, Protestants, particularly Puritans, believed in predestination, the idea that God had already chosen the saved and the damned. If one's fate was predetermined, why toil endlessly? Yet Puritans held that hard work and self-sacrifice were essential for good stewardship of their earthly communities. Many also believed that material success—wealth, influence, the respect of one's peers—was a sign of God's favor and a glimpse of His divine plan for them.

So deeply embedded is this work ethic in American culture that its values—thrift, perseverance, and relentless ambition—are seen as virtues even in a secular context. We celebrate those who demonstrate grit and discipline, regardless of whether we share their beliefs. One of the clearest manifestations of this is in entrepreneurship, a subject explored elsewhere in this book for its cultlike tendencies. These culty elements could not exist without the seamless alignment between the Protestant work ethic and entrepreneurial culture. So thoroughly has this mindset shaped American life that it implicitly endorses many of the defining characteristics of modern ambition.

You can't talk about American culture without mentioning the American Dream. Over the roughly 250 years since the country's founding, the dream has evolved—sometimes emphasizing freedom, sometimes prosperity—but it has never disappeared. What endures are its most aspirational and inspiring elements, the "dreamiest" parts that fuel the collective imagination.

But basking in the glow of the American Dream often obscures the darker realities woven into the fabric of American history. The genocide and displacement of Indigenous peoples, the horrors of chattel slavery—these are not footnotes but central to the story of how the American Dream was built. Yet they fade into the background when the dream takes center stage. This cognitive dissonance—celebrating the greatness of our nation while ignoring its true history—is also central to the myth of the American Dream (and a core ideological tenet of Trump's promise to Make America Great Again).

So what is this dream, exactly? The term *American Dream* was coined by James Truslow Adams in his 1931 book *The Epic of America*. He described it as "a dream of a social order in which each man and each woman shall be able to attain to the fullest stature of which they are innately capable, and be recognized by others for what they are, regardless of the fortuitous circumstances of birth or position." Elsewhere, he referred to it as "a better, richer, and happier life for all our citizens of every rank."[13] Adams's words capture the heart of the American ethos, echoing the soaring language of the Declaration of Independence and the Constitution—documents that Americans treat as sacred texts, reminders of what the country aspires to be. The power of the Dream lies in its ostensible inclusivity—the idea that anyone, regardless of background, can rise and thrive.

By 1776, the American Dream had already taken root. Its seeds came over with the earliest settlers, carried in their pockets and planted in the fertile soil of ambition, optimism, and religious zeal. From those roots also grew the idea of American exceptionalism, a concept often invoked to justify national actions, noble or otherwise. While the American Dream centers on the limitless potential of each individual—immigrant, colonist, or citizen—American exceptionalism speaks to the supposed uniqueness and destiny of the nation itself.

Whether or not one believes in predestination, the Protestant work ethic continues to shape American culture and fuel the myth of the American Dream. So deeply embedded is this ethic that it has been repackaged and repurposed across countless contexts, especially in business. It serves as a thought-stopping cliché, to obscure systemic inequality with feel-good narratives of self-reliance. Entrepreneurs who "bootstrap" their ideas are celebrated for their scrappiness. We admire their grit, applauding their willingness to sacrifice today for the promise of success tomorrow. Yet we rarely interrogate the systems that enable certain people to bootstrap in the first place: access to credit, family support networks, higher education, mentorship, and a media environment eager to elevate stories that fit a familiar mold—often featuring white, male founders.

It's worth pausing to examine the phrase "pulling yourself up by your bootstraps." It began as a joke—literally. In the nineteenth century, it described something absurd or impossible, like lifting yourself off the ground by tugging at your own shoes. But over time, America turned this sarcastic metaphor into a badge of honor, a rallying cry for the self-made.[14] Today *bootstrapping* is everywhere—from startups launched without outside funding to computers initiating their own startup sequence. It embodies the myth of self-reliance, the belief that with hard work alone, one can create something out of nothing. But like many enduring myths, it glosses over reality: Even the most successful bootstrappers usually had help along the way.[15]

So how does this connect to America's founding mythology? Precisely *because* the story has been simplified over time, it resonates. It reinforces itself through systems that seem to confirm its truth and sustainability. The outline is familiar:

1. A group of visionaries, driven by righteous indignation, left the Old World in search of something better.

2. Upon arriving in the New World, they toiled, struggled, and sacrificed to bring their vision to life.

3. In doing so, they created a unique and exceptional society where *anyone* can succeed—if they follow the same formula.

This, in essence, is the American Dream. Its details shift, but the core message remains: Hard work powers excellence, and America rewards strivers with success—be it fame, fortune, or respect.

America's founding mythology draws from both Pilgrim and Puritan legacies. The Pilgrims had the audacity to break from the establishment and create a new world rooted in their ideals. Contemporary Americans often admire that courage and shared vision. The Puritans, on the other hand, sought to purify rather than leave, distinguishing themselves from the morally impure— and seizing the economic opportunities that came with doing so. Their rigid intolerance of dissent or deviation became a defining trait, and that too is part of their enduring legacy.

The Legacy of Slavery and Cognitive Dissonance

In 1607 a ship of colonists arrived in what is now known as Virginia. Unlike their northern counterparts, these settlers had no ideological reasons for coming to the New World; they were drawn purely by economic opportunity. The Jamestown colony, named for King James I, was essentially a business venture operated by the Virginia Company, with its labor producing goods for export to England.

John Smith, one of Jamestown's early leaders, was a pragmatist. While he lacked the religious fervor of the Pilgrims or Puritans, he shared their belief in hard work. Jamestown's settlers—mostly men and boys—had varying levels of commitment, and Smith quickly grew frustrated with those unwilling to contribute. Survival was precarious, with food shortages and violent conflicts with the Powhatans. So Smith imposed a strict rule: If you don't work, you don't eat. This policy had the intended effect—death rates declined, Jamestown's infrastructure improved, and goods were finally sent back to England. Ultimately, the colony found economic stability through the cultivation of tobacco, along with other cash crops like indigo, sugar, and cotton, though Smith's leadership was unpopular among those unwilling to submit to his strict discipline.

Agricultural labor was intensive, and rather than pay wages and have to depend on the unreliable settler workforce, the English turned to slavery. By 1619 enslaved Africans were being brought to Jamestown, and by 1662 slavery was codified in law. Thus marked the official beginning of America's sinister practice of stripping people of their humanity in order to use them as tools, justified by racist ideologies designed to assuage the moral qualms of the enslavers. Myths circulated that enslaved people were better off in captivity, naturally suited to labor, or content with their oppression—arguments that, while absurd, were instrumental in normalizing and perpetuating slavery.

These theories and countless others like them would be laughable if they weren't effective for easing the cognitive dissonance of enslavers and perpetuating the institution of slavery in the colonies, and eventually within America itself. It is important to recognize how important these lies were in normalizing and reinforcing slavery, and how over time they would be reshaped and applied to other forms of labor exploitation. Even Thomas Jefferson embodied this contradiction. He proclaimed that all men had a right to life, liberty, and the pursuit of happiness, yet personally enslaved 607 people.[16] Although he recognized slavery as morally corrupt and sought to limit its expansion, he also believed that emancipated slaves should be deported, holding firm to a belief in white superiority. His own life depended on the forced labor of others, a hypocrisy starkly reflected in his treatment of his enslaved children he fathered through the sexual exploitation of Sally Hemings.

The institution of slavery casts a long shadow over every aspect of contemporary American life. The legacy of white supremacy remains deeply entrenched, gripping our institutions, shaping our collective subconscious, and influencing the conscious beliefs of many today. Perhaps most insidious is America's enduring cognitive dissonance—the mindset that allows us to champion American exceptionalism and moral superiority while being fully aware of the facts that contradict these claims: slavery, the genocide of Native Americans, Japanese internment, one of the highest incarceration rates in the world, the most mass shootings of any nation on Earth—the list goes on.[17] This ability to hold conflicting realities, coupled with a culture of us-versus-them thinking, makes Americans particularly susceptible to cultlike ideologies.

A Brief History of Cults in the US

Cults are deeply rooted in American culture. From the moment Europeans set foot on this land, they were forming high-control, separatist groups—the Pilgrims and Puritans fled religious persecution only to turn around and enforce their own brand of rigid, exclusionary doctrine. The early US became a breeding ground for groups with a strong us-versus-them mentality, each convinced they had the *real* truth and that the rest of the world was doomed, wrong, or both.

Tara Isabella Burton's *Strange Rites: New Religions for a Godless World* profiles many of the United States' modern alternative spiritual movements, but it also offers a compelling historical overview of the nation's distinctive religious evolution, framed within the broader context of the traditionally recognized "Great Awakenings." The 1730s and 1740s saw what some historians refer to as the First Great Awakening, when evangelical Christianity swept across the thirteen colonies in the form of revival tents.[18] This can also be seen as the birth of the highly emotional and fanatical version of Christianity that Americans so love today, where connection to God is defined by altered states and the loss of self. People rejected the rationalism of the Enlightenment unitarians and deists in favor of emotional preaching and an intense personal experience of the Holy Spirit.

By the early nineteenth century, religious experimentation was everywhere. The evangelical Christian movement spread even further during this Second Great Awakening, accompanied by the growth of new denominations like Methodists and Baptists, and a growing number of fringe offshoots such as the egalitarian (and celibate, hence their demise) Shaker movement, as well as the polyamorous Oneida Community. Inspired by the revivals of his youth, Joseph Smith claimed to receive divine visions, publishing the Book of Mormon in 1830 and starting the Church of Jesus Christ of Latter-day Saints. While not all these groups were destructive, most shared one core trait: a belief that they were the chosen ones, the enlightened, and everyone else was lost, misguided, or actively working against them.

But things really started getting culty with the New Thought meta-physical movements of the early 1900s, which emphasized positive thinking, the power of the mind, and the idea that individuals can shape their reality through spiritual and mental discipline—principles popularized a hundred or so years later with books like *The Secret* and concepts like manifesting. Emerging from transcendentalism, the New Thought movement was loosely Christian and encompassed a diverse and highly individualistic hodgepodge of groups and leaders, from the spiritual healing of Christian Science, to the occultism of Theosophy, to the channeling and seances of spiritualism, as well as a growing interest in Eastern spiritual traditions.[19] Part of the Third Great Awakening, which also saw the rise of Pentecostalism, Jehovah's Witnesses, and socially minded and activist churches, the New Thought movement laid the groundwork for what we now think of as New Age or alternative spiritualty—and perhaps the most quintessentially American contribution to Christianity of all: the prosperity gospel.

The prosperity gospel is a decidedly American invention. Heavily influenced by the New Thought movement, it teaches that faith, positive thinking, and financial giving lead to material wealth and success. Rooted in the belief that thoughts shape reality, New Thought introduced ideas like the law of attraction and divine abundance, which were later rebranded in prosperity gospel theology as "name it and claim it" teachings.[20] This movement also adopted New Thought's emphasis on spiritual healing, suggesting that faith can cure sickness as well as generate financial prosperity. The "seed faith" doctrine, which promotes giving money to religious leaders in expectation of multiplied blessings, further ties material gain to spiritual devotion. These ideas gained traction through figures like E. W. Kenyon and Oral Roberts, but modern televangelists such as Joel Osteen and Kenneth Copeland have globalized the message.

The prosperity gospel is the height of cognitive dissonance: distorting core Christian teachings like humility, self-sacrifice, and the dangers of wealth, reducing faith to a formula for financial success, and implying that poverty or illness results from a lack of belief. Believers in the prosperity gospel conveniently overlook the very clear warnings in the Bible about leaders who exploit religion for personal gain. Instead they follow preachers who accumulate wealth while promising material blessings to followers, fitting the very description of those Saint Paul cautioned against. In contemporary American culture, prosperity theology fuels megachurches and televangelism; preachers get rich while burdening followers with unrealistic promises of wealth in exchange for faith and financial contributions.[21]

While the First and Second Great Awakenings are widely recognized by historians, the Third, and particularly the Fourth, are less universally accepted and remain subjects of debate. The Fourth Great Awakening typically refers to a period of social and cultural upheaval in the US during the late 1960s through the 1970s, which saw the rise of fringe new religious movements at the same time that evangelical Christianity was regaining influence, which shaped political realignments and sparked debates over what economic historian Robert Fogel described as "spiritual inequality." This period also marked the beginning of what we now think of as culture wars and the religious right. When it comes to cults, this is usually the era most people think of, when disillusioned young people (like my grandparents) sought meaning outside mainstream society, which led to the rise of high-control groups. Charles Manson convinced his followers they were soldiers in an impending apocalyptic race war he termed "Helter Skelter." The Children of God rebranded Christianity with a focus on love and salvation, but their practices included exploitation and abuse. Synanon began as a well-meaning drug rehab program but spiraled into a violent and authoritarian empire, leaving a lasting impact on 12-step and other recovery communities that can be felt to this day. Despite many high-profile exposés of its abuses, Scientology—blending self-help, pseudoscience, and religious doctrines involving past lives and extraterrestrial influences—continues to maintain a stronghold in Hollywood. These groups thrived by offering members a distinct identity (us), a compelling cause, and a clear enemy (them)—be it the government, societal systems, or outsiders perceived as unenlightened.

The 1980s and '90s saw the rise and fall of high-control groups like Osho's Rajneesh movement, which built a compound in Oregon and gained notoriety for a bioterror attack on the local community, and which today still operates meditation centers in over eighty countries.[22] No one can forget Heaven's Gate, a group that took the whole us-versus-them thing to the extreme, rejecting the material world and embracing death as escape. Around the same time, the Branch Davidians, a splinter group of Seventh-day Adventists led by David Koresh, engaged in a fifty-one-day standoff with federal agents in Waco, Texas, that ended in a fire that killed seventy-six people.

Cults of this time also adopted new packaging—self-help, corporate training, and wellness movements wrapped in a thin veneer of empowerment. But underneath was the same old control, coercion, and strict division between insiders and outsiders. In today's world, cults haven't vanished; they've simply adapted to modern platforms and methods. Social media transformed conspiracy movements like QAnon into global phenomena by convincing followers that they alone possess the truth and everyone else is deceived. In 2025 QAnon may be no more, but it doesn't need to be—its conspiracy theories and us-versus-them mentality are thoroughly entrenched in mainstream culture and politics.

As explored in other chapters, modern cults can take the form of MLMs, toxic workplaces, self-help movements, insular online communities, and, arguably, many organized religious groups. America's unique culture has infused them with many culty attributes. And then, of course, there's politics. Every election cycle, Americans are told that if *they* win, it's the end of democracy, the destruction of values, or the total collapse of the country. It's no longer a disagreement—it's war. Both major political parties fuel this fire by painting the other side as not just wrong but dangerous.[23] Compromise is weakness. Skepticism is betrayal. So we dig in, picking media that feeds our worst fears, unfollowing or cutting off people who don't agree with us. Our political divides now feel like religious schisms, with true believers on both sides convinced the other is leading us straight to ruin.[24] It's the same script, over and over—on different battlegrounds.

Us versus them is rooted in our tribal instincts, and it has the power to make people feel special, protected, part of something bigger. And it works—over and over again, in every kind of group imaginable. But the moment you stop and ask *Who benefits from this division?*—that's when you might finally see the game for what it is.

The Psychology of Groupthink and Mass Movements

Today's movements—from #BlackLivesMatters to Trumpian populism, from evangelical Christianity to alternative wellness—operate in a digital world where ideas spread faster than ever, and groupthink is amplified by social media algorithms. Mass movements no longer require physical gatherings or a single charismatic leader; they need only a compelling narrative, a strong in-group identity, and a shared enemy.

The Black Lives Matter protests of 2020 showcased the power of decentralized movements. Millions of people rallied against police brutality without a singular leader, unified instead by viral footage and collective outrage. Meanwhile, the January 6 insurrection was an example of how us-versus-them rhetoric, combined with mass disinformation and a charismatic figure (Trump), could drive people to violent extremism. Both movements reveal the same underlying truth: When people feel like they're part of something greater than themselves, and when they believe an enemy is threatening their way of life, they will go to extraordinary lengths to defend their cause.

From the American Revolution to white nationalism, mass movements often follow the same pattern. They thrive on a binary mindset, a sense of moral high ground, and our deep need to fit in. Whether these movements drive progress or cause harm hinges on what happens when critical thinking bumps up against group identity. Because once a movement reaches the point where asking questions is risky, it's veering into cult territory. At the heart of every mass movement is *groupthink*—a psychological phenomenon observed by American psychologist Irving Janis during his analysis of the Bay of

Pigs fiasco, where seemingly smart people collectively made very bad decisions. Groupthink occurs when people's desire for group cohesion overrides their critical thinking, leading to irrational or dysfunctional outcomes. The eight symptoms of groupthink described below are adapted from Janis's work on decision-making failures:

1. **Perceived invulnerability:** Overconfidence leads the group to take dangerous or reckless actions.

2. **Rationalization and denial:** The group dismisses warnings and avoids reevaluating flawed beliefs.

3. **Moral justification:** The group assumes its actions are inherently good, ignoring possible ethical issues.

4. **Stereotyped views of others/enemies:** Outsiders are seen in overly simplistic, negative terms, which reduces the need for thoughtful engagement.

5. **Silencing dissent:** Members who disagree are pressured to conform and not speak out.

6. **Internal suppression:** Individuals keep quiet about their own doubts or concerns to avoid disrupting harmony.

7. **False consensus:** A lack of voiced disagreement is mistaken for unanimity among members.

8. **Self-designated "mindguards":** Some members take it upon themselves to block dissenting views or information that might disrupt group unity.[25]

Like the ten aspects of cult behavior I outline in this book, these eight symptoms of groupthink are pervasive in groups of all kinds to varying degrees. Whether in a cult, a mainstream religion, a small town, a social movement, a financial bubble, or a high school clique, I would bet that everyone has at some point participated in groupthink. Humans are social creatures, wired to seek approval and avoid rejection, so it is easy to get swept up in what everyone else seems to be doing. The key is in recognizing when the stability of the group requires conformity in order to operate, when individuality is suppressed in favor of consensus. If your group or movement cannot function without silencing dissent, rejecting diverse opinions, or squashing critical discussion, then it might be time for you to go.

Mass movements don't just happen—they're carefully constructed, step by step, using psychology, social pressure, and reinforced norms to draw individuals into a shared ideology. In *The True Believer*, Eric Hoffer explains that mass movements attract people who feel alienated or disillusioned and offer them a sense of purpose by immersing them in a collective identity. Loyalty and exclusivity can then be weaponized, whether through social proof, authority pressure, or scarcity tactics, as people are subtly manipulated into aligning more closely with the group.[26] Even the most well-intentioned political and social movements exploit us-versus-them rhetoric to deepen divisions, making people more loyal to their side while vilifying the opposition.

Radicalization is not limited to cults or extremist cells. In *Dying to Win: The Strategic Logic of Suicide Terrorism*, political scientist Robert Pape shows that us-versus-them narratives serve ideological purposes but also fuel extreme loyalty. When people believe their group faces an existential threat, they may defend it with actions they once found unimaginable. This shift isn't about intelligence, morality, or even ideology—it's rooted in human psychology. The more we understand how movements shape identity, enforce norms, and weaponize our values, the better we can recognize the warning signs before we're in too deep to turn back.

A movement becomes a high-control group when the "us" identity requires the loss of personal identity. High-control groups want more than your agreement; they want your entire sense of self to be indistinguishable from the collective. Because once your identity is fully tied to the group, you'll do whatever it takes to maintain your place within it. And that's where the real exploitation begins, with your labor. And ultimately, your ability to work is really what a cult is after.

Chapter 8

Exploitation of Labor: Nobody Wants to Work Hard Anymore

I n 2022 a global tech giant—long considered a rare outlier in an otherwise cutthroat industry—fell into the hands of one of the world's most polarizing billionaires. The takeover was swift, chaotic, and public. For employees, it felt less like a leadership change and more like the opening scene of a survival game.

Employees felt their psychological safety erode, and their fear of saying the wrong thing crept into meetings with the new chief, whose unpredictable reactions kept people on edge. Some were even warned to "be careful"—not out of paranoia, but because a growing culture of fear made missteps feel consequential.[1] Then came the ultimatum: Work "hardcore" hours without complaint, or walk away. There was no middle ground.

What followed blurred the line between ambition and madness. Photos began surfacing online: senior staff curled up in sleeping bags on office floors, bright fluorescent lights overhead. These weren't leaked as warning signs—they were at least partially staged and paraded as badges of honor. Sacrifice had become spectacle.[2]

They'd seen it coming, but that didn't make it easier. The rules had changed overnight. Miss a deadline, and you might not be back the next day. Say the wrong thing, and your access could vanish by morning.

Productivity was a blood sport, and failure meant exile. Surveillance was silent but constant—expectations rising, hours stretching, boundaries dissolving. Family, sleep, health—everything was expendable in the name of endurance.[3]

The message was clear: If you weren't willing to sacrifice everything, you didn't belong. This wasn't a company. It was a cult of performance, ruled by fear, fueled by ego, and justified by the illusion of innovation.

* * *

The man driving this cultural shift was, of course, Elon Musk, and the company in question was Twitter. What began as Musk's attempt to reinvent a tech giant quickly turned into a case study in just how far modern workplaces can push employees under the banner of progress and efficiency, all led by a charismatic, larger-than-life leader. This wasn't about working hard—it was about proving unwavering devotion to the cause, even if it broke you. Employees, many of whom would be eliminated regardless, were mercilessly told by Musk that they would need to work strenuously to keep the company afloat. "Those who are able to go hard core and play to win, Twitter is a good place," he said. "And those who are not, totally understand, but then Twitter is not for you."[4]

After Donald Trump announced that he'd appoint Musk as Director of the Department of Government Efficiency—an entirely new position Trump promised to create—Musk wasted no time setting the tone. He made it crystal-clear that anyone interested in being part of his task force would need to commit to working eighty-plus hours per week. If the Twitter takeover was any indication, it's not hard to imagine what that might look like: exhaustion spun as dedication, sacrifice demanded without question, and a culture that celebrates pushing human limits as if it's the ultimate virtue.

Musk took the Silicon Valley startup cult's "move fast and break things" mentality and ran with it—straight into the US government.

Whether it's SpaceX launching rockets before regulators can blink, Starlink shaping battlefield communications with zero accountability, or Tesla pushing self-driving tech that still can't seem to stop hitting emergency vehicles, Musk operates like the rules are just suggestions— for other people, not him. He's turned disruption into a power move, forcing government agencies to work around *his* timeline, not the other way around. Agencies have been left scrambling to keep up, bending regulations and making exceptions because, well, Musk gets results. He's mastered the art of positioning himself as the untouchable innovator—the guy who's too essential to be slowed down by things like safety, ethics, or, you know, the inconvenience of democracy. In this view, the startup world's fixation on speed and disruption has gone mainstream. Musk illustrates that convincing people you're indispensable can prompt the rules to bend around you.

Cults Are Always About Labor

It was like a light bulb went on when, in my thirties, I heard Dr. Janja Lalich say that *cults are always about labor* and that "most cults are doing labor trafficking."[5] It was the missing piece that made my childhood make sense in a way I didn't even realize I'd been struggling to understand. The realization hit me like a punch in the gut: I'd been labor-trafficked around the world by the Children of God. They exploited us as unpaid actors in child entertainment videos that we, as kids and teenagers, were then forced to sell on the streets. We kids also did much of the physical labor needed to run huge compounds that housed up to 250 people. Teenage boys did construction. Teenage girls worked around the clock as nannies. I was a full-time commune cook at eleven. The "troubled" kids were punished by being forced to scrub pail after pail of dirty diapers. We did it all, without a second thought, because we were raised to believe that work was devotion.

But that wasn't the first time I'd started piecing together the connection between cults and labor. When I was around twenty-two, a young lieutenant in the Army, I found myself devouring memoirs of former cult members, desperately trying to make sense of my own past. In *Beyond Belief: My Secret Life Inside Scientology and My Harrowing Escape*, Jenna Miscavige Hill's account of her childhood in Scientology, I first recognized not only the emotional control but the specific ways child labor was used.[6] It turns out cults don't just thrive on blind devotion—they run on the backs of unpaid labor, especially that of children who are too young, isolated, and indoctrinated to realize they're being exploited.

More than a religious movement, the Children of God cult was essentially a criminal entertainment syndicate, and I spent my entire childhood being trafficked as a performer within it. From the time I could walk and talk, I was singing and dancing on the streets of cities all over the world, along with 7,000 other kids, forced to perform to fund the group's survival and send money up to its leaders. We were recorded on video, too, creating child entertainment that was distributed globally under the guise of spreading "God's love." This wasn't small-time either—we performed at the White House *twice* in the '90s and once for the president of Brazil. The group also produced actors like Rose McGowan and Joaquin and River Phoenix, all kids who grew up performing for this machine. It was exploitation, pure and simple, but the cult spun it as "spreading the gospel." We were used like products to keep their operations running.

Many cults have a documented history of using unpaid labor as part of their operations.[7] And when it comes to the ideal workforce, kids are the perfect choice—easy to indoctrinate, cheap to maintain, completely dependent, and too young to realize they're being exploited. They grow up inside the system, working not just for survival but for salvation—and love. Children are uniquely situated to be exploited because they are wired to seek love and approval from caregivers. In cults, as in abusive families, that attachment system gets distorted because they learn that love is conditional. Affection and acceptance are only given when the child behaves and works "correctly." A child's natural fear of abandonment becomes weaponized, as many children would rather endure abuse than lose the only family or community they know. The cult leader is perceived as both godlike and as a kind of surrogate parent, often even more powerful than the child's actual parents. Pleasing the leader can feel like the most important goal in life, as if their value and salvation depend on it.[8] The only world these kids know is the one their leaders have constructed, and there's no union, no minimum wage, and no escape.[9]

Mainstream churches and religious institutions across America also run on unpaid labor, though it is framed as volunteering and service—and young people are a big part of that system.[10] From the moment children are old enough to stack chairs or hand out bulletins, they're expected to pitch in as part of their "spiritual development." It's framed as service or giving back, but the truth is that many of these organizations simply wouldn't function without free labor. Teenagers end up doing the heavy lifting—setting up events, running Vacation Bible School, and working long, grueling hours on mission trips. Some churches even make volunteering a requirement for youth leadership or religious scholarships, so service feels more like a toll you must pay to belong. Volunteering can be deeply valuable. It builds confidence, time management, empathy—all good things. The problem is when it's wrapped in spiritual obligation and quietly enforced, instead of being a real choice. When work is tied to faith, obedience, or standing in the community, pushing back becomes unthinkable. After all, who wants to be the selfish one complaining about "giving back" when everyone else is doing it with a smile?

In Mormon communities, male members are expected to give two full years of their young adult lives to missionary work, usually footing the bill themselves. The message is clear: Your time, your energy, and your very identity belong to the church. The Amish have a comparable setup, but instead of sending kids off to knock on doors (which is labor, by the way), they're put to work on the land or in family businesses; many also labor in construction. It's framed as a way to teach discipline and community values. And in many ways, it does. But it also has another effect: By limiting formal education to the eighth grade (a practice upheld by the Supreme Court in *Wisconsin v. Yoder*) and immersing teens in tightly controlled environments, communities effectively anchor the next generation to the only world they've ever known. Plenty of former Amish describe how difficult it is to navigate the outside world with only a middle school education and no exposure to broader cultural or technological systems. That's not incidental—it's structural.[11]

Unlike the Mormon church or the Amish, Synanon wasn't even pretending to be a traditional religion—it was supposed to be a drug rehab program. But Charles "Chuck" Dederich demanded members' labor. Kids were put to work, too, not just in chores but in the literal dirty work of the "rehabilitation" process. Children as young as six were cleaning up after sick, strung-out addicts—fetching rags, emptying puke buckets, tending to people too far gone to even lift their heads. Dederich called it therapy and an "experiment" in communal living, but really, it was exploitation. Children were absorbed into the system, and their labor fueled the organization while their childhoods slipped away. Much like my experience in the Children of God, Synanon's children weren't raised by their parents but by the group, shuffled into communal "schooling" and trained for a lifetime of devotion to the cause. Some of them, like Dederich's own daughter, eventually escaped and spoke out about the physical and emotional abuse they endured.[12]

You may be surprised to learn that businesses and nonprofits you know and love were founded and may even still run on the unpaid labor of members. The Oneida Community, founded in the mid-1800s by John Humphrey Noyes, started out as a religious community built around communal living, polygamy, and endless labor. Noyes preached "perfectionism," the idea that people could achieve spiritual purity through shared work, communal property, and some pretty unconventional practices—like complex marriage, where everyone was "married" to everyone else. The group's self-sufficiency was the point. Members grew their own food, made furniture, canned produce, built their own housing, and ran light manufacturing operations. Labor was central to both their survival and their theology: Noyes preached that spiritual purity came through shared work and collective living. Everyone contributed—men, women, and children—rotating through farming, domestic tasks, and industrial production.[13] Eventually, they got really good at manufacturing, especially silverware, which became their main source of income. By the late 1800s, the religious experiment crumbled, but the labor stuck around. The group rebranded itself into a business and eventually became Oneida Limited, now a household name in silverware and flatware.[14]

You wouldn't expect it, but Celestial Seasonings—the tea company known for its cozy boxes and calming blends—has an origin story tied to *The Urantia Book*, a 2,000-page pseudo-religious text that claims to be a divine revelation from celestial beings. In addition to bizarre teachings—such as the belief that Jesus was an alien (remember the thing about cults loving space?)—even more disturbingly, it is steeped in racist and eugenicist ideology. The book, which influenced co-founder Mo Siegel's business philosophy and even appeared in early marketing, promotes ideas such as a hierarchy of races and the elimination of so-called inferior groups. Although *The Urantia Book* itself is not classified as a destructive cult, experts note that some of its offshoot groups are. Its teachings helped shape the values and messaging behind the brand in its early years—another example of fringe beliefs finding their way into mainstream culture. It's a reminder that even your favorite bedtime brew may have roots in something far more unsettling than herbal folklore.[15]

Speaking of tea, the Yogi Tea brand, popular for its Ayurvedic blends, was founded by Yogi Bhajan, the controversial leader of Kundalini Yoga in the US and founder of 3HO (Healthy, Happy, Holy Organization), which has been accused of cultlike activity like isolation, arranged marriages, and rigid dress codes. The tea company's roots are deeply embedded in 3HO's communal labor system, where followers worked in kitchens, offices, or yoga centers for free or for minimal stipends, believing their service was part of their spiritual practice. Multiple allegations of sexual abuse, spiritual manipulation, labor exploitation, and authoritarian control came out after Bhajan died in 2004.[16] The company has since distanced itself from 3HO and Yogi Bhajan, but his image and quotes are still featured on their products.

Then there are the restaurant fronts—places like the Yellow Deli and Common Ground Cafe, both run by the Twelve Tribes cult, where children grow up waiting tables and baking bread, all in the name of religious devotion. Kids in the Twelve Tribes are raised to see constant work as a form of spiritual devotion, which makes it easy for leaders to justify putting them to work in the kitchens, cleaning, or doing other behind-the-scenes labor. They often work long hours alongside adults, denied education, rest, and a normal childhood. They are unpaid and unseen by customers who have no idea their sandwich was made with the help of child labor.[17]

Now let's talk about Girl Scouts (and give the entire nonprofit sector a long, skeptical side-eye while we're at it). On the surface, it looks wholesome—girls selling cookies to support their troop activities and learn entrepreneurial skills. But when you think about it, the Girl Scouts are operating a multimillion-dollar business powered by the unpaid work of children. According to an online article by Brian Flaherty, who explores the economics of Girl Scout cookies, those iconic boxes bring in hundreds of millions of dollars every year. Yet after paying the bakers, most of the money goes to each girl's local Girl Scout council (and their surprisingly well-paid employees), with her troop receiving a portion of the rest from a communal pot. An individual girl can sometimes use her "portion" of the troop's profit to fund Girl Scout activities or other rewards (according to one account, this comes out to about $0.09 per box sold),[18] but she doesn't receive any money directly.[19] Meanwhile, it's the girls (and often their mothers) who are doing the heavy lifting—pounding the pavement, braving the cold at cookie booths, managing orders and inventory, and juggling the pressure of sales goals. What's marketed as a fun, empowering experience can start to feel like an unpaid sales job. It's worth noting that the national Girl Scouts of the USA does not directly profit from cookie sales, though they receive a small amount in licensing fees from the bakeries that produce the cookies. In 2023 this royalty income amounted to $9.3 million, or about 9.1 percent of the national Girl Scout organization's annual revenue.

Honestly, I'm relieved my kid decided to quit Scouts before we got too deep into it. Because the more I reflect on it, the stranger it seems. How did we collectively decide it's normal for little girls to prop up a business for free? We call it "character building," and it certainly can be, but it also teaches girls how to work hard without pay while someone else reaps the rewards. It's not so different from those cult "fundraising" activities I was forced into—just with better branding and better snacks.

In all these cases, the line between volunteering, spiritual duty, and straight-up trafficking gets blurred beyond recognition. Cult leaders, church leaders, and business leaders alike dress it up as character building, but let's call it what it is: unpaid labor. Sure, there's a wide range of harm across these organizations (if your kid loves the Girl Scouts and genuinely feels empowered, more power to her). But if we strip away the sacred missions and the lofty ideals of the very worst offenders, we're left with a harsh truth: Cults are just organized crime syndicates that run on free labor. They recruit, they indoctrinate, and extract—demanding time, money, and endless work from members—all while dodging taxes and labor laws under the guise of religion or self-improvement. The mafia runs protection rackets, but cults run salvation rackets—promising enlightenment, purpose, or an exclusive path to heaven, in exchange for absolute obedience and relentless effort. They rely on coercion, fear, and emotional manipulation to maintain control, just like any criminal enterprise. And when someone tries to leave? They're hit with retaliation—whether it's public shaming, financial ruin, severed relationships, or outright threats. The only difference between a cult and the mob is that cults usually don't need guns to keep their members in line—they use love, belonging, and fear of abandonment instead.

There's nothing wrong with real, unpressured volunteering—it can be a great way to give back and create meaning in one's life. And it can be argued that there's something inherently anti-cult about removing labor from the confines of the cult of capitalism. But we need reasonable limits, especially for kids, who aren't in a position to advocate for themselves. Service can cross the line into exploitation, and that's a line that both cults and way too many churches are willing to blur. Volunteering and being of service, when done responsibly, are about building community—not being used by it.

The Cult of Busyness

When I first started thinking about doing a PhD, one of the questions I wanted to tackle was: How much labor—mental, emotional, physical—does it take for something to fully monopolize someone's mind? Not just in terms of productivity, but total internal takeover. My guess was that it might only take twenty to thirty hours a week, though as far as I know, there have been no official studies on this. I'd seen firsthand how systems—military, religious, cultural—leverage that time to entrench control. Whether through official order or unspoken expectations, they make labor and busyness the medium through which identity and autonomy are reshaped.

I used to tell my boss, "You know, when we're all living at home and just coming to work in uniform every day, the Army doesn't feel that culty. But the minute we go away together—deploy to training or combat—it's really culty." He'd give me this tiny, knowing smirk, the kind that said, *Keep going—you're on to something,* and tell me to think more about it. He was one of the only leaders who actually encouraged me when I started comparing my Army experience to the cult I grew up in.

What I was feeling, but couldn't yet articulate, was how much busyness itself was being used as a form of labor for control. Once I started thinking about isolation (explored more in chapter 5) as a core feature of cults and total institutions, the patterns became impossible to ignore. Physical isolation was the easy part to name. I'd lived it—on a separatist cult commune, and later, deep in the Louisiana swamps for Army war games, or deployed to Afghanistan. But what stayed with me were the mental and emotional forms of separation, the ones created not by fences or geography, but by time. Constant activity. Constant demands. Constant motion.

I started to see it everywhere. People weren't in communes or barracks, but they were just as cut off in their thinking and social interactions as I'd been—so immersed in their jobs, their hobbies, their belief systems that they didn't have the bandwidth to think beyond them. CrossFit. Organic eating. Faith healing. Marathon training and TikTok (me, guilty on these). Recovery communities and hot yoga (my co-writer Amy, guilty on these). What all of them had in common wasn't just commitment—it was schedule saturation. And schedule saturation is a kind of labor that wears down your resistance while masquerading as discipline or devotion.

Cults have long understood that busyness itself is labor, and that labor is a form of control. Control doesn't require putting up walls or moving to remote locations—sometimes all you need is an overpacked schedule. By keeping members running from task to task, meeting to meeting, cult leaders leave no room for independent thought or personal reflection. People get too tired to question anything. The relentless pace ensures they're too busy to build connections with anyone outside who might challenge the group's control. The pace also isolates them from *themselves.* Janja Lalich calls it being "isolated from your own mind." She writes, "How can that happen? If your day starts at seven a.m., and ends at midnight, and is extremely active and filled with group events, it becomes difficult to turn inward and reflect. By the end of the day when your head hits the pillow, you just do not have the energy to stay awake."[20]

Jehovah's Witnesses' entire structure is built around spiritual labor—meetings multiple times a week, personal study, door-to-door preaching, volunteering at conventions, construction projects. Their publishing arm, the Watchtower Bible and Tract Society Printery, also runs on volunteer labor.[21] All this spiritual busyness keeps members so focused on the mission that there's no time left for relationships outside the faith—or room to question their own beliefs. It's isolation through activity, and it works.

Through this kind of time manipulation, high-control groups keep members constantly occupied. The goal isn't productivity—it's distraction. With their attention diverted elsewhere, members have little room for personal reflection or independent thought. If every moment is filled with tasks, rituals, or meetings, people are less likely to question what's happening around them. In the military, from day one of basic training, recruits are thrown into a whirlwind of drills, inspections, and tightly scheduled routines. It's a deliberate approach that overwhelms the mind, strips away individual autonomy, and fosters compliance through sheer mental and physical exhaustion. The parallels to cult indoctrination are hard to miss.

The obsession with busyness is deeply rooted in American culture. As explored in the previous chapter, the Protestant work ethic ("idle hands are the devil's workshop") has been drilled into us for generations. Kids are told to "stay busy" or risk falling behind, overscheduled with sports and tutoring and other activities, and set up to equate downtime with failure. In our society, exhaustion is celebrated, and chronic overwork becomes the price of acceptance.[22]

And the impact goes beyond fatigue—it leads to disconnection. A *PBS NewsHour* discussion on loneliness pointed to time as one of the key culprits: "People are busy. People are spending more time at work. We just don't have enough free time to connect with the people we care about."[23] Whether it's a cult keeping you occupied with endless tasks, a military schedule designed to leave no room for thought, or a culture that glorifies the grind, the result is the same: isolation. And once you're isolated, it's a lot harder to see a way out.

The Cult of American Labor Culture

Labor exploitation in the US has been baked into the system for centuries, from slavery to modern-day sweatshops. As we've explored in previous chapters, American labor practices have a lot in common with what you see in high-control groups—where people are expected to sacrifice their personal lives, health, and well-being for someone else's goals.

Let's start with the most egregious example: slavery. For centuries, enslaved Africans were forced into brutal, unpaid labor that built much of this country's early wealth. And when slavery "ended," things didn't magically improve—sharecropping in the South kept many formerly enslaved people and poor farmers stuck in a vicious cycle of debt and poverty. Then came industrialization, where factory workers—including kids—faced grueling hours, dangerous conditions, and barely enough pay to survive, and many didn't. Monopolistic companies ran the show, so profits always came before workers' well-being. Economic exploitation was the foundation of a culture that normalizes control, obedience, and sacrifice, making the US uniquely fertile ground for cultlike systems to thrive.[24]

In the late nineteenth and early twentieth centuries, company towns sprang up across the country, especially in industries like coal, steel, lumber, and textiles, where an employer essentially owned the entire community, including housing, stores, schools, churches, and other amenities. Workers typically paid rent to the company and bought goods from company-owned stores, often at inflated prices. Some towns—and sharecropping farms in the South—paid workers in scrip (a form of company-issued currency), which could only be used within the company town, essentially trapping workers in a closed economy and making it nearly impossible to leave. Paternalistic employers controlled every aspect of their employees' lives, claiming to "take care" of workers and their families while actually crushing autonomy. Dissent could lead not only to firing but eviction, casting the worker and their family out of their community with nothing.[25] It mirrored the structure of a cult: total control disguised as care, and punishment for anyone who tried to walk away. (Modern corporations such as Meta and Google are reinventing company towns by providing things like housing, food, and other services on their campuses—Meta's massive headquarters in Menlo Park, California, offers a barbershop and laundry services—so employees can focus on their work and never have to leave.[26])

By the early twentieth century, many people had had enough. Labor unions like the AFL (American Federation of Labor) and

IWW (Industrial Workers of the World) started pushing back, organizing strikes and protests to demand better pay, shorter hours, and safer workplaces. Then came tragedies like the Triangle Shirtwaist Factory fire of 1911, where 146 garment workers—mostly young immigrant women—died because of unsafe working conditions. As the Triangle Shirtwaist Factory Fire Memorial website explains, the owners "felt vulnerable to union organizers who felt that the workers were treated poorly," so they "decided that the best defense against union infiltration was to lock the workers in." The tragic fire caused public outrage to finally hit a tipping point. This era brought major wins for workers, like the Fair Labor Standards Act of 1938, which introduced the minimum wage, banned most child labor, and capped the workweek. The New Deal era of the 1930s was another game-changer, bringing things like unemployment insurance and collective bargaining rights. These reforms were critical, but they didn't dismantle the deeper system—one built on obedience, control, and the idea that sacrifice is virtue. Even as conditions improved on paper, the underlying culture remained eerily compatible with the logic of high-control groups.

Labor rights were much slower to take hold in US agriculture than in industrial sectors. During the New Deal era, when major labor protections were introduced, agricultural and domestic workers were explicitly excluded from many key laws, including the right to unionize and earn a minimum wage. This exclusion was largely driven by racism and political compromise—Southern lawmakers sought to maintain the plantation-style economy reliant on cheap Black labor. By preserving control over agricultural labor through legal exclusion, the system didn't just overlook exploitation—it codified a structure of dependence and domination that echoed the very logic of cultic control.[27]

On the west coast, specifically in California's Central Valley, farm labor in the 1920s and early 1930s depended heavily on Filipino immigrants (like my co-writer Amy's grandfather). At the time, the Philippines were a US territory and immigration was mostly unrestricted, so Filipinos were actively recruited for cheap labor with promises of the American Dream. In 1942 the Bracero program began importing laborers from Mexico under similar exploitative conditions. White growers, taking advantage of these workers' lack of legal rights, frequently played different racial groups against one another—using Mexicans as strikebreakers when Filipinos walked out, and vice versa. These strategies did more than exploit cheap labor—they manufactured division, turning marginalized groups into tools of control, which made organizing harder and employer dominance easier, much like in cult systems where loyalty is enforced by isolation and internal competition.

Divide-and-conquer has been a recurring theme in American labor history, with race being weaponized to fracture solidarity and maintain employer control. But there are some powerful examples of multiracial labor solidarity, such as the 1934 West Coast Waterfront Strike, when Black and white longshoremen organized to build the International Longshore and Warehouse Union, one of the most progressive and anti-racist unions in US history. In the 1930s and 1940s, Black and white auto workers in Detroit united to join the United Auto Workers, turning Detroit into a hub of interracial labor activism, and later, civil rights support. And in September 1965, at the height of harvest season, Filipino farmworkers, led by organizer Larry Itliong, sparked the famous Delano grape strike, soon joined by Cesar Chavez and Mexican farmworkers, and the United Farm Workers union was born. These moments of cross-racial organizing stand out precisely because they disrupted the control system—briefly breaking the cultlike spell of isolation, fear, and hierarchy that had long kept workers divided and dependent.

Some states, like California, eventually legislated their own protections for farmworkers—but to this day, these workers still lack full federal collective bargaining rights. US agriculture still runs on exploited labor—often that of migrant and even child workers. Fresh produce comes at the cost of grueling hours in harsh conditions; undocumented workers are often forced to accept dangerous, low-wage jobs with little to no healthcare or protection. Shockingly, children as young as twelve can legally work full-time in the fields under loopholes that wouldn't be tolerated in other industries.[28] The system banks on this vulnerability to keep profits high while masking the brutal reality behind idyllic images of sunlit farms and fresh markets. Corporate agriculture is a modern extension of a high-control system that thrives on obedience, invisibility, and the moral justification of suffering, which makes it eerily aligned with cults.

Childcare workers in America face a different kind of exploitation. These are the people we trust to nurture our kids, yet they're paid near minimum wage, often without healthcare, paid leave, or job security. The system leans on outdated, sexist assumptions—most childcare workers are women, disproportionately women of color, and are expected to accept low wages under the belief that caregiving is simply women's work. Despite the skill and emotional labor involved, their work is devalued as something natural and expected. Meanwhile, families are drowning in sky-high childcare costs, which perpetuates a broken system where nobody wins. Like in cult dynamics, the system disguises exploitation as virtue—framing sacrifice as love, and low wages as moral duty—while demanding total devotion with little in return. If we claim to be a country that values children and families, we need to start by valuing the people who care for our kids.

The restaurant industry is textbook normalized exploitation. Servers and bartenders are expected to survive on tips, with base pay sometimes as low as $2.13 an hour—a federal minimum for tipped employees that has remained unchanged since 1991. Kitchen staff face grueling hours in sweltering conditions, often barely making above minimum wage. Managers push a toxic hustle culture, cramming schedules and demanding cheerfulness despite exhaustion—even as they slash shifts, change schedules abruptly, and expect fewer workers to shoulder the same load. Sexual harassment is the norm, and time off is taboo—if you can't handle it, someone else is waiting to take your place. Benefits like healthcare or paid sick days are rare, which forces workers to choose between a paycheck and their well-being. It's a classic high-control setup: low pay, emotional manipulation, and the constant threat of replacement—all disguised as "just how the industry works."[29]

Worse still, human trafficking is a documented issue within the industry.[30] Vulnerable workers—often immigrants (and their children)—are sometimes lured in with promises of legitimate jobs, only to be trapped in conditions that border on modern slavery. Their passports get confiscated, so escape is nearly impossible. Investigations from outlets like *The New York Times* show this isn't a fringe problem—it's a systemic one, rooted in a culture that commodifies labor and shrugs off abuse.[31]

In Hollywood, fame is glamorized while decades of labor abuse—especially toward children—remain hidden beneath the surface. As the documentary series *Quiet on Set: The Dark Side of Kids TV* reveals, child actors often endure grueling schedules and relentless pressure, sacrificing their education, mental health, and autonomy in the process. Although legal protections exist, they are rarely enforced with any real accountability. In practice, children are treated like miniature professionals, expected to perform flawlessly, often isolated from their peers and deprived of a normal childhood. The very people entrusted with protecting them—directors, producers, even family members—are frequently complicit. The unspoken mantra of the Hollywood machine is clear: The pursuit of fame justifies any means. So child stars can be left burned out, emotionally scarred, and financially exploited when their earnings are mismanaged or outright stolen. For every child who "makes it," countless others pay the price of a childhood they never got to live. It's a cultlike economy of control—obedience is rewarded, dissent is punished, and the illusion of opportunity is used to justify systemic harm.

Jeanette McCurdy's memoir *I'm Glad My Mom Died* lays bare the brutal truth: Beyond demanding long hours or setting impossible expectations, the industry systematically strips young performers of agency. Their labor becomes a product. Their identities become brands. And the fact that they are still children is all but forgotten. The documentary series *Quiet on Set* further exposes the toxic culture behind children's television, particularly at Nickelodeon, where young actors endured abusive and dangerous environments, including sexual misconduct. This industry sexualizes kids from an early age and places them under constant public scrutiny. Paparazzi stalk them. Tabloids feast on their pain. Their breakdowns become headlines. The consequences are devastating: Drew Barrymore entered rehab at thirteen. Macaulay Culkin emancipated himself at fourteen to escape parental control of his money. Mary-Kate Olsen sought treatment for anorexia at eighteen. Corey Haim died at thirty-eight after a long struggle with addiction. River Phoenix, first abused as a child in the Children of God, died at twenty-three from a drug overdose. Lindsay Lohan, Amanda Bynes, and Britney Spears all became cautionary tales—relentlessly pursued, publicly shamed, and discarded by the same culture that once celebrated them. Behind every child star's bright smile is often a darker story—one of control, exploitation, and a system that fails to treat kids like the kids they still are. The high-control Hollywood system prioritizes profit and image over safety and autonomy, using the tools of cults: isolation, coercion, and the erasure of self.

Reclaiming Rest

The combination of dependency, shame, and constant busyness is what makes labor exploitation so effective. It's why cults demand endless service, why corporations push employees to "give 110 percent," and why society shames people for resting. Work that stops being just labor and becomes a tool of control takes on a whole new purpose. If someone's entire identity is tied to their work, then questioning the value of that work feels like questioning their own worth. That's why systems of control—whether cults, corporations, or governments— want to exploit people's labor: to keep people obedient, dependent, and just too damn tired to question the whole thing.

But I do wonder: Are we finally starting to reject the sacred assumptions of capitalism's cultic system? The loudest voices clutching their pearls over the "labor shortage" in America keep shouting that "nobody wants to work hard anymore," while ignoring that younger generations are perhaps seeing through the lie. Maybe millennials and Gen Z aren't lazy—we're just done believing that "working for the man" is a worthy, transcendent mission for our lives. We've figured out that climbing the corporate ladder isn't worth sacrificing our health, happiness, and sense of self on the altar of hustle culture. But the devoted members of capitalism's cult can't handle that cognitive dissonance. Because if they start questioning the system, they have to face the fact that the people benefitting the most are the ones at the top, reaping the rewards of everyone else's exhaustion and exploitation.

One person leading the movement to escape from grind culture is Tricia Hersey, founder of The Nap Ministry and author of the books *Rest Is Resistance: A Manifesto* and *We Will Rest! The Art of Escape.* Her work centers on healing the generational exhaustion felt by American Black women through intentional, radical, liberatory rest. In a blog post titled "Rest Is Anything That Connects Your Mind and Body," she explains:

> I took to rest and naps and slowing down as a way to save my life, resist the systems telling me to do more and most importantly as a remembrance to my Ancestors who had their Dream-Space stolen from them. This is about more than naps. It is not about fluffy pillows, expensive sheets, silk sleep masks or any other external, frivolous, consumerist gimmick. It is about a deep unraveling from white supremacy and capitalism. These two systems are violent and evil. History tells us this and our present living shows this. Rest pushes back and disrupts a system that views human bodies as a tool for production and labor. It is a counter narrative. We know that we are not machines. We are divine.

Hersey reminds us that caring for ourselves in a culture determined to strip away our autonomy and agency is, in itself, a radical act of political rebellion—especially for those whose labor has been historically, systematically, and violently exploited, particularly Black women. If we are to truly break free from the cults of capitalism, white supremacy, and patriarchy, we must disrupt the American economy that is built on shame and embody a deeper truth: Our worth is not defined by our work.

Chapter 9

High Entrance and Exit Costs: It Costs What to End My Membership?

For Karen, a lonely stay-at-home mom, the idea of being a #bossbabe and running her own business felt like a lifeline. Her world had been reduced to diapers, bottles, and exhaustion, feeling invisible in her own life. Then, suddenly, there it was—a community of She-EOs who promised support, success, and a sisterhood of women all taking charge of their futures. Weekly Zoom calls, hyped-up Facebook groups, and a flood of feel-good messaging made her feel seen and inspired for the first time in ages. She wasn't just a mom anymore—she was an entrepreneur. She was doing more than selling clothes; she was buying into purpose, independence, and the dream of financial freedom. So when she was told the upfront investment was a "small price to pay" to start her empire, it felt worth it.

For Becky, the hook was different. She was stuck in a corporate job that drained her—no room to grow, no control over her schedule, and definitely no recognition for her hard work. The pitch was exactly what she was waiting to hear: Be your own boss. Work from anywhere. Build a business on your terms. It felt like a way out from under the glass ceiling she'd been banging her head against for years. She invested what she was told was a small risk to unlock "unlimited potential" and dove in headfirst. But pretty soon, the cracks started showing. Sales were inconsistent, the pressure to recruit more people turned into a constant hustle, and no matter how hard she worked, the numbers just didn't add up.

* * *

Multi-level marketing ventures entail costs and challenges beyond the initial investment. New MLM recruits are usually hit with the same pitch right away: "Start with your friends and family!" Sell to them, recruit them, get them to buy in. But what's not mentioned is how awkward—and sometimes devastating—that can be. Pushing overpriced products on the people closest to you can strain relationships, fast. One Reddit user summed it up bluntly: "Joining an MLM destroyed my extended family."[1]

And the financial pressure doesn't stop there. MLMs love to host flashy conferences, summits, and retreats—events that promise attendees the secrets to success. But between flights, hotels, and registration fees, buying those secrets can drain your bank account fast.[2] The Federal Trade Commission (FTC) warns that MLMs often require recruits to buy training materials, marketing kits, and attend expensive seminars, all adding up to significant financial strain.[3]

The result is a predictably toxic mix of money problems, social isolation, and emotional exhaustion. Many people find themselves in too deep to walk away, convinced that if they just try a little harder, they'll finally make it. But the reality is bleak: For most, the effort doesn't pay off and the money never comes—or worse, they end up losing money. And when the dream crumbles, they're left broke, burned out, and disillusioned, wondering how they ever got roped in to begin with.

For women like our hypothetical Karen and Becky, the realization hits like a slow-moving train: The system isn't designed for them to succeed. By the time they start asking questions, they are already deep in debt, holding boxes of unsold inventory they can't afford to keep but can't bring themselves to toss. The supportive "sisterhood" that once felt so warm turns icy when they stop toeing the line. Leaving doesn't mean just financial loss—they lose the social circle they've come to rely on. Take LuLaRoe: More than one hundred of its sellers filed for bankruptcy by 2019, with nearly half reporting an average of over $4,100 in unsold merchandise.[4] By the time their dream crumbled, the hustle that was supposed to set them free had turned into a nightmare. The emotional impact on sellers was significant too; many felt regret and shame, and felt wronged by a system that was not designed for their success.

Cult experts call MLMs "commercial cults" and it's not hard to see why—the math just doesn't math.[5] MLMs sell a dream: financial freedom, being your own boss, living life on your terms. The reality? One study found that nearly 99 percent of people in MLMs lose money once you factor in the endless products, fees, and promotional materials "consultants" are pressured to buy.[6] And if an MLM seems to prioritize recruitment over product sales, that's a major red flag. According to the FTC, this shifts it into pyramid scheme territory—which is illegal.[7]

Pyramid schemes are considered investment fraud. They focus on recruiting rather than selling products, requiring participants to "buy in" or invest to join, with promises of passive and easy income. The money primarily comes from new recruits paying to join, not from real customers buying real products. And when recruitment slows, the entire structure tends to collapse. MLMs are legal as long as their income comes from actual product sales. But anytime the model shifts—say, if the financial incentive to recruit outweighs commission from sales—it's likely veering into pyramid scheme territory. These elements were central to LuLaRoe's legal troubles—to join, reps had to purchase inventory with no reasonable return policy; and the real money came from recruiting, not selling clothes; and the money flowed straight to the handful of folks at the top. Everyone stuck at the bottom of the pyramid was hustling just to break even.[8]

MLMs like LuLaRoe, Herbalife, doTerra, Arbonne, and countless supplements and wellness products rely on classic cult approaches to keep people hooked. They love-bomb new recruits with praise and promises of success. They have an us-versus-them mentality. Anyone who questions the system is jealous, negative, or not willing to hustle hard enough. And when doubts creep in, the companies roll out the same thought-stopping clichés—"You're building your dream" or "Success is just around the corner." It's emotional manipulation dressed up in a sparkly, motivational package.

MLMs aren't entrepreneurship—they're a trap. Just like any cult, they use deceptive recruiting to sell empowerment while exploiting the people who buy in, keeping them working tirelessly so the leaders at the top can keep cashing in. It's all smoke and mirrors. And in the end, the house always wins.

Sunk Cost Fallacy and the Real Price of Entrance Costs

Some groups demand financial investments for entry, but the true cost often runs much deeper. The more you put in, the harder it becomes to walk away—because leaving means losing everything you've invested. Economists call this the *sunk cost fallacy*: our tendency to keep investing in something that no longer serves us simply because we've already poured time, money, or effort into it. We fear "wasting" our past investment, even if staying causes greater harm.

Sunk costs cannot be recovered, yet we're wired with a cognitive bias that tells us to stick with it, so we ignore the potential future benefits of abandoning it. It's a big reason why people stay in bad relationships, dead-end jobs, and, yes, cults. Admitting you were wrong, that you spent years or even decades chasing a lie, feels unbearable. As with abused spouses defending their abusers, cult members will make excuses for their leader or rationalize failure as a test of faith. That's how cults keep people hooked, even after spectacular collapse.

People regularly talk about exit costs, but rarely about *entrance costs*—everything you have to pay, literally or figuratively, to fully commit.

Sometimes it's just money: the membership fee, the inventory you're forced to buy, the pricey conferences and retreats sold as "investments" in your future. But more often it's deeper: the time you pour in, the relationships and opportunities you give up, the way you reshape your beliefs, identity, and life to match the group's world.

In cults, entrance costs can be extreme. You might drain your savings, cut ties with family, quit your job, or move across the country to prove you're "all in." And the more of yourself you give, the harder it becomes to acknowledge how much you've already lost or what you may be sacrificing to stay. As Mark Twain reportedly said, "It's easier to con a man than to convince him that he has been conned."*

And while cults and MLMs appeal to different kinds of needs—emotional connection versus financial opportunity—they share a system that raises the cost of leaving. The more you invest, the harder it is to walk away, because leaving means admitting your sacrifices might have been in vain.

Joining the Children of God in the 1970s wasn't as simple as just showing up. Once the love-bombing wore you down and you were ready to "forsake all and follow Jesus," you were expected to hand over everything: your savings, possessions, even the clothes on your back. If you owned a home or land, like my grandmother's family, or earned passive income, like Jeremy Spencer of Fleetwood Mac (who joined in 1971 and is said to have handed over his lifetime royalties), you were told to sign it over. If you had a job, like my grandfather, you were expected to quit and live on the compound full-time, essentially becoming a beggar for God. The cult claimed it was straight out of the Bible—the new Christians had gathered all their things and "laid them down at the apostles' feet: and distribution was made unto every man according as he had need."[9] But in practice, it meant you had no

---

* But alas, according to the Center for Mark Twain Studies website, Mark Twain never actually said this. ("The Apocryphal Twain," June 10, 2022, https://marktwainstudies .com/the-apocryphal-twain/it-is-easier-to-con-a-man-than-to-convince-him-he-has-been -conned)

fallback if you wanted to leave. Once you were in, you were *all in*: no safety net, no backup plan, just total dependence on the cult.

High entry costs are plentiful outside the cult world—some are called "barriers to entry." But not all barriers are financial, and not all costs are unfair. After all, training to be a doctor or musician takes time and money, but that's not a scam, it's just what the job requires. Still, the pattern shows up elsewhere: expensive degrees you're told you need to succeed, licensing fees that professions require, the hefty buy-in to join an exclusive club. Some costs are justified—but others exist mainly to extract and deepen commitment. And once you've sunk time, money, and effort, walking away can feel like failure.[10]

An academic I spoke with—who asked to remain anonymous because, well, they're still in academia—described entrance and exit costs perfectly. The parallels to my own experience as both a fifteen-year-old who left a cult and a former Army captain trying to fit into the workforce were uncanny:

> [Academia's] entrance costs: the price of admission; the lost wages while pursuing a PhD and/or doing a postdoc; delaying life events to accommodate that degree or preparation for a faculty position; loss of sleep because there is not a single hour you are awake when you couldn't theoretically be working (thinking, reading, planning) even if you're not "on campus"; relocating your home at least once, if not several times over however many years of postdoc-ing, often in different countries; and your transferrable/generalizable skills from working on incredibly niche projects.
>
> Exit costs: loss of your social circle, your home (esp. if you live on campus), your ideals of the pursuit of knowledge as a noble career, years of your life spent specializing to a career with low upward mobility prospects, the feeling of not ever having a "real job" so feeling unqualified for the workforce, your economic or social status symbols (esp. if you don't finish the degrees) which

can be tied to your self-esteem, reconciling your utopian ideals to the workforce, having to re-learn how to talk to/interact/ make friends with non-academics outside of the relatively easy framework of academia, feeling directionless once your "purpose" is removed.

Entrance costs can be plain cash. MLMs require big upfront investments for inventory you might never sell. Professional organizations sell the illusion of career advancement, for huge membership fees. Churches solicit tithes as proof of devotion. It all feels like investing in your future—but once the money's gone, it's hard to admit it might not pay off.

Then there are large group awareness trainings, where personal growth gets slapped with luxury pricing. These programs cost thousands—sometimes tens of thousands—for multiday intensives promising personal transformation. NXIVM charged $7,500 for a single "executive success" session.[11] Landmark Forum, Tony Robbins, and others use the upsell: advanced courses, one-on-one coaching, endless upgrades to "unlock your full potential." It's a spiral. People drain their savings, convinced they're building a better future, while the promised breakthroughs never quite arrive. Meanwhile, high-pressure tactics keep them hooked.[12]

And then there's college—even getting *in* costs money. AP exams, test-prep books, tutors, application fees, transcript fees, travel for campus visits, clothes for interviews—it adds up fast. Consultants to "boost" your application? Thousands more. By the time a student is admitted, many families have already spent more than they can afford, and many others don't have the resources to even compete. And graduate school? Medical, law, and MBA students face punishing schedules—endless classes, clinicals, internships. Hobbies vanish. Social lives disappear. Relationships suffer. Even basic self-care takes a backseat. According to the American Medical Association, approximately half of US medical students report experiencing burnout, which makes them more susceptible to depression compared to their non-medical peers.[13] And when someone dares to ask for better conditions, they're told, "You knew what you signed up for," as if that excuses everything.

It's the same in competitive sports and music. Elite leagues, travel tournaments, private lessons, equipment, audition fees—the costs are staggering. If your kid shows promise, the price only climbs: advanced coaches, elite programs, maybe even moving across the country. Talent without financial privilege doesn't get you very far. And again, the sunk cost fallacy kicks in. After years of lessons, training, and sacrifice, quitting feels impossible. In sports, this might mean tolerating abuse or dangerous regimens. In the arts, it can mean accepting toxic mentors or industry exploitation because "that's how it works."

But entrance costs aren't always as obvious as handing over a wad of cash. Take the military. On paper, enlisting looks like a straight shot to stability, education, and purpose, but the hidden entrance costs are steep. There's the unpaid prep—studying for the ASVAB (the Department of Defense's version of standardized testing), training for fitness tests—while juggling regular life. There's the emotional toll of leaving your home, friends, and everything familiar. The mental adjustment is massive. You enter a world where your personal autonomy is limited by strict rules, rigid hierarchies, and a culture that demands conformity. Most recruits have no clue about the long-term costs—injuries that don't heal, deployment trauma that sticks with you, or the uphill battle of figuring out civilian life after you get out.[14] The military's pitch sounds like an opportunity, but those entrance costs are higher than just signing your name on the dotted line—there's a reason we call it "signing away your life."

Some people push back when I draw comparisons between the military and cults. Their favorite argument is always, "At least in the military, you know what you're signing up for." But in both cases, you can't truly know what you're in for until much later. Then reality hits. As one sergeant barked at me: "I don't care what your recruiter told you. I own you now."

Margaret Singer said it best: "You usually do not learn the full story (and real purpose) of the cult until long after becoming embedded in the group."[15] Cult veteran or Army vet, most of us would agree: The life you're living six months later rarely matches the one you signed up for.

Time is another entrance cost that goes unnoticed, especially when it comes to our work. Late nights to "show initiative," unpaid weekends, endless meetings—it's baked into nonprofit culture ("for the greater good"), corporate culture ("be a team player"), and government jobs (endless red tape). The expectation to be always available seeps in quietly but ends up stealing your life: the Slack notifications on our phones, the habit of checking work email at night. Especially in the post-pandemic world where so many people work from home, the boundary between work and personal life has become even blurrier.

In work, school, the military, or a creative pursuit, our commitments require us to let go of certain things in order to focus on what we value most. Maybe we skip a party to study for a test, or pinch pennies to attend that writers' conference. The key word here is *choose*. Sacrifice, in itself, isn't a bad thing—it can even be empowering when it's in service of something we genuinely want and care about, and when it doesn't come at the cost of our well-being. But when those sacrifices no longer feel like choices, but obligations—driven by fear instead of passion—that's when you risk giving *yourself* up.

Which brings us full circle to exit costs. Because maybe the biggest, most hidden cost of all is having to go back to the people you left behind and say: "I was wrong."

The High Cost of Walking Away

For Karen, leaving the MLM was like ripping off a Band-Aid, only to find the wound underneath still raw and painful. She had spent thousands of dollars on inventory that she couldn't move, and walking away meant giving up the "business opportunity" she'd convinced herself would change her life. But worse than the financial fallout was the social fallout. The women she'd called her "sisters"—the ones who'd cheered her on during calls and bombarded her with motivational quotes—stopped responding to her texts, unfriended her, and cut her off completely. She was losing a community. The hardest part was the guilt. She had internalized so much of the MLM's messaging that she felt like a failure, like her inability to succeed was a reflection of her worth, instead of realizing the system itself was set up for her to fail.

For Becky, the exit was quieter, but still painful. After realizing she was spending more on conferences and products than she was making, she stopped attending the weekly "team calls" and posting sales pitches on Instagram. Her upline didn't confront her directly, but the silence was deafening. The women who had once bombarded her with emojis and encouraging messages when she hit a "personal best" went radio silent. Becky also had to face the reality of lost time. She had spent so many nights messaging strangers, attending virtual pep rallies, and pushing herself to meet quotas that she'd neglected her real friends and family. Rebuilding those relationships felt overwhelming, especially since so many people had written her off as "that MLM girl." Walking away meant confronting the shame she felt about everything she'd sacrificed to stay in the game for so long.

Both these women found themselves in a new, uncertain reality—lonelier and poorer perhaps—but finally free.

In every listicle telling you how to stay away from cults, you'll find a reference to exit costs. And very rarely does that mean only money, although we know cults are always after that too. The term *exit costs* captures all the ways leaving a high-control group can wreck a person's life: socially, financially, and psychologically. Exit costs are the invisible weight pressing down on every decision to leave, keeping people stuck even when they know they should run.

Social Exit Costs

Social ostracism is a nearly inevitable cost of leaving a high-control group. Members who walk away often lose their support systems, including family and friends who remain loyal to the group. The emotional toll is staggering, especially because the group has worked so hard to make you believe it's your only real family. For members of tight-knit groups—whether a religious cult, a "family"-oriented workplace, or a sorority or fraternity—leaving is framed as betrayal. If you've spent years, or your entire life, investing in this community, the idea of starting over can feel paralyzing. High-control groups exploit that fear. They warn you that life outside the group is bleak, dangerous, or doomed to failure.

When I was excommunicated from the cult at fifteen, it felt like losing everything in one brutal instant.* One day, I had a family, a home, and a role in the world—even if it was oppressive—and the next, I was nothing. Suddenly I was out in the world I'd been taught to fear, with no money, no education, and barely any family to rely on (though one incredible older sister took me in). Excommunication was like being erased from existence.

Many high-control groups enforce strict shunning practices to ensure that leaving feels like the end of your life. The Children of God wasn't unique in this. Jehovah's Witnesses, for example, use "disfellowshipping," in which baptized members who commit serious sins and are deemed unrepentant are formally removed from the congregation—parents won't speak to their own children, siblings become strangers, and lifelong friends will cross the street to avoid you.[16] In

* The concept of "excommunication" was complicated in the Children of God—and in my story specifically. You'll notice I sometimes say I "escaped" and other times that I was "excommunicated." Technically, because I had sex with someone outside the group, I would have been automatically excommunicated—unless I agreed to go through what they called a "partial excommunication." Essentially, that meant six months of imprisonment, including extra labor, reindoctrination, and endless readings of group doctrine. I said, "Nah, I'm out." (Though in *Uncultured*, I do talk about wavering and how my mom encouraged me to leave rather than recommit and submit to the punishments.) So, my parents arranged for me to live with my stepsister in Texas. There was no formal paperwork—our group didn't really operate that way—but excommunication in cases like mine was more or less automatic.

Separately, many cult survivors use the phrase "escaped a cult" regardless of the exact circumstances of their exit. Experts have affirmed that this language is valid—especially for children who were born into these groups, given no choice in joining, and never taught anything about the outside world.

2024 the Norwegian government revoked the Jehovah's Witnesses' legal registration and access to state funding, citing their shunning practices as the primary reason. That decision was overturned in 2025, but the government has appealed to the Supreme Court, where the case remains pending as of June 2025.[17]

Other American churches employ similar tactics, often under the guise of "church discipline." Evangelical, Baptist, and other conservative communities frequently excommunicate members who question doctrine, challenge leadership, or have lifestyles deemed "sinful." Pastors sometimes publicly name and shame people from the pulpit. Former members are treated as though they've betrayed both God and their loved ones. A notable example is Mars Hill Church, an evangelical megachurch founded in Seattle in 1996 and led by Mark Driscoll. Members who voiced concerns about leadership or doctrine were labeled unrepentant and dangerous, exiled from the community, and publicly shamed. After a 2014 investigation into the alleged abuse, Driscoll resigned, and the church dissolved its several campuses across several states.[18]

Even when groups don't explicitly demand shunning, the social result is the same. Former members of the Church of Jesus Christ of Latter-day Saints report feeling a subtle but unmistakable chill. They may not be excommunicated, but they're outsiders. Friends stop calling, family interactions grow stiff, and invitations disappear. Some are even labeled "apostates," a word heavy with meaning inside the church, one that signals someone who has not just left but betrayed the faith.[19] The exclusion isn't always loud or dramatic—relationships fade, glances are exchanged, and a once tightly knit community feels like a world they can't go back to.

And shunning isn't just a religious practice. Former members of Alcoholics Anonymous, for example, report being distanced or quietly judged by people who once supported them—regardless of whether they remain sober. Some are told they're "in denial" or "headed for relapse." My co-writer, Amy Reed, spent many years in AA and remembers this dynamic well. When someone decided AA wasn't for them, it was as if the relationship just quietly ended. Nothing was explicitly said, but everyone seemed to understand: That person was no longer part of the group. Phrases like "they went back out" or "they're doing more research" carried a heavy implication, code words that framed former members as unstable, uncertain, or unsafe—"slippery" people to be avoided, as if doubt itself were contagious. Maintaining sobriety, it seemed, required maintaining distance. In this way, shunning functioned as a silent safeguard. If someone stopped showing up to meetings, they simply disappeared. And for those who left, the shame of being cast out—or fear of being seen as a failure—could make it difficult to return or seek support elsewhere. The result is often a painful cycle of guilt, isolation, and disconnection.

When I left the Army at twenty-eight, the response was shockingly similar to what I experienced when I was excommunicated at fifteen. Though the military says "everyone transitions eventually," my departure was met with social exit costs: I was abruptly pulled from my position, isolated from colleagues, and given a lower evaluation. People spoke of my future in ominous tones, not realizing I'd already rebuilt my life once before. Critics often insist the military can't be a cult because "you're free to leave anytime." But my second rule of cults is that the cult will forgive any sin—except the sin of leaving.[*]

That rule applies even in the most gilded institutions—including one that calls themselves "The Family." We saw it play out in real time when Harry and Meghan stepped back from the British royal family. They were instantly cut off—financially, socially, and emotionally. The media turned on them, their security detail was revoked, and the family went silent. Meanwhile, Prince Andrew, accused of sexual abuse of minors, retained his residence and family ties. The message? Any sin is forgivable, except leaving.

Beyond personal relationships, leaving a high-control group means giving up the shared sense of purpose and identity the group provided. Life inside is highly organized and full of meaning. When you leave, you're losing your framework for existing. The emptiness left behind

---

[*] The first rule, as I wrote in *Uncultured*, is "You're not in a cult."

can feel overwhelming. Beyond losing people you love, you feel like you no longer belong anywhere. These social costs aren't incidental—they're strategic. The more a group controls your relationships and purpose, the harder it is to walk away.

One of the most defining aspects of being human is how deeply social we are. We rely on our communities not just for connection but for safety, identity, and survival. That's why social shunning cuts so deep—it doesn't just hurt, it destabilizes us. Rejection can feel like a kind of death.

Most of us carry such memories. Being iced out of a childhood friend group for speaking up, for being different, for not fitting in. For many, that pain only deepens with age: being rejected by family or faith communities for being gay, for questioning a belief, for refusing to conform. The fear of exile is so powerful that people choose silence over truth, compliance over authenticity. It's easier to stay in a toxic church, social circle, or political tribe than risk rocking the boat—and being thrown overboard.

Hate, after all, is its own kind of cult. And as we learned in the chapter about us-versus-them thinking, hate can build powerful community. A cruel, conditional kind—but community nonetheless. And in America, it often looks a lot like home.

Once you see how steep the social costs of leaving can be—the ones that technically don't "cost" anything—it becomes easier to understand the weight of financial exit costs. Because leaving a group you were told you were "free to leave anytime" comes with a bill. And sometimes that bill is steep.

Financial Exit Costs

Leaving a cult can trigger financial penalties—like forfeiting the assets, savings, or property you "donated" to the group. These traps are often invisible to outsiders, but for members, fear of losing everything they've built or having to start over from scratch is overwhelming. That's what makes financial exit costs such a powerful tool for control: They drain not just your wallet but your hope. And when hope disappears, so does the will to leave.

But these costs aren't only about assets. High-control groups often make their members reliant on them for basic needs like food, housing, and even employment. In the Children of God, you lived and worked in the commune; there was no outside job to fall back on if you left. In extreme religious groups like the FLDS and Twelve Tribes, members work for church-owned businesses, meaning their entire livelihood is tied to the institution. It's not much different from corporate setups where employees live in company housing and are locked into "free" meal plans—think oil rigs and remote fracking operations, cruise ships, amusement parks, agricultural and meatpacking labor camps, boarding schools, and tech companies with on-site campuses. In exchange for a place to live and all their needs being "taken care of," people are likely to put up with more abuse than they would otherwise.*

If you want to climb the spiritual ladder in Scientology, you better bring your checkbook. Nothing in this "religion" comes cheap—not enlightenment, not self-improvement, and definitely not freedom. Auditing, the church's signature form of spiritual counseling, can cost up to $800 per hour, and members are encouraged—some might say pressured—to buy in bulk. Think of it like therapy, except instead of working through childhood trauma, you're trying to rid yourself of invisible alien soul parasites, and instead of insurance covering the sessions, you're on the hook for a bill that rivals a small mortgage. Introductory courses may only be $35, but they don't count toward the mandatory advanced courses, each costing hundreds more.[20] Before long, many Scientologists find themselves thousands of dollars deep; some even mortgage their homes and take on more debt just to stay in.[21] And then there's the "freeloader debt"—a retroactive bill for

---

* People often agree that trading labor for room and board can be a fair arrangement. But if we follow the common guideline of spending no more than 20–25% of your paycheck on housing, a 40-hour workweek shows a different picture: Working more than 8–10 hours per week in exchange for room and board crosses into exploitation.

discounted or free services you received while working for the church, which you're obligated to pay back if you ever leave (in 2008, one family reportedly paid $147,183 in freeloader debt to cover trainings and services received by their two children while they were serving in the Sea Org[22]). It's the spiritual equivalent of quitting a job and getting a retroactive invoice for your training.

Financial entrapment is one of the most insidious tools these groups use. Debt isn't a side effect—it's a tactic. The fear of losing everything, from social connections to their life savings, keeps many people locked in place, unable to take the exit even when they desperately want to. Yet every one of these organizations insists "You're free to leave."

Silicon Valley's "golden handcuffs" of benefits are wrapped in sleek packaging: Stock options, bonuses, and equity can make staying seem worth it. But those options usually come with a four-year vesting schedule and a one-year cliff. Quit before year one and you get nothing. After that, shares vest slowly, keeping you chasing a payout that might never come. Meanwhile, long hours and toxic leadership wear you down. Performance bonuses and raises tied to tenure subtly nudge you to stay past your breaking point. For leadership roles, noncompete agreements ensure that leaving is professionally crippling. Agreements might bar employees from working for competitors for months, sometimes years, trapping them in a limbo where they can't take their experience anywhere else without a legal battle.

Medicine has its own brutal exit costs. The average med school debt as of 2023 was over $200,000, a burden taken on with the assumption of a stable, high-paying future.[23] But physicians are burning out at record rates, often feeling like cogs in a broken machine. Leaving medicine can mean a major salary drop, plus the loss of benefits like malpractice insurance, continuing education stipends, and conference support. Even when the job becomes unbearable, the financial structure is built to keep doctors in place.

Divorce, too, comes with financial costs. Ending a marriage means untangling a life that's been legally, financially, and socially fused, and that process can be expensive. Lawyers alone can cost a fortune—as much as a down payment on a house if things get ugly. Dividing assets, retirement accounts, businesses, and homes often involves penalties, forced sales, and long-term losses. Women, especially those who have taken on the caregiving roles, see significant income drops post-divorce—an average of 41 percent, according to the US Government Accountability Office—while men's household income fell by 23 percent.[24] Add in relocation, paying a mortgage or rent on a single income, restarting a career, rebuilding a life from scratch, and hopefully therapy for you and the kids (if you can afford it), and it's clear why many people stay in marriages they'd rather leave.

Underlying all of this is the concept of sunk costs. When you've poured years of your life and all your savings into something, the idea of leaving can feel like throwing all of that away and admitting it was all for nothing. That logic keeps people in cults, soul-crushing jobs, toxic relationships, MLM schemes, and broken systems. You convince yourself it's better to stick it out than admit you made a bad investment. That lie is the glue that holds these institutions together.

Psychological Exit Costs

Fear is foundational for maintaining control—whether it's fear of eternal damnation, failure, or the dangers of the outside world. In religious groups, members are warned that leaving means spiritual ruin or divine punishment. In AA, members often receive messaging that leaving means relapse and death. In secular groups, like workplaces or MLMs, the fear of failure and the shame of quitting can act as powerful psychological shackles that keep members tethered even when they're miserable. The intention is the same: Instill the belief that leaving equals doom.

Dr. Alexandra Stein emphasizes that fear is a key part of totalist control:

Isolation and engulfment alone are not enough. To brainwash a person—so that they will do your bidding regardless of their own survival-interest—the group must lock in their control of that person's emotional and cognitive life. This is the essence of totalist indoctrination. To isolation and engulfment must be added a third ingredient: threat. Any kind of threat will do, so long as the isolation and engulfment has already been established as the only safe haven.[25]

The outside world is dangerous, cruel, and meaningless without the group's protection—a paranoid worldview that is deeply internalized by the group's members.

Jim Jones told his isolated followers terrifying stories about the racist, capitalist, CIA-controlled outside world that wanted to destroy them. He drilled into them that defectors would be hunted down and tortured by enemies, and if they ever tried to leave, they'd not only be killed, but they'd be the reason the rest of the group was slaughtered too. It made revolutionary suicide sound not only noble, but logical. Similar narratives played out in the Children of God, where we were taught that "Systemites" (aka all outsiders) were cruel, brainwashed agents of Satan. When bad things would happen to "backsliders," especially if it was the suicide of a former member (a tragically common thing among cult survivors), that was proof.[26] Heaven's Gate also used apocalyptic framing: Earth was doomed, and members were told they were on a divine mission to leave the planet before it was "recycled." Anyone who left the group risked eternal separation from the "Next Level," forfeiting their only shot at transcendence.

The threat doesn't even have to be dramatic to be effective. It just has to be consistent. Cults know that once they've broken someone down, given them a new identity, and flooded their nervous system with fear, the mere suggestion that they might be alone, unloved, or unsuccessful "out there" is often enough to keep them tethered for years. What makes these psychological costs so powerful is their subtlety. The threats come wrapped in concern: *We're just worried for you. You'll be lost without us. You'll never find this kind of support again. No one will ever love you like I do.*

In many groups, members communicate these threats without even realizing it. Having been manipulated themselves, they sincerely believe that they are helping by trying to keep you from leaving. Whether it's the well-meaning folks "being of service" in AA, or that sweet old lady gently urging you to stay in the church fold, what looks like care is often control in disguise. And that kind of control—masked as love or concern—is the hardest to recognize, and even harder to resist.

Perhaps the largest psychological cost of leaving a high-control environment is figuring out who you are without the group. When every aspect of your life—what you believe, how you dress, who you love—has been dictated for you, walking away means dismantling the scaffolding of your identity. In the Children of God, we were told that the group was our family, our purpose, our salvation. So when I was excommunicated, I was losing *me*. It felt like peeling off every layer of myself, only to realize I wasn't sure what was left underneath. The pain was beyond physical and social—it was existential. Prolonged exposure to such coercive environments can lead to complex psychological distress known as religious trauma syndrome. Symptoms include confusion, anxiety, depression, and difficulty with decision-making, all of which make it even harder for individuals to distance themselves from the group and recover their autonomy.[27]

This identity rupture is echoed across other institutions. In the military, especially for career soldiers, your rank, uniform, even the way you speak, all become part of your identity. The "real world" is messy and ambiguous by comparison—no clear mission, no built-in camaraderie. And then there's the guilt: *Did I let my team down? Did I take the easy way out? Was that war even honorable?* The psychological exit costs linger for years, making it hard to move forward when a part of you still feels left behind.

Corporate environments aren't much different. One article on the job site Welcome to the Jungle flat-out says that the methods managers and HR use to enforce employee bonding and efficiency aren't so different from those used by cults.[28] TechTarget dives into how toxic work environments can instill a culture of fear that causes employees to feel "punished, rejected, guilty, defensive, and humiliated."[29] That kind of fear doesn't just make people quiet—it paralyzes them.

Self-improvement and spiritual groups often hook people through identity entanglement—entwining a person's sense of self with the group's beliefs, values, and purpose to the point where separating personal identity from group identity becomes nearly impossible—all while presenting themselves as paths to enlightenment but operating like high-demand organizations. "Healing" becomes another trap— one that pathologizes doubt and frames departure not as liberation, but as failure. And the scariest part? The void it leaves behind. No guru to supply the answers. No built-in community to mirror your worth back to you. Just you, standing alone. Terrified, but maybe for the first time, real. In a *Guardian* article that captures the emotional and existential impact of leaving the self-help and spiritual "healing" world, a survivor reports: "I was at saturation point with healing. I realised I had to stop trying to heal and recover from recovery."[30]

Leaving a religion means giving up beliefs, but moreover you're losing *certainty*. The framework that once gave your life meaning and direction is unraveling. Without it, you're in freefall. You feel guilt, shame, and the slow sting of exile from a community that once embraced you. And then there's the grief—because even if you know leaving was necessary, you're still mourning a version of yourself that once found comfort in faith, in ritual, in belonging. The hardest part often isn't always the walking away—it's figuring out who you are on the other side. The psychological toll of this deconstruction can mirror the symptoms of post-traumatic stress disorder (PTSD), because when your worldview and community vanish overnight, your nervous system doesn't know the difference between emotional exile and physical danger.[31]

Similar identity crises are reported across fields like education, the nonprofit sector, public safety, and the arts. When your work is deeply tied to your identity, walking away can feel like giving up on yourself. But eventually, you may realize that caring doesn't pay the bills, passion doesn't prevent burnout, and the system was never designed to sustain you. You grieve the version of you who believed you could change the world. You mourn the dreams you thought you'd realize, and wrestle with the guilt of finally choosing yourself. Teachers, first responders, and artists often describe the transition out of their field as a profound loss of meaning. Without that role, who are you?

First responders like firefighters, paramedics, and law enforcement have a particularly difficult transition. Their world is built on high-stakes camaraderie, trust, and shared trauma. Outside that world, nothing feels the same. The rush of the job—the sirens, the split-second decisions, the life-or-death stakes—is impossible to replicate, so civilian life feels dull and meaningless by comparison.[32] People may spend years numbing their PTSD with other work, but without that structure, the demons can creep in. The world moves on, but for them, the weight of what they've seen lingers. Finding purpose again feels like trying to breathe without oxygen. People who retire from public safety roles often face a profound identity crisis. Retirees commonly experience a loss of camaraderie and purpose, emphasizing the importance of preparing for these feelings and developing outside interests and support to ease the transition.[33]

At the core of it all, exit costs work because they tap into the deepest human fears: rejection, failure, and losing ourselves. This loss of identity, purpose, and belonging is what makes psychological exit costs so heavy. The grief is real. So is the fear. But these costs aren't signs that you've failed—they're signs that you've been deeply invested, shaped, and, in some cases, exploited.

High-control systems are built to make leaving feel impossible. But walking away isn't erasure—it's reclamation. You're not abandoning your identity; you're rebuilding it. And beyond the fear is something those systems never wanted you to find: your own freedom.

Recovering and Rebuilding

Leaving a high-control group isn't the end of the story—it's the start of a long, messy, deeply personal process. Many former members describe leaving a cult as a kind of psychological death—an idea echoed by cult expert Margaret Singer, who says, "The pariah image (from shunning) takes on an enormous proportion and comes to fit the image that seems a fate worse than death."[34] When you walk away, you lose your world, your people, your beliefs, your rhythm of life. Everything collapses. And standing at the edge of that wreckage, staring into the unknown, is terrifying. That's why so many people stay, even after the lies and abuse are exposed, even after the harm is done. Because the familiar pain can feel safer than the freefall into nothingness.

This is especially true for cults, but it echoes across other spaces where you've lost yourself: a career, a church, a cause, a relationship, a political identity, a community that promised meaning, belonging, purpose—and demanded everything in return.

The first thing many of us need is a lifeline, a new support system. High-control groups often isolate you until you're dependent on them and forget how to stand on your own. Leaving can feel like falling off a cliff with no one to catch you. But support groups, hobby communities, even Reddit threads—those can be a safe landing zone. Finding new people who understand you proves that you can belong somewhere else, that you're not alone in this.

Then comes the anger. For so long, we were taught to repress it, taught it was sinful, selfish, unspiritual, ungrateful, or proof that we were broken. But anger is not the enemy—it's evidence. It's your nervous system rising up to say, *What happened was wrong.* Rage is a natural response to betrayal and injustice. When we stop stuffing it down, it becomes fuel. It sharpens our instincts and returns our voice. And in that fire, we stop making excuses for what hurt us and start reclaiming our story.

Therapy can be an important part of healing—especially with someone who understands cult dynamics, religious trauma, spiritual abuse, coercion, or ideological entrapment. Whether it's unpacking years of fear and control or learning to trust yourself again, therapy can offer you space to grieve, rebuild coping and relationship skills, set boundaries, and begin imagining a life that isn't shaped by the group.

Of course, every healing journey is different—what works for one person may not work for another. Therapy is just one path, not a universal prescription. If you or someone you know has experienced a cult, consider finding support from a qualified mental health professional who understands this kind of trauma. I strongly recommend the International Cultic Studies Association website (icsahome.com), which offers a wealth of resources for cult survivors and their loved ones, as well as for researchers and mental health professionals.

One of the hardest parts of healing is figuring out who you are without the group. They often dictate everything: how you speak, who you can love, what you're allowed to want. So recovery means asking questions like "What do *I* want? What do *I* think? What are *my* values?" Sometimes reclaiming yourself starts as small as getting a haircut you weren't allowed to have or reading a book that was forbidden. Sometimes it means rebuilding your entire moral compass from scratch. However it begins, it can feel overwhelming—but also be the most liberating part of it all. (And I highly recommend wearing wacky outfits. Take up space. Be loud. Be weird on purpose.)

There's also real grief. For the people you left, for the beliefs you lost, even your sense of self. And the people who stay behind often see you as a threat, a traitor, a cautionary tale. That rejection cuts deep, especially when part of you has internalized those messages. Trying to reconnect with others can reopen that wound again and again. And sometimes, the only path forward is acceptance. Some relationships won't come back. And that is a brutal but necessary grief.

Leaving can leave you untethered, adrift without a "why." But that void can be fertile. You get to build a new why, one that's entirely your own. It might be a cause, a career, a creative passion, or simply learning how to be happy and how to live without shame. Many survivors find healing in helping others leave, by raising awareness, by turning pain into purpose. Especially for those of us whose labor was exploited, choosing where and how to give ourselves again can be an act of profound reclamation.

When you've been manipulated for so long, letting new people in is scary. When you've been used, trust becomes a minefield. But healing and learning to trust again start with small risks: A therapist.

A support group. A coworker who knows you only for who you are now. A friend who listens without trying to fix you. A kind stranger who reminds you that not everyone wants to control you. Learning to trust again—yourself, others, and the world—is part of the work.

But perhaps the most radical act of recovery is this: reclaiming joy. Cults, high-control groups, and toxic systems steal joy and turn pleasure into something shameful. So laugh, dance, sleep in, paint for no reason. Let your joy be loud, messy, and unapologetic. Joy doesn't have to prove its worth to matter. Sometimes the most defiant thing you can do is simply let yourself feel good again.

Eventually, many of us feel the urge to give back—not out of obligation, but out of deep empathy. Through telling our stories or quietly supporting someone else who's leaving, the act of helping can be healing too. It doesn't erase what happened, but it gives our pain purpose. It reminds us that life after the group isn't just possible—it is rich and beautiful.

Recovery isn't linear. There's no checklist, no perfect story arc. But the act of walking away, of choosing your freedom, is already a victory. It may feel like a death, but it's also the start of a new life—one where you decide what's sacred, what matters, and what's worth living for.

Chapter 10

The Ends Justify the Means: What Red Flags?

It started quietly, just a cryptic post on an obscure online forum. A breadcrumb here, a quirky question there, and before anyone realized what was happening, it had snowballed into a full-blown movement. Was it a cult? A conspiracy theory? Some kind of bizarre role-playing game? Nobody knew for sure, and that was part of the allure. This force sweeping America seemingly had something for everyone—a promise of secret knowledge, a righteous mission, and a chance to be part of a global battle between good and evil. It gave people a sense of purpose and a place to channel their anger in a world that felt increasingly unstable.

The power of this movement lay in its simplicity and adaptability. Followers could fill in the blanks with whatever fit their worldview, connecting dots that often didn't exist. It turned confusion into clarity, frustration into righteous action. People who felt overlooked or powerless suddenly had a mission: to save the world from an unseen enemy. Millions of others validated the narrative, reinforcing the sense of belonging that high-control groups thrive on. For some, it was harmless escapism, but for many, it became all-consuming.[1]

It came to a head on January 6, 2021. Cognitive dissonance, weaponized to the extreme, spilled over as the very people who had once sworn to defend democracy became its domestic enemies—military veterans, teachers, parents, and neighbors stormed the US Capitol, convinced they were fighting for a righteous cause. QAnon had done what cults do best: give people a narrative so compelling, with such clear good guys and bad guys, that they were willing to destroy everything they once believed in to protect it. What started as a fringe conspiracy became a movement that reshaped lives, ruined families, and tried to unravel democracy.

My Ex-Husband and the Path to Radicalization

One Sunday in February 2021, I saw an email pop up with a name I hadn't thought about in years: Major William Jeffrey Poole. My first thought was this had to be about my ex-husband's top-secret clearance review. It wasn't unusual for investigators to reach out to ex-spouses, even if the marriage had ended a decade earlier. I sighed, ready to tell them what little I could. Sure, he'd been controlling and toxic during our marriage, but they wouldn't care about that. They'd want to know if he'd committed treason or plotted the overthrow of the US government. For your typical US Army major, these are just check-the-box questions, the answers a resounding "no."

Not this time.

The email wasn't about clearance. Jeff had been accused of advocating armed insurrection against the government—including killing fellow service members. There would be a military tribunal to determine whether they'd kick him out for violent white-nationalist rhetoric. My heart pounded as my mind rifled through old memories, searching for clues I might have missed. I pictured him now, a self-proclaimed white supremacist, and to my surprise, I wasn't shocked. The signs had been there; I just hadn't recognized them for what they were.

As a former military intelligence officer, I'd been trained to spot indicators of violence in terrorist networks overseas. But when it came to my own ex-husband, I hadn't connected the dots. How had the Army missed it? How had I?

Jeff, like so many others, had fallen into a cult. His cult didn't have a commune or a single charismatic preacher, but the mechanics of control were the same. I knew them intimately. In the Children of God, isolation, an urgent mission, and a strict us-versus-them mentality trained me and thousands of others to follow unquestioningly. Our prophet warned us the outside world was dangerous, corrupt, and doomed. We were the chosen ones, and any sacrifice—of autonomy, of safety, even our lives—was worth it.

When I joined the Army, I saw the same ingredients. Basic training was isolation, indoctrination, and a special mission to protect and serve. Everything was designed to reprogram us to live and breathe Army values. Loyalty to the mission was paramount, and we learned to suppress any prick of conscience that suggested otherwise. I had already been programmed to ignore the voice in my head telling me something was wrong, so this came easily to me.

In the Army, I noticed how seamlessly hateful language slipped into everyday conversation. Racist slurs weren't aimed at just insurgents but also against our Afghan partners and civilians, dehumanizing them into enemies or obstacles. In the cult, we had our own words—"systemites," "backsliders," "apostates"—to erase outsiders' humanity. As an intelligence officer, I studied how terrorist groups used the same techniques to fuel violence.

So no, I wasn't surprised to learn that Jeff had become a self-described racist, bigot, National Socialist (the political party of Hitler), and an advocate of domestic terrorism. What did surprise me was his self-awareness of how it happened. In one Reddit post under investigation, he wrote:

> [Liberal media] bias will continue to push people into right wing discussion spaces, as they're the only ones that still allow free and open discussion on all topics. And that, in turn, will push more people to the extreme political right.

It happened to me. 3 years ago, I was a pretty moderate guy, on the fence between Sanders & Trump as I saw them both as status quo breakers. Then they sold our /r/politics and /r/worldnews to agenda driven interests, and it was obvious. Then they banned /r/fatpeoplehate and then /r/cringeanarchy. Again and again, they silenced people and banned places that allowed people to say whatever they wanted. They wiped out all the right wing political facebook pages in Italy weeks before an election. So I kept seeking out places where people were free to say whatever they wanted, and reading the ideas, and statistics and memes I found along the way. Now I'm so far right I don't believe in democracy anymore (democracy is mob rule, and the mob is easily controlled by the media, so democracy is media rule, aka the 'elite'), and I think violence is the only way to break the stranglehold that these cultural marxists have on our society.[2]

Though Sanders and Trump seemed ideologically opposite, I immediately understood why both appealed to Jeff—who's the type of white man angry about the world diversifying and modernizing without centering guys like him. The type of man who once walked up to me—his wife—after I gave a valedictorian speech (after escaping a cult with no formal education), only to tell me the other guy's speech was "funnier."

In *Mediocre: The Dangerous Legacy of White Male America*, Ijeoma Oluo tells us:

These [Bernie bros] were white men who felt personally wronged by our system and were dedicated to Sanders' campaign for their own self-interests. The anger they voiced over the cruelties of establishment politics, their disdain for "liberal elites," and their feeling of exclusion from modern-day "identity politics" felt like a funhouse mirror of the grievances of white male Trump supporters.[3]

Both candidates appealed to the emotions of working-class white men. Both positioned themselves as outsiders who wanted to shake up a broken system. But Trump did something Sanders didn't—he transformed that frustration into cultural resentment. He gave that anger a face, an easily identifiable enemy: immigrants, liberals, feminists, trans people, anyone who could be categorized as other. He gave voice to white men's sense of lost status in an increasingly diverse country, appealing to their grief and rage with promises to help them "take their country back." Sanders, by contrast, envisioned a country that worked for everyone—including the very people Trump vilified. His message was rooted in solidarity and structural change, not scapegoating. But when Sanders exited the race, he left behind a vacuum—especially among voters who already distrusted the system. Trump swooped right in to fill that space, fuel their distrust, and deepen their belief that the whole game was rigged against them.

Looking back, I see how inevitable Jeff's shift was. I think of my ex-husband back when he was just Lieutenant Poole—he was bright, passionate about making a difference in the world, thinking about maybe entering politics after the military. I can see how his desire to fit in drove him more than most people—at first with fraternities and shooting clubs, and then in the Army, moving from a support role into combat arms, following the drive to be more elite, more glorified.

As we've explored throughout this book, radicalization thrives on isolation and the promise of belonging. People who become radicalized aren't gullible or uneducated—they feel disconnected, unseen, or like they're not enough. High-control groups promise them significance.[4] And so many young white men, across the political spectrum, feel isolated by today's world—not understanding that the cult of patriarchy demanded that isolation of them in the first place. They have been taught to reject vulnerability, suppress emotion, and measure worth through dominance, leaving them disconnected from each other and from themselves.

As discussed in chapter 2, all humans have a fundamental need to matter and be recognized by others—a "quest for significance," according to researchers Katarzyna Jasko, Gary LaFree, and Arie Kruglanski. The people most likely to be drawn into violent ideologies tend to be those who feel socially isolated—often divorced or lacking close relationships. They're disconnected from grounding social structures that might keep them tethered to reality.[5] This pattern shows up in cults, extremist movements, and institutions like the US military. My own experience, and the work of scholars like Alexandra Stein and Lorne Dawson, makes it clear: What extremist groups offer isn't just ideology—it's emotional attachment, camaraderie, and a sense of meaning that feels like love.

As Jeff climbed the Army ranks, he simultaneously moved into more elite, more masculine, more white spaces—systems built to reward stoicism, obedience, and a willingness to sacrifice. His drive to fit in, to be part of something bigger, made him vulnerable to the rhetoric and ideology that eventually consumed him. And Jeff wasn't an anomaly. An NPR analysis found that nearly one in five Capitol rioters charged were military veterans: Ashli Babbitt, the one person directly killed in the ensuing violence that day; Larry Brock, the man with the zip ties dangling from his belt, which he'd brought as handcuffs; and Jacob Chansley, the so-called QAnon Shaman—all veterans.[6] Their radicalization wasn't an accident. The same conditioning that made them effective soldiers—obedience, group cohesion, and mission focus—also left them susceptible to extremist recruitment, which prizes veterans for their skills, discipline, and perceived legitimacy.[7]

MAGA and its extremist offshoots have infiltrated countless aspects of American life, turning workplaces, school boards, and family gatherings into battlegrounds for ideological warfare.[8] The same high-control mechanisms we've explored in this book—fear, us-versus-them thinking, a charismatic leader, and so on—are all at play. The rhetoric of "Make America Great Again" taps into deep-seated fears about loss and change; it offers a seductive story about returning to a nostalgic (and imagined) past where everything made sense and everyone knew their place.[9] It creates a mission, a crusade that justifies everything from disrupting public meetings to storming the Capitol. For many people, it fills a void, providing a sense of purpose and community in a fractured world. MAGA doesn't just rally individuals—it radicalizes them, convincing ordinary people that they're part of a historic battle where any means justifies the end of saving their version of America.[10]

Necessary Evil and the Cult of Winning

Throughout this book, we've explored the many red flags that signal a group becoming toxic. But what's critical to understand is that these signs of control often *are* the very means by which members believe they will achieve their ultimate goals. In these environments, people are willing to accept a shifting definition of what is "necessary" to win—and the importance of *winning at all costs*. And when winning becomes the only goal, anything can be justifiable.*[11]

Nowhere is this mentality more visible today than in the MAGA movement. On November 8, 2016, much of America watched in disbelief as Donald Trump became the forty-fifth president of the United States. Then, eight years and an attempted armed insurrection later, we watched it happen again. People have struggled to understand the unwavering support he commands, especially from groups that traditionally champion "morality" and "family values." After all, Trump—a thrice-divorced man embroiled in scandals and now a convicted felon—seems to contradict everything these groups claim to stand for. Yet to anyone familiar with the psychology of cults, this steadfast allegiance isn't surprising at all.

Cults don't arise with overt extremism; they emerge gradually, fueled by hope, fear, and identity. Followers don't believe they are joining a destructive movement—they believe they're answering a higher calling.[12] And the larger the group grows, the less it feels like extremism at all. Cult mentality can emerge anywhere people surrender their loyalty to a leader who they believe embodies their identity. I've

* As noted earlier, I'm cautious about citing Steven Hassan due to his documented transphobic views. However, he was among the first to widely publish on the concept of Trumpism as a cult, and while he is by no means the only voice in this area, his work has been influential. For that reason, I reference him here—albeit with reservations.

been told that 77 million people (the number of Americans who voted for Trump in 2024) can't be in a cult. But numbers don't inoculate a group from cult dynamics. In fact, the larger the group, the stronger the social pressure is to conform.

Growing up in the Children of God, I learned that we were chosen and the rest of the world was doomed. When the apocalypse we were promised didn't arrive in 1993, our leaders simply shifted the narrative: God had given us more time. The prophecy had failed, but the faith remained. This, too, is how political cults survive failed prophecies— by redefining winning and moving the goalposts.

Donald Trump has followed a familiar blueprint. He has positioned himself as the lone protector against an array of existential threats: the "deep state," immigrants, liberal elites, the media, political opponents—and now with Trump 2.0, DEI initiatives, government workers, higher education, and the trans community. He has painted them as enemies out to destroy America, fostering a siege mentality among his followers. This constant sense of threat makes the group more insular, more paranoid, and more loyal.[13] In this climate of fear, Trump's flaws aren't disqualifying; they're seen as badges of authenticity. He is being attacked *because* he's right. The more the world condemns him, the more his followers cling to him and deepen their self-image as persecuted victims.

This psychological investment enables a disturbing trend: people fully embracing "the ends justify the means" thinking.[14] Trump supporters who once championed constitutional originalism now cherry-pick which amendments they uphold, invoking the Second Amendment while ignoring birthright citizenship and the separation of powers. Executive overreach, defying court orders, silencing dissent— methods that would spark outrage if used by political opponents—are excused or celebrated when used in service of their cause. Democracy is no longer the goal. As my ex-husband bluntly put it, "I don't believe in democracy anymore."

Examples of ends justifying the means are everywhere. Trump supporters accepted or actively spread false claims about the 2020 election being stolen, despite overwhelming evidence to the contrary, because keeping Trump in power was seen as essential to saving America. The violent storming of the Capitol on January 6 was rationalized as necessary patriotism—a defense of the nation rather than an attack on democracy. Personal scandals that would have ended other political careers were overlooked because the policies Trump promised—such as judicial appointments, immigration crackdowns, and fighting "wokeness"—were seen as more important than integrity. Harsh immigration practices, like the separation of families at the border, were accepted as unfortunate but necessary deterrents. Disinformation, conspiracy theories, and doctored memes were willingly spread to damage political opponents and reinforce the movement's narrative. Authoritarian calls for investigations into political enemies, often without clear legal basis, were cheered as righteous efforts to "drain the swamp."[15] In each case, people abandoned traditional moral or democratic principles in service of a larger goal. In each case, the mentality is the same: *The stakes are too high to play fair.* When America itself is seen as being on the brink of destruction, anything is justifiable to prevent that outcome—even destroying the democratic principles Trump's followers claim to defend.

But this phenomenon isn't unique to MAGA. It is a pattern deeply rooted in how extremist groups grow. Willingness to abandon the truth is not incidental—it's foundational. In high-control groups, lying to outsiders is considered morally righteous. In the Children of God, these lies were called "deceivers yet true," a warped belief that lying was virtuous if it protected the mission. Systemites weren't worthy of the truth. Telling them the whole story might confuse them— or worse, they'd find a way to twist it against us. So we spun stories, omitted details, and sometimes outright lied about, for instance, where donations were really going. It didn't count as deception if it was serving God.

As described by Singer and Lalich in *Cults in Our Midst*, other groups use different names for lying. In some evangelical circles, it's called "heavenly deception" or "transcendental trickery." Others justify lying when "talking to the Babylonians," cautioning followers not to "cast your pearls before swine." In Mormon splinter groups, it's known as "lying for the Lord." Among mainstream Mormons, it's framed more gently: "It's not secret; it's sacred." Whatever the term, the message is the same: Some people don't deserve the truth.[16] This kind of lying reinforces us-versus-them thinking and turns secrecy into a virtue. When you're convinced you're one of the few who truly "gets it," every act of concealment feels like proof of your specialness. And that kind of secrecy binds you more tightly to the group, making it even harder to leave or to trust anyone on the outside.

As Janja Lalich explains, deception in cults isn't aimed only at outsiders—it becomes internalized. Members are often deliberately kept in the dark about leadership misconduct, inner conflict, the actual size or influence of the group, and how the outside world truly sees them. Over time, the group begins lying to itself as much as it lies to everyone else.[17] This bubble of misinformation is reinforced by leaders and inner circles to ensure people can't make real assessments about what's happening. And when the whole group is repeating the same myths, those myths start to feel like reality. "Fake news" is the only news they hear. Truth becomes subjective. Loyalty replaces honesty. And secrecy becomes sacred.

In the military, secrecy is institutionalized—need-to-know briefings, redacted missions—because too much transparency could jeopardize the mission. Secrecy extends to interactions with families and civilians, where leaders soften facts about deployments, injuries, or mental health to "protect the team" or maintain morale. Everyone knows no unit completes every required training every year—and yet those sign-offs roll up the chain. It's not always lying in the traditional sense, but it's a learned manipulation of information, where shaping the truth becomes second nature.

In corporate America, the same dynamics play out with a shinier gloss. Steve Jobs famously used his "reality distortion field" to bend inconvenient facts and shape perceptions to match his vision. As Emily Chang wrote in *Brotopia*, acceptable lying, especially in startup culture, is often seen as part of the game.[18] Elizabeth Holmes was treated as a cautionary tale—but she was really a sacrificial lamb for the collective lie all startups tell to survive and scale. Across industries and ideologies, the pattern repeats: Protect the mission, even if it means bending the truth. Lying becomes holy, deception becomes virtue, and the first compromises of integrity are cloaked in righteousness.

Nietzsche's concept of pia fraus, or "pious fraud," is disturbingly at home in these worlds of startup myth and charismatic leadership. He used the term to describe the lies told in service of a supposedly greater moral or spiritual truth—deceptions that are justified because they preserve the illusion necessary for maintaining order or belief. In cults, religions, and increasingly in corporations, pia fraus becomes the sacred glue holding the whole thing together. The story is massaged, the numbers fudged, the device doesn't quite work but the pitch deck says otherwise. What matters is that you believe in the mission. That's why a reality distortion field can be hailed as visionary leadership, and why an Elizabeth Holmes can channel her inner prophet, faking the miracle until it's too late to admit it never existed. Pia fraus is why so many people in tech and startup idolize Peter Thiel,* who, in his book *Zero to One: Notes on Startups, or How to Build the Future*, openly embraces strategic misdirection as a business practice, alongside monopolistic ideology and the founder-as-savior archetype, describing startups as small, cultlike tribes—all in glowing terms.[19]

In these systems, the fraud is the faith. And the more people you can get to believe in the righteousness of your deception, the holier the lie becomes. History shows us that no cult, no authoritarian movement, starts with obvious extremism. It begins with a shared mission, a feeling of righteousness, and an us-versus-them worldview. From there, small

---

* It's worth pointing out Thiel's famous quote from his 2009 essay "The Education of a Libertarian" in the online journal *Cato Unbound*: "I no longer believe that freedom and democracy are compatible." His words are eerily similar to my extremist ex-husband's: "I don't believe in democracy anymore."

ethical compromises accumulate. Members are told their sacrifices are necessary for the greater good. Slowly, almost imperceptibly, the group crosses lines its members once swore they would never cross.

As my friend and manager Lizy Freudmann perfectly put it: "The defining feature of a line in the sand is that it's easily erased." By the time the line is crossed—whether it's lying to outsiders, participating in violence, endorsing abuse, or willfully ignoring harm—it doesn't feel like a line at all. It feels like loyalty, purpose, and righteousness. And that's why the slow descent into extremism is so terrifying—it happens so gradually that by the time you look back, you can't recognize who you were before.

The End Was Always the Point

At the heart of many high-control groups lies a dangerous certainty: the belief that the future is already written. This is the essence of teleological thinking—the conviction that history is moving toward a predetermined outcome, whether ordained by God, destiny, or some inevitable arc of progress. People inside the system feel reassured by the belief. If everything is unfolding exactly as it should, then there's no need to question, resist, or reimagine. Doubt becomes irrelevant. Morality becomes secondary to momentum.

When a group leader insists that a particular outcome is fated, they reframe members' obedience as virtue and dissent as heresy. If the future is locked in, then any action taken in its service—no matter how extreme—is the justifiably correct one. A lie becomes strategy. A crime becomes sacrifice. Violence becomes prophecy fulfilled.

Teleological thinking also creates a closed loop. If one path is inevitable, then every alternative is not just wrong but dangerous. Compromise turns into treason. Debate becomes attack. Soon people stop asking if they're doing the right thing—they start asking how quickly they can get there. It's a shortcut to extremism, where the "greater good" eclipses moral nuance and individual conscience. If the end is guaranteed—if your cause is just and preordained—then what's a little rule-bending, or a "white" lie*, or a strategically leaked war plan (#signalgate)? If the future is locked in, anything done in its service feels justified. And studies show that this kind of binary thinking isn't a personality quirk—it's a key cognitive trait linked to extremism.[20]

Paired with this belief in destiny is its shadow twin: apocalyptic thinking—the conviction that the end of the world is not only coming but must come, and soon. In many high-control groups, the apocalypse is something to be prepared for, even welcomed. Cults are especially fluent in this logic. The promise of imminent collapse creates urgency, loyalty, and a heightened sense of purpose. When you believe the world is about to end, ordinary life becomes trivial. Personal safety, long-term planning, relationships—all of it fades in importance compared to the role you've been assigned in the dramatic grand finale.

From the Puritans' vision of a "New Jerusalem" to nineteenth-century millennial movements like the Millerites—whose "Great Disappointment" gave birth to new sects like the Seventh-day Adventists when the second coming didn't happen as predicted—the story of America is full of prophetic endings and divine missions. Leaders have used apocalyptic fervor to justify colonization, war, revolution, and social cleansing. The vocabulary has changed over time, but the emotional logic remains: We are the elect, the world is corrupt, and judgment is coming.

As some scholars have pointed out, modern political movements and conspiracy theories continue to echo these early apocalyptic impulses—the end-of-the-world narrative is as American as apple pie.[21] Trump's 2024 campaign framed the political landscape as the "final battle," with him as the last hope to save America from collapse. His supporters—saturated with conspiratorial messaging about stolen elections, an immigrant invasion, and cultural decay—genuinely believe the country teeters on the edge of ruin. Some Christian nationalists have even interpreted scripture to justify violent political

---

* Note the coded language here. "White" signals harmless, implying dark or black is dangerous.

objectives, convinced they're fighting a holy war.[22] Surveys now show that a growing number of Americans—especially within right-wing circles—believe political violence is warranted to "save" the nation.[23] In that light, extreme actions feel not just acceptable but necessary. Trump's embrace of conspiracy theories and extremist rhetoric led directly to January 6—not only the riot, but the manifestation of apocalyptic thinking. His followers believed they were defending their country from annihilation.

A convergence of teleological and apocalyptic thinking is where things get truly dangerous. When people believe not only that the future is inevitable but that the present must be purged to reach it, anything becomes permissible. These frameworks go beyond rationalizing authoritarianism—they demand it. After all, if you're racing toward salvation or collapse, who has time for due process or debate?

This mindset permeates mainstream politics, social movements, and public discourse. We hear it in slogans like "the right side of history" or "this is our last chance." We see it in doomsday headlines, existential campaign ads, and climate narratives that alternate between urgency and despair. Teleology and apocalypse aren't just religious ideas anymore—they're political strategies. And when fear and destiny work together, they can override logic, suppress dissent, and make people feel morally obligated to obey.

This psychological landscape is fertile ground for high-control leaders, who offer more than answers—they offer destiny. They don't predict collapse—they orchestrate it. And for their followers, the cost of leaving reaches existential levels: To walk away is to abandon the only story that makes sense of their suffering.

That's why ruptures are so rare, and so painful when they happen. Because to leave a group steeped in apocalyptic teleology is to say: *Maybe the world isn't ending. Maybe there is no grand plan. Maybe we were wrong.*

And that kind of uncertainty is its own kind of apocalypse.

The Mirror of Extremism

We like to think we're immune to extremism, but we're likely picturing violent mobs and fringe groups. Extremism actually begins with something much quieter: a longing to belong, a desire for clarity, a need to feel safe in an overwhelming world. The same psychological forces that bind people to cults—fear, isolation, identity, us-versus-them—exist in the mainstream. They're part of the human experience, woven into our politics, our workplaces, our wellness circles, our spiritual communities, our families. Extremism, in all its forms, is simply the most visible symptom of deeper cultural wounds—unaddressed inequalities, unmet emotional needs, and systemic failures, dressed up as ideology—that drive people to seek comfort in binary answers and rigid groups.

Movements like MAGA make the reflection sharper. For many followers, it isn't really about politics—it's about pain, finally feeling seen after years of invisibility, and finding their purpose in the promise to restore something lost. The "loss" they mourn often stems from a privileged position built on generations of systemic inequality and abuse, but their feelings are real, whether we like them or not. The rhetoric of persecution and the rallying cry to restore greatness are more than slogans. They're lifelines for people who feel forgotten, betrayed, or overwhelmed by a system that no longer seems to serve them. Like any high-control group, MAGA became a tribe—a community offering purpose, clarity, and a shared enemy. And in that tribe, loyalty is currency. As much as it mirrors a traditional cult, MAGA also reveals the unmet needs of millions of Americans who are simply desperate for meaning.[24]

What makes extremism so dangerous isn't its boldness—it's how quietly it seeps in. Cults don't start with mass suicide or pledges to storm the Capitol. They start with small things: a shared belief, an inspiring leader, a feeling of belonging. They start with language—words like *awakening, truth, resistance, patriotism*. And before long, that language becomes identity, and identity becomes dogma. The

254   Daniella Mestyanek Young

most dangerous ideas aren't shouted—they're whispered in living rooms, reinforced in group chats and family dinners, slowly absorbed until they feel like common sense (and sometimes accidentally texted to a journalist or two).[25]

Social proof—the psychological tendency to look to others for cues on how to think and behave, and how to determine what's safe, what's normal, and what's good—makes it even harder to question. According to Dr. Robert Cialdini in *Influence*, we evolved this way for survival. If everyone's running from the tiger, you probably should too. But in modern systems, that instinct can backfire.[26] As J. Richard Hackman says in *Leading Teams: Setting the Stage for Great Performances*, humans will do almost anything to be accepted by a group they voluntarily joined.

How often do you actually stop and question a group norm? How often do you ask why you're clapping, nodding, agreeing? Do you just assume it's okay because everyone else is doing it? Psychotherapist Santiago Delboy writes that our need for approval can show up in obvious ways—excessive people-pleasing, avoiding confrontation—but it also reveals itself in subtler forms like having an agreeable personality or being easygoing.[27] In short, we will do almost anything to fit in. Until, one day, we don't recognize ourselves.

That's how we got to January 6. People like Peter Stager—who likely called himself a patriot and believed Blue Lives Matter—didn't wake up that morning planning to beat a police officer with a flagpole. "That entire building is filled with treasonous traitors," he was caught on video saying. "Death is the only remedy for what's in that building."[28] I doubt he saw the irony in his words. I'm sure, in that moment, he truly believed he was doing a service to his country, his cause, his team. He didn't see the holes in his logic—because that's how cognitive dissonance and cult-think work.

We are all at risk. We are seeing cultlike movements reemerge across American life, much like they did during the political and cultural turmoil of the 1960s. Modern spaces—from gyms to coaching seminars—capitalize on the need for belonging and clarity in a confusing world. Wherever there's uncertainty, there's someone promising clarity. Wherever there's disconnection, someone is selling belonging. Methods of coercion are startlingly adaptable, because the human needs they exploit are universal.

Because that's the thing about extremism: Binary thinking feels good. It's clean. It's simple. It tells you who you are, what you believe, and who your people are. It tells you who to trust—and who to hate. But nuance is harder. Questioning is harder. Yet that discomfort is where truth lives.

I've spent my life answering the same questions: How could anyone stay in a group like the Children of God? How could anyone follow a man who preached religious prostitution and sanctioned child abuse? But inside a group, almost anything can become normal—especially when it meets your deepest psychological needs. The Children of God has operated for over fifty years. Why? Because cults that last often do a lot of things *right*, whether by accident or design. Maslow's hierarchy of needs tells us that once people have food and safety, their next craving is belonging. Building on that, David McClelland suggested we're all driven by three key motivators: the need for affiliation, the need for achievement, and the need for power.[29] Cults, in all their forms, know how to check all those boxes. They don't just manipulate people. They meet them where they're most vulnerable.

So the real question is not "How could they believe that?" It's "Where does that same logic live in me?"

Extremism works because it's comforting. It makes complexity disappear. It gives you certainty—an idea explored in Eric Hoffer's *The True Believer*. What we fail to recognize is how fast the slide can be, how quickly we can come to believe that the ends justify the means, how easily we can find ourselves obeying a leader who says it's okay to harm others—even our own children—and not know how to walk away.

We all have our cults. Groups we believe in. Ideas we defend without question. Maybe they're political, religious, familial, professional. And maybe they're benign—until they're not. They become dangerous the moment we stop asking questions. The moment they demand we choose them over our own values, and we say yes.

But sometimes, the spell breaks. Not all at once—but gradually, something starts to feel off. A crack forms: a contradiction too blatant to ignore, a moment of real harm that jars the nervous system awake. The logic that once seemed airtight begins to unravel, and the belief system that once felt like truth starts to look more like a cage. Sometimes it's as subtle as realizing the utopia that was promised isn't coming—and maybe never was.

For some, it starts with the hypocrisy—watching a leader preach sacrifice while living in luxury. For others, it's witnessing the mistreatment of someone else—a friend, a child, a partner—and feeling that gut-level recognition: *This isn't right.* Sometimes it's political—followers growing disillusioned when policies start to hurt their businesses, their families, their 401ks. These are moments of cognitive dissonance: when the mind can no longer hold two conflicting beliefs at once, and something's got to give. Ex-cult members almost always describe a moment like this—not just when the spell weakened, but when it fractured. When they stepped back, even just for a second, and said, "Wait a minute. This doesn't make sense." Ex-Mormons have a phrase for it: the moment the "shelf breaks."[30] It's the moment when the weight of all the unanswered questions finally crashes down. And while that moment can feel like the end—a collapse of identity, faith, or belonging—it's actually the beginning. It's the first real step toward freedom.

Leaving isn't easy. It means questioning everything that once gave your life meaning. It means facing the ache of "What if I was wrong?" But people do it. All the time. And each time, it's a testament to the strength of the human spirit—not just to survive indoctrination, but to unlearn it. Education, exposure to new perspectives, and supportive relationships are lifelines during this process. Just hearing a different viewpoint or encountering someone who contradicts the group's narrative can begin to widen those initial cracks. The more people reengage with the outside world, the harder it becomes for the cult's totalizing story to hold. Freedom comes not from flipping a switch, but from slowly, stubbornly reclaiming one's ability to think independently again.

The thing about extremism—whether in cults, conspiracies, or toxic ideologies—is that it arrives dressed as hope. Then it builds slowly, layer by layer, with just enough logic to make you believe you're choosing it. That's why the red flags matter: the suppression of dissent, the glorification of loyalty, the pressure to cut off outsiders, the belief that nuance is dangerous and questioning is betrayal. These are signs of any system that trades humanity for control—and they're showing up everywhere. In political movements. In workplaces. In wellness communities and religious institutions. Even in our own relationships. The only real antidote is awareness. When we begin to see these control tactics for what they are—not mystical sacred truths, not destiny, not justice, but manipulation—we start to reclaim our power. Whether we're disentangling from a high-control group, a conspiracy theory, or just a toxic belief system that's lived in our heads too long, that clarity is everything. The real victory isn't just in walking away—it's learning to live in the whole beautiful, confusing spectrum between binaries. It's in rebuilding a life where questioning is safe, where doubt is allowed, and where complexity is welcomed instead of feared. That's where healing begins.

Extremism shows us what happens when we cling to certainty and belonging at the cost of truth. But it also illuminates what's possible when people begin to wake up. There is no single answer, no perfect system, no utopia. But there is this: the ability to think for ourselves, to choose complexity over simplicity, and to keep walking—together—toward something more human.

And that, maybe, is the real story: not how people get trapped—but how they find their way out.

Humans are a profoundly social species. As Yuval Noah Harari explains in *Sapiens*, many thousands of years ago we learned that groups made us stronger. As we gathered in larger communities, we developed stories, myths, and religions to regulate behavior, build trust, and help us coexist more peacefully. Shared narratives allowed us to cooperate in increasingly large and complex groups. From those beginnings, we went on to build systems—political, economic, religious, and social structures—designed to outlast and outperform any individual. These systems became the source of human power and dominance over the natural world. But while we designed them to be strong, we also built those systems in our own image—flawed, biased, and afraid. And now many of them no longer work for the vast majority of people. Systems persist not because they are fair or functional, but because they are self-sustaining, as designed.[31] Yet despite their flaws, we can no longer live outside them. The myth of rugged individualism is just that—a myth. According to research from the National Bureau of Economic Research, excessive emphasis on individualism undermines collective responses to urgent problems, such as public health crises or climate change—the increasingly tragic effects of which we're seeing on a national and global scale every day.[32]

Real change will take collective courage. It will take communities willing to name what isn't working, to question what we've accepted for too long, and to build something better in its place. Individual action, while valuable, is not enough to confront the scale of today's systemic problems. Whether we're talking about inequality, polarization, or global environmental collapse, meaningful change requires collective solutions—by communities that are connected, informed, and working together. Community, not individualism, is our best hope for addressing systems that no longer serve us, especially now, as the logic of those systems is breaking down.

Chapter 11

Just Groups

Dear Reader,

Imagine entering a space where the air crackles with electricity, the kind of energy that makes your chest feel tight and your skin tingle, where anticipation hums in every breath and a strange excitement radiates from the crowd. The people here, thousands of them, are adorned with handmade tokens, beads and charms clinking together in intricate bracelets, each one a tiny offering. Their clothing is more than fashion; it's coded, symbolic, chosen with near-religious devotion to honor distinct phases of a shared mythology.

There's a ritualistic energy in the air, like the moment before a sermon or a sacred rite. Faces shine with fervor, eyes wide with reverence. Strangers clasp hands, chant lyrics in unison, and cry without shame. It's not just a gathering—it's a pilgrimage. You feel it in your chest, the unmistakable sensation that you are entering something larger than yourself, something that demands not just your attention but your transformation.

Then the lights drop.

The opening notes drift in—familiar, haunting. The crowd erupts. The roar is so unified it doesn't feel like individual voices but a single, unstoppable wave of sound. It's not applause; it's an invocation. For a moment, it feels like nothing outside exists. Time bends. Reality tilts. You are no longer merely an observer. You are inside a story, one that stretches across decades and emotional lifetimes.

The journey that follows is seamless, hypnotic. Each chapter flows into the next: innocence to heartbreak, glitter to grit, rebellion to rebirth. Every costume change, every lighting cue, every breathless pause is part of the ritual. The songs aren't performed; they're lived, reenacted, devoured. The experience becomes an emotional deluge, waves of joy and pain crashing in so rapidly that you can barely stay afloat. The intensity leaves you lightheaded, dissociated; your body and mind can't keep up with the flood of emotions. Singing along doesn't feel optional; it's mandatory, a call to unify, and as your voice blends into the sea of thousands, you feel seen, understood, and part of something much bigger than yourself.

Yet that unity comes at a cost: To belong here, you give up a little bit of yourself. Not forever, perhaps, but for the duration of this ecstatic surrender. To fully immerse yourself, you have to shed your individuality, even if only for the night. Your voice disappears into the mass. Your memories fuse with the lyrics. Your boundaries soften until you're not sure whose story is being told. Is it hers, or is it yours?

By the time the final chorus fades and the lights return to their earthly glow, you're wrung out, exhilarated, and vaguely disoriented. You look around at the glitter-covered faces, the smeared mascara, the strangers who now feel like kin. You've just spent hours in the world of one woman's art and emotion, a place built meticulously and inhabited so fully that leaving it feels like waking from a dream.

Only then, as you step outside and catch your breath, does it hit you: This wasn't just any concert. This was *the* concert. You've just lived through the Eras Tour. You've just been inducted—body, heart, and soul—into the world of Taylor Swift.

* * *

If you were a teenager when *Fearless* came out—old enough to be falling in love for the first time, sneaking drinks at high school parties, and dreaming about something bigger—you probably grew up *with*

Taylor. Her heartbreaks mirrored your own. Her reinventions tracked your coming-of-age. Each album felt like a collective diary entry you didn't know you needed until you hit play.

And then there are the millennial women—along with Gen X and older—who didn't discover their inner Swiftie until adulthood. For so many who grew up in the '80s and '90s, speaking your mind or talking about your feelings like they actually *mattered* wasn't merely discouraged—it was culturally punished. Girls were trained in the fine art of silence, told in a thousand little ways that our voices were too loud, our feelings too much, ambitions too threatening. So when Taylor sings—clear-eyed and unapologetic—about betrayal, rebirth, and burning it all down, it feels like more than nostalgia; it's a reckoning. Like a kind of vicarious healing session in glitter and stadium lighting. The scream-singing session we needed back then but rarely got. It's a collective exorcism of girlhoods when we were told to step back and be humble, while boys were told to step forward and take charge. And for those whose adolescence was disrupted by trauma, who never got to fully grow into ourselves, it can feel like something close to transcendence—a simultaneous experience of grief and restoration (which, let's be honest, could be the subject of a whole other book).

But if you're like my daughter, born into a world where Taylor has always existed, it's not about growing up *with* Taylor—it's about growing up *under* her. Taylor's voice is one of the first your nervous system recognizes as safe. Her mythology isn't reflective but foundational. For my daughter, there is no "before," only immersion. And that kind of early and total cultural saturation brings with it a different kind of power—and a different kind of risk.

Regardless of how you enter Taylor's universe, once you're in it, the concert doesn't end when the lights come up—it imprints itself on your soul, leaving a mark you can't shake off. The community around you feels sacred, a tribe bound together by shared lyrics, inside jokes, and unwavering devotion to the woman at the center. And like any high-control experience, it's a transformation. You walk out of that arena feeling both exhilarated and drained, cracked open in a way that feels intimate yet collective. The indoctrination doesn't require force. Sometimes all it takes is one night.

You can leave such a concert emotionally raw, soul buzzing, heart vibrating on a new frequency, and not brainwashed—you're just temporarily expanded. And that's a beautiful thing. But it's also when you're most vulnerable. That's when the Hare Krishna guy or the Twelve Tribes woman in her flowing skirt is waiting outside, pamphlet in hand, smile just a little too wide, ready to offer you "real" transcendence. Because they know the music softened you. The shared experience made you porous. And now someone's waiting to catch you in that in-between moment—before your critical thinking kicks back in, before the spell wears off. Group experiences don't need to be manipulative to make you suggestible. The danger isn't always *inside* the concert. Sometimes it's who's waiting for you just outside the door.

And it's important to say: Not every moment of deep collective emotion is manipulation. Not every fandom is a cult. After a concert you can feel lit up, transformed, more connected to yourself and others. You can be changed without being coerced. But openness isn't neutral. It's a state of possibility—and vulnerability. It makes you more receptive. More trusting. More permeable.[1]

And that's when it gets tricky. Because the concert, or the fandom, or Taylor Swift herself may not be trying to control you, but someone else might be waiting in the wings. Emotionally expanded people are easier to influence. So proselytizers set up outside concerts, cult recruiters hang out near college campuses and wellness expos, and charismatic entrepreneurs love the post-retreat high.

We All Need Groups

Our ancestors learned—many thousands of years ago—that forming groups enhanced their survival. Before we had language, fire, or shelter, we had each other. Alone, a human was vulnerable: slow, soft, clawless. But together? We were powerful. We hunted cooperatively, protected one another, and passed down crucial knowledge. According to the

Smithsonian's Human Origins Program, the emergence of complex social behavior was one of the key factors that distinguished early humans from other primates.[2]

Over time, our bodies evolved to reflect this interdependence. According to Dr. Stephen Porges, creator of polyvagal theory, our nervous systems developed *in the company of others*—we are literally wired for connection. From birth, we scan for eyes, faces, and emotional cues. Human infants, unlike many animals, are profoundly dependent, not only for physical survival but for emotional and neurological development. Through attuned caregiving—mutual gaze, soothing vocal tones, gentle touch—infants learn to manage stress, develop trust, and form the blueprint for future relationships—a process known as coregulation. As we grow, these early patterns of coregulation extend outward into families, communities, and social groups. Systems like the vagus nerve and mirror neurons enable empathy, attunement, and synchronization with those around us, embedding our need for connection into our very biology.[3]

Humans need groups because we evolved as fundamentally social creatures. Our survival, from the earliest stages of human evolution, depended on cooperation, shared resources, and collective protection. Living in groups allowed early humans to hunt more effectively, care for children communally, and defend against predators or rival tribes.[4] This evolutionary pressure shaped not only our behaviors but also our brains: We developed complex social cognition, emotional attunement, and language to navigate group life. Belonging to a group was quite literally a matter of life or death—those who were excluded or exiled faced a much higher risk of dying.

But our need for connection goes beyond biology. Psychologically, we seek bonds that help us feel seen, safe, and grounded. Social ties regulate our stress, shape our identity, and help us make sense of the world. Groups offer belonging, structure, and shared meaning— all essential for emotional well-being. Even in modern life, where survival no longer hinges on the tribe, the drive to connect persists, so we're drawn to religious communities, workplaces, fandoms, and movements. When healthy, these groups provide support, motivation, and a buffer against loneliness.[5]

Research backs this up. Scholars have consistently found that strong social bonds are linked to better physical health, longer life expectancy, improved emotional well-being, and greater resilience in the face of adversity. Belonging isn't just a comfort—it's a core psychological need that shapes our development and protects our mental and physical health. In other words: We don't just like being in groups—we need them.[6]

We didn't develop language only to share food or warn about predators. We used it to create stories, myths, rituals, and rules. We encoded our behaviors and beliefs into culture, and those cultures became systems—far more powerful than any individual. From tribes to towns, religions to corporations, from Girl Scout troops to multi-billion-dollar fan empires, we built society out of stories we all agreed to believe.

Because that's what a group is, at its core: humans with a shared belief. A mutual performance. A pact.

And when it's good, it's magic. Whether it's a fandom, a workplace, a book club, a team, a marriage, a found family, or a political cause, being part of something bigger than yourself can be profoundly fulfilling. It taps into three key psychological needs: feeling connected, being accepted, and being seen or validated. The group reflects you back to yourself—but shinier. It tells you: You're one of us. You matter. You are home.[7]

Identity Versus Control

Just as a group can elevate you, it can also erase you. Our deep need for connection makes us vulnerable to manipulation. The same mechanisms we evolved to keep us safe and bonded can be hijacked by systems that exploit our social instincts. When a group offers belonging, shared rituals, and emotional attunement—especially during moments of personal crisis or disconnection—it can feel neurologically regulating, even if the group is coercive. Coregulation feels like safety to us, even when it's embedded in control. People often stay in environments that are externally harmful but internally soothing because their nervous systems are responding to perceived connection, not reason. This evolutionary design helps explain our deep craving for community—but also the ways it can bind, exploit, and entrap.

The line between healthy group dynamics and subtle manipulation is thin, and often invisible when you're hovering over it. We like to believe we'd know when something's off, but conformity is sneaky. It doesn't usually look like brainwashing. It looks like biting your tongue in a meeting, like nodding along with a conversation when you don't really agree, like "going along to get along." Even smart, thoughtful people fall into groupthink, where the desire for harmony overrides good judgment.

Fandoms are one of the clearest illustrations of collective energy that could tip in either direction. If you've ever screamed the bridge to your favorite song with a stadium full of strangers, you know the power. The rituals, the hashtags, the shared language that only makes sense to "us"—it feels like home. But that intimacy can quickly shift into conformity. Suddenly, there's right and wrong ways to be a fan. A hierarchy of who's "real." An expectation of loyalty that leaves no room for critique. Research has shown that high levels of celebrity worship are associated with obsessive behavior, fantasy proneness, and attachment-related traits—psychological dynamics that can lead to a blurring of personal identity with that of the admired celebrity, sometimes described as identity merging.[8] Parasocial relationships—those one-sided emotional bonds with people who don't know you exist—aren't inherently harmful, but they can blur boundaries, become obsessive, or be exploited by brands, influencers, or cultish figures to sell products or ideologies.[*] These ties can even influence financial decisions: Recent research shows that emotional resonance with internet celebrities can drive impulse buying.[9]

---

[*] Is it exploitation of the parasocial bond when public figures use their platforms to promote causes they genuinely believe in? How many Swifties lean left politically because Taylor does? I'll be the first to admit—I'm not mad at it.

But here's the thing: You can be a Swiftie and not be in a cult—because "Swiftie" is an identity, not a group. It's a cultural affiliation, a personal label, a way of saying *These songs meant something to me.* There's nothing inherently manipulative about loving music, or even building your whole personality around it. The difference is the same one I always give when people ask, *What's the line between a religion and a cult?* A religion is an idea, a belief system, a worldview. A cult is a group. Groups can certainly be powered by ideas and belief systems. Cults give you worldviews. But ideas, like identities, on their own aren't cults. And you can be a Christian, a Muslim, or a Buddhist all by yourself.

It's the same with fandom. You can be a Swiftie in solitude, a quiet appreciator of lyrics that once held your teenage heart together. You can even have a Swiftian worldview (I sometimes joke that I was knocked off my horse on the road to Damascus by the song "Tim McGraw" and converted to Swiftianity). None of that makes it a cult. A cult is a group that exerts power over its members in specific, measurable ways—and it must be a group to start with. No group, no cult. That's the key distinction. Identity, even fervent identity, isn't dangerous on its own. When identity gets absorbed into a controlling system, things get...well, culty.

But there is some truly concerning behavior in the Swiftie universe: obsessive online sleuthing, full-scale doxxing of critics, refusal to tolerate any hint of nuance or dissent, digital dogpiling that turns an offhand comment into a days-long character assassination campaign. And then there's the monetization: the multiple album variants with one different Polaroid or bonus track, the merch drops, the parasocial intimacy wrapped in capitalist brilliance. It can all feel...intense. Cult adjacent, even. But intensity alone doesn't make a cult. Neither does passion. What matters is the presence of a group exerting control. If Swifties ever start requiring loyalty pledges, cutting people off from their families, punishing them for listening to Olivia Rodrigo, or making them pick up glitter after the party for free[*]—then we'll talk.

---

[*] If you know, you know.

Until then, it's a fandom—maybe a very committed one, maybe a little unhinged at times—but not a cult. Not yet, anyway.*

Identity isn't a cult. What makes something a cult is the level of control and the harm it causes. Fandom isn't a problem, unless people within it are acting abusively. The same goes for identity and affinity groups—whether it's a choice like political affiliation or niche hobby interest, or something you're born with like race, sexual or gender identity, or neurodivergence. Affinity groups based on shared identities support individual expression and empower their members. They allow disagreement and evolution. Cults, by contrast, demand conformity,

---

*Just as this book was about to go to press, Taylor Swift's album *The Life of a Showgirl* dropped, and with it the song "Opalite," which immediately drew criticism for being racist. Intentional or not, the lyric "Sleepless through the onyx night but now the sky is opalite" was seen by some as contrasting her fiancé Travis Kelce's past relationship with a Black woman ("onyx night"—onyx is a black gemstone) with his current one with Taylor ("opalite"—opals are usually milky white in color), fueling accusations of racial undertones. While it's impossible for anyone to know what Taylor was thinking when she wrote this line, it's also impossible for me not to, at the very least, see it as an insensitive, ignorant, and careless use of racially charged language (see the footnote on page 6 about "black and white" thinking). There are several lines throughout the album that can be seen as references to her partner's ex—and that alone should have given Taylor pause, as she's well aware of her fans' propensity to take action against those she feels slighted by, and it would be all too easy for these actions—inspired by a white woman, against a Black woman—to turn racist.

Ultimately, I decided to keep this chapter as originally written, because using Taylor Swift as an example of extreme fandom, and as a tool to explain the difference between identity and a cult, is still valid. But I also recognize how this is problematized by her imperfections as an icon. Putting anyone on a pedestal will always be problematic, but in our celebrity-obsessed culture, we do it often. I have been as guilty as anyone.

Time will tell how Taylor and her fans respond to what is, at best, a tragic lapse in judgment by a woman of incredible privilege and platform, or at worst, a racist dog whistle. Will fans stick by her no matter what, digging their heels in and doubling down on their devotion to their leader? Or will they, like me, question their loyalty and, as painful as it may be, consider letting go of their identity of "Swiftie" in order to stay true to themselves and their values? I have joked in this book about being a convert to Swiftianity, but maybe now that's an affiliation that I, along with other white women fans, must deconstruct.

Taylor herself has said that fans should see her art as a mirror, and when I looked in *Showgirl's* mirror, I didn't like what I saw.

suppress dissent, and often punish departure with emotional, social, or financial consequences. Understanding this distinction is vital. When we conflate interest- or identity-based communities with cults, we risk undermining the value of genuine connection—and worse, we risk demonizing a whole group of people.

Belonging is beautiful. It's one of our most essential human needs. But if belonging demands your silence, your conformity, or your emotional labor in exchange for love or legitimacy, that's not a community—that's control. Real community lets you question the rules without losing your seat at the table. It lets you leave and still be welcome. It doesn't force you to choose between authenticity and acceptance. Because if you have to surrender your critical thinking to stay, you were never truly safe to begin with.

At the end of the day, it's on us to stay aware of how our groups operate and what they're asking of us. Being part of something bigger can be beautiful, but only if it's reciprocal. Ask yourself regularly: *Does this group give me as much as it takes? Am I free to express myself, to disagree? Can I leave without losing myself?* Staying self-aware and questioning the dynamics around you is how you protect your individuality while still enjoying the sense of community that groups provide.

Protecting yourself doesn't mean closing off but rather recognizing when you've been emotionally opened—and giving yourself a buffer before you say yes to the next thing. It means knowing that being moved doesn't mean you owe anyone your trust. You can be transformed by a moment and still say no to the pamphlet. You can let something beautiful move through you without becoming someone else's recruit.

What About Good Cults?

The number one question I get asked—by far—is: "Are there good cults?" And every time, I pause. Not because I don't know the answer, but because I understand the underlying desire for a loophole. People want to believe that if the mission is noble enough, or the results impressive enough, then perhaps control and coercion are justifiable.

But I don't believe in "good cults." Manipulation, by its very nature, strips individuals of their agency. Even if a group is feeding the hungry or saving lives—if it relies on fear, guilt, secrecy, or control, then it's not truly good. It's merely efficient. And efficiency isn't synonymous with morality. (Just ask DOGE.)

What's particularly telling is that it's mostly men who pose the question about good cults. This pattern reveals a deeply ingrained patriarchal belief that power structures are neutral and can be flipped or rebranded to serve benevolent purposes. It suggests that the issue isn't with the existence of control but with who wields it. This mindset overlooks the fundamental problem: Any system built on coercion and manipulation is inherently flawed, regardless of the intentions of those in charge. True leadership doesn't seek to control but to empower— without strings attached.

As someone who grew up in a cult, I find all definitions of cults— even my own—to be inadequate. The complexity of such groups defies simple categorization. So instead of starting with a definition, I ask: *What are we really trying to say when we use the word "cult"?* I've come to understand that when we say someone is "in a cult," we mean they've fallen under the coercive control of a group. That's the crux of it. Therefore, the opposite of a cult isn't a "good cult" but a group that doesn't manipulate its members. The opposite of a cult leader isn't a benevolent dictator, but a leader who doesn't rely on coercion at all.

By this point in the book, I hope you're not expecting a simple answer or a neat little recipe for what makes a group *good*. The intelligence officer in me wants to remind you: It's always *low* threat, never *no* threat. I used to think I'd use what I know about organizational dynamics to help groups become better, more ethical, more human. But eventually I had to admit something to myself: I don't actually care about groups. How can I know if they want to be good? I'm not even sure they *can* be—not while they're operating under the triple cult systems of capitalism, patriarchy, and white supremacy. And let's be honest, most of them are.

So what's the point of this book—of my work?

After years of asking myself that question, I found the answer: I do this for the *individual*. As someone raised from day one to sacrifice myself for the group, I believe the most radical thing I can do is help *you*—not your workplace, not your church, not your family system, but *you*. If all this book does is help you name the weirdness that happened when your boss insisted all the women wear pantyhose, or when your "accountability group" started policing your food choices, then good. If it helps you trust that moment in your gut when something felt off—even if no one else said anything—then I've done my job.

The answer to what makes a group "good" is not easy, and anyone who tries to give you an easy answer is probably trying to cult you or con you. A nineteen-year-old Stanford dropout was never going to solve a global blood-testing problem that stumped the best scientists in the world. But Elizabeth Holmes sold us the myth of the visionary disruptor, and a lot of powerful people bought it. Startups and MLMs, predatory coaching and the law of attraction, the prosperity gospel and the American Dream itself—for most people, they will always promise way more than they can ever deliver. Myths don't survive because they're true. They survive because we *want* to believe in simple answers.

People then ask me, "So what *is* the answer then?" The truth is, I don't know. If we've learned anything from this journey through the ten features of cultiness, it's that the line between devotion and indoctrination is thinner than we think. There is no bright flashing "Now Entering Cult Territory" sign. What I know is that people really want groups. Systems. Our ancestors' tribes helped them sleep at night knowing they're "safe." We don't join cults—we join communities. We sign up for connection, for answers, for hope. We walk in looking for purpose and belonging. I can't give you that. Honestly, I don't think anyone can.

And maybe that's the real issue. We're both asking the wrong questions and asking the wrong people for answers. The people most likely to rebuild better groups probably don't look like me. Historically, people with my lack of melanin have not been the ones doing ethical group leadership. But deeper than that, I think we're relying on groups to fix problems that come from the absence of community. Somewhere along the way, we gave up connection and replaced it with cultic substitutes: brands, influencers, online movements, workplaces that call themselves "family." Maybe it's not just capitalism. Maybe it's the way American individualism has replaced community with content.

That vacuum—of meaning, of support, of shared responsibility—is what makes us vulnerable. It's why people get pulled into MLMs, extremist politics, manipulative relationships, or unhealthy friend circles. It's why Goop gets to sell you "vagina eggs" and why influencer wellness culture gets a bigger platform than public health and actual doctors. When true community disappears, control steps in to replace it. And control always comes with a cost.

So in the spirit of community, and trying to ask the right people better questions, I want to pass the mic to someone whose work has helped me better understand the difference between being part of a community and being held by a group—Rebecca Slue, known online as the White Woman Whisperer—whose wisdom, humor, and boundary-setting skills are exactly what we need as we figure out where we go from here.

(And don't worry, she's not starting a cult. I checked.)

From Groups to Community: A Shift from Performance to Presence

By Rebecca Slue
The White Woman Whisperer

In a world increasingly fractured by identity and ideology, many of us long to belong. But too often, we confuse *fitting in* with *belonging*, mistaking tightly organized groups for genuine community. This confusion isn't just semantic—it speaks to a deeper cultural conditioning, one that values structure over connection, performance over presence, and conformity over compassion.

The distinction between "group" and "community" is a matter of foundational values and relational truth. Groups are built to be functional, often around a cause, a mission, or a leader. They offer clarity and control—qualities especially appealing to people who have experienced chaos. Communities, on the other hand, are built on care. They are not tools for performance nor vehicles for status; they are living ecosystems where authenticity, not adequacy, is the threshold for entry.

Many who seek out "good groups" are not really seeking connection—they're seeking safety in certainty. This instinct, while understandable, is ultimately limiting. It leads to what can be described as *cult shopping*: moving from one group to another in search of the "right" values, the "best" practices, the "purest" intentions. But this pursuit of ideological purity often leads us away from the messiness—and richness—of real human relationships.

Groups and communities arise from different emotional soil. Groups are often defined by their borders—who is in, who is out, and how to behave to stay included. Community, by contrast, is boundary-aware but not boundary-obsessed. It centers presence over power, curiosity over control. Where groups fear open conflict, communities make space for it. Where groups prioritize harmony—often dishonest and fragile—communities value honest disruption. Because they know conflict is not combat. It is how we grow.

In groups, questioning is perceived as a threat. In communities, it is seen as a gift. A sign that someone cares enough to risk discomfort for the sake of connection.

To truly belong in a community, we must learn to practice distress tolerance and discernment. We must recognize the difference between discomfort and danger, between the survival instinct of safety-seeking and the learned reflex of comfort-chasing. This is not easy work. It requires that we de-center ourselves in the stories of others, so that we can *center ourselves in our own*. We must sit with the discomfort of emotional honesty, and resist the pull of groupthink and self-silencing.

Groups often resolve conflict by removing the source—through avoidance, aggression, or triangulation. This "resolution" is more about removing discomfort than restoring trust. But in community, conflict is metabolized rather than eradicated. It is addressed relationally, not reactively. People in community listen not fearfully but carefully, trusting that telling the truth, even when it hurts, is a form of love.

We've been taught, often by well-meaning mentors, to "go along to get along," to "not rock the boat," or "not stir the pot." But what if the boat needs to be rocked? What if what's in the pot is harmful, and silence is complicity?

I find it telling that toxic groups often embody the same traits identified by Kenneth Jones and Tema Okun as the fifteen tenets of white supremacy culture in *Dismantling Racism: A Workbook for Social Change Groups*.* These include:

- Perfectionism
- Sense of urgency
- Paternalism
- Binary thinking
- Worship of the written word
- Quantity over quality
- Individualism
- "I'm the only one"
- One right way
- Right to comfort
- Fear of open conflict

---

* It's important to clarify that this list of characteristics was originally intended as a tool for anti-racist organizational development, and its application here is broader than its initial context. Okun has spoken openly about the informal and collaborative process behind the list's creation, its intended nuance, and the ways it has been misinterpreted, misused without discernment, and even weaponized—particularly by the political right. (Grim, "Tema Okun on Her Mythical Paper," 2023)

- Progress as bigger/more

- Objectivity

- Power hoarding

- Defensiveness[10]

These traits don't appear only in explicitly racist institutions; they permeate corporate, academic, activist, and spiritual spaces—anywhere group identity is protected above personal accountability or collective care. These aren't "bad habits"— they're structural dynamics that reproduce hierarchy and harm under the guise of order, efficiency, or tradition.

This is the essence of community accountability. It doesn't mean perfection. It means participation. It means asking not "How do I stay out of trouble?" but "How do I show up with care?" Communities are made up of people who don't always agree—and are willing to stay in the room when they don't.

A group elevates you when you perform well, then isolates or discards you when you don't. A community grounds you whether you're shining or struggling. In groups, power is hoarded; in community, power is shared. Groups see people as resources to be used. Communities see people *as* resources— valuable for who they are, not just for what they produce.

This difference is not abstract—it shows up in daily inter- actions. In a group, your worth may depend on how well you adhere to unspoken rules, how perfectly you perform profes- sionalism, politeness, or positivity. In a community, your worth is not up for debate. Your value is not earned through perfor- mance but honored through presence.

The difference can also be seen in leadership. In groups, leaders often become gatekeepers. In communities, leadership is fluid. Every member has the capacity to lead through wisdom, care, and example—not command. A leader in community is not the loudest voice or the most polished speaker, but the person willing to risk vulnerability for the sake of connection.

To shift from group dynamics to community consciousness, we must abandon binary thinking: good/bad, right/wrong, us/them. We must embrace nuance and hold space for contradiction. We must stop trying to *win* and start trying to *understand*.

Real freedom begins when we stop trying to earn a seat at the table, and instead start asking why the table was set that way in the first place. Maybe the point isn't to sit at the top—but to sit on the ground, in a circle, in shared humanity. Maybe the ultimate success isn't climbing to the penthouse of power, but planting roots in a hut of humility.

Groups seek certainty. Communities make room for change. Groups focus on control. Communities foster connection. In groups, the question is "How do I stay in?" In communities, the question is "How do we stay with each other?"

In the end, community is not something you find. You *create* it—through showing up honestly, listening deeply, and learning to love without the armor of perfection. Abandoning the value systems that measured you by performance alone is not easy—it's disorienting, even painful. But uncertainty is not the same as danger, and struggle is not the same as suffering. You are more prepared than you know.

You've made it this far—surviving within inhumane systems that silenced your instincts and dimmed your voice. Imagine what might unfold if you turned that same devotion inward, toward belief in yourself. No one knows the shape of your freedom better than you. And the truth is, it's not something to earn—it's something to remember.

It's time to take your mind back. Stop trying to prove you're enough, and start trusting that you already are.

As Rebecca so eloquently describes, the distinction between a group and a community is essential. A group is defined by structure, purpose, or task. You join to *do* something—complete a project, follow a mission, achieve a goal. Roles tend to be fixed or hierarchical, power is often centralized, and there are clear boundaries around who's in and who's out. There are also unspoken (or explicit) norms about how to behave, think, and speak in order to be considered "one of us."[11]

A community, by contrast, is defined by mutual care. You belong not to prove your value but simply to be with others. A healthy community empowers rather than controls. It encourages connection and growth, not dependency or fear. Community respects your boundaries rather than crossing them—or pressuring you to move them. Shared values and goals may exist, but they never override your personal identity. A community's boundaries are permeable: joining is voluntary, and leaving is met with respect. Disagreement, discussion, and questioning are welcome. Transparency is the norm. Leadership is accountable, ideally shared or rotating, and decisions are made with input from everyone.

A group asks, "What can you do for us?" A community asks, "How can we care for each other?"

When asked what marked the first sign of civilization, American anthropologist Margaret Mead pointed to a 15,000-year-old healed human femur. In a pre-civilization, survival-of-the-fittest world, a broken leg would likely have meant death. Yet this bone had healed—proof that someone had stayed behind, that a community had carried and cared for an injured member who might easily have been seen as a liability. For Mead, this showed that human civilization began not with competition, but with connection.[12]

I can't name a single group that gets it all right. Does that mean we should avoid groups entirely? Of course not. We're human. The point is, we are not perfect, and neither are our groups. Even the best ones will still show some flicker of cultiness.

As imperfect as AA is, Amy still says she's grateful to the group and probably couldn't have gotten sober without it. And as much as she hates the pseudo-spiritual cultiness of American yoga culture, she still goes to her hot yoga studio multiple times a week—some might say religiously—though she refuses to say "namaste" at the end of class or buy anything from Lululemon. These small rebellions, while seemingly inconsequential, can remind us of our autonomy and agency. We can still say no—even when we're choosing to say yes.

As for me, as much as I criticize social media for being largely responsible for the culting of modern America, I am still on TikTok every day, knitting furiously, wearing my wild outfits, ranting to anyone who will listen, and collecting my "followers." As much as I critique the US military, I am still immensely proud of my service and will never stop supporting veterans. I suppose this is what it means to live in the nuance between extremes—to hold conflicting truths, to be in constant conversation with them.

So no, I can't tell you how to build a "good group." What I've tried to do in this book is sharpen your awareness, so you can feel when something's off. So you can notice the subtle shifts—from collaboration to compliance, from consensus to conformity, from community to cult. Because once you can name the shift, you don't need a rulebook. You need yourself. You need your instincts, your boundaries, your exit plan. And maybe, if enough of us do that, we'll get closer to building something better.

Your friendly neighborhood intelligence officer,
    Captain Daniella Mestyanek Young
    Scholar of cults, extreme groups, and extremely bad leadership

Ten Ways to Tell if Your Group Is Trending Culty

This checklist will help you reflect on your experience with a group, organization, or community. Each of the ten sections corresponds to a hallmark of high-control systems, drawn from the framework in *The Culting of America*. If multiple sections resonate, it doesn't mean you're in a cult—but it may be time to take a closer look at what the group is demanding, and what it's giving in return.[*]

1. LEADERSHIP AND AUTHORITY

- ☐ The group is built around a singular founder, guru, or leader who is treated as extraordinary or divinely inspired.
- ☐ The leader's words are taken as truth, even when they contradict themselves.
- ☐ Dissenters are discredited, dismissed, or exiled.

---

[*] This checklist, like my ten-part cultiness spectrum, is informed by the work of established cult scholars, including, but not limited to, Janja Lalich's four structural pillars from *Bounded Choice*, Margaret Singer's six conditions of thought reform in *Cults in Our Midst*, and Robert Jay Lifton's eight criteria outlined in *Thought Reform and the Psychology of Totalism*.

☐ You find yourself defending a leader's actions you once would have questioned.

The danger of charismatic leadership is that people will follow without question—not just because they agree, but because they want to believe.

2. SACRED ASSUMPTIONS

☐ Your group has a belief you must accept without question in order to belong.

☐ Alternative perspectives are dismissed as dangerous, ignorant, or unenlightened.

☐ Mantras, quotes, or origin myths are repeated until they become unchallengeable truth.

The sacred assumption—the one thing you must believe to be a member in good standing—becomes a lens through which members see everything.

3. TRANSCENDENT MISSION

☐ The mission is so urgent or righteous that it justifies extreme sacrifice.

☐ Members are encouraged to suppress doubts for the sake of the cause.

☐ The mission feels like the only thing that gives your life meaning.

When everything is about saving lives or changing the world, there's no room left for your own needs or doubts.

4. SELF-SACRIFICE

☐ You are expected—or you feel pressured, even subtly—to change significant aspects of your appearance, personality, or other parts of your identity in order to fit in.

☐ Exhaustion, burnout, or overwork are celebrated as proof of devotion.

☐ You feel guilty when you put your interests, hobbies, family, or other things that feed your soul before the group.

Exhaustion becomes proof. Sacrifice becomes moral currency. And what begins as devotion becomes identity.

5. ISOLATION

☐ Your world has shrunk since you joined the group.

☐ You feel misunderstood by those outside or avoid people who don't "get it."

☐ Outside perspectives are dismissed as negative or unsafe.

It doesn't take walls or gates to isolate people. All it takes is a shared narrative that the outside world is dangerous, wrong, or not worth your time.

6. LANGUAGE AND THOUGHT CONTROL

☐ The group uses special jargon that outsiders wouldn't understand.

☐ Dissenting opinions are reframed as negativity, weakness, or sin.

☐ You find it hard to describe your experience without using the group's words.

Language becomes the border wall of belief. Once you're speaking their words, you're thinking their thoughts.

7. US-VERSUS-THEM MENTALITY

☐ Members are told they are more enlightened, chosen, or awakened than outsiders.

☐ People who leave the group are described as broken, bitter, or lost.

☐ Disagreement is treated as blasphemy.

What starts as a tight-knit community can quickly consume your identity by demanding loyalty and framing outsiders as threats.

8. EXPLOITATION OF LABOR

☐ You are expected to give more than you receive—your time, body, or energy.

☐ Unpaid labor, "volunteering," or constant work are reframed as spiritual practice or community service.

☐ Rest and boundaries are treated as selfishness.

Cults are organized crime syndicates that run on free labor. They recruit, they indoctrinate, and they extract.

9. HIGH ENTRANCE AND EXIT COSTS

☐ You have sacrificed money, relationships, or identity to join or stay.

☐ Walking away feels like betraying something sacred—or like starting over from scratch.

☐ Your doubts are minimized by reminders of everything you'd lose if you left.

The second rule of cults is that the cult will forgive any sin...except the sin of leaving.

10. ENDS JUSTIFY THE MEANS

☐ Harm is tolerated or justified in pursuit of the group's goals.

☐ Lies are reframed as strategy. Dissent is reframed as heresy.

☐ The group measures success in devotion, not ethics.

This is how lying becomes holy, deception becomes virtue, and the first compromises of integrity are cloaked in righteousness.

How to Interpret Your Results

SO...HOW CULTY IS YOUR GROUP?

This checklist isn't a diagnostic tool or a gotcha quiz. It's a reflection guide. That said, if you're staring at a lot of checked boxes and feeling a little sick to your stomach, you're not alone—and you're not wrong to be concerned.

Here's a rough breakdown to help you assess where things might land on the culty spectrum.

0–2 SECTIONS CHECKED: NOT CULTY (BUT STAY CURIOUS)

You're likely in a healthy group, or at least one that hasn't tipped into control territory. Some strong personalities or quirky traditions might be present, but your autonomy is intact. Keep asking questions. Stay grounded in your own values. And if anything shifts, trust your gut.

Think: Your book club has a few strong opinions, but nobody's banning Oprah.

3–5 SECTIONS CHECKED: KINDA CULTY (TIME TO PAY ATTENTION)

There are some red flags flapping in the wind. You might be in a high-demand environment that's trending culty. Maybe it's your workplace, your family, your yoga studio, or your online community. These groups often start out as helpful, healing, or even revolutionary—but that doesn't mean they stay that way. The danger here is slow creep.

Think: You joined for the mission. Now you're skipping holidays, quoting the founder, and haven't had a day off since 2022.

6+ SECTIONS CHECKED: SUPER CULTY (YOU MIGHT BE IN TROUBLE)

Okay, this group is checking a lot of boxes. Maybe it started with good intentions, but now you're isolated, exhausted, and finding it harder to think clearly outside the group's framework. That's not your fault—that's how high-control systems are designed to work. If leaving feels impossible, or even dangerous, it's not just a red flag. It's a whole damn parade.

Start thinking about what freedom might look like—and know that help exists.

Think: You're explaining away things you used to find horrifying. You're working for free. You're terrified of what happens if you leave.

The Bottom Line

A single charismatic leader does not a cult make. Nor does loving a mission, using a little jargon, or feeling deep belonging. But if those things combine with control, isolation, and sacrifice that outweighs the benefits promised (in this lifetime), then something deeper is happening. And you deserve to name it.

It's not about whether a group is a full-blown cult. It's about how culty it's bccoming—and whether you're still free inside it.

Take what works. Leave the rest. And take your power with you when you go.

Quick Reference Guide
to Culty Things

This guide isn't comprehensive, but it's a quick-and-dirty map of culty behavior—whether it shows up in religious movements, startups, fandoms, fitness groups, activist circles, or anywhere else people collect.

How to Spot a Cult (My Definition)

A cult is a group that:

- Follows a **charismatic leader** (and often his **Skinny White Woman**)
- Centers around a **sacred assumption**
- Pursues a **transcendent mission**
- Requires **self-sacrifice** of its members
- **Limits** access to the outside world
- Creates a **distinct insider language**
- Enforces an **us-versus-them mentality**
- **Exploits** members' labor
- Builds up **high exit costs**
- Believes **the ends always justify the means**

The 3 Rules of Cults

1. The first rule of cults: You're not in a cult.

2. The second rule of cults: The only unforgivable sin is leaving.
3. The third rule of cults: Even if he did it, that doesn't mean he's guilty.

Favorite Linguistic Tricks of Cults

- **Call and response** chanting
- **Loaded language** that rewrites reality
- **Thought-stopping clichés** to shut down questions
- **Softened language** for insider bad behavior
- **Dehumanizing language** for outsiders

The 10 Commandments for Good Groups (aka How Not to Be Culty)

1. Thou shalt not rape the children (or stand by those who do).
2. Thou shalt have other gods before me.
3. Thou shalt question all things too sacred to question.
4. Thy mission must be achievable, in this lifetime.
5. Thou shalt never call thyself a "family." Ever.
6. Thou shalt loudly declare that information is never bad.
7. Thou shalt keep insider jokes and lingo to a minimum.
8. Thou shalt not chant thy own last name.
9. Thou shalt compensate physical and emotional labor.
10. Thou shalt beware of exit costs and shunning.

How Cult Leaders Keep You from Leaving

They keep you:

- Isolated

- Hungry
- Busy
- Skinny
- Tired
- Poor
- Pregnant

Guru Gotcha Checklist (aka Cult Leader Bingo)

- Claims to be **uniquely special**
- **Plays hot/cold** "come here, go away" games
- **Tests your loyalty** constantly
- **Lacks intellectual humility**
- Pretends to be an **expert in everything**
- **Trance talk** (thanks, Dr. Janja Lalich)
- **Charges for** "presence," "energy," "access"
- Hands out **life advice** they aren't qualified to give
- **Demands purity** from followers
- Controls followers' **appearance and attitude**
- **Badmouths** other leaders
- **Blames** systemic failures on individuals
- **Blurs sexual boundaries** (often with help from the Skinny White Woman)
- Asks you to **quit your job** and follow them
- **Threatens** you if you leave (or even if you think about it)

Toxic Group Red Flags

- Obsessively sells their **unique answers**

- **Badmouths ex-members**
- **Attacks critics** with vitriol
- Worships the founder's **origin story**
- Parrots the same **defensive responses**
- Forces secretive, sudden **goodbyes**
- Meets criticism with **cliché shutdowns**
- Fosters **heavy secrecy** culture
- Has **high turnover** of members
- Blames individuals for **organizational failures**
- Causes **unstable** work/life balance
- Results in **life takeover** (aka scope creep)
- Pushes the group as part of **your identity**
- Uses **enforced positivity** ("Don't bring up a problem unless you have a solution")
- Enforces **anti-gossip rules** ("Shut up and suffer quietly")

The Bottom Line

If your group looks, sounds, and acts like the above...it might not just be "passionate." It might be culty.

And "a little bit culty" always gets worse—unless someone leaves or speaks up.

Book Club Discussion Questions

- *What cults are you in?* The book asks this question early on. What came to mind for you? Did your perspective on any group you're part of change as you read?

- What do you make of the argument that "cult" exists on a spectrum, not a binary? How does that change your understanding of groups like the military, tech startups, or fandoms?

- The authors argue that all cults have a "sacred assumption" at their core—something unquestioned and central. Can you identify a sacred assumption in one of your own groups? Is it ever discussed or challenged?

- Which figures (personal, professional, or public) have held a disproportionate amount of influence in your thinking or behavior? What made them so compelling?

- Did you recognize any cultlike language patterns in communities you've been part of? How does specialized language reinforce belonging—or control?

- Which kinds of exit costs (social, financial, psychological) have you faced or witnessed when someone tries to leave a group? What surprised you about how these costs keep people tethered?

- The book explores how a "transcendent mission" can justify harm. Have you ever seen a noble mission used to excuse toxic behavior or overwork?

- How did the book challenge your own belief systems or assumptions? Were there moments you found yourself resisting what was being said?

- What distinguishes healthy influence from coercive control? Were you surprised by how blurry that line can be?

- Chapter 7 dives into nationalism and the myth of the "chosen nation." How do you see American identity overlapping with cultlike dynamics? What makes those myths powerful or dangerous?

- Which social roles (like being a parent or a "good worker") came into focus for you in a new way? Where do you see cultural expectations becoming cultic?

- After reading this book, what changes—big or small—do you want to make in how you engage with the groups you're part of? What new questions are you asking?

Acknowledgments

Daniella

This book is the result of a lifetime of trying to understand the impossible—how groups change people, and how people try to change the world through groups. To those who've survived: Thank you for your courage, your vulnerability, and your refusal to stay silent. I carry your stories with me.

To my family of origin: This book wouldn't exist without what I inherited from you—both the darkness and the light. And to my chosen family: Thank you for helping me see the difference.

To the readers of *Uncultured*, the TikTok followers who helped me crowdsource this book into what it is now, the cult nerds in my DMs, the veterans who whispered "me too," and the survivors who entrusted me with their truths—you gave this book its momentum. You reminded me that telling the truth about harmful groups isn't dangerous—it's necessary.

To the experts and scholars who shaped this work—Dr. Janja Lalich, Dr. Alexandra Stein, Dr. Robert Cialdini, and so many others—thank you for creating the intellectual scaffolding that made it possible to name what so many of us have lived through. I only hope I've done your work justice.

To Ada Lee, who helped me with research—I didn't know if I was gonna get this done!

To my co-writer and editor, Amy—thank you for fiercely protecting the heart of this book while cutting the fat around it. For every page you pushed me to go deeper, sharper, braver—thank you. Thank you for all the work and research that you added to this complex narrative that we have woven over two and a half years (and a forty-eight-page bibliography!). And thank you for toning down my snark, so that I'm less polarizing on the page than I am on social media. Thank you, Amy. There wouldn't be this, if there hadn't been you.

To my publisher, Saeah Wood, and the entire team who believed in a book that dares to say "You're probably in a cult"—thank you for taking the risk.

To my husband, who has seen the toll this work takes, and still tells me to go harder. To my child, who gives me the reason to imagine better systems. And to the girl I used to be, who escaped a cult with nothing but a hunger to understand the world: This one's for you.

Amy

As someone who has preferred working mostly solo on my own creative projects, my partnership with Daniella feels nothing short of miraculous. Our strengths balance each other in ways that feel like creative alchemy, grounded in mutual trust, honesty, and shared values. Daniella, your integrity and vision inspire me, and I'm deeply honored and grateful you've entrusted me with your stories—first *Uncultured*, then this book, and hopefully many more to come.

Deep gratitude to our fierce editorial team: Rukshani Lye, for your profound knowledge, guidance, and research superpowers; Matthew Hoover for your deep wisdom and skill; and Christa Evans for your care and attention to detail. Thank you for whipping our mess of ideas and words into shape. Thank you to Elizabeth Evey and Ivica Jandri-jević for the beautiful cover and design. And thank you Saeah Wood, for your inexhaustible enthusiasm and big ideas, and for thinking outside the box even when I insist on staying inside it.

Working on this book has naturally made me reflect on the groups and communities I've been part of throughout my life. Though I have certainly not been immune to toxic groups, it could have been so much worse. I think what kept me from ever going too far was the gift of a deep inner knowing of myself, a fierce independence, and a healthy skepticism. Nature versus nurture aside, I owe much of that to my parents. Mom and Dad, thank you for standing out from the pack, and for teaching me to do the same.

I made some mistakes early on trying to fit in with the wrong groups in middle school—charismatic, often abusive leadership included—but I was lucky to find my way to real community in high school and beyond. To my Seattle and Oakland weirdos, many of whom are still my dearest friends: I'm so grateful we found each other. I'm always telling my daughter to look for the people whose weirdness compliments hers, the ones who never ask her to be anything but her quirky, unique self. Thank you for being that for me, and for teaching me how friendship works.

Thank you to my Jossey-Bass lunchroom bffs who wouldn't let me get a "stress test" from the Scientologists at the BART station. As much as I tried to convince you I was going undercover, you knew better.

My feelings about AA are complicated, but I know this: What made my early experience overwhelmingly positive was the community I found within it. To my old East Bay AA crew—you know who you are—thank you for saving my life. The Big Book is flawed and sexist and far from trauma-informed, and peer-led groups of wounded people will always carry their wounds, but you helped fill in the gaps. Thank you for making my first few years of recovery a lot less culty than they could have been.

Thank you to the OG Recovery Dharma crew—you know who you are too. Were we culty while we tried to build something that wasn't a cult? Probably, yeah. But cultiness is a spectrum, and I think we did pretty good, all things considered.

Thank you to everyone who still includes me in their groups even though I am a curmudgeonly non-joiner.

Thank you to my best-ever group, my new little hodgepodge of a family: Doug, Elouise, Caleb, Daisy. Thank you for complimenting my weirdness with yours.

And finally, to everyone out there doing the relentless, courageous, often invisible work of untangling yourselves and others from the groups and systems that cause harm—this book is for you. May we liberate ourselves, each other, and this country from all the cults we are in.

Note on Content and Intent

This book draws on publicly available sources, interviews, scholarly research, and the authors' own experiences. The narrative includes analysis, personal interpretation, and commentary intended to foster education, awareness, and public discussion.

While efforts have been made to ensure factual accuracy, the book should not be read as a legal, psychological, or clinical diagnosis of any individual or group. The content reflects the authors' understanding at the time of writing and is not intended to represent the views of any person or institution.

Some names and identifying details have been changed to protect individuals' privacy. Where real persons or organizations are discussed, the intent is to report, analyze, and critique behaviors and systems, not to defame or harm. Any similarities to individuals not explicitly named or discussed are purely coincidental.

The content is provided under the principles of fair use for educational, critical, and journalistic purposes. The authors and publisher expressly disclaim all liability for any actions taken or not taken based on the material presented herein. Readers are encouraged to conduct their own research and consult professionals where needed.

Notes

Prologue

1. Alexandra Dean, *Secrets of Playboy*, "Playboy Legacy."
2. Alexandra Dean, *Secrets of Playboy*, "Behind 'The Girls Next Door.'"
3. Madison, *Down the Rabbit Hole*.
4. PLBY Group, "2024 Financial Results."
5. Gardner, "Children of God sex cult survivors come out of the shadows."

Introduction: Good Cult/Bad Cult

1. Parker et al., "American Veteran Experience."
2. Obama, "Farewell Address," 22:50.

Chapter 1 (Part I): Charismatic Leadership

1. Brown and Farrell, *Cult of We*, 21.
2. Brown and Farrell, *Cult of We*, 245.
3. Brown and Farrell, *Cult of We*, 319–24.
4. Croom, "Psychopaths in Corporate Leadership."
5. Croom, "Psychopaths in Corporate Leadership."
6. "Charisma," *Psychology Today*.
7. Lebowitz, "7 Ways to Increase Your Charisma."
8. Beckert and Zafirovski, *International Encyclopedia of Economic Sociology*, 53.
9. Best, "Power, Authority and the State."
10. Beckert and Zafirovski, *International Encyclopedia of Economic Sociology*, 53.
11. Weber, "Nature of Charismatic Authority."
12. Montell, *Cultish*, 27.
13. Robbins, "Charisma."
14. Khurana, *Searching for a Corporate Savior*, 51–80.
15. Lambert, "Cult of the Charismatic CEO."
16. Beres et al., "Medical Medium."
17. Burleigh, "Gen Alpha Is Snubbing the Careers."
18. Conroy, "An Apocalyptic Cult."
19. Montell, *Cultish*, 57.
20. Montell, *Cultish*, 58.
21. Reiterman and Jacobs, *Raven*, x.

22. Naipaul, *Journey to Nowhere*, 297.
23. McChrystal et al., *Leaders*, xiii.
24. McChrystal et al., *Leaders*, 388.
25. McChrystal et al., *Leaders*, 391.
26. US Department of the Army, "TRADOC Regulation 350-6."
27. Sadun, "Myth of the Brilliant, Charismatic Leader."
28. McChrystal et al., *Leaders*, xiii.
29. Howson, "Types of Authority."
30. Dr. Janja Lalich, Zoom interview by the author, June 12, 2023.
31. Cohan, "4 Startling Insights."
32. Bilton, "Talented Ms. Holmes."
33. Wiedeman, "Art of Failing Up."
34. Ferranti, "Civil Rights Leader to Cult Murderer."
35. Reiterman and Jacobs, *Raven*, 328, 446.
36. Hough, *Leaving Isn't the Hardest Thing*, 19.
37. Cohan, "4 Startling Insights."
38. Beres et al., *Conspirituality*, 95.
39. Eva Orner, *Bikram*.
40. Brown and Farrell, *Cult of We*, 254.
41. Edmonson, *Scarred*, 24.
42. Rosman, "Rise and Fall of WeWork?"
43. Hong and Piccoli, "Sentenced to 120 Years in Prison."
44. Popkin and Farivar, "Holmes Admits Whistleblower Was Right."
45. Lowenstein, "'Bad Blood' Review."
46. Carlin, "True Story Behind 'WeCrashed.'"
47. Robbins, "Charisma."
48. Wallis and Bruce, "Sex, Violence and Religion," 115–27.
49. Lambert, "Cult of the Charismatic CEO."
50. Lalich, interview by the author.

Chapter 1 (Part II): ...And His Skinny White Woman

1. Kelvas, "What Is Thin Privilege?"; Haslam and Ryan, "The Glass Cliff."
2. Montell, *Cultish*, 59.
3. Gross, "The Mistress Syndrome," April 11, 2016, https://amandakgross.com/2016/04/11/the-mistress-syndrome (now inaccessible).
4. Gross, *White Women, Get Ready*, 18.
5. Arruza et al., *Feminism for the 99%*, 12.
6. Schuller, *Trouble with White Women*, 231.
7. Lelwica, "Religion of Thinness."
8. Edmonson, *Scarred*, 25.
9. Schuller, *Trouble with White Women*, 222, 227.
10. Lowenstein, "'Bad Blood' Review."
11. Carreyrou, *Bad Blood*, 174–75.

12. Cohan, "4 Startling Insights."
13. Dickson, "Toxic Ladyboss."
14. Sudakov, "The Deep End."
15. Center for Countering Digital Hate, "The Disinformation Dozen."
16. Kruse, "Casey DeSantis Problem."

Chapter 2: Sacred Assumption

1. Erickson, "Alcoholics Anonymous Most Effective Path to Alcohol Abstinence."
2. Dodds, *Sober Truth*, 1.
3. McCauley and Moskalenko, "Mechanisms of Political Radicalization."
4. Cialdini, *Influence*, 126.
5. Gurr, *Why Men Rebel*.
6. Cialdini, *Influence*, 88–89.
7. Bulwer, *Misguided*, 53.
8. Jasko et al., "Quest for Significance and Violent Extremism."
9. Kruglanski et al., "Significance-Quest Theory."
10. Singer and Lalich, *Cults in Our Midst*, 20.
11. Singer and Lalich, *Cults in Our Midst*, 23.
12. knitting.cult.lady, TikTok video, July 5, 2025, https://www.tiktok.com/@knitting.cult.lady?lang=en.
13. Lalich, *Bounded Choice*, 1–2.
14. Stein, *Terror, Love and Brainwashing*, 53.
15. Stein, *Terror, Love and Brainwashing*, 53.
16. Borum, *Psychology of Terrorism*, 26.
17. Venhaus, "Why Youth Join al-Qaeda."
18. Harari, *Sapiens*, 23–25
19. Harari, *Sapiens*, 38.
20. Borum, *Psychology of Terrorism*.
21. Borum, "Etiology of Radicalization," 21–22.
22. Dawson, "Study of New Religious Movements."
23. Lalich, *Bounded Choice, 7*.
24. Lalich, *Bounded Choice*, 251.
25. Erickson, "Alcoholics Anonymous Most Effective Path to Alcohol Abstinence."
26. Stein, *Terror, Love and Brainwashing*, 24.
27. Narcotics Anonymous, *Narcotics Anonymous White Booklet*.
28. Stein, *Terror, Love and Brainwashing*, 24.
29. Stein, *Terror, Love and Brainwashing*, 24.
30. Lalich, *Bounded Choice*, 15.
31. Festinger et al., *When Prophecy Fails*.
32. Festinger, *Theory of Cognitive Dissonance*.
33. Festinger et al., *When Prophecy Fails*.
34. Singer and Lalich, *Cults in Our Midst*, 9.
35. Singer and Lalich, *Cults in Our Midst*, 14.

36. Montell, *Cultish,* 33.
37. Mestyanek Young, *Uncultured*, 199.
38. Dawson, "Study of New Religious Movements," 18.
39. Smith, "Deprogramming from AA."
40. Lalich, *Bounded Choice,* 26, 231.

Chapter 3: Transcendent Mission

1. Holmes, "Lab Testing Reinvented," at 2:47.
2. Fuller and Masko, "Theranos: The Unicorn That Wasn't."
3. Hoffer, *True Believer.*
4. Lalich, *Bounded Choice*, 17.
5. North, "How #SaveTheChildren Is Pulling American Moms into QAnon."
6. Lalich, *Bounded Choice*, 56–57.
7. Lalich, *Bounded Choice*, 214–15.
8. Patrick, *Let Our Children Go!*, 58.
9. Hicks, "What Hymns Early Mormons Sang and How They Sang Them."
10. Mansfield, *Mormonizing of America*, 37.
11. "Sara" (pseudonym), direct message on TikTok, March 2023, formerly available at @groupbehaviorgal (account since deleted).
12. "Erin" (pseudonym), comment on TikTok video, March 2023, formerly available at @groupbehaviorgal (account since deleted).
13. Awana, "Global Impact"
14. Erikson, *Identity.*
15. Isenhardt et al., "Identity Diffusion and Extremist Attitudes in Adolescence."
16. Gereluk, "Whole-School Approach."
17. Levenson, "Congresswoman Apologizes."
18. Jones, "Generation Moves On."
19. Popik, "Christians in Action."
20. Mansfield, *Mormonizing of America*, 33.
21. Jensen et al., "PIRUS."
22. Samet, *Looking for the Good War*, 339.
23. Samet, *Looking for the Good War*, 75.
24. Hughes, "Those Who Fight Our Wars."
25. Saslow, *Rising Out of Hatred.*
26. Saslow, "White Flight of Derek Black."
27. Dreisbach and Anderson, "Nearly 1 in 5 Defendants."
28. Arnott, *Corporate Cults*, 4–5.
29. Achor et al., "9 Out of 10 People."
30. Torres, "4 Ways Elizabeth Holmes Manipulated."
31. Chang, *Brotopia*, 29.
32. Chang, *Brotopia*, 32.
33. Arnott, *Corporate Cults,* ix.

Chapter 4: Self-Sacrifice

1. Reddebrek, "Starvation Army."
2. Reddebrek, "Starvation Army"; Del Valle, "Salvation Army Says It Doesn't Discriminate"; Moreno, "Salvation Army Withdraws."
3. Gariepy, *Christianity in Action*.
4. Geddes, "Shaping and Sustaining a Community in Covenant."
5. Goffman, *Asylums*, xiii.
6. Madison, *Down the Rabbit Hole*, 5.
7. Arain et al., "Maturation of the Adolescent Brain."
8. Goffman, *Asylums*, 19–26.
9. Jenkinson, "Investigation into Cult Pseudo-Personality."
10. Singer and Lalich, *Cults in Our Midst*, xxiv.
11. Singer and Lalich, *Cults in Our Midst*, 10.
12. Tampa Bay Times, "Salvation Army Changes Rules for Married Officers"; Hart, "Officers Given 'Farewell Orders'"; Docter, "Changes of Appointment."
13. Silvestrini and Chen, "'It's a Sign of Weakness.'"
14. Petersen, "Dark Side of Capitalism."
15. Sharkey, "2025 Mother's Day Index."
16. Wolf, *Beauty Myth*, 53.
17. Singer and Lalich, *Cults in Our Midst,* 8.
18. Kennedy and Bailey, *The Synanon Fix*; McCormack, Bulwer, Misguided, 53.Outside the Limits of the Human Imagination"; Kapur, "Return of the Utopians"; Remnick, "The Spirit Level."
19. Lalich, *Take Back Your Life*, 19.
20. Lalich, "Declaration of Janja Lalich."
21. Lalich, *Take Back Your Life*, 41.
22. Scott, "Revisiting the Total Institution," 9.
23. Adler, "Medical Medium and the True Believer."
24. Gray, "Bias of 'Professionalism' Standards."
25. Singer and Lalich, *Cults in Our Midst*, 117.
26. Martinez, "Ranks Push Back on Criticism of Pregnant Women in the Military."
27. Strings, *Fearing the Black Body*, 6.
28. National Center for Complementary and Integrative Health, "Detoxes and Cleanses."
29. Novotney, "Boys and Men Make Up One Third."
30. Novotney, "Unrecognized Eating Disorders."
31. Robinson and Baronio, "Hyper-Masculine Content Floods Social Media."
32. Morin, "Men's Modesty, Religion, and the State."
33. Morin, "Men's Modesty, Religion, and the State."
34. Church of Jesus Christ of Latter-day Saints, "Temple Garments."
35. AR670.com, "Undergarments."
36. Hassan, *The BITE Model of Authoritarian Control*.
37. Bologna, "Personality Traits in Cult Leaders."

38. Hassan, "The BITE Model of Authoritarian Control."
39. Neilson et al., "Traditional Masculinity Ideology."
40. Langone, "Large Group Awareness Trainings."
41. Astor, "Tony Robbins Apologizes."
42. Raab, "What Is Spiritual Bypassing?"
43. Cullen, "Suppressing Emotions Can Harm You"; Chapman et al., "Emotion Suppression and Mortality Risk"; Srivastava et al., "Social Costs of Emotional Suppression."

Chapter 5: Isolation

1. Groth, *Kingdom of Happiness*, 227.
2. Groth, *Kingdom of Happiness*, 227.
3. Lalich, *Take Back Your Life*, 41.
4. Singer and Lalich, *Cults in Our Midst*, 114.
5. Stein, *Terror, Love and Brainwashing*, 31.
6. Lalich, *Take Back Your Life*, 35.
7. Crouse et al., "Buddy Team Assignment Program."
8. Szalavitz, *Help at Any Cost*, 9.
9. Stein, *Terror, Love and Brainwashing*, 47.
10. Montell, *Cultish*, 82.
11. Singer and Lalich, *Cults in Our Midst*, 118.
12. Lalich, *Take Back Your Life*, 32.
13. Singer and Lalich, *Cults in Our Midst*, 88.
14. Singer and Lalich, *Cults in Our Midst*, 117.
15. Singer and Lalich, *Cults in our Midst*, 285.
16. Polyportis et al., "Persuasive Communication in Sustainable Food Transitions."
17. Federal Trade Commission, "FTC Proposes Rule to Ban Noncompete Clauses."
18. Stack, "Tithing Requirement for Entry into LDS Temples."
19. Masci, "How Income Varies among U.S. Religious Groups."
20. Taylor, "Increase in Monthly Missionary Contribution."
21. Church of Jesus Christ of Latter-day Saints, "Missionary Finances Guidelines."
22. Bialik, "Americans Unhappy with Family, Social or Financial Life."
23. Agnew, "Meet the Queen of the 'Trad Wives'."
24. Dunlop, "189. Escaping Tradwife Cults and Christian Patriarchy."
25. Crouse et al., *Child Care Industry Trends*.
26. Stein, *Terror, Love and Brainwashing*, 63.
27. Singer and Lalich, *Cults in Our Midst*, 29.
28. LaGarde, "What's Really Going on at Zappos?"
29. Valeska et al., "Nondisclosure Agreements in the Trump White House."
30. Salter, *Organised Sexual Abuse*.
31. Reiterman and Jacobs, *Raven*, 258–60.
32. Chapman, *American Cult*, 75–84.
33. Stout, *Sociopath Next Door*, 96.
34. Bialik, "Americans Unhappy with Family, Social or Financial Life."

35. Tolin, "Banned Books List 2025."
36. Dow et al., "COVID-19 Pandemic and the Search for Structure."
37. Singer and Lalich, *Cults in Our Midst*, 114.
38. Institution of Engineering and Technology, "Facebook Did Not Act on Own Evidence."

Chapter 6: Distinguishable Vernacular

1. Diseko, "Woman Encouraging Her Followers to Visualise Death."
2. *Jon Kasbe,* The Deep End.
3. Beres et al., *Conspirituality*, 13.
4. Beres et al., *Conspirituality*, 15.
5. Boroditsky, "How Language Shapes Thought."
6. Noah, *Born a Crime*, audiobook, chap. 3, "Trevor, Pray," 29:59.
7. Montell, *Cultish*, 13.
8. Singer and Lalich, *Cults in Our Midst*, 57.
9. Montell, *Cultish*, 82.
10. United States Patent and Trademark Office, filing for "MAKE AMERICA GREAT AGAIN."
11. Singer and Lalich, *Cults in Our Midst*, 57.
12. Montell, *Cultish*, 57.
13. Emmorey, "Language"
14. Singer and Lalich, *Cults in Our Midst*, 57.
15. Montell, *Cultish*, 43.
16. Herman and Chomsky, *Manufacturing Consent*.
17. Poole, "Worst Examples of Management-Speak."
18. Ingersoll and Bender, "41 Phrases."
19. Marriott, "Jargon Is Choking Us."
20. Petersen, "Wellness Mommy Bloggers."
21. Singer and Lalich, *Cults in Our Midst*, 9.
22. Pearson, "'Spiritual' Experience of SoulCycle."
23. Scheeres, *A Thousand Lives*; Serratore, "Manson Family Murders."
24. Patrick, *Let Our Children Go!*, 71.
25. Doyle, "Amazon Center in Tennessee Fosters Family-like Culture"; Bezos, "1997 Letter to Shareholders"; Döpfner, "Jeff Bezos Interview."
26. Hawkins, "Tesla's 'Ultra Hardcore' Work Culture."
27. Perry et al., "Physiological and Psychological Effects of Group Chanting."
28. Keeler et al., "Neurochemistry and Social Flow of Singing."
29. Geirland, "Go with the Flow."
30. Lalich, *Take Back Your Life*, 125.
31. Singer and Lalich, *Cults in our Midst*, 128.
32. Basso et al., "Dance on the Brain."
33. Grinder and Bandler, *Trance-Formations*.
34. Montell, *Cultish*, 58.

35. Wright, "Jonestown Appeal."
36. Insider, "How Cults Actually Work (Nxivm)."
37. STARZ, "Seduced."
38. Dubrow and Dubrow Eichel, "Manipulation of Spiritual Experience."
39. Rinder, *A Billion Years.*
40. Streep, "5 Kinds of Blame-Shifting."
41. Schneid, "What Is DEI and What Challenges Does It Face?"
42. Huynh, "'Us' vs. 'Them' Dichotomy."
43. Trafton, "In the Blink of an Eye"; Alpuim and Ehrenberg, "Why Images Are So Powerful."
44. Grace, "Extremist Memes More Dangerous."
45. Marschall, *Drawing Power,* 5.
46. Mara Einstein, interview by the author, November 2024.
47. Stack, "Teaching LDS Polygamy in Primary."
48. Tucker, "Danger of Chick Tracts."
49. ExJW Caleb, "This Jehovah's Witness Cartoon."
50. Montell, *Cultish,* 43.
51. Lalich, *Take Back Your Life,* 123.

Chapter 7: Us-Versus-Them Mentality

1. Konnikova, "18 U.S. Presidents."
2. Foubert, "'Rapebait' E-mail Reveals Dark Side."
3. Biddix et al., "Influence of Fraternity and Sorority Involvement."
4. Minow and Einolf, "Sorority Participation and Sexual Assault Risk."
5. Nuwer, "Greek Letters Don't Justify."
6. North Carolina State University, "Hazing Statistics and Research."
7. Ispa-Landa and Oliver, "Hybrid Femininities."
8. Easton, "Greek Life on Campus."
9. Gallup and Purdue University, "Fraternities and Sororities."
10. Gibson, "Black and Brown First-Generation Fraternity Men."
11. Rensink, "Genocide of Native Americans."
12. Weber, *Protestant Ethic and the Spirit of Capitalism.*
13. Adams, *Epic of America,* 404–05.
14. Zimmer, message to ADS-L mailing list.
15. Bologna, "'Pull Yourself Up by Your Bootstraps' Is Nonsense."
16. Thomas Jefferson Foundation, "Business of Slavery at Monticello."
17. Statista Research Department, "Countries with the Largest Number of Prisoners."
18. Burton, *Strange Rites,* 39.
19. Horowitz, *One Simple Idea.*
20. Koch, "Prosperity Gospel and Economic Prosperity."
21. Bowler, *Blessed.*
22. Abbott, "Utopia and Bureaucracy."
23. Dodge, "Us Versus Them."

24. McCoy and Press, "When Democracies Become Perniciously Polarized."
25. Janis, *Groupthink.*
26. Hoffer, *True Believer.*

Chapter 8: Exploitation of Labor

1. Crawford, "My Time Working at Twitter."
2. Conger and Mac, *Character Limit*, 316.
3. Conger and Mac, *Character Limit*, 298.
4. Conger, Isaac, Mac, and Hsu, "Two Weeks of Chaos."
5. Lalich, interview; Durvasula, "What Is a Cult? With Dr. Janja Lalich."
6. Hill, *Beyond Belief*, 35–37.
7. Stein, *Terror, Love and Brainwashing*, 18–24.
8. Kern and Jungbauer, "Long-Term Effects of a Cult Childhood."
9. Stein, *Terror, Love and Brainwashing*, 108.
10. Williams, "Engagement of Young Adults in the Church."
11. Mission to Amish People, "Former Amish Testimonies."
12. Kennedy and Bailey, *The Synanon Fix.*
13. Coffee, "Utility of Liberal Capitalism."
14. VCU Libraries Social Welfare History Project, "Oneida Community."
15. Giller, "Bizarre History of Sleepytime Tea."
16. Deslippe, "Construction of Yogi Bhajan's Kundalini Yoga."
17. New York State Department of Labor, "Child Labor Violations at Common Sense Farm."
18. Flaherty, "Girl Scout Economics."
19. Girl Scouts – Diamonds, "Where the Girl Scout Cookie Money Goes."
20. Lalich, *Take Back Your Life*, 26.
21. ExJW Panda Tower, "Slaving Away as UNPAID Workers."
22. Schwartz and Severson, "Glorify Overwork and Refuse to Rest."
23. Yang and Santos, "Why Americans Are Lonelier."
24. Stelzner and Beckert, "Contribution of Enslaved Workers."
25. Hirsch, "America's Company Towns."
26. Guynn, "Welcome to Zucker Burg."
27. Linder, "Farm Workers and the Fair Labor Standards Act."
28. Hsu, "Children as Young as 12."
29. Penn State News, "Tipping and Smiling Are Both Expected."
30. Zhang, "Organization, Operation, and Victimization Process of Labor Trafficking."
31. Ojavalo, "What Is Modern Slavery?"

Chapter 9: High Entrance and Exit Costs

1. u/psado, "DO NOT Let Your Friends or Family Do MLM," Reddit, r/personalfinance, November 30, 2015. https://www.reddit.com/r/personalfinance/comments/3vqm65/psado_not_let_your_friends_or_family_do_mlm.

2. Liu, "Behavioral Economics of Multilevel Marketing."
3. Federal Trade Commission, "Multi-Level Marketing Businesses and Pyramid Schemes."
4. Truth in Advertising, "LuLaRoe Distributors in Bankruptcy."
5. Petrarca, "Why Americans Can't Resist Multilevel Marketing."
6. Taylor, "MLM's Abysmal Numbers."
7. Federal Trade Commission, "Multi-Level Marketing Businesses and Pyramid Schemes."
8. Northrup, "LuLaRoe Sales Reps' Problems."
9. Acts 4:34-35 in the King James Version (KJV)
10. Fuller et al., "Emerging Degree Reset."
11. Martin, "Critical Analysis of the Executive Success Programs."
12. Booda, "Ethical Ecstasy."
13. Murphy, "To Thwart Medical Student Burnout."
14. BestMind Behavioral Health, "Military Transition to Civilian Life."
15. Singer and Lalich, *Cults in Our Midst*, 23.
16. Jehovah's Witnesses, "Disfellowshipping Is a Loving Provision."
17. AvoidJW.org, "Jehovah's Witnesses in Norway Appeal."
18. Cosper, "Episode 1: Who Killed Mars Hill?"
19. Roberts, "Profile of Apostasy."
20. Nededog, "How Scientology costs members up to millions of dollars."
21. Krueger, "Scientology Accused of Not Paying."
22. Tobin, "Court Can't Take On Couple's Dispute."
23. American Medical Association, "Medical Student Financial FAQ."
24. Creative Planning, "How Women Are Financially Affected."
25. Stein, *Terror, Love and Brainwashing*, 82–83.
26. Edmondson and Ames, *A Little Bit Culty*.
27. Winell, "Religious Trauma Syndrome."
28. Lottret, "Is Your Company Starting to Look."
29. Hetler, "13 signs of a toxic workplace culture."
30. Ewens, "After Becoming Obsessed with Self-Help."
31. Perspectives Holistic Therapy, "Recovering from Religious Trauma."
32. Coon, "What Happens After Retirement"
33. Scism, "Retiring from Public Safety."
34. Singer and Lalich, *Cults in Our Midst*, 273.

Chapter 10: The Ends Justify the Means

1. Temes and Kovačević, "Rise of QAnon."
2. Myers, "Army Wants to Kick Out."
3. Oluo, *Mediocre,* 73–74.
4. Jasko et al., "Quest for Significance," 4.
5. Jasko et al., "Quest for Significance," 2.
6. Dreisbach and Anderson, "Nearly 1 in 5 Defendants."
7. Atuel and Castro, "3T Model of Military Veteran Radicalization."

8. Cushman, "Resentment, Online Living, and Sacred Soldiers."
9. Behler et al., "Making America Great Again?"
10. Youngblood, "Extremist Ideology as a Complex Contagion."
11. Hassan, *Cult of Trump*, 122.
12. Hassan, *Cult of Trump*, 85.
13. Hassan, *Cult of Trump*, 10.
14. Hassan, *Cult of Trump*, 169.
15. Hassan, *Cult of Trump*, 121.
16. Singer, *Cults in Our Midst*, 21.
17. Durvasula, "What Is a Cult? With Dr. Janja Lalich."
18. Chang, *Brotopia*, 30.
19. Thiel, *Zero to One*, 33–36, 100–2, 116, 197.
20. Lewsey, "Psychological 'Signature' for the Extremist Mind."
21. Borden, "Trump's America Echoes Our Puritan Past."
22. Allam, "Pro-Trump Christian Extremists Use Scripture."
23. Smith, "Nearly One in Four Americans Believe Political Violence."
24. Webber et al., "Road to Extremism."
25. Ross, "Inside Meadows' Phone on Jan. 6."
26. Cialdini, *Influence*, 87.
27. Delboy, "Dilemma of the People-Pleasing Chameleon."
28. US Attorney's Office, District of Columbia, "Arkansas Man Sentenced for Assaulting Law Enforcement."
29. PeopleShift, "McClelland's Motivation Theory."
30. Halverson, "Broken Shelves."
31. Harari, *Sapiens*, 77.
32. Bazzi et al., *Rugged Individualism and Collective (In)Action*.

Chapter 11: Just Groups

1. Warren, *Doomsday Cults*, 190.
2. Smithsonian Institution, "Human Characteristics: Social Life."
3. Porges, "The Polyvagal Theory."
4. Apicella and Silk, "Evolution of Human Cooperation."
5. Fitch et al., "Social Cognition and the Evolution of Language."
6. Holt-Lunstad et al., "Social Relationships and Mortality Risk."
7. Grant, "Cultic Lifecycle."
8. Brooks, "FANatics."
9. Chen, Yeh, and Lee, "Impact of Internet Celebrity Characteristics."
10. Jones and Okun, *Dismantling Racism*; Okun, "White Supremacy Characteristics."
11. Tiayon, "Do You Find Belonging in Groups or Communities?"
12. Goleman, *Emotional Intelligence*, 77–78.

Bibliography

A REBEL POST. "Values Gone Wrong: The Case of Enron Corporation." The Rebel Playbook for Employee Engagement. https://www.rebelplaybook.com/interviews/values-gone-wrong-enron-corporation.

ABC NEWS. "Doomsday Psychology: The Appeal of Armageddon." May 19, 2011. https://abcnews.go.com/Health/MindMoodNews/21-doomsday-psychology-appeal-armageddon/story?id=13638739.

ABC NEWS. "Feds Cite Amish for Child Labor Violations." July 30, 2001. https://abcnews.go.com/US/story?id=92732&page=1.

ABDUR-RAHMAN, NAHLAH. "Black Professors School Social Media Users Via 'Tiktok' University." Black Enterprise, January 27, 2025. https://www.blackenterprise.com/tiktok-university-black-professors-hillmantok.

ABURROW, YVONNE. "The Sunk Cost Fallacy." Changing Paths Resources, December 6, 2024. https://changingpathsresources.ca/2024/12/05/the-sunk-cost-fallacy.

ABBOTT, CARL. "Utopia and Bureaucracy: The Fall of Rajneeshpuram, Oregon." *Pacific Historical Review*, February 1, 1990, https://pdxscholar.library.pdx.edu/cgi/viewcontent.cgi?article=1039&context=usp_fac.

ACHOR, SHAWN, ANDREW REECE, GABRIELLA ROSEN KELLERMAN, ET AL. "9 Out of 10 People Are Willing to Earn Less Money to Do More-Meaningful Work." *Harvard Business Review*, November 6, 2018. https://hbr.org/2018/11/9-out-of-10-people-are-willing-to-earn-less-money-to-do-more-meaningful-work.

ADAMS, JAMES TRUSLOW. *The Epic of America*. Little, Brown, and Company, 1931.

ADLER, DAN. "The Medical Medium and the True Believer." *Vanity Fair*, April 26, 2023. https://www.vanityfair.com/style/2023/04/the-medical-medium-and-the-true-believer.

AGENTALPANDA. "CMV: There's No Myth in the Whole 'Myth of Self Made Billionaires.'" Reddit, https://www.reddit.com/r/changemyview/comments/zg3o5w/cmv_theres_no_myth_in_the_whole_myth_of_self_made.

AGNEW, MEGAN. "Meet the Queen of the 'Trad Wives' (And Her Eight Children)." *Sunday Times*, July 20, 2024. https://www.thetimes.com/magazines/the-sunday-times-magazine/article/meet-the-queen-of-the-trad-wives-and-her-eight-children-plfr50cgk.

ALBERTY, ERIN. "Popular New Zealand Podcast Takes Critical Look at Mormon Church's Abuse 'Helpline.'" Axios Salt Lake City, November 20, 2024. https://www.axios.com/local/salt-lake-city/2024/11/20/heavens-helpline-new-zealand-podcast-mormon-church-abuse.

ALCOHOLICS ANONYMOUS. *Alcoholics Anonymous: The Story of How Many Thousands of Men and Women Have Recovered from Alcoholism.* Alcoholics Anonymous World Services, 1939. https://www.aa.org/the-big-book.

ALCOHOLICS ANONYMOUS. *Twelve Steps and Twelve Traditions.* Alcoholics Anonymous World Services, 1953. https://www.aa.org/twelve-steps-twelve-traditions.

ALCOHOLICS ANONYMOUS. *Questions and Answers on Sponsorship.* Alcoholics Anonymous World Services, 2022. https://www.aa.org/sites/default/files/literature/P-15_1124.pdf.

ALEXANDER, KERRI LEE. "Tarana Burke." National Women's History Museum, 2020. Accessed June 7, 2025. https://www.womenshistory.org/education-resources/biographies/tarana-burke.

ALHARIRI, SARA. "I Escaped a 'Troubled Teen' Program—They Deprived Us of Sleep & Controlled Our Lives, 20 of My Friends Are Dead Now." The Irish Sun, July 23, 2024. https://www.thesun.ie/news/13462728/escaped-troubled-teen-program-deprived-sleep-friends-died/.

ALLAM, HANNAH. "Pro-Trump Violent Extremists Use Scripture to Justify Violent Rhetoric." *Washington Post,* July 13, 2024. https://www.washingtonpost.com/politics/2024/07/13/trump-christian-nationalist-violent-rhetoric.

ALLEN, KELLY-ANN. "The Importance of Belonging Across Life." *Psychology Today,* June 20, 2019. https://www.psychologytoday.com/us/blog/sense-of-belonging/201906/the-importance-of-belonging-across-life.

ALMEIDA, TERESA. "Five Signs You Might Be in a Corporate Cult." London School of Economics and Political Science, June 5, 2024. https://blogs.lsc.ac.uk/businessreview/2024/06/05/five-signs-you-might-be-in-a-corporate-cult.

ALPUIM, MARGARIDA, AND KATJA EHRENBERG. "Why Images Are So Powerful — and What Matters When Choosing Them." Bonn Institute, August 3, 2023. https://www.bonn-institute.org/en/news/psychology-in-journalism-5.

AMERICAN MEDICAL ASSOCIATION. "Medical Student Financial FAQ: Insight on Loan Forgiveness and More." February 22, 2024. https://www.ama-assn.org/medical-students/medical-school-life/medical-student-financial-faq-insight-loan-forgiveness.

AMSLER, SARAH. "58 Awful Corporate Jargon Phrases You Can't Escape." TechTarget, July 29, 2023. https://www.techtarget.com/whatis/feature/Awful-corporate-jargon-phrases-you-cant-escape.

ANTI-DEFAMATION LEAGUE. "QAnon." Updated October 28, 2022. https://www.adl.org/resources/backgrounder/qanon.

AP CENTRAL. "AP Exam Fees." Accessed July 18, 2025. https://apcentral.collegeboard.org /exam-administration-ordering-scores/ordering-fees/exam-fees.

APICELLA, COREN L., AND JOAN B. SILK. "The Evolution of Human Cooperation." *Current Biology* 29, no. 11 (2019): R447–R450. https://doi.org/10.1016/j.cub .2019.03.036.

AR670.COM. "Undergarments." *Online Guide for the AR 6701 Army Regulation*. December 21, 2018. https://www.ar670.com/2018/12/21/undergarments.

ARAIN, M., M. HAQUE, L. JOHAL, ET AL. "Maturation of the Adolescent Brain." *Neuropsychiatric Disease and Treatment* 9 (2013): 449–461. https://doi.org/10.2147 /NDT.S39776.

ARNOTT, DAVE. *Corporate Cults: The Insidious Lure of the All-Consuming Organization.* AMACOM Books, 1999.

ARRUZA, CINZIA, TITHI BHATTACHARYA, AND NANCY FRAZIER. *Feminism for the 99%: A Manifesto.* Verso, 2019.

ASTOR, MAGGIE. "Tony Robbins Apologizes for Saying Women Use #MeToo to Gain 'Significance.'" *New York Times*, April 9, 2018. https://www.nytimes.com/2018/04 /09/business/tony-robbins-me-too-apology.html.

ATUEL, HAZEL R., AND CARL A. CASTRO. "The 3T Model of Military Veteran Radical-ization and Extremism: Exploring Risk Factors and Protective Strategies." *Frontiers in Sociology* 10 (March 11, 2025). https://doi.org/10.3389/fsoc.2025.1500774.

AVOIDJW.ORG. "Jehovah's Witnesses in Norway Appeal to the European Court of Human Rights Over Shunning Policy." April 24, 2025. https://avoidjw.org/news /norway-appeal-childrens-rights-court-shunning/.

AWANA. "Global Impact." Accessed June 20, 2025. https://www.awana.org/global -impact.

AZARIAN, BOBBY. "Trump Is Gaslighting America Again — Here's How to Fight It." *Psychology Today*, August 31, 2018. https://www.psychologytoday.com/us/blog/ mind-in-the-machine/201808/trump-is-gaslighting-america-again-here-s-how -fight-it.

BALTUS, HOWARD. "Delving into the Minds of Trump Supporters." Democrats Abroad, September 19, 2024. https://www.democratsabroad.org/341101/delving_into_the _minds_of_trump_supporters.

BANDURA, ALBERT. "Moral Disengagement in the Perpetration of Inhumanities." *Personality and Social Psychology Review* 3, no. 3 (1999): 193–209. https://doi.org /10.1207/s15327957pspr0303_3.

BARKAN, STEVEN E. "3.5: Resocialization and Total Institutions." In *Sociology: Understanding and Changing the Social World*, 2nd ed. University of Minnesota Libraries, 2016. https://open.lib.umn.edu/sociology/chapter/4-5-resocialization-and -total-institutions. [Source no longer available.]

BARRY, ELOISE. "Theranos Founder Elizabeth Holmes Faces Trial for Fraud. Here's What to Know About the Case." *Time*, August 25, 2021. https://time.com/6092115/elizabeth-holmes-trial.

BASIL, MICHAEL D. "Identification as a Mediator of Celebrity Effects." *Journal of Broadcasting & Electronic Media* 40, no. 4 (1996): 478–495. https://eric.ed.gov/?id=EJ537899.

BASSO, JULIA C., MEDHA KUMARI SATYAL, AND RACHEL RUGH. "Dance on the Brain: Enhancing Intra- and Inter-Brain Synchrony." *Frontiers in Human Neuroscience* 14 (2021): 584312. https://doi.org/10.3389/fnhum.2020.584312.

BAZZI, SAMUEL, MARTIN FISZBEIN, AND MESAY GEBRESILASSE. *Rugged Individualism and Collective (In)Action During the COVID-19 Pandemic*, NBER Working Paper No. 27776. National Bureau of Economic Research, September 2020. http://www.nber.org/papers/w27776.

BECKERT, JENS, AND MILAN ZAFIROVSKI. *International Encyclopedia of Economic Sociology*. Routledge, 2006.

BERES, DEREK, MATTHEW REMSKI, AND JULIAN WALKER. "Episode 156: Medical Medium (w/ Dan Adler)." *Conspirituality* (podcast). June 1, 2023. https://www.conspirituality.net/episodes/156-medical-medium-dan-adler.

BERES, DEREK, MATTHEW REMSKI, AND JULIAN WALKER. *Conspirituality: How New Age Conspiracy Theories Became a Health Threat*. PublicAffairs, 2023.

BESTMIND BEHAVIORAL HEALTH. "Challenges of the Military Transition to Civilian Life." Accessed June 29, 2025. https://bestmindbh.com/blog/challenges-of-the-military-transition-to-civilian-life.

BEZOS, JEFFREY P. "1997 Letter to Shareholders." 1997 Annual Report. Amazon.com, Inc., 1998. https://media.corporate-ir.net/media_files/irol/97/97664/reports/Shareholderletter98.pdf.

BHANDARI, SANDHYA. "Reality TV Distorts People's Perception of True Reality." *Washburn Review*, February 21, 2023. https://washburnreview.org/42994/features/reality-tv-distorts-peoples-perception-of-true-reality.

BEHLER, ANNA MARIA C., ATHENA CAIRO, JEFFREY D. GREEN, ET AL. "Making America Great Again? National Nostalgia's Effect on Outgroup Perceptions." *Frontiers in Psychology* 12 (2021). https://doi.org/10.3389/fpsyg.2021.555667.

BEST, SHAUN. "Power, Authority and the State." In *Introduction to Politics and Society*, 6-39. SAGE Publications Ltd, 2002. https://doi.org/10.4135/9781446220832.n2.

BIALIK, KRISTEN. "Americans Unhappy with Family, Social or Financial Life Are More Likely to Say They Feel Lonely." Pew Research Center, December 3, 2018, https://www.pewresearch.org/short-reads/2018/12/03/americans-unhappy-with-family-social-or-financial-life-are-more-likely-to-say-they-feel-lonely.

BIEBER, CHRISTY. "Revealing Divorce Statistics in 2025." *Forbes*, November 20, 2024. https://www.forbes.com/advisor/legal/divorce/divorce-statistics.

BIDDIX, J. PATRICK, MALINDA M. MATNEY, ERIC M. NORMAN, ET AL. "The Influence of Fraternity and Sorority Involvement: A Critical Analysis of Research (1996–2013)." *ASHE Higher Education Report* 39, no. 6 (2014). https://doi.org/10.1002/aehe.20012.

BILTON, NICK. "The Talented Ms. Holmes." *Vanity Fair*, October 2016. https://archive.vanityfair.com/article/share/b843ef57-9c53-4b35-92f2-059dca6f86ae.

BLITZ, MATT. "The Popular Oneida Silverware and the Polyamorous Religious Cult That Started It All." Today I Found Out, July 1, 2016. https://www.todayifoundout.com/index.php/2016/07/oneida-silverware-socialist-sexual-polygamous-religious-community.

BOLOGNA, CAROLINE. "The 9 Most Common Personality Traits in Cult Leaders." HuffPost, March 8, 2024. https://www.huffpost.com/entry/cult-leaders-personality-traits-common_l_65c17191e4b0dbc806adcdba.

BOLOGNA, CAROLINE. "Why the Phrase 'Pull Yourself Up by Your Bootstraps' Is Nonsense." HuffPost, August 9, 2018, https://www.huffpost.com/entry/pull-yourself-up-by-your-bootstraps-nonsense_n_5b1ed024e4b0bbb7a0e037d4.

BOND, SHANNON. "Just 12 People Are Behind Most Vaccine Hoaxes on Social Media, Research Shows." NPR, updated May 14, 2021. https://www.npr.org/2021/05/13/996570855/disinformation-dozen-test-facebooks-twitters-ability-to-curb-vaccine-hoaxes.

BONNER, MICHAEL, AND GRAHAM ELLENDER. "Military Training: Does It Predispose Service Personnel to Negative Mental Health Issues?" *Journal of Mental Health Disorders* 2, no. 1 (2022): 11–18.

BOODA, DAVE. "Ethical Ecstasy: Can We Combine Intensity and Integrity?" Boodaism, May 2025. https://boodaism.com/lgat.

BOOT, MAX. *The Savage Wars of Peace: Small Wars and the Rise of American Power.* Basic Books, 2002.

BORDEN, JANE. "Donald Trump's America Echoes Our Puritan Past." *Vanity Fair,* March 21, 2025. https://www.vanityfair.com/news/story/donald-trumps-america-echoes-our-puritan-past.

BORODITSKY, LERA. "How Language Shapes Thought." *Scientific American*, February 1, 2011. https://www.scientificamerican.com/article/how-language-shapes-thought.

BORUM, RANDY. *Psychology of Terrorism.* Mental Health Law & Policy Faculty Publications 571, 2004. https://digitalcommons.usf.edu/mhlp_facpub/571.

BORUM, RANDY. "The Etiology of Radicalization." In *The Handbook of the Criminology of Terrorism*, edited by Gary LaFree and Joshua D. Freilich, 17–32. WileyBlackwell, 2016. https://doi.org/10.1002/9781118923986.ch1.

BORUM, RANDY. "Radicalization into Violent Extremism II: A Review of Conceptual Models and Empirical Research." *Journal of Strategic Security* 4, no. 4 (2010): 19–36. https://doi.org/10.5038/1944-0472.4.4.2.

BOTH, ALEXANDRA. "The Great Reshuffling Revisited: Why Are Americans Moving?" *RentCafe*, December 4, 2024. https://www.rentcafe.com/blog/rental-market /market-snapshots/top-reasons-for-moving-us.

BOWLER, KATE. *Blessed: A History of the American Prosperity Gospel*. Oxford University Press, 2013.

BRADBURY, SHELLY. "Long Days, No Pay: Twelve Tribes Cult Exploits Followers for Free Labor, Ex-Members Say." *Denver Post*, March 7, 2022. https://www.mercurynews .com/2022/03/07/twelve-tribes-cult-labor-exploitation-yellow-deli.

BROOKS, SAMANTHA K. "FANatics: Systematic Literature Review of Factors Associated with Celebrity Worship, and Suggested Directions for Future Research." *Current Psychology* 40 (February 2021): 864–86. https://doi.org/10.1007/s12144-018-9978-4.

BROWN, ANGELO KEVIN. "Fake It Until You Make It!: The Crimes and Trial of Anna Sorokin (Delvey)." In *Cases on Crimes, Investigations, and Media Coverage*, edited by Liam James Leonard. IGI Global Scientific Publishing, 2022. https://arch.astate.edu/clac -scrim-facpub/2.

BROWN, ELIOT, AND MAUREEN FARRELL. *The Cult of We: WeWork, Adam Neumann, and the Great Startup Delusion*. Crown, 2021.

BRUCE, STEVE. "EVP—Enron's Was Chiseled in Marble." HR Daily Advisor, April 2, 2015. https://hrdailyadvisor.blr.com/2015/04/02/evp-enrons-was-chiseled-in-marble.

BRUNI, FRANK. "A Pox on Campus Life." *New York Times,* December 2, 2014. https: //www.nytimes.com/2014/12/03/opinion/frank-bruni-a-pox-on-campus-life.html.

BUENING, SARAH, AND ELLE COWLEY. "Buening & Cowley: Mormon Missionary Trips Do More Harm Than Good." *Daily Utah Chronicle*, April 29, 2022. https: //dailyutahchronicle.com/2022/04/29/buening-cowley-mormon-missionary.

BULWER, PERRY. *Misguided: My Jesus Freak Life in a Doomsday Cult*. New Star Books, 2023.

BURLEIGH, EMMA. "Gen Alpha Is Snubbing the Careers That Boomers Dreamed Of." *Fortune*, May 2025. https://fortune.com/article/gen-alpha-dream-careers -youtuber-influencer-social-media.

BURTON, BONNIE. "Star Trek Fans Are Not Pleased About the New US Space Force Logo." CNET, January 24, 2020. https://www.cnet.com/culture/entertainment/star-trek -fans-are-not-pleased-about-the-new-us-space-force-logo.

BURTON, TARA ISABELLA. *Strange Rites: New Religions for a Godless World*. PublicAffairs, 2020.

BUSH, GEORGE W. "Address to a Joint Session of Congress and the American People" (speech, United States Capitol, Washington, DC, September 20, 2001). White House Archives. https://georgewbush-whitehouse.archives.gov/news/releases/2001 /09/20010920-8.html.

CAFFIER, JUSTIN. "The Heaven's Gate Nikes and the Sneakerheads Who Collect Them." Vice, March 16, 2017. https://www.vice.com/en/article/the-heavens-gate-nikes-and-the-sneakerheads-who-collect-them.

CALOGERO, RACHEL M. "A Test of Objectification Theory: The Effect of the Male Gaze on Appearance Concerns in College Women." *Psychology of Women Quarterly* 28, no. 1 (2004): 16–21.

CAREATC. "5 Reasons Why Physicians Are Leaving the Practice (And Where They Want to Go)." Health Industry News, July 9, 2024. https://www.careatc.com/blog/5-reasons-why-physicians-are-leaving-the-practice-and-where-they-want-to-go.

CAREY, BENEDICT. "Have You Heard? Gossip Turns Out to Serve a Purpose" *New York Times,* August 16, 2005. https://www.nytimes.com/2005/08/16/science/have-you-heard-gossip-turns-out-to-serve-a-purpose.html.

CARLIN, SHANNON. "The True Story Behind *WeCrashed*" *Time*, March 18, 2022. https://time.com/6158804/wecrashed-true-story.

CARNEGIE, MEGAN. "Hustle Culture: Is This the End of Rise-and-Grind?" BBC, April 17, 2023. https://www.bbc.com/worklife/article/20230417-hustle-culture-is-this-the-end-of-rise-and-grind.

CARPENTIER, MEGAN. "How LuLaRoe Made Its Founders Rich While So Many Others Went Bankrupt." Yahoo! Entertainment, September 8, 2021. https://www.yahoo.com/entertainment/lularoe-made-founders-rich-while-162100316.html.

CARREYROU, JOHN. *Bad Blood: Secrets and Lies in a Silicon Valley Startup.* Alfred A. Knopf, 2018.

CARUSO, SKYLER. "What Happened to Synanon Founder Charles 'Chuck' Dederich? All About the Cult Leader Who Died in 1997." *People*, April 2, 2024. https://people.com/what-happened-to-synanon-founder-charles-dederich-8622934.

CENTER FOR COUNTERING DIGITAL HATE. "The Disinformation Dozen: Why Platforms Must Act on Twelve Leading Online Anti-Vaxxers." March 24, 2021. https://counterhate.com/research/the-disinformation-dozen.

CHANG, EMILY. *Brotopia: Breaking Up the Boys' Club of Silicon Valley.* Penguin, 2018.

CHAPMAN, BENJAMIN P., KEVIN FISCELLA, ICHIRO KAWACHI, PAUL DUBERSTEIN, AND PETER MUENNIG. "Emotion Suppression and Mortality Risk over a 12-Year Follow-Up." *Journal of Psychosomatic Research* 75, no. 4 (October 2013): 381–85. https://doi.org/10.1016/j.jpsychores.2013.07.014.

CHAPMAN, ROBYN, ED. *American Cult: A Graphic History of Religious Cults in America from the Colonial Era to Today*, illustrated by Lara Antal. Silver Sprocket, 2021.

CHEN, OZ. "My Review of Landmark Forum (Los Angeles)." December 2018. https://ozchen.com/landmark-forum-review.

CHEN, TSER, TSAI YEH, AND FANG LEE. "The Impact of Internet Celebrity Characteristics on Followers' Impulse Purchase Behavior: The Mediation of Attachment and Parasocial Interaction." *Journal of Research in Interactive Marketing* 15, no. 3 (2021).

CHERRY, KENDRA. "What Is Conformity?" Verywell Mind, Updated on June 22, 2024. https://www.verywellmind.com/what-is-conformity-2795889.

CHILDCARE AWARE OF AMERICA. "Child Care in America: 2024 Price & Supply." https://www.childcareaware.org/price-landscape24/.

CHRISTENSEN, LYNNE, AND LEWIS E. MARSHALL. "Cults and Mind Manipulation: Pathology or Path of Righteousness." 21stC (Columbia University), accessed June 14, 2025. https://www.columbia.edu/cu/21stC/issue-1.4/mbmcult.html.

CHURCH OF JESUS CHRIST OF LATTER-DAY SAINTS. "Temple Garments." Accessed July 7, 2025. https://newsroom.churchofjesuschrist.org/article/temple-garments.

CHURCH OF JESUS CHRIST OF LATTER-DAY SAINTS. "Missionary Finances Guidelines." Accessed June 16, 2025, https://www.churchofjesuschrist.org/tools/help/missionary-finances.

CIALDINI, ROBERT B. *Influence: The Psychology of Persuasion*. 1984. Reprint, HarperCollins, 2007. E-book.

CLAYTON, JAMES. "Elizabeth Holmes: Has the Theranos Scandal Changed Silicon Valley?" BBC News, January 3, 2022. https://www.bbc.com/news/technology-58469882.

COFFEE, KEVIN. "The Oneida Community and the Utility of Liberal Capitalism." *Radical Americas* 4, no. 1 (2019). https://doi.org/10.14324/111.444.ra.2019.v3.1.003.

COFFEY, MAUREEN. "Still Underpaid and Unequal." Center for American Progress. July 19, 2022. https://www.americanprogress.org/article/still-underpaid-and-unequal.

COHAN, PETER. "4 Startling Insights Into Elizabeth Holmes From Psychiatrist Who's Known Her Since Childhood." *Forbes*, February 17, 2019. https://www.forbes.com/sites/petercohan/2019/02/17/4-startling-insights-into-elizabeth-holmes-from-psychiatrist-whos-known-here-since-childhood.

COLVIN, ALEXANDER J. S., AND HEIDI SHIERHOLZ. "Noncompete Agreements." Economic Policy Institute. December 10, 2019. https://www.epi.org/publication/noncompete-agreements.

CONGER, KATE, MIKE ISAAC, RYAN MAC, ET AL. "Two Weeks of Chaos: Inside Elon Musk's Takeover of Twitter." *New York Times,* November 11, 2022. https://www.nytimes.com/2022/11/11/technology/elon-musk-twitter-takeover.html.

CONGER, KATE, AND RYAN MAC. *Character Limit: How Elon Musk Destroyed Twitter.* Penguin, 2024.

CONNER, CHRISTOPHER T. "QAnon, Authoritarianism, and Conspiracy within American Alternative Spiritual Spaces." *Frontiers in Sociology* 8 (2023): 1136333. https://doi.org/10.3389/fsoc.2023.1136333.

CONROY, J. OLIVER. "An Apocalyptic Cult, 900 Dead: Remembering the Jonestown Massacre, 40 Years On." *Guardian*, November 17, 2018. https://www.theguardian.com/world/2018/nov/17/an-apocalyptic-cult-900-dead-remembering-the-jonestown-massacre-40-years-on.

COOK, JOHN. "Stephen Colbert Wants to Know: Is Zappos CEO Tony Hsieh Really a Cult Leader?" GeekWire, August 2, 2011. https://www.geekwire.com/2011/stephen-colbert-tony-hsieh-cult-leader/.

COON, DANNY. "What Happens After Retirement." Bulletproof First Responder, March 7, 2020. https://bulletprooffirstresponder.com/what-happens-after-retirement.

CORBEL, KÉVIN. "When Your Company is Looking More and More Like a Cult." Welcome to the Jungle, January 2, 2024. https://www.welcometothejungle.com/en/articles/company-looking-like-a-cult.

COSPER, MIKE (HOST). "Episode 1: Who Killed Mars Hill?". The Rise and Fall of Mars Hill (podcast). June 21, 2021. https://www.christianitytoday.com/podcasts/the-rise-and-fall-of-mars-hill/who-killed-mars-hill-church-mark-driscoll-rise-fall/

CRANE, GENEVIEVE SLY, AND BENJAMIN NUGENT. "Are Frats and Sororities Really Just Cults?" Electric Literature, October 2, 2020. https://electricliterature.com/fraternity-sorority-benjamin-nugent-genevieve-sly-crane.

CRAWFORD, ESTER. "An Epilogue to My Time Working at Twitter." Medium, July 26, 2023. https://esthercrawford.medium.com/an-epilogue-to-my-time-working-at-twitter-24a126098246.

CREATIVE PLANNING. "How Women Are Financially Affected by Divorce." Creative Planning, April 3, 2024. https://creativeplanning.com/insights/financial-planning/how-women-are-financially-affected-by-divorce.

CROOM, SIMON. "12% of Corporate Leaders are Psychopaths. It's Time to Take This Seriously." *Fortune*, June 6, 2021. https://fortune.com/2021/06/06/corporate-psychopaths-business-leadership-csr.

CROUCH, IAN. "Did the Vikings Cut Chris Kluwe for His Gay-Rights Activism?" *New Yorker*, January 3, 2014. https://www.newyorker.com/sports/sporting-scene/did-the-vikings-cut-chris-kluwe-for-his-gay-rights-activism.

CROUSE, GILBERT, ROBIN GHERTNER, AND NINA CHIEN. "Child Care Industry Trends During the Recovery from the COVID-19 Pandemic." US Department of Health and Human Services, Office of the Assistant Secretary for Planning and Evaluation, 2022. https://aspe.hhs.gov/sites/default/files/documents/71981d3ec3a1d02537d86d827806834b/Child-Care-Trends-COVID.pdf.

CULLEN, KATHERINE. "Suppressing Emotions Can Harm You—Here's What to Do Instead." *Psychology Today*, December 23, 2022. https://www.psychologytoday.com/us/blog/the-truth-about-exercise-addiction/202212/suppressing-emotions-can-harm-you-heres-what-to-do.

CUSHMAN, PHILIP. "Resentment, Online Living, and Sacred Soldiers in Trumpist America: Toward Understanding the Emergence of a Populist Cult." *Journal of Theoretical and Philosophical Psychology* 44, no. 2 (2024): 80–94. https://doi.org/10.1037/teo0000259.

CUTLER, R. J., DIRECTOR. *Big Vape: The Rise and Fall of Juul*. United States: Netflix, 2023. TV miniseries.

CZARNECKA, BARBARA. "Women's Hair in Lager Narratives." *Folia Litteraria Polonica* 8, no. 46 (2017): 105–119. https://doi.org/10.18778/1505-9057.46.07.

DA COSTA, CELINNE. "Stop Idolizing Hustle Culture and Do This Instead." *Forbes*, August 26, 2021. https://www.forbes.com/sites/celinnedacosta/2019/04/28/stop-idolizing-hustle-culture-and-do-this-instead.

DASKALOPOULOS, ALLY, NADIA HERNANDEZ, FELIX JASON, ET AL. "Thinking Outside the Bubble: Addressing Polarization and Disinformation on Social Media." Center for Strategic and International Studies, September 17, 2021. https://journalism.csis.org/thinking-outside-the-bubble-addressing-polarization-and-disinformation-on-social-media.

DAVENPORT, CHARLES R. "Understanding the Manipulative Tactics of Cults." Davenport Psychology., February 12, 2024. https://davenportpsychology.com/2024/02/12/understanding-the-manipulative-tactics-of-cults.

DAVIES, CHRISTIE. "Goffman's Concept of the Total Institution: Criticisms and Revisions." *Human Studies* 12, no. 1/2 (1989): 77–95.

DAVIS, VIOLA. *Finding Me*. HarperOne, 2022.

DAVIS, WES. "Amazon Teamsters in NYC Have Voted to Authorize a Strike." The Verge, December 16, 2024. https://www.theverge.com/2024/12/16/24322383/amazon-warehouse-delivery-drivers-unions-teamsters-strike-labor-safety-senate-report.

DAWSON, LORNE L. "The Study of New Religious Movements and the Radicalization of Home-Grown Terrorists: Opening a Dialogue." *Terrorism and Political Violence* 22, no. 1 (2009): 1–21.

DEAN, ALEXANDRA, DIRECTOR. *Secrets of Playboy*. Aired January 24, 2022, on A&E. https://www.aetv.com/shows/secrets-of-playboy.

DEANS, BOB. "Captain John Smith." *Time*. April 26, 2007. https://time.com/archive/6680849/captain-john-smith.

DEIKMAN, ARTHUR J. *The Wrong Way Home: Uncovering the Patterns of Cult Behavior in American Society*. Beacon, 1990.

DELBOY, SANTIAGO. "The Dilemma of the People-Pleasing Chameleon: The Struggle of Seeking Validation While Losing Oneself in Relationships." *Psychology Today*, last modified April 9, 2025. https://www.psychologytoday.com/us/blog/relationships-healing-relationships/202503/the-dilemma-of-the-people-pleasing-chameleon.

DEL VALLE, GABY. "The Salvation Army Says It Doesn't Discriminate against LGBTQ People. Critics Say That's Not True." *Vox*, December 16, 2019. https://www.vox.com/the-goods/2019/12/16/21003560/salvation-army-anti-lgbtq-controversies-donations.

DEPARTMENT OF THE ARMY. *Army Regulation 670-1: Wear and Appearance of Army Uniforms and Insignia.* Washington, DC: Department of the Army, 2017. https://milreg.com/File.aspx?id=1385.

DESLIPPE, PHILIP. "Reappraising the Construction of Yogi Bhajan's Kundalini Yoga." *Sikh Formations: Religion, Culture, Theory* 20 (2024). https://doi.org/10.1080/17448727.2024.2320015.

DEVILBISS, KERRY. "Out of the Rooms: Why I Left AA." Workit Health. https://www.workithealth.com/blog/why-i-left-aa.

DICKSON, E. J. "How 'Lean In' Feminism Created Elizabeth Holmes and the Toxic Ladyboss." *Rolling Stone*, March 22, 2019. https://www.rollingstone.com/culture/culture-features/elizabeth-holmes-theranos-documentary-lean-in-feminism-811433.

A DICTIONARY OF SOCIOLOGY. "Degradation Ceremony." Encyclopedia.com, accessed January 10, 2025. https://www.encyclopedia.com/social-sciences/dictionaries-thesauruses-pictures-and-press-releases/degradation-ceremony.

DIGIOVANNA, SAM. "Retiring from Public Safety: The Big Breakup." Lexipol, June 28, 2024. https://www.lexipol.com/resources/blog/retiring-from-public-safety-the-big-breakup.

DISCOVERY FREEMASONRY. "Famous Freemasons." United Grand Lodge of England. https://www.ugle.org.uk/discover-freemasonry/famous-freemasons.

DISEKO, LEBO. "Teal Swan: The Woman Encouraging Her Followers to Visualise Death." BBC News, November 22, 2019. https://www.bbc.com/news/world-us-canada-50478821.

DITTMANN, MELISSA. "Lessons from Jonestown." *Monitor on Psychology* 34, no. 10 (2003): 36.

DIXIT, PRANAV. "Meta Keeps 'Block List.'" Business Insider, February 2025. https://www.businessinsider.com/meta-secret-block-lists-bar-rehiring-some-former-employees-2025-2.

DIXON, LUCAS J., MATTHEW J. HORNSEY, NICOLE HARTLEY, ET AL. "The Psychology of Attraction to Multi-Level Marketing." *Journal of Consumer Affairs* 57, no. 3 (Fall 2023): 1213–35. https://doi.org/10.1111/joca.12526.

DOCTER, BOB. "Changes of Appointment." *Caring* magazine (Salvation Army), December 12, 2016. https://caringmagazine.org/changes-of-appointment.

DODES, LANCE. *The Sober Truth: Debunking the Bad Science Behind Twelve-Step Programs and the Rehab Industry.* Beacon Press, 2015.

DODGE, JEFF. "Us Versus Them: The 'Wicked Problem' of How We Talk to Each Other in 2020." College of Liberal Arts, Colorado State University. September 29, 2020. https://libarts.source.colostate.edu/us-vs-them-the-wicked-problem-of-how-we-talk-to-each-other-in-2020.

DÖPFNER, MATHIAS. "Jeff Bezos Interview with Axel Springer CEO on Amazon, Blue Origin, Family." Business Insider, April 28, 2018. https://www.businessinsider.com/jeff-bezos-interview-axel-springer-ceo-amazon-trump-blue-origin-family-regulation-washington-post-2018-4.

DOW, BENJAMIN J., AMBER L. JOHNSON, CYNTHIA S. WANG, ET AL. "The COVID-19 Pandemic and the Search for Structure: Social Media and Conspiracy Theories." *Social and Personality Psychology Compass* 15, no. 9 (2021): e12636. https://doi.org/10.1111/spc3.12636.

DOYLE, MEG. "Amazon Center in Tennessee Fosters Family-Like Culture Among Nearly 800 Employees." News Channel 9, November 29, 2024. https://newschannel9.com/news/local/amazon-center-in-tennessee-fosters-family-like-culture-among-nearly-800-employees.

DREISBACH, TOM, AND MEG ANDERSON. "Nearly 1 In 5 Defendants in Capitol Riot Cases Served in the Military." NPR, January 21, 2021. https://www.npr.org/2021/01/21/958915267/nearly-one-in-five-defendants-in-capitol-riot-cases-served-in-the-military.

DUBROW, LINDA, AND STEVE K. DUBROW EICHEL. "The Manipulation of Spiritual Experience: Unethical Hypnosis in Destructive Cults." Cult Recovery 101. Accessed July 18, 2025. https://cultrecovery101.com/cult-recovery-readings/the-manipulation-of-spiritual-experience-unethical-hypnosis-in-destructive-cults.

DU MEZ, KRISTIN KOBES. *Jesus and John Wayne: How White Evangelicals Corrupted a Faith and Fractured a Nation*. LiveRight, 2020.

DUNLAP, TORI, HOST. Financial Feminist (podcast), "189. Escaping Tradwife Cults and Christian Patriarchy with Tia Levings." *Financial Feminist* (podcast), September 30, 2024. Her First 100k. https://herfirst100k.com/financial-feminist-show-notes/189-escaping-tradwife-cults-and-christian-patriarchy-with-tia-levings.

DURVASULA, RAMANI, HOST. *Navigating Narcissism with Dr. Ramani* (podcast). Season 2, episode 15, "What Is a Cult? With Dr. Janja Lalich." June 22, 2023. https://podcasts.apple.com/us/podcast/what-is-a-cult-with-dr-janja-lalich/id1629909313.

DZIAK, MARK. "Great Man Theory." *Research Starters: Religion and Philosophy*. EBSCO. Accessed June 6, 2025. https://www.ebsco.com/research-starters/religion-and-philosophy/great-man-theory.

EASTON, CHELSEA. "Greek Life on Campus: A Data-Driven Look at the Impact on College Students." myFraternity Life, March 18, 2025. https://myfraternitylife.org/2025/03/18/greek-life-on-campus-a-data-driven-look-at-the-impact-on-college-students/.

EDMONSON, SARAH. *Scarred: The True Story of How I Escaped NXIVM, the Cult that Bound My Life*. Chronicle Books, 2019.

EDMONDSON, SARAH, AND ANTHONY "NIPPY" AMES, HOSTS. *A Little Bit Culty* (podcast). "Sex Cult Nun: Faith Jones on Breaking Way from the Children of God (Part 2)." November 3, 2022. https://alittlebitculty.com/episode/sex-cult-nun-faith-jones-on-breaking-way-from-the-children-of-god-part-2.

EHRENREICH, BARBARA. *Bright-Sided: How the Relentless Promotion of Positive Thinking Has Undermined America.* Metropolitan, 2009.

EIDELSON, JOSH. "The Gig Economy Is Coming for Millions of American Jobs." Bloomberg, February 7, 2021. https://www.bloomberg.com/news/features/2021 -02-17/gig-economy-coming-for-millions-of-u-s-jobs-after-california-s-uber-lyft-vote.

EISENSTEIN, PAUL A. "Iacocca Bows Out, but Does Not Close the Door." *Christian Science Monitor*, December 31, 1992. https://www.csmonitor.com/1992/1231 /31091.html.

EGNER, KATE. "Slavery in Colonial America." American Battlefield Trust. Accessed June 22, 2025. https://www.battlefields.org/learn/articles/slavery-colonial-america.

EGWUONWU, NNAMDI, AND RAQUEL CORONELL URIBE. "'So Evil' and 'Dangerous': Trump Doubles Down on Calling Democrats 'Enemies from Within.'" NBC News, updated October 16, 2024. https://www.nbcnews.com/politics/2024-election/trump -democrats-enemies-within-rcna175628.

EMMOREY, KAREN. "Language: Do Bilinguals Think Differently in Each Language?" *Current Biology* 29, no. 21 (2019): R1133–R1135. https://doi.org/10.1016 /j.cub.2019.09.009.

ERICKSON, MANDY. "Alcoholics Anonymous Most Effective Path to Alcohol Abstinence." *Stanford Medicine,* March 11, 2020. https://med.stanford.edu/news/all-news /2020/03/alcoholics-anonymous-most-effective-path-to-alcohol-abstinence.html.

ERIKSON, ERIK H. *Identity: Youth and Crisis.* W. W. Norton, 1968. Internet Archive. Accessed July 7, 2025. https://archive.org/details/300656427ErikHEriksonIdentity YouthAndCrisis1WWNortonCompany1968.

ERWIN, SANDRA. "U.S. Space Force Says Its New Seal Is Not a Starfleet Knockoff." SpaceNews, January 25, 2020. https://spacenews.com/u-s-space-force-says -its-new-seal-is-not-a-starfleet-knockoff.

EVERETT, RACHEL SCOTT. "A Nation Adrift: Confronting Another Trump Presidency— How the Rise of an Oligarchy Threatens America's Future and What We Can Do About It." *RVA Magazine*, January 24, 2025. https://rvamag.com/community/a-nation -adrift-confronting-another-trump-presidency.html.

EWENS, HANNAH. "After Becoming Obsessed with Self-Help, I Had to Heal from 'Healing.'" *Guardian*, March 23, 2025. https://www.theguardian.com/lifeandstyle/2025 /mar/23/after-becoming-obsessed-with-self-help-i-had-to-heal-from-healing.

EXJW CALEB. "This Jehovah's Witness Cartoon Is BEYOND Twisted." YouTube video, 17:25. January 22, 2025. https://www.youtube.com/watch?v=PFQ7rynmtvs.

EXJW PANDA TOWER. "Jehovah's Witnesses | Slaving Away as UNPAID Workers." YouTube video, 22:41, January 10, 2022. https://www.youtube.com/watch?v =xMtq8CthL8s.

FAMILY INSTITUTE. "Dehumanizing Language." Northwestern University, March 26, 2021. https://www.family-institute.org/behavioral-health-resources/dehumanizing-language.

FAN, XIAOYU, ROSYA IZYANIE SHAMSHUDEEN, AND MOHAMAD SALEEH RAHAMAD. "The Guiding Role of Social Media in the Socialization of Celebrity Fans." *Studies in Media and Communication* 12, no. 2 (2024): 50. https://doi.org/10.11114/smc.v12i2.6608.

FASIH, SUHA. "The Fast-Fashion Dilemma: Unraveling Forced Labor in Global Supply Chains." *Law Journal for Social Justice*, October 31, 2024. https://lawjournalforsocialjustice.com/2024/10/31/the-fast-fashion-dilemma-unraveling-forced-labor-in-global-supply-chains.

FEDERAL BUREAU OF INVESTIGATION. "Jonestown." https://www.fbi.gov/history/famous-cases/jonestown.

FEDERAL TRADE COMMISSION. "Federal Trade Commission Returns More Than $149 Million to Consumers Harmed by AdvoCare Pyramid Scheme." May 5, 2022. https://www.ftc.gov/news-events/news/press-releases/2022/05/federal-trade-commission-returns-more-149-million-consumers-harmed-advocare-pyramid-scheme.

FEDERAL TRADE COMMISSION. "FTC Proposes Rule to Ban Noncompete Clauses, Which Hurt Workers and Harm Competition." January 5, 2023. https://www.ftc.gov/news-events/news/press-releases/2023/01/ftc-proposes-rule-ban-noncompete-clauses-which-hurt-workers-harm-competition.

FEDERAL TRADE COMMISSION. "Multi-Level Marketer AdvoCare Will Pay $150 Million to Settle FTC Charges It Operated an Illegal Pyramid Scheme." October 2, 2019. https://www.ftc.gov/news-events/news/press-releases/2019/10/multi-level-marketer-advocare-will-pay-150-million-settle-ftc-charges-it-operated-illegal-pyramid.

FEDERAL TRADE COMMISSION. "Multi-Level Marketing Businesses and Pyramid Schemes." Last modified April 2021. https://consumer.ftc.gov/articles/multi-level-marketing-businesses-pyramid-schemes.

FERRANTI, SETH. "How Jim Jones Went From Civil Rights Leader to Cult Murderer." Vice, April 10, 2017. https://www.vice.com/en/article/ezw344/how-jim-jones-went-from-civil-rights-leader-to-cult-murderer.

FESTINGER, LEON. *A Theory of Cognitive Dissonance*. 1957. Reprint, Stanford University Press, 1968. Accessed June 18, 2025. https://archive.org/details/FestingerLeonATheoryOfCognitiveDissonance1968StanfordUniversityPress.

FESTINGER, LEON, HENRY W. RIECKEN, AND STANLEY SCHACHTER. *When Prophecy Fails*. Martino, 2009. Originally published 1956, University of Minnesota Press.

FINEMAN, MEREDITH. *Brag Better: Master the Art of Fearless Self-Promotion*. Portfolio, 2020.

FITCH, W. TECUMSEH, LUDWIG HUBER, AND THOMAS BUGNYAR. "Social Cognition and the Evolution of Language: Constructing Cognitive Phylogenies." *Neuron* 65, no. 6 (March 25, 2010): 795–814.

FLAHERTY, BRIAN. "Girl Scout Economics: Thin Mints, Thick Margins." Alts.co, March 17, 2024. https://alts.co/girl-scout-economics-thin-mints-thick-margins.

FLANDERS, CHRIS. "Experience: My Yoga Class Turned Out to Be a Cult." *Guardian*, June 26, 2020. https://www.theguardian.com/lifeandstyle/2020/jun/26/experience-my -yoga-class-turned-out-to-be-a-cult.

FOLKENFLIK, DAVID. "A Look at the Rhetoric Around the Storming of U.S. Capitol." NPR, January 6, 2021. https://www.npr.org/2021/01/06/954149242/a-look-at-the-rhetoric -around-the-storming-of-u-s-capitol.

FOUBERT, JOHN. "'Rapebait' E-mail Reveals Dark Side of Frat Culture." CNN, October 9, 2013. https://www.cnn.com/2013/10/09/opinion/foubert-fraternities-rape.

FRAGA, KALEENA. "The Real Story of Mormon Underwear, the Sacred Temple Garments Worn Day and Night by Members of the LDS Church." All That's Interesting, February 28, 2024. https://allthatsinteresting.com/mormon-underwear-temple-garment.

FREEDOM TO READ. "Bannings and Burnings in History." Accessed July 8, 2025. https: //www.freedomtoread.ca/resources/bannings-and-burnings-in-history.

FULLER, JOSEPH B., CHRISTINA LANGER, JULIA NITSCHKE, ET AL. "The Emerging Degree Reset." Harvard Business School Project on Managing the Future of Work. February 2022. https://www.hbs.edu/managing-the-future-of-work/Documents /research/emerging_degree_reset_020922.pdf.

FULLER, JOSEPH B., AND JOHN MASKO. "Theranos: The Unicorn That Wasn't. Harvard Business School Case 319-068." Harvard Business School Publishing. February 2019; revised September 2019.

G., STACY. "Work Hard Play Hard = Bro Culture: 20 Job-Search Red Flags" Medium, February 28, 2023. https://sgarrels.medium.com/a-job-searchers-glossary-20-job -speak-buzzwords-what-they-mean-ed80a8c99791.

GABRIELSON, RYAN, AND J. DAVID MCSWANE. "A Christian Health Nonprofit Saddled Thousands with Debt as It Built a Family Empire Including a Pot Farm, a Bank and an Airline." ProPublica, February 25, 2023. https://www.propublica.org/article /liberty-healthshare-healthcare-sharing-ministries-obamacare.

GALLUP AND PURDUE UNIVERSITY. "Fraternities and Sororities: Understanding Life Outcomes." Gallup. 2014. https://nicfraternity.org/wp-content/uploads/2019/02 /Fraternities-and-Sororities-Report-5-27-2014.pdf.

GARCIA-NAVARRO, LULU, HOST. "Google Changed Work Culture. Its Former Hype Woman Has Regrets." *First Person* (podcast). *New York Times*, February 23, 2023. https: //www.nytimes.com/2023/02/23/opinion/google-big-tech-work-culture.html.

GARAMONE, JIM. "Space Force Personnel to Be Called Guardians." DOD News, US Department of Defense, December 19, 2020. https://www.defense.gov/News /News-Stories/Article/article/2452910/space-force-personnel-to-be-called-guardians.

GARDNER, SIMON. "Children of God sex cult survivors come out of the shadows." March 13, 2016. https://www.cbc.ca/news/canada/ottawa/children-of-god-survivors -1.3481788.

GARIEPY, HENRY. *Christianity in Action: The History of the International Salvation Army.* Wm. B. Eerdmans, 2009.

GAVIN, ROBERT. "Doctor Who Branded Women for Raniere Loses Medical License." *Times Union*, October 1, 2021. https://www.timesunion.com/news/article/NXIVM -loyalist-Danielle-Roberts-loses-license-for-16501584.php.

GDOWSKI, MILAN, AND ROGAN OAKES. "Yellow Deli: A Good Place to Eat or a Cult on the Street?" *The Owl*, October 25, 2023. https://bhsowl.org/6984/features/yellow -deli-a-good-place-to-eat-or-a-cult-on-the-street.

GEDDES, EVA R. "Shaping and Sustaining a Community in Covenant: Retention of Salvation Army Officers in the U.S.A. Eastern Territory." PhD diss., Nyack College, 2014, 124. https://www.proquest.com/docview/1561159048.

GEIRLAND, JOHN. "Go with the Flow." *Wired*, September 1, 1996. https://www.wired .com/1996/09/czik.

GERELUK, DIANNE. "A Whole-School Approach to Address Youth Radicalization." *Educational Theory* 73, no. 3 (June 2023): 434–451. https://doi.org/10.1111/edth .12581.

GIBSON, MARLON LADELL. "The Narrative Experiences of Black and Brown First-Generation Fraternity Men in Historically White Fraternities." PhD diss., University of Georgia, 2021. https://nicfraternity.org/wp-content/uploads/2022/06/ MLG-Final-Dissertation-7-19-21.pdf.

GIDDENS, ANTHONY. *The Constitution of Society: Outline of the Theory of Structuration.* University of California Press, 1979.

GILLER, MEGAN. "Cults, Conspiracies, and the Utterly Bizarre History of Sleepytime Tea." Cult Education Institute, February 12, 2016. https://culteducation.com/group/1289 -general-information/29190-cults-conspiracies-and-the-utterly-bizarre-history-of-sleepytime-tea.html.

GINGERICH, EMMA. *Runaway Amish Girl: The Great Escape.* Tate, 2014.

GIRL SCOUTS – DIAMONDS OF ARKANSAS, OKLAHOMA AND TEXAS. "More Questions About Where the Girl Scout Cookie Money Goes." Accessed June 30, 2025. https: //www.girlscoutsdiamonds.org/content/dam/girlscoutsdiamonds-redesign /documents/cookies/More%20Questions%20about%20Where%20Cookie%20 Money%20Goes.pdf.

GOFFMAN, ERVING. "On the Characteristics of Total Institutions." Presented at the Walter Reed Institute's Symposium on Preventive and Social Psychiatry, April 1957.

GOFFMAN, IRVING. *Asylums: Essays on the Social Situations of Mental Patients.* Transaction Publishers, 2009. Originally published in 1961 by Doubleday & Company, Inc.

GOLDEN, BERNARD. "Shaming Is an Aggressive Act." *Psychology Today*, January 5, 2023. https://www.psychologytoday.com/us/blog/overcoming-destructive-anger/202301 /shaming-is-an-aggressive-act.

GOLDSMITH, BEN, AND LARS J. K. MOEN. "Trump's Personality Cult Plays a Part in His Political Appeal." *Scientific American*, June 4, 2024. https://www.scientificamerican .com/article/trumps-personality-cult-plays-a-part-in-his-political-appeal.

GOLEMAN, DANIEL. *Emotional Intelligence: Why it Can Matter More than IQ.* Bantam Books, 1995.

GONZALEZ, CRISTINA. "Avoiding Sunk Cost Fallacy to Prioritize Well-Being." Performing Well Blog, September 16, 2024. https://umperformingwell.wordpress.com/2024/09/16 /avoiding-sunk-cost-fallacy-to-prioritize-well-being.

GOSHA, RYAN. "Lying Flat, Anti-Work and Quiet Quitting—A Crisis within Capitalism." Medium, August 25, 2022. https://ryangosha.medium.com/lying-flat-anti-work-and -quiet-quitting-a-crisis-within-capitalism-843f63f7bfc7. [Source no longer available. Author deleted article.]

GRACE, ERIN. "Extremist Memes More Dangerous Because of Their Viral Nature and Coded Messaging." Nebraska Examiner, March 15, 2023. https://nebraskaexaminer. com/2023/03/15/extremist-memes-more-dangerous-because-of-their-viral-nature -and-coded-messaging.

GRANT, SHAELEN. *The Cultic Lifecycle: A Thematic Analysis of Fulfillment and Fear in Cult Membership.* Master's thesis, City University of New York, 2022. https: //academicworks.cuny.edu/jj_etds/265.

GRAY, AMBER D. "International Cult Awareness Month: The BIG Why." International Cult Awareness Month, August 2, 2023. https://internationalcultawareness.org/2023 /08/02/international-cult-awareness-month-the-big-why/.

GRAY, AYSA. "The Bias of 'Professionalism' Standards." *Stanford Social Innovation Review*, June 4, 2019. https://doi.org/10.48558/TDWC-4756.

GREEN, ANN. Ann Green's Nonprofit Blog. https://anngreennonprofit.com.

GREENE, JAY. "Amazon's Employee Surveillance Fuels Union Efforts: 'It's Not Prison, It's Work.'" *Washington Post,* December 2, 2021. https://www.washingtonpost.com /technology/2021/12/02/amazon-workplace-monitoring-unions.

GREENHOUSE, STEVEN. "Foes of Idle Hands, Amish Seek an Exemption From a Child Labor Law." *New York Times,* October 18, 2003. https://www.nytimes.com/2003/10/18/us /foes-of-idle-hands-amish-seek-an-exemption-from-a-child-labor-law.html.

GRIM, RYAN, HOST. "Tema Okun on Her Mythical Paper on White Supremacy." *Deconstructed* (podcast), season 10, episode 5, February 3, 2023. https://theintercept .com/2023/02/03/deconstructed-tema-okun-white-supremacy.

GRINDER, JOHN, AND RICHARD BANDLER. *Trance-Formations: Neuro-Linguistic Programming and the Structure of Hypnosis.* Real People, 1981.

GROSS, AMANDA K. *White Women, Get Ready: How Healing Post-Traumatic Mistress Syndrome Leads to Anti-Racist Change.* Otterpine, 2021.

GROSS, TERRY. "How a Rising Star of White Nationalism Broke Free from the Movement." NPR, September 24, 2018. https://www.npr.org/2018/09/24/651052970/how-a -rising-star-of-white-nationalism-broke-free-from-the-movement.

GROTH, AIMEE. *The Kingdom of Happiness: Inside Tony Hsieh's Zapponian Utopia*. Atria, 2017.

GURR, TED ROBERT. *Why Men Rebel*. Princeton University Press, 1970.

GUSTO. "Crash Course: Offering Equity to Your Employees." https://go.gusto.com /rs/110-WOX-868/images/An%20Entrepreneur%E2%80%99s%20Guide%20to%20 Employee%20Equity.pdf.

GUTIERREZ, KATIE. "How I Lost Myself to Motherhood." *Time*, May 21, 2022. https: //time.com/6177113/motherhood-sacrifice-roe-v-wade.

GUYNN, JESSICA. "Welcome to Zucker Burg." *Los Angeles Times*, August 10, 2012. https: //www.latimes.com/archives/la-xpm-2012-aug-10-la-fi-facebook-company-town -20120810-story.html.

HACKMAN, J. RICHARD. *Leading Teams: Setting the Stage for Great Performances*. Harvard Business School Press, 2002.

HAIMOWITZ, IAN. "No One Is Immune: The Spread of Q-anon Through Social Media and the Pandemic." CSIS, December 17, 2020. https://www.csis.org /blogs/strategic-technologies-blog/no-one-immune-spread-q-anon-through-social -media-and-pandemic.

HALVERSON, JARED M. "Broken Shelves or Continuing Revelation? Extending the Shelf Life of Faith." *Religious Educator* 25, no. 3 (2024). https://rsc.byu.edu/vol-25-no-3 -2024/broken-shelves-continuing-revelation-extending-shelf-life-faith.

HARARI, NOAH YUVAL. *Sapiens: A Brief History of Humankind*. Harper, 2015.

HART, ROBIN. "Salvation Army Officers Given 'Farewell Orders.'" *Advocate-Messenger*, May 30, 2019. https://amnews.com/2019/05/30/salvation-army-officers-given-farewell -orders.

HARVARD BUSINESS REVIEW. "Implementing Strategic Goals for Organizational Success." September 2022. https://hbr.org/sponsored/2022/09/implementing-strategic -goals-for-organizational-success.

HASLAM, S. ALEXANDER, AND MICHELLE K. RYAN. "The Road to the Glass Cliff: Differences in the Perceived Suitability of Men and Women for Leadership Positions in Succeeding and Failing Organizations." The Leadership Quarterly 19, no. 5 (2008): 530–546. https://web.archive.org/web/20131225013107/http://blog.aelios.com /mbawg/wp-content/uploads/2010/05/The-glass-cliff.pdf. Hassan, Steven. "The BITE Model of Authoritarian Control: Undue Influence, Thought Reform, Brainwashing, Mind Control, Trafficking, and the Law." PhD diss., Fielding Graduate University, 2021. https://doi.org/10.13140/RG.2.2.12755.60965.

HASSAN, STEVEN. *The Cult of Trump: A Leading Cult Expert Explains How the President Uses Mind Control*. Free Press, 2019.

HASSAN, STEVEN A. "Multi-Level Marketing Groups Operate Much Like Cults." *Psychology Today*, January 14, 2022. https://www.psychologytoday.com/us/blog /freedom-mind/202201/multi-level-marketing-groups-operate-much-cults.

HASSAN, STEVEN A. "Phobias: A Tool of Cult Indoctrination." *Psychology Today*, September 27, 2022. https://www.psychologytoday.com/us/blog/freedom-mind /202209/phobias-tool-cult-indoctrination.

HAWKINS, ANDREW J. "Tesla's 'Ultra Hardcore' Work Culture—As Told by Its Employees." The Verge, August 16, 2023. https://www.theverge.com/2023/8/16/23833447 /tesla-elon-musk-ultra-hardcore-employees-land-of-the-giants.

HEAVEN'S GATE OFFICIAL WEBSITE. Archived December 12, 1997. https://web.archive .org/web/19971212001005/http://www.heavensgate.com.

HELLER, ZOË. "What Makes a Cult a Cult?" *New Yorker*, July 5, 2021. https://www .newyorker.com/magazine/2021/07/12/what-makes-a-cult-a-cult.

HELLING, STEVE. "Children of God Cult Survivor Speaks Out: 'We Were Told Sex Was How to Show God's Love.'" *People,* May 31, 2019. https://people.com/crime /children-of-god-cult-survivor-speaks-out-sex-gods-love.

HELMORE, EDWARD. "Nxivm Trial: Keith Raniere Found Guilty on All Counts in Sex Cult Case." *Guardian,* June 19, 2019. https://www.theguardian.com/us-news/2019 /jun/19/nxivm-trial-keith-raniere-verdict-guilty-allison-mack.

HENRY, ZOE. "How Tony Hsieh Has Built a Cult of Personality." *Inc.*, March 3, 2017. https://www.inc.com/zoe-henry/why-tony-hsieh-is-a-cult-leader.html.

HERMAN, EDWARD S., AND NOAM CHOMSKY. *Manufacturing Consent: The Political Economy of the Mass Media*. Pantheon Books, 1988.

HETLER, AMANDA. "13 Signs of Toxic Workplace Culture and How to Combat It." TechTarget, July 11, 2025. https://www.techtarget.com/whatis/feature /Signs-of-toxic-workplace-culture.

HETZNER, CHRISTIAAN. "Elon Musk Is Hiring for His DOGE Taskforce—But You'll Need to Work 80 Hours per Week on Unglamorous Cost-Cutting." Inkl, November 15, 2024. https://www.inkl.com/news/elon-musk-is-hiring-for-his-doge-taskforce-but -you-ll-need-to-work-80-hours-per-week-on-unglamorous-cost-cutting.

HEYRMAN, CHRISTINE LEIGH. "Puritanism and Predestination." National Humanities Center. Accessed June 18, 2025, https://nationalhumanitiescenter.org/tserve /eighteen/ekeyinfo/puritan.htm.

HICKS, MICHAEL. "What Hymns Early Mormons Sang and How They Sang Them." *BYU Studies Quarterly* 47, no. 1 (2008): article 5. https://scholarsarchive.byu.edu /byusq/vol47/iss1/5.

HILL, JENNA MISCAVIGE. *Beyond Belief: My Secret Life Inside Scientology and My Harrowing Escape.* HarperCollins, 2013.

HILLARY. "The Challenge of Retaining Talent in Silicon Valley's Competitive Market." Tech Bullion, November 1, 2024. https://techbullion.com/the-challenge-of-retaining-talent-in-silicon-valleys-competitive-market.

HILLIARD, RYAN. "How to Leave a Cult." People Leave Cults, February 3, 2023. https://www.peopleleavecults.com/post/how-to-leave-a-cult.

HILTON, PARIS, EXECUTIVE PRODUCER, AND ALEXANDRA DEAN, DIRECTOR. *This Is Paris*. Documentary film. YouTube Originals, 2020. https://www.youtube.com/watch?v=wOg0TY1jG3w.

HIRING OUR HEROES. "The Hidden Financial Costs of Military Spouse Unemployment." US Chamber of Commerce Foundation. https://www.hiringourheroes.org/resources/hidden-financial-costs-military-spouse-unemployment.

HIRSCH, MICHELE LENT. "America's Company Towns, Then and Now." *Smithsonian Magazine*, September 4, 2015. https://www.smithsonianmag.com/travel/americas-company-towns-then-and-now-180956382.

HISTORY.COM EDITORS. "Heaven's Gate Cult Members Found Dead." History, February 9, 2010. https://www.history.com/this-day-in-history/march-26/heavens-gate-cult-members-found-dead.

HOFFER, ERIC. *The True Believer: Thoughts on the Nature of Mass Movements*. Harper & Row, 1951.

HOLMES, ELIZABETH. "Lab Testing Reinvented." TEDMED 2014. YouTube video, 17:42. October 7, 2014. https://www.youtube.com/watch?v=ZWSlwSYJ9SE.

HOLT-LUNSTAD, JULIANNE, TIMOTHY B. SMITH, AND J. BRADLEY LAYTON. "Social Relationships and Mortality Risk: A Meta-Analytic Review." *PLOS Medicine* 7, no. 7 (July 27, 2010): e1000316. https://doi.org/10.1371/journal.pmed.1000316.

HOME SCHOOL LEGAL DEFENSE ASSOCIATION'S GENERATION JOSHUA. "History." Accessed June 23, 2025. https://generationjoshua.org/about/history.

HONG, NICOLE, MICHAEL ROTHFELD, AND TIFFANY MAY. "How a Persecuted Religious Group Grew Into a Global Movement." *New York Times,* August 16, 2024. https://www.nytimes.com/2024/08/16/nyregion/shen-yun-falun-gong.html.

HONG, NICOLE, AND SEAN PICCOLI. "Keith Raniere, Leader of Nxivm Sex Cult, Is Sentenced to 120 Years in Prison." *New York Times*, October 27, 2020. https://www.nytimes.com/2020/10/27/nyregion/nxivm-cult-keith-raniere-sentenced.html.

HOPKINS, JERRY. "The Fourth Great Awakening—Timeline Movement, 1950–1980." Association of Religion Data Archives. Accessed June 23, 2025. https://www.thearda.com/us-religion/history/timelines/entry?etype=3&eid=6.

HOROWITZ, MITCH. *One Simple Idea: How Positive Thinking Reshaped Modern Life*. Random House, 2014.

HOUGH, LAUREN. *Leaving Isn't the Hardest Thing*. Hodder & Stoughton, 2022.

HOWSON, ALEXANDRA. "Types of Authority." EBSCO. 2021. https://www.ebsco.com/research-starters/social-sciences-and-humanities/types-authority.

HSU, ANDREA. "Children as Young as 12 Work Legally on Farms, Despite Years of Efforts to Change Law." NPR, June 12, 2023. https://www.npr.org/2023/06/12/1181472559/child-labor-farms-agriculture-human-rights-congress.

HSU, ANDREA. "Why the Pandemic Is Forcing So Many Women to Leave Their Jobs." NPR, November 14, 2020. https://www.npr.org/2020/11/14/935018298/why-the-pandemic-is-forcing-so-many-women-to-leave-their-jobs

HUGHES, SEAN PATRICK. "Those Who Fight Our Wars Don't Write 'Blank Checks' to America." *Washington Post,* October 22, 2017. https://www.washingtonpost.com/news/checkpoint/wp/2017/10/22/those-who-fight-our-wars-dont-write-blank-checks-to-america-the-soldiers-slain-in-niger-knew-that.

HUNTER, JOHN. "Brainwashing in a Large Group Awareness Training? The Classical Conditioning Hypothesis of Brainwashing" Dissertation, 2015. https://researchspace.ukzn.ac.za/server/api/core/bitstreams/ed760dd4-8b6b-4b8e-83c4-a2e8ff9990a3/content.

HUNTER, JOHN. "LGATs and Fight Club. Dissecting a Delusion." The Fincher Analyst, November 26, 2019. https://thefincheranalyst.com/articles/lgats-and-fight-club-dissecting-a-delusion.

HURST, DANIEL. "Commissioner Condemns 'Failure of Leadership' in Australian Defence Force, Urges Greater Focus on Wellbeing of Personnel." *Guardian,* September 9, 2024. https://www.theguardian.com/australia-news/article/2024/sep/09/commissioner-condemns-failure-of-leadership-in-australian-defence-force-urges-greater-focus-on-wellbeing-of-personnel.

HUTCHINGS, JAMES. "Sweet Charity?: Salvation Army or Starvation Army?" The Anarchist Library. Accessed July 20, 2025. https://theanarchistlibrary.org/library/james-hutchings-sweet-charity-salvation-army-or-starvation-army.

HUYNH, NINA. "The 'Us' vs. 'Them' Dichotomy That Leads to Dehumanization." Vox, February 12, 2015. https://blogs.ubc.ca/ninatnhuynh/2015/02/12/the-us-vs-them-dichotomy-that-leads-to-dehumanization.

IMMERWAHR, DANIEL. *How to Hide an Empire: A History of the Greater United States.* Farrar, Straus and Giroux, 2019.

INDIGO MARKETING AGENCY. "What Really Happens at a Tony Robbins Event?" Accessed July 20, 2025. https://indigomarketingagency.com/what-really-happens-at-a-tony-robbins-event/.

INGERSOLL, JEFFREY, AND JEREMY BENDER. "41 Phrases Only People in the Military Will Understand." Business Insider, November 1, 2014. https://www.businessinsider.com/phrases-only-people-in-the-military-know-2014-10.

INSIDER. "How Cults Actually Work (Nxivm)." Insider, YouTube video, 34:09. October 31, 2024. https://www.youtube.com/watch?v=5bb1EtTnvaw.

INSTITUTION OF ENGINEERING AND TECHNOLOGY. "Facebook Did Not Act on Own Evidence of Algorithm-Driven Extremism." *E&T Magazine,* updated October 9, 2023.

https://eandt.theiet.org/2020/05/27/facebook-did-not-act-own-evidence-algorithm
-driven-extremism.

INTEGRATIVE PSYCH. "Unmasking Toxic Positivity: The Dangers of Forced Positivity in Mental Health." Accessed July 18, 2025. https://www.integrative-psych.org/resources/unmasking-toxic-positivity-the-dangers-of-forced-positivity-in-mental-health.

INTERNATIONAL CULT AWARENESS MONTH. "Week 1: Understanding Cults and Coercive Control." https://internationalcultawareness.org/week-1-understanding-cults/.

INTERNATIONAL CULTIC STUDIES ASSOCIATION WEBSITE. Accessed June 30, 2025. https://www.icsahome.com.

INTROVIGNE, MASSIMO. "Scientology, Secular Courts, and Disconnection/Fair Game Policies: 3. The Origins of Disconnection." Bitter Winter, November 12, 2022. https://bitterwinter.org/scientology-3-the-origins-of-disconnection.

INVERSE. "Cults, Conspiracies, and the Twisted History of Sleepytime Tea." Inverse, January 28, 2018. https://www.inverse.com/culture/10731-cults-conspiracies-and-the-twisted-history-of-sleepytime-tea.

IRWIN, JULIE. "Loyalty to a Leader Is Overrated, Even Dangerous." *Harvard Business Review*, December 16, 2014. https://hbr.org/2014/12/loyalty-to-a-leader-is-overrated-even-dangerous.

ISAAC, JAMES, AND IRWIN ALTMAN. "Interpersonal Processes in Nineteenth Century Utopian Communities: Shakers and Oneida Perfectionists." *Utopian Studies* 9, no. 1 (1998): 26–49, http://www.jstor.org/stable/20719741.

ISENHARDT, ANNA, MARIA KAMENOWSKI, PATRIK MANZONI, ET AL. "Identity Diffusion and Extremist Attitudes in Adolescence." *Frontiers in Psychology* 12 (September 28, 2021): 711466. https://doi.org/10.3389/fpsyg.2021.711466.

ISPA-LANDA, SIMONE, AND MARIANA OLIVER. "Hybrid Femininities: Making Sense of Sorority Rankings and Reputation." *Gender and Society* 34, no. 6 (2020): 893–921. https://www.jstor.org/stable/26967175.

IYYANI, VIVEK. "About Quiet Quitting, Lying Flat, Wheelbarrows and Sensors." March 8, 2025. https://www.vivekiyyani.com/about-quiet-quitting-lying-flat-wheelbarrows-and-sensors.

JACK. "Challenges of the Military Transition to Civilian Life." BestMind Behavioral Health, June 11, 2024. https://bestmindbh.com/blog/challenges-of-the-military-transition-to-civilian-life.

JACKSON, SARAH. "Facebook CEO Mark Zuckerberg Told Staff That Sheryl Sandberg Had 'Good Skin' and They Should Have 'a Crush' on Her, New Book Says." Business Insider, July 13, 2021. https://www.businessinsider.com/mark-zuckerberg-staff-should-have-a-crush-on-sandberg-book-2021-7.

JAIME, ANGIE. "Paris Hilton Shares Story of Alleged Abuse While Testifying Before Congress." *Teen Vogue*, June 27, 2024. https://www.teenvogue.com/story/paris-hilton-shares-story-of-traumatic-abuse-while-testifying-before-congress.

JALONICK, MARY CLARE, ERIC TUCKER, FARNOUSH AMIRI, ET AL. "Trump 'Lit That Fire' of Capitol Insurrection, Jan 6 Committee Report Says." PBS News, December 23, 2022. https://www.pbs.org/newshour/politics/trump-lit-that-fire-of-capitol-insurrection-jan-6-committee-report-says.

JANIS, IRVING L. "Groupthink." *Psychology Today* 5, no. 6. November, 1971. 84–90. https://web.archive.org/web/20100401033524/http://apps.olin.wustl.edu/faculty/macdonald/GroupThink.pdf.

JANIS, IRVING L. *Groupthink: Psychological Studies of Policy Decisions and Fiascoes*. 2nd ed. Houghton Mifflin, 1982.

JANIS, IRVING L. *Victims of Groupthink*. Houghton Mifflin, 1972.

JASKO, KATARZYNA, GARY LAFREE, AND ARIE KRUGLANSKI. "Quest for Significance and Violent Extremism: The Case of Domestic Radicalization." *Political Psychology* 38, no. 5 (2017): 815–831. https://doi.org/10.1111/pops.12376.

JEHOVAH'S WITNESSES. "Why Disfellowshipping Is a Loving Provision." *The Watchtower–Study Edition*, April 2015. https://www.jw.org/en/library/magazines/w20150415/disfellowshipping-a-loving-provision.

JENKINSON, GILLIE. "An Investigation into Cult Pseudo-Personality: What Is It and How Does It Form?" *Cultic Studies Review* 7, no. 3 (2008): 199-224.

JENSEN, MICHAEL, SHEEHAN KANE, AND ELENA AKERS. "PIRUS: Mass Casualty Extremist Offenders with U.S. Military Backgrounds." National Consortium for the Study of Terrorism and Responses to Terrorism (START). June 2023. https://www.start.umd.edu/sites/default/files/publications/local_attachments/PIRUS-Mass%20Casualty%20Extremist%20Offenders%20with%20Military%20Background-Final%20%283%29.pdf.

JONES, DAVID W. "5 Errors of the Prosperity Gospel." Gospel Coalition, June 15, 2015. https://www.thegospelcoalition.org/article/5-errors-of-the-prosperity-gospel.

JONES, KENNETH, AND TEMA OKUN. *Dismantling Racism: A Workbook for Social Change Groups*. ChangeWork, 2001.

JONES, SARAH. "A Generation Moves On." *New York*, May 30, 2023. https://nymag.com/intelligencer/2023/05/the-joshua-generation-moves-on.html.

JP MORGAN WORKPLACE SOLUTIONS. "Unvested Stock—Everything You Should Know." July 1, 2022. https://www.globalshares.com/insights/unvested-stock.

KAMRATH, ANGELA E. "Why and How Schools Began in the United States: The Puritans Supported Education for Bible Literacy." American Heritage Education Foundation. August 31, 2017. https://americanheritage.org/schools-begin-united-states.

KANG, JAY CASPIAN. "Tony Hsieh and the Emptiness of the Tech-Mogul Myth." *New Yorker*, May 9, 2023. https://www.newyorker.com/news/our-columnists/tony-hsieh -and-the-emptiness-of-the-tech-mogul-myth.

KAPUR, AKASH. "The Return of the Utopians." *New Yorker*, October 3, 2016. https: //www.newyorker.com/magazine/2016/10/03/the-return-of-the-utopians.

KARASU, SYLVIA R. "The Weaponization of Hair: And How It Can Be Used to Oppress, Punish, Seduce, and Rebel." *Psychology Today*, November 29, 2023. https://www .psychologytoday.com/us/blog/the-gravity-of-weight/202311/the-weaponization -of-hair.

KASBE, JON, DIR. *The Deep End.* Aired on Freeform, May 18–June 8, 2022. https: //www.imdb.com/title/tt19387554.

KEELER, JASON R., EDWARD A. ROTH, BRITTANY L. NEUSER, ET AL. "The Neurochemistry and Social Flow of Singing: Bonding and Oxytocin." *Frontiers in Human Neuroscience* 9 (2015): 518. https://doi.org/10.3389/fnhum.2015.00518.

KELLY, JOSEPH, AND PATRICK RYAN. "History of Large Group Awareness Trainings (LGAT)." Intervention 101, February 9, 2020. http://www.intervention101.com /2019/09/history-of-large-group-awareness.html.

KELVAS, DANIELLE. "What Is Thin Privilege?" *Within Health*, updated August 24, 2023. https://withinhealth.com/learn/articles/what-is-thin-privilege.

KENDALL, DIANA, JANE LOTHIAN MURRAY, AND RICK LINDEN. *Sociology in Our Times.* 2nd Canadian edition. Nelson Education Limited, 2000.

KENNEDY, RORY, AND MARK BAILEY, EXECUTIVE PRODUCERS AND DIRECTORS. *The Synanon Fix.* Documentary series. HBO Documentary Films/Moxie Films. Aired April 1–22, 2024.

KERN, CORNELIA, AND JULIA JUNGBAUER. "Long-Term Effects of a Cult Childhood on Attachment, Intimacy, and Close Relationships: Results of an In-Depth Interview Study." *Clinical Social Work Journal* 50 (June 2022): 207–17. https://doi .org/10.1007/s10615-020-00773-w.

KENT, STEPHEN. "Lustful Prophet: A Psychosexual Historical Study of the Children of God's Leader, David Berg." *Cultic Studies Journal* (1994): 135–188. https://www .researchgate.net/publication/232542050_Lustful_prophet_A_psychosexual _historical_study_of_the_children_of_God%27s_leader_David_Berg.

KHOMAMI, NADIA. "Arts Sector's Use of Unpaid Interns for Some Roles Could Be Illegal, Experts Say." *Guardian*, February 26, 2025. https://www.theguardian.com/ culture/2025/feb/26/arts-sectors-use-of-unpaid-interns-for-some-roles-could-be -experts-say.

KHORRAM-MANESH, AMIR, AND FREDERICK M. BURKLE. "Sociopathic Narcissistic Leadership: How About Their Victims?" *World Medical & Health Policy* 16, no. 1 (2024): 19–36. https://doi.org/10.1002/wmh3.588.

KHURANA, RAKESH. *Searching for a Corporate Savior: The Irrational Quest for Charismatic CEOs.* Princeton University Press, 2002.

KIABA, JEN. "Toxic Positivity and the Thought-Terminating Cliché." May 29, 2021. https://www.jenkiaba.com/lessons-on-leaving/toxic-positivity-thought-terminating-cliche.

KIM, JAE YUN, TROY CAMPBELL, STEVEN SHEPHERD, ET AL. "Passion Exploitation: The Legitimization of Exploiting Other People's Passion for Work." Academy of Management Proceedings, 2016. https://www.researchgate.net/publication/320788469_Passion_Exploitation_The_Legitimization_of_Exploiting_Other_People's_Passion_for_Work.

KING, ANDREW. "1 Big Thing: Why Ohio Veterans Are Struggling." Axios, November 8, 2024. https://www.axios.com/newsletters/axios-columbus-69bcbb70-9d47-11ef-8c78-9f8894f0f67a.

KING, ERNEST W., AND FRANKLIN G. MIXON. "Religiosity and the Political Economy of the Salem Witch Trials." *Social Science Journal* 47, no. 3 (2010): 678–688. https://doi.org/10.1016/j.soscij.2010.01.008.

KLEIN, LINDA KAY. *Pure: Inside the Evangelical Movement That Shamed a Generation of Young Women and How I Broke Free.* Atria Books, 2018.

KNIGHT, JOANNA. "Employee Belonging: Why Celebrating Individuality Is the Recipe For Business Success." *Forbes*, July 21, 2023. https://www.forbes.com/councils/forbesbusinesscouncil/2023/07/21/employee-belonging-why-celebrating-individuality-is-the-recipe-for-business-success.

KOCH, BRADLEY A. "The Prosperity Gospel and Economic Prosperity: Race, Class, Giving, and Voting." PhD diss., Indiana University, 2009. https://hdl.handle.net/2022/8654.

KONNIKOVA, MARIA. "18 U.S. Presidents Were in College Fraternities: Do Frats Create Future Leaders, or Simply Attract Them?" *Atlantic*, February 21, 2014. https://www.theatlantic.com/education/archive/2014/02/18-us-presidents-were-in-college-fraternities/283997.

KOZIOL, JILL. "America Runs on Mothers' Sacrifice—and It's Not OK." Motherly, May 12, 2022. https://www.mother.ly/parenting/america-runs-on-mothers-sacrifice.

KRAKAUER, JON. *Under the Banner of Heaven: A Story of Violent Faith.* Random House, 2003. Audiobook.

KRUEGER, CURTIS. "Church of Scientology Accused of Not Paying Bills." *Tampa Bay Times*, June 30, 1991. https://www.tampabay.com/archive/1991/06/30/church-of-scientology-accused-of-not-paying-bills.

KRUGLANSKI, ARIE W., ERICA MOLINARIO, KATARZYNA JASKO, ET AL. "Significance-Quest Theory." *Perspectives on Psychological Science* 17, no. 4 (2022): 1050–71. https://doi.org/10.1177/17456916211034825.

KRUSE, MICHAEL. "The Casey DeSantis Problem: 'His Greatest Asset and His Greatest Liability.'" Politico, May 19, 2023. https://www.politico.com/news/magazine /2023/05/19/casey-ron-desantis-wife-profile-00097456.

LAGARDE, KATELYN. "What's Really Going on at Zappos? The Impact of Holacracy on Workforce, Culture and Morale." OpenView, March 16, 2016. https://openviewpartners .com/blog/impact-of-holacracy-at-zappos.

LAKRITZ, TALIA. "19 Former Child Stars Who Have Opened Up About the Price of Fame." Business Insider, updated March 29, 2024. https://www.businessinsider.com /child-stars-how-fame-affected-them-2021-1.

LALICH CENTER ON CULTS AND COERCION WEBSITE. Accessed July 20, 2025. https://www .lalichcenter.org.

LALICH, JANJA. Bounded Choice: True Believers and Charismatic Cults. University of California Press, 2004.

LALICH, JANJA. "Declaration of Janja Lalich in Opposition to Motion for Summary Adjudication." Superior Court of the State of California, County of San Mateo, August 16, 1995. https://www.lalichcenter.org/blog/declaration-ananda-trial/.

LALICH, JANJA. Take Back Your Life: Recovering from Cults and Abusive Relationships. Bay Tree, 2006.

LAMBERT, CRAIG. "The Cult of the Charismatic CEO." Harvard Magazine, September–October 2002. https://www.harvardmagazine.com/2002/09/the-cult-of-the -charisma.html.

THE LANCET. "Theranos and the Scientific Community: At the Bleeding Edge." Lancet 399, no. 10321 (January 15, 2022): 211, https://doi.org/10.1016/S0140-6736 (22)00052-6.

LANGONE, MICHAEL D. "Large Group Awareness Trainings." Cult Observer 15, no. 1 (1998). https://www.icsahome.com/elibrary/topics/articles/large-group-awareness -trainings-langone.

LASSILA, KATHRIN. "A Brief History of Groupthink." Yale Alumni Magazine, January/ February 2008. https://yalealumnimagazine.org/articles/1947-a-brief-history-of -groupthink.

LAVOIE, JENNIFER. "Under Grace: Legal Isolation and the Children of the Old Order Amish." Modern American 2, no. 1 (Spring 2006): 32–34. https://digitalcommons.wcl .american.edu/tma/vol2/iss1/10.

LAZO, LUZ, AND EMILY GUSKIN. "1 in 7 Residents of the D.C. Area Moved During the Pandemic, Poll Finds." Washington Post, August 17, 2021. https://www.washingtonpost .com/transportation/2021/08/17/dc-move-pandemic-poll.

LEBOWITZ, SHANA. "7 Ways to Increase Your Charisma, According to Psychologists." Inc., June 28, 2023. https://www.inc.com/business-insider/how-to-become-more -charasmatic-according-to-psychological-research.html.

LEE, JENNIFER E. C., SANELA DURSUN, ALLA SKOMOROVSKY, ET AL. "Correlates of Perceived Military to Civilian Transition Challenges Among Canadian Armed Forces Veterans." *Journal of Military, Veteran and Family Health* 6, no. 2 (April 2020). https://doi.org/10.3138/jmvfh-2019-0025.

LEE, LLOYD. "The Former Twitter Director Who Went Viral for Sleeping in the Office Was Deeply Concerned About Employee Burnout." Business Insider, August 25, 2024. https://www.businessinsider.com/twitter-director-esther-crawford-sleeping -in-office-photo-employee-burnout-2024-8.

LEGAL INFORMATION INSTITUTE. "18 U.S. Code §1592." Cornell Law School. https: //www.law.cornell.edu/uscode/text/18/1592.

LEIGH, HEATHER. "'It's Harsh, It's Rough': Parents Are Drowning in Childcare Costs, But What's the Solution?" ABC Action News, May 29, 2024. https://www.abcactionnews. com/news/state/its-harsh-its-rough-parents-are-drowning-in-childcare-costs-but -whats-the-solution.

LELWICA, MICHELLE. "The Religion of Thinness." *Temenos: Nordic Journal of Comparative Religion* 47, no. 2 (2011): 257–279, https://journal.fi/scripta/article/view /67400.

LEVENSON, MICHAEL. "Congresswoman Apologizes for Making an Approving Reference to Hitler." *New York Times*, January 8, 2021. https://www.nytimes.com/2021/01/08 /us/mary-miller-hitler-remarks-controversy.html.

LEVOY, GREGG. "The Real Attention Deficit Disorder: The Hunger for Attention." *Psychology Today*, February 2023. https://www.psychologytoday.com/us/blog /passion/202302/the-real-attention-deficit-disorder-the-hunger-for-attention.

LEWSEY, FRED. "Psychological 'Signature' for the Extremist Mind Uncovered." University of Cambridge. Accessed July 20, 2025. https://www.cam.ac.uk/stories /extremistmind.

LIFTON, ROBERT JAY. *Thought Reform and the Psychology of Totalism: A Study of "Brainwashing" in China*. UNC Press, 1989. First published 1961.

LIN, YII-JAN. "Unearthed Skeletons Are Part of America's Chilling Apocalyptic Story." Religion News Service, October 31, 2024. https://religionnews.com/2024/10/31 /unearthed-skeletons-are-part-of-americas-chilling-apocalyptic-story.

LINDER, MARC. "Farm Workers and the Fair Labor Standards Act: Racial Discrimination in the New Deal." *Texas Law Review* 65 (1987). https://nationalaglawcenter.org /wp-content/uploads/assets/bibarticles/linder_racial.pdf.

LINNE, BLAIR, AIXA DE LÓPEZ, SHARON DICKENS, ET AL. (HOSTS). "The Prosperity Gospel: How It Can Mislead and Harm." *Glo* (podcast), June 13, 2023. https://www .thegospelcoalition.org/podcasts/glo/prosperity-gospel-mislead-harm.

LIU, HEIDI. "The Behavioral Economics of Multilevel Marketing." *Hastings Business Law Journal* 14, no. 1 (2018): 109–138. https://repository.uclawsf.edu/hastings_business _law_journal/vol14/iss1/3.

LIZZIE IN LACE. "EXPOSING LULAROE: Why I Quit Selling Lularoe (Things the LulaRich Documentary Left Out)." YouTube video, 46:58. September 18, 2021. https://www.youtube.com/watch?v=Ct4RlKQ8fFE.

LONG, HEATHER. "Donald Trump Trademarks 'Make America Great Again." 7 News WSVN, October 8, 2015. https://wsvn.com/news/donald-trump-trademarks-make-america-great-again/.

LOTTRET, CHLOÉ. "Is Your Company Starting to Look a Bit Like a Cult?" Welcome to the Jungle, January 4, 2022. https://www.welcometothejungle.com/en/articles/company-looking-like-a-cult.

LOWENSTEIN, ROGER. "'Bad Blood' Review: How One Company Scammed Silicon Valley. And How It Got Caught." *New York Times*, May 21, 2018. https://www.nytimes.com/2018/05/21/books/review/bad-blood-john-carreyrou.html.

LUCAS, GAVIN. "Steve Jobs' Reality Distortion Field Explained." Medium, accessed June 29, 2025. https://gavinlucas22.medium.com/steve-jobs-reality-distortion-field-explained-5ac3c8e5f992.

LUK, SHARON. "To Extinguish: On Aaron Bushnell and the Casualties of Nonviolence." Social Text (Columbia University), March 15, 2024. https://socialtextjournal.org/periscope_article/to-extinguish-on-aaron-bushnell-and-the-casualties-of-nonviolence.

LUPTON, ROBERT. *Rethinking Mission Trips*. Urbane, 2011.

MADISON, HOLLY. *Down the Rabbit Hole: Curious Adventures and Cautionary Tales of a Former Playboy Bunny*. Dey Street, 2015.

MANSFIELD, STEVEN. *The Mormonizing of America*. Worthy, 2012.

MARRIOTT, JAMES. "From PhDs to Politics, Jargon Is Choking Us." *The Times*, December 9, 2024. https://www.thetimes.com/comment/columnists/article/from-phds-to-politics-jargon-is-choking-us-hzbj7fp62.

MARSCHALL, RICHARD. *Drawing Power: A Compendium of Cartoon Advertising*. Fantagraphics, 2011.

MARTIN, PAUL. "A Critical Analysis of the Executive Success Programs Inc." School of Computer Science, Carnegie Mellon University, February 13, 2023. https://www.cs.cmu.edu/~dst/NXIVM/esp10.html.

MARTINEZ, LUIS. "Ranks Push Back on Criticism of Pregnant Women in the Military." *ABC News*, March 12, 2021. https://abcnews.go.com/Politics/ranks-push-back-criticism-pregnant-women-military/story?id=76415696.

MASCI, DAVID. "How Income Varies Among U.S. Religious Groups." Pew Research Center, October 11, 2016. https://www.pewresearch.org/short-reads/2016/10/11/how-income-varies-among-u-s-religious-groups.

MAYER, MILTON. *They Thought They Were Free: The Germans 1933–45*. Harper & Row, 1955.

MCADAMS, DAN P. "The Mass Psychology of Trumpism." *New Lines*, February 21, 2024. https://newlinesmag.com/argument/the-mass-psychology-of-trumpism.

MCCAULEY, CLARK, AND SOPHIA MOSKALENKO. "Mechanisms of Political Radicalization: Pathways Toward Terrorism." *Terrorism and Political* Violence 20, no. 3 (2008): 415–33.

MCCHRYSTAL, GENERAL STANLEY, JEFF EGGERS, AND JASON MANGONE. *Leaders: Myth and Reality.* Penguin, 2018.

MCCORMACK, WIN. "Outside the Limits of the Human Imagination." *New Republic*, March 27, 2018. https://newrepublic.com/article/147657/outside-limits-human -imagination.

MCCOY, JENNIFER, AND BENJAMIN PRESS. "What Happens When Democracies Become Perniciously Polarized?" Carnegie Endowment for International Peace, January 18, 2022. https://carnegieendowment.org/2022/01/18/what-happens-when -democracies-become-perniciously-polarized-pub-86190.

MCCRACKEN, THERESA, AND ROBERT B. BLODGETT. *Holy Rollers: Murder and Madness in Oregon's Love Cult.* Caxton, 2002.

MCCURDY, JENNETTE. *I'm Glad My Mom Died*. Simon & Schuster, 2022.

MCGINNIS, KELSEY KRAMER. "Worship Music Is Emotionally Manipulative. Do You Trust the Leader Plucking the Strings?" *Christianity Today*, May 26, 2023. https: //www.christianitytoday.com/2023/05/worship-music-emotionally-manipulative -leader-hillsong.

MCGRATH, A. HOPE. "'A Slave in Uncle Sam's Service': Labor and Resistance in the US Army, 1865–1890." *Labor* 13, no. 3–4 (2016): 37–56. https://muse.jhu.edu/article /636900.

MCKIM, JENIFER B. "'Working Like a Slave': Why Human Trafficking in Restaurants Is Underreported." WGBH, January 17, 2023. https://www.wgbh.org/news /local/2023-01-17/working-like-a-slave-why-human-trafficking-in-restaurants-is -underreported.

MCLAUGHLIN, KELLY, AND NICOLE EINBINDER. "How NXIVM, a So-Called Self-Help Company, Crumbled After Former Members Exposed It as a Cult That Abused Sex Slaves." Business Insider, June 19, 2010. https://www.businessinsider.com /what-is-nxivm-keith-raniere-explainer-2019-4.

MELO, YANAN RAHIM NAVAREZ. "The Gospel Belongs to the 'Heathen,' Not White Saviors." Sojourners, October 12, 2022. https://sojo.net/articles/gospel-belongs -heathen-not-white-saviors.

MELTON, J. GORDON. "Branch Davidian." Britannica, April 15, 2025. https://www .britannica.com/topic/Branch-Davidian.

MELTON, J. GORDON. "The Family International." Britannica, March 28, 2025. https: //www.britannica.com/topic/The-Family-International.

MILITARY ONESOURCE (US DEPARTMENT OF DEFENSE). "Military Pay." Accessed June 20, 2025. https://www.militaryonesource.mil/resources/millife-guides/military-pay.

MINDFULNESS SUPERVISION. "What Does No Privacy Do to a Person?" December 4, 2022. https://mindfulness-supervision.org.uk/what-does-no-privacy-do-to-a-person.

MINOW, JACQUELINE, AND CHRISTOPHER EINOLF. "Sorority Participation and Sexual Assault Risk." Violence Against Women 15, no. 7 (June 2009): 835–851. https://doi.org/10.1177/1077801209334472.

MIREL, JEFFREY, AND SIMONA GOLDIN. "Alone in the Classroom: Why Teachers Are Too Isolated." *Atlantic,* April 17, 2012. https://www.theatlantic.com/national/archive/2012/04/alone-in-the-classroom-why-teachers-are-too-isolated/255976.

MISSION TO AMISH PEOPLE. "Former Amish Testimonies." Accessed June 25, 2025. https://www.mapministry.org/news/former-amish-testimonies.

MOMS FOR AMERICA. "Republican Congresswoman Mary Miller Quotes Hitler During Rally." Video, 0:31. *Guardian,* January 10, 2021. https://www.theguardian.com/us-news/video/2021/jan/11/republican-congresswoman-mary-miller-quotes-hitler-during-rally-video.

MONTAGNE, RENEE. "Research: Long Connection Between Fraternities and Sexual Assault." *NPR*, November 28, 2014. https://www.npr.org/2014/11/28/367154308/research-long-connection-between-fraternities-and-sexual-assault.

MONTELL, AMANDA. *Cultish: The Language of Fanaticism.* Harper Wave, 2021.

MOORE, PAM. "Lonely After a Move?" *Washington Post,* December 10, 2021. https://www.washingtonpost.com/wellness/2021/12/10/how-to-combat-loneliness-move.

MORAN, ANDREW. "50 Annoying and Overused Corporate Jargon." Career Addict, July 19, 2022. https://www.careeraddict.com/corporate-jargon.

MORGAN, EMMA. "Losing Yourself: Cults, Greeks, and Sociological Theories of Self and Identity." Honors program thesis, Rollins College, 2021. https://scholarship.rollins.edu/honors/138.

MORE-LOVE.ORG. "About." Accessed July 4, 2025, https://more-love.org/about.

MORENO, ANN DAILEY. "Salvation Army Withdraws Controversial 'Let's Talk About Racism' Guide." *WPDE*, November 30, 2021. https://wpde.com/news/nation-world/salvation-army-withdraws-controversial-lets-talk-about-racism-guide.

MORIN, KAREN M. "Men's Modesty, Religion, and the State: Spaces of Collision." *Men and Masculinities* 16, no. 3 (2013): 307–328. https://doi.org/10.1177/1097184X13482128.

MOUNTAIN PACIFIC. "Weakness Leaving the Body: The Myth of Pain." September 26, 2023. https://mpqhf.org/weakness-leaving-the-body-the-myth-of-pain.

MOYA, ANDRÉS. "Violence, Psychological Trauma, and Risk Attitudes: Evidence From Victims of Violence in Colombia." *Journal of Development Economics,* 131 (2018): 15–27. https://doi.org/10.1016/j.jdeveco.2017.11.001.

MUNDIN, FRANCIS. "6 Law Student Mental Health Statistics." Law Crossing, January 9, 2024. https://www.lawcrossing.com/article/900055264/6-Law-Student-Mental -Health-Statistics.

MURGIA, CARLA IPPOLITO NOTARNICOLA, ROSARIO CARUSO, ET AL. "Spirituality and Religious Diversity in Nursing: A Scoping Review." *Healthcare* (Basel, Switzerland) 10, no. 9 (August 2022): 1661. https://doi.org/10.3390/healthcare10091661.

MURPHY, BILL, JR. "GM Has a 2-Word Dress Code, and It's Actually Brilliant." *Inc.*, June 8, 2018. https://www.inc.com/bill-murphy-jr/this-giant-company-has-a-2-word-dress -code-its-actually-kind-of-brilliant.html.

MURPHY, BRENDAN. "Medical Student Financial FAQ: Insight on Loan Forgiveness, Repayment." American Medical Association, January 5, 2025. https://www.ama-assn. org/medical-students/medical-school-life/medical-student-financial-faq-insight-loan -forgiveness.

MURPHY, BRENDAN. "To Thwart Medical Student Burnout, Make It Easier to Seek Time Off." American Medical Association, June 13, 2023. https://www.ama-assn.org/medical- students/medical-student-health/thwart-medical-student-burnout-make-it-easier -seek-time.

MURRAY, JENNY. "Review: Smile or Die: How Positive Thinking Fooled America and the World by Barbara Ehrenreich." *Guardian,* January 9, 2010. https://www.theguardian .com/books/2010/jan/10/smile-or-die-barbara-ehrenreich.

MYERS, MEGHANN. "The Army Wants to Kick Out an Avowed White Supremacist Officer, but They Won't Admit It." Military Times, May 25, 2021. https://www .militarytimes.com/news/your-military/2021/05/25/the-army-wants-to-kick-out -an-avowed-white-supremacist-officer-but-they-wont-admit-it.

NAIPAUL, SHIVA. *Journey to Nowhere: A New World Tragedy.* Penguin, 1982.

THE NAP MINISTRY. "Rest Is Anything That Connects Your Mind and Body." February 21, 2022. https://thenapministry.wordpress.com/2022/02/21/rest-is-anything-that -connects-your-mind-and-body.

NARCOTICS ANONYMOUS. *Narcotics Anonymous White Booklet.* 1986. https://na.org/e-lit /white-booklet.

NATIONAL ALLIANCE FOR EATING DISORDERS. "Understanding Eating Disorders: A Quick Guide to Orthorexia Nervosa." July 8, 2022. https://www.allianceforeating disorders.com/orthorexia-nervosa/.

NATIONAL CENTER FOR COMPLEMENTARY AND INTEGRATIVE HEALTH. "'Detoxes' and 'Cleanses': What You Need to Know." Last modified July 2, 2025. https://www .nccih.nih.gov/health/detoxes-and-cleanses-what-you-need-to-know.

NATIONAL INSTITUTE OF MENTAL HEALTH. "Psychotherapies." February 2024. https://www.nimh.nih.gov/health/topics/psychotherapies.

NATIONAL PARK SERVICE. "African Americans at Jamestown." December 6, 2024. https: //www.nps.gov/jame/learn/historyculture/african-americans-at-jamestown.htm.

NATIONAL PARK SERVICE. "A Short History of Jamestown." Accessed June 20, 2025. https: //www.nps.gov/jame/learn/historyculture/a-short-history-of-jamestown.htm.

NEDEDOG, JETHRO. "How Scientology costs members up to millions of dollars, according to Leah Remini's show." Business Insider, December 14, 2016. https: //www.businessinsider.com/scientology-costs-leah-remini-recap-episode-3-2016-12.

NEILSON, E. C., R. S. SINGH, K. L. HARPER, ET AL. "Traditional Masculinity Ideology, Posttraumatic Stress Disorder (PTSD) Symptom Severity, and Treatment in Service Members and Veterans: A Systematic Review." *Psychology of Men & Masculinities*, 21, no. 4 (2020): 578–92. https://doi.org/10.1037/men0000257.

NEJAT SOCIETY. "What Is a Destructive Cult? How Can We Recognize It? Part One." Accessed July 20, 2025. https://dlb.nejatngo.org/File/Books_EN/Banisadr_Des _Cults/Destructive_cult_1.pdf

NEUROLAUNCH. "Cult Behavior: Recognizing and Understanding Manipulative Group Dynamics." September 22, 2024. https://neurolaunch.com/cult-behavior.

NEWSINENGLISH.NO. "State Wins Over Jehovas Witness' Complaint." March 4, 2024. https: //www.newsinenglish.no/2024/03/04/state-wins-over-jehovas-witness-complaint.

NEW YORK STATE DEPARTMENT OF LABOR. "Department of Labor Finds Multiple Child Labor Violations at Common Sense Farm as a Result of Twelve Tribes Investigation." June 5, 2018. https://apps.cio.ny.gov/apps/mediacontact/public/view.cfm?parm =2CF2601B-9936-D8DD-DFC640F525B8799D.

NG, SIK HUNG, AND FEI DENG. "Language and Power." *Oxford Research Encyclopedia of Communication.* August 22, 2017. https://doi.org/10.1093/acrefore/9780190228613 .013.436.

NGUYEN, BRITNEY. "The Career, Rise, Fall, and Return of Adam Neumann, the Controversial WeWork Cofounder Who Is Back with Another Real-Estate Start Up." Business Insider, updated August 16, 2022. https://www.businessinsider.com/wework -ceo-adam-neumann-bio-life-career-2019-8.

NOAH, TREVOR. *Born a Crime: Stories from a South African Childhood.* Narrated by the author. Audible Studios, 2016. 8 hr, 4 min.

NORTH, ANNA. "How #SaveTheChildren Is Pulling American Moms into QAnon." *Vox*, September 18, 2020. https://www.vox.com/21436671/save-our-children-hashtag -qanon-pizzagate.

NORTH CAROLINA STATE UNIVERSITY, DIVISION OF ACADEMIC AND STUDENT AFFAIRS. "Hazing Statistics and Research." Accessed July 20, 2025. https://hazing.dasa.ncsu.edu /resources/hazing-research.

NORTHRUP, LAURA. "4 Things to Know About LuLaRoe Sales Reps' Problems with the Company." *Consumer Reports*, updated March 2, 2017. https://www.consumerreports .org/consumerist/4-things-to-know-about-lularoe-sales-reps-problems-with-the -company/.

NOT THE GOOD GIRL. "She Lost $40,000 in Amway." YouTube video, 1:12:33. February 15, 2021. https://www.youtube.com/watch?v=3kqFe2Wb6TQ.

NOVOTNEY, AMY. "Boys and Men Make Up One Third of All People with Eating Disorders, but Most Aren't Getting the Care They Need." American Psychological Association, September 27, 2024. https://www.apa.org/topics/eating-disorders/boys-men.

NOVOTNEY, AMY. "Unrecognized Eating Disorders in Boys and Young Men." *Monitor on Psychology* 55, no. 7 (October 1, 2024): 30. https://www.apa.org/monitor/2024/10/eating-disorders-boys-men.

NOYES, JOHN HUMPHREY. *Dixon and His Copyists.* Oneida Community, 1871.

NUWER, HANK. "Greek Letters Don't Justify Cult-Like Hazing of Pledges." *Chronicle of Higher Education* 46, no. 14 (1999): B7.

NYE, JOSEPH S., JR. "What Is a Moral Foreign Policy?" *Texas National Security Review* 3, no. 1 (November 2019): 96–108. https://tnsr.org/2019/11/what-is-a-moral-foreign-policy.

OBAMA, BARACK. "President Obama's Farewell Address." January 10, 2017. https://obamawhitehouse.archives.gov/farewell.

OJALVO, HOLLY EPSTEIN. "What Is Modern Slavery? Investigating Human Trafficking." *New York Times*, March 6, 2012. https://archive.nytimes.com/learning.blogs.nytimes.com/2012/03/06/what-is-modern-slavery-investigating-human-trafficking.

OKRENT, ARIKA. "Merriam-Webster's Word of the Year Is 'Culture.'" Mental Floss, December 15, 2014. https://www.mentalfloss.com/article/60713/merriam-websters-word-year-culture. [Source no longer available]

OKUN, TEMA. "White Supremacy Culture Characteristics." Whitesupremacyculture.info. Accessed September 26, 2025. https://www.whitesupremacyculture.info/characteristics.html. Oluo, Ijeoma. *Mediocre: The Dangerous Legacy of White Male America.* Basic, 2020.

O'NEIL, BILL. "Where Does the Money from Girl Scout Cookies Go?" WXII 12 News, January 29, 2021. https://www.wxii12.com/article/local-scout-leader-says-troops-get-76-box/35362285.

O'NEILL, LAUREN. "The Cult of Thinness Is Making a Depressing Comeback." Vice, November 28, 2022. https://www.vice.com/en/article/thin-is-in-cult-making-comeback.

ORANGE. "Introduction." In *The Orange Papers.* https://orangepapers.eth.limo/orange-intro.html.

ORNER, EVA, DIRECTOR. *Bikram: Yogi, Guru, Predator.* Netflix, 2019. https://www.netflix.com/title/80221584.

OXFORD REFERENCE. "Total Institution." https://www.oxfordreference.com/display/10.1093/oi/authority.20110803105035774.

PALMADA, BELINDA. "How the Royal Family Uses Queen Elizabeth's $57M Lodge." Realestate.com.au. Accessed May 15, 2025. https://www.realestate.com.au/news/how-royal-family-use-queen-elizabeths-57m-lodge.

PANDA, GAYATRI. "The Mental Health of Startup Employees: What Founders Can Do to Foster Well-Being." Forbes, November 12, 2024. https://www.forbes.com/councils/forbesbusinesscouncil/2024/11/12/the-mental-health-of-startup-employees-what-founders-can-do-to-foster-well-being.

PAPE, ROBERT A. Dying to Win: The Strategic Logic of Suicide Terrorism. Random House, 2005.

PARGAMENT, KENNETH I., AND JULIE J. EXLINE. "Religious and Spiritual Struggles." American Psychological Association, November 1, 2020. https://www.apa.org/topics/belief-systems-religion/spiritual-struggles.

PARK, ROSA. "The Psychology Behind 'Escaping Twin Flames.'" First Session, November 18, 2024. https://www.firstsession.com/resources/the-psychology-behind-escaping-twin-flames-vulnerability-and-loneliness.

PARKER, KIM, RUTH IGIELNIK, AMANDA BARROSO, ET AL. "The American Veteran Experience and the Post-9/11 Generation." Pew Research Center, September 10, 2019. https://www.pewresearch.org/social-trends/2019/09/10/the-american-veteran-experience-and-the-post-9-11-generation.

PARKS, JENNIFER. "Installations and Logistics Leadership Visits MCLB Albany." US Department of Defense, March 10, 2023. https://www.defense.gov/News/Releases/Release/Article/3325544/department-of-defense-releases-fiscal-year-2022-annual-report-on-sexual-assault-i.

PARVEZ, HANAN. "The Psychology of Changing Your Name." PsychMetric, December 10, 2024. https://www.psychmechanics.com/psychology-of-changing-your-name.

PASSIKOF, ROBERT. "The Few, The Proud, The Marines." Forbes, November 9, 2014. https://www.forbes.com/sites/robertpassikoff/2014/11/09/the-few-the-proud-the-marines.

PATRICK, TED. Let Our Children Go!. Dutton, 1976.

PATTERSON, THOM. "What to Know Before Pledging a Fraternity or Sorority." CNN, updated August 25, 2018. https://www.cnn.com/2018/04/12/us/fraternity-sorority-overview.

PBS. "The 1934 Waterfront Strike: Solidarity on the Docks." Video, 8:32. April 18, 2023. https://www.pbs.org/video/the-1934-waterfront-strike-solidarity-on-the-docks-istzx6.

PCOM SOUTH GEORGIA. "Understanding Medical Student Burnout Causes, Symptoms and How to Recover." August 4, 2022. https://www.pcom.edu/south-georgia/news/understanding-student-burnout.html.

PEARCE, EILUNED, JACQUES LAUNAY, AND ROBIN I. M. DUNBAR. "The Ice-Breaker Effect: Singing Mediates Fast Social Bonding." *Royal Society Open Science* 21 (2015): 50221. https://doi.org/10.1098/rsos.150221.

PEARSON, LAURA. "Is the 'Spiritual' Experience of Soulcycle Sacred or Inane?" *Chicago Reader*, May 5, 2016. https://chicagoreader.com/arts-culture/is-the-spiritual -experience-of-soulcycle-sacred-or-inane.

PENN STATE NEWS. "When Tipping and Smiling Are Both Expected at Work, So Is Sexual Harassment." June 25, 2018. https://www.psu.edu/news/research/story /when-tipping-and-smiling-are-both-expected-work-so-is-sexual-harassment.

PEOPLESHIFT. "McClelland's Motivation Theory." February 2019. https://people-shift .com/articles/mcclellands-motivation-theory..

PERLSTEIN, RICK. "Our Cults, Ourselves." The American Prospect, October 9, 2024. https://prospect.org/politics/2024-10-09-our-cults-ourselves/.

PERRY, GEMMA, VINCE POLITO, AND WILLIAM FORDE THOMPSON. "Exploring the Physiological and Psychological Effects of Group Chanting in Australia: Reduced Stress, Cortisol and Enhanced Social Connection." *Journal of Religion and Health* 63 (2024): 4793–815.

PERSPECTIVES HOLISTIC THERAPY. "Recovering from Religious Trauma and Spiritual Abuse." Accessed June 28, 2025. https://www.perspectivesholistictherapy.com/blog /recovering-from-religious-trauma-and-spiritual-abuse.

PETERSEN, SARA. "Wellness Mommy Bloggers and the Cultish Language They Use." *Harper's Bazaar*, August 25, 2021. https://www.harpersbazaar.com/culture/features /a36595860/wellness-mommy-bloggers-and-the-cultish-language-they-use.

PETERSEN, TYRONE. "The Dark Side of Capitalism: Prioritizing Profit over People." *Medium*, February 11, 2024. https://medium.com/@thefearlessgrind2023/the-dark -side-of-capitalism-prioritizing-profit-over-people-5bf839edb745.

PETERSON, HAYLEY. "LuLaRoe is Facing Mounting Debt, Layoffs, and an Exodus of Top Sellers, and Sources Say the $2.3 Billion Legging Empire Could Be Imploding." Business Insider, November 20, 2018. https://www.businessinsider.com/lularoe-legging -empire-mounting-debt-top-sellers-flee-2018-11.

PETRARCA, MARISA. "Why Americans Can't Resist Multilevel Marketing Schemes." *Artful Living*, September 21 2022. https://artfulliving.com/multilevel-marketing -schemes-2022.

PETTER, OLIVIA. "'They Mix Social Media Branding with the Deep Pull of Religion': SoulCycle, OneTaste, and the Cult of Wellness." *Independent*. April 1, 2021. https://www .the-independent.com/life-style/wellness-cult-soulcycle-onetaste-b1825478.html.

PEW RESEARCH CENTER. "Political Polarization in the American Public." June 12, 2014. https://www.pewresearch.org/politics/2014/06/12/political-polarization-in-the -american-public.

PJSPEARS212. "Is Alcoholics Anonymous a Cult?...What Are Your Thoughts?" Reddit. https://www.reddit.com/r/cults/comments/16wu8me/is_alcoholics_anonymous_a _cult_what_are_your.

PLBY GROUP, INC. "PLBY Group Reports Fourth Quarter and Full Year 2024 Financial Results." *GlobeNewswire*, March 13, 2025. https://www.globenewswire.com/news -release/2025/03/13/3042626/0/en/PLBY-Group-Reports-Fourth-Quarter-and -Full-Year-2024-Financial-Results.html.

POLYPORTIS, ATHANASIOS, LEONIE PEIFFER, ANNE-MARIE VAN PROOIJEN, ET AL. "Navigating Anti-Vegan Perspectives for Persuasive Communication in Sustainable Food Transitions." Paper presented at Etmaal van de Communicatiewetenschap 2025, Brugge, Belgium, February 2025. https://www.researchgate.net/publication /389814315_Navigating_anti-vegan_perspectives_for_persuasive_communication _in_sustainable_food_transitions.

POOLE, STEVEN. "10 of the Worst Examples of Management-Speak." *Guardian*, April 25, 2013. https://www.theguardian.com/books/2013/apr/25/top-10-worst -management-speak.

POPIK, BARRY. "Christians in Action (Central Intelligence Agency or CIA Nickname)." February 8, 2012. https://barrypopik.com/blog/christians_in_action_central _intelligence_agency_or_cia_nickname.

POPKIN, BEN, AND CYRUS FARIVAR. "Elizabeth Holmes Admits Whistleblower Was Right and Reporter Was 'Mishandled.'" NBC News, November 30, 2021. https:// www.nbcnews.com/business/business-news/elizabeth-holmes-admits-whistleblower -was-right-reporter-was-mishandle-rcna7123.

PORGES, STEPHEN W. *The Polyvagal Theory: Neurophysiological Foundations of Emotions, Attachment, Communication, and Self-regulation.* W. W. Norton, 2011.

PRICKETT, MATTHEW. "Inside the Childrens House." Rowan CHSS, YouTube video, 42:07. January 22, 2018. https://www.youtube.com/watch?v=WymYpctLlWo.

PRINCE HARRY. *Spare*. Random House, 2023.

PROJECT PLAY. "Cost to Play Trends." Aspen Institute, 2022. https://projectplay.org /state-of-play-2022/costs-to-play-trends.

PSYCHOLOGY TODAY. "Charisma." Accessed July 2023. https://www.psychologytoday. com/us/basics/charisma.

QUART, ALISSA. *Bootstrapped: Exposing the Myth of the Self-Made and the Rugged Individualist, From "Little House" to Horatio Alger.* Ecco, 2023.

RAAB, DIANA. "What Is Spiritual Bypassing?" *Psychology Today*, updated May 31, 2024. https://www.psychologytoday.com/us/blog/the-empowerment-diary/201901 /what-is-spiritual-bypassing.

RAINE, SUSAN. "Flirty Fishing in the Children of God: The Sexual Body as a Site of Proselytization and Salvation." *Marburg Journal of Religion* 12, no. 1 (2015). https: //doi.org/10.17192/mjr.2007.12.3608.

RAMSBERGER, PETER F., PETER LEGREE, AND LISA MILLS. "Evaluation of the Buddy Team Assignment Program, Final Report," FR 02-20 (Human Resources Research Organization, July 29, 2002). Prepared for US Army Research Institute for the Behavioral and Social Sciences. https://apps.dtic.mil/sti/tr/pdf/ADA408486.pdf.

RAMSLAND, KATHERINE. "Heaven's Gate." Crime Library. Archived March 5, 2005. https://web.archive.org/web/20050305162149/http://www.crimelibrary.com /notorious_murders/mass/heavens_gate/1.html?sect=8.

RC. "I Am a Horrible Person: Saying 'No' to Girl Scouts and Their Cookies, Too." Strange Culture Blog, January 18, 2009. http://www.strangecultureblog.com/2009/01 /i-am-horrible-person-saying-no-to-girl.html.

REDDEBREK. "The Starvation Army: Twelve Reasons to Reject the Salvation Army." Libcom.org, December 20, 2013. https://libcom.org/article/starvation-army-twelve -reasons-reject-salvation-army.

REITERMAN, TIM, AND JOHN JACOBS. *Raven: The Untold Story of the Rev. Jim Jones and His People*. Penguin, 2008.

RELIGION NEWS BLOG. "Polygamy Garb Born of Rules: Garment Rules Used to Control Women's Individuality, Former Cult Members Say." April 18, 2008. https://www .religionnewsblog.com/21208/flds-84.

REMINI, LEAH, AND MIKE RINDER, EXECUTIVE PRODUCERS AND HOSTS. *Leah Remini: Scientology and the Aftermath*. TV series. A&E, 2016–2019.

REMINI, LEAH, AND REBECCA PALEY. *Troublemaker: Surviving Hollywood and Scientology*. Ballantine, 2015.

REMNICK, DAVID. "The Spirit Level." *New Yorker*, November 8, 2004. https://www .newyorker.com/magazine/2004/11/08/the-spirit-level.

RENSINK, BRENDEN. "Genocide of Native Americans: Historical Facts and Historiographic Debates." In *Genocide: A Critical Bibliographic Review*, vol. 8, ed. Samuel Totten and Robert K. Hitchcock. Transaction, 2011.

RESNICK, BRIAN. "The Dark Psychology of Dehumanization, Explained." Vox, March 7, 2017. https://www.vox.com/science-and-health/2017/3/7/14456154 /dehumanization-psychology-explained.

RICE, NICHOLAS, AND NATALIA SENANAYAKE. "Delta's New Rule That Flight Attendants Must Wear 'Proper Undergarments' Has Commenters Buzzing." *People*, September 21, 2024. https://people.com/delta-has-new-rule-that-flight-attendants-must-wear -proper-undergarments-8715893.

RIEPE, MARK. "What Is the Sunk Cost Fallacy and How Does It Work?" Schwab Center for Financial Research, May 12 2025. https://www.schwab.com/learn/story/dont -look-back-how-to-avoid-sunk-cost-fallacy.

RIGHETTI, F., J. K. SAKALUK, R. FAURE, ET AL. "The Link Between Sacrifice and Relational and Personal Well-Being: A Meta-Analysis." *Psychology Bulletin* 146, no. 10 (2020): 900–921.

RINDER, MIKE. *A Billion Years: My Escape from a Life in the Highest Ranks of Scientology.* Gallery, 2024.

ROBBINS, THOMAS. "Charisma." In *Encyclopedia of Religion and Society.* Hartford Institute for Religion and Society, Hartford Seminary, 1998. https://web.archive .org/web/20060526114911/http://hirr.hartsem.edu/ency/charisma.htm.

ROBERTS, ALLEN D. "Profile of Apostasy: Who Are the Bad Guys, Really?" *Dialogue: A Journal of Mormon Thought* 31, no. 4 (Winter 1998): 143–62. https://www .dialoguejournal.com/articles/profile-of-apostasy-who-are-the-bad-guys-really.

ROBERTSON, MARY, AND EMMA SCHWARTZ, DIRECTORS. *Quiet on Set: The Dark Side of Kids TV.* Investigation Discovery, aired March 17–April 7, 2024.

ROBINSON, LUCY, AND JOSEPH BARONIO. "As Hyper-Masculine Content Floods Social Media, a 'Healthier' Men's Movement Is Stepping Up." ABC News (Australia), May 8, 2024. https://www.abc.net.au/news/2024-05-09/toxic-masculinity-social -media-content-impacts-teenage-boys/103810334.

ROGAL, LAUREN. "Secrets, Lies, and Lessons from the Theranos Scandal." *Hastings Law Journal* 72 (August 2021): 1663–1702. https://hastingslawjournal.org/wp-content /uploads/Rogal_7-TRANSMIT.pdf

ROMANIUK, M., AND C. KIDD. "The Psychological Adjustment Experience of Reintegration Following Discharge from Military Service: A Systematic Review." *Journal of Military and Veterans' Health* 26, no. 2 (April 2018).

ROOS, DAVE. "What's the Difference Between Puritans and Pilgrims?" History.com. July 31, 2019. https://www.history.com/news/pilgrims-puritans-differences.

ROSE, JOEL. "Even if It's 'Bonkers,' Poll Finds Many Believe QAnon and Other Conspiracy Theories." NPR, December 30, 2020. https://www.npr.org/2020/12/30/951095644 /even-if-its-bonkers-poll-finds-many-believe-qanon-and-other-conspiracy-theories.

ROSMAN, KATHERINE. "How to Explain the Rise and Fall of WeWork?" *New York Times,* July 18, 2021. https://www.nytimes.com/2021/07/18/books/review/the-cult-of-we -eliot-brown-maureen-farrell.html.

ROSS, GARRETT. "POLITICO Playbook PM: Inside Meadows' Phone on Jan. 6." Politico, April 25, 2022. https://www.politico.com/newsletters/playbook-pm /2022/04/25/inside-meadows-phone-on-jan-6-00027516.

ROSSI, EUGENE JOSEPH. "'Helter Skelter': Lyrics Matter." American Bar Association, March 1, 2024. https://www.americanbar.org/groups/litigation/resources/litigation -journal/2024-winter/helter-skelter-lyrics-matter.

ROTHFELD, MICHAEL, AND NICOLE HONG. "Shen Yun Is Said to Be Under Federal Investigation over Possible Visa Fraud." *New York Times,* February 6, 2025. https: //www.nytimes.com/2025/02/06/nyregion/shen-yun-federal-investigation.html.

RUDENSKY, MIRA. "The Global Rise of Quiet Quitting." *Brown Political Review,* November 21, 2022. https://brownpoliticalreview.org/global-rise-of-quiet-quitting.

SABIN, SAM. "Musk's 'Move Fast, Break Things' Ethos Threatens U.S. Security." Axios, February 9, 2025. https://www.axios.com/2025/02/09/elon-musk-doge-federal-it -national-security.

SADUN, RAFFAELLA. "The Myth of the Brilliant, Charismatic Leader." *Harvard Business Review*, November 23, 2022. https://hbr.org/2022/11/the-myth-of-the-brilliant -charismatic-leader.

SALTER, MICHAEL. *Organised Sexual Abuse*. Routledge, 2013.

SAMET, ELIZABETH. *Looking for the Good War: American Amnesia and the Violent Pursuit of Happiness*. MacMillan, 2021.

SANDAY, PEGGY REEVES. *Fraternity Gang Rape: Sex, Brotherhood, and Privilege on Campus*. 2nd ed. New York University Press, 2007.

SASLOW, ELI. *Rising Out of Hatred: The Awakening of a Former White Nationalist*. Narrated by Scott Brick. Penguin Random House Audio, 2018. 9 hr., 12 min.

SASLOW, ELI. "The White Flight of Derek Black." *Washington Post*, October 15, 2016. https://www.washingtonpost.com/national/the-white-flight-of-derek-black/2016 /10/15/ed5f906a-8f3b-11e6-a6a3-d50061aa9fae_story.html.

SASSE, BEN. *Them: Why We Hate Each Other—and How to Heal*. St. Martin's Press, 2018.

SAUL, EMILY. "Nxivm Defense Quotes 'Mockingbird,' Churchill in Bombastic Opening." *New York Post,* May 7, 2019. https://nypost.com/2019/05/07/nxivm-defense -quotes-mockingbird-churchill-in-bombastic-opening.

SCHEERES, JULIA. *A Thousand Lives: The Untold Story of Hope, Deception, and Survival at Jonestown*. Free Press, 2011.

SCHNEID, REBECCA. "What Is DEI and What Challenges Does It Face amid Trump's Executive Orders?" *Time*, January 25, 2025. https://time.com/7210039/what-is -dei-trump-executive-order-companies-diversity-efforts.

SCHULLER, KYLA. *The Trouble with White Women: A Counterhistory of Feminism*. PublicAffairs, 2021.

SCHWARTZ, TONY, AND ERIC SEVERSON. "Why We Glorify Overwork and Refuse to Rest." *Harvard Business Review*, August 28, 2023. https://hbr.org/2023/08/why-we -glorify-overwork-and-refuse-to-rest.

SCIENTOLOGY. "What Does 'Suppressive Person' Mean?" Accessed July 20, 2025. https: //www.scientology.org/faq/scientology-attitudes-and-practices/what-is-a-suppressive -person.html.

SCISM, REX. "Retiring from Public Safety: The Big Breakup." Lexipol, February 28, 2022. https://www.lexipol.com/resources/blog/retiring-from-public-safety-the-big -breakup.

SCOTT, SUSIE. "Revisiting the Total Institution: Performative Regulation in the Reinventive Institution." *Sociology* 44, no. 2 (2010): 213–31. https://doi.org/10.1177/0038038509357198.

SELIGMAN, MARTIN. *Learned Optimism: How to Change Your Mind and Your Life.* Pocket, 1998.

SERRATORE, ANGELA. "What You Need to Know About the Manson Family Murders." *Smithsonian Magazine*, July 25, 2019. https://www.smithsonianmag.com/history/manson-family-murders-what-need-to-know-180972655.

SHARKEY, SARAH. "Mother's Day Index 2025: Mom's Annual Salary Climbs 4%, Now More Than $145,000." Insure.com. Accessed June 30, 2025. https://www.insure.com/life-insurance/the-mothers-day-index.html.

SHERRILL, MIKIE. "Sherrill Calls for Investigations into Elon Musk's Vast Conflicts of Interest and Self-Dealing at Federal Agencies." Press release, March 21, 2025. https://sherrill.house.gov/media/press-releases/sherrill-calls-for-investigations-into-elon-musk-s-vast-conflicts-of-interest-and-self-dealing-at-federal-agencies.

SILTANEN, ROB. "The Real Story Behind Apple's 'Think Different' Campaign." *Forbes*, December 14, 2011. https://www.forbes.com/sites/onmarketing/2011/12/14/the-real-story-behind-apples-think-different-campaign.

SILVESTRINI, MOLLY, AND JESSICA A. CHEN. "'It's a Sign of Weakness': Masculinity and Help-Seeking Behaviors Among Male Veterans Accessing Posttraumatic Stress Disorder Care." *Psychological Trauma* 15, no. 4 (May 2023): 665–71. https://doi.org/10.1037/tra0001382.

SIMPSON, ERIKA. "Unmasking Cults: Examining the Parallels Between Trumpism and Chinmoyism to Understand Extremism and Offer Peacemakers' Support." *Peace Review*, March 2025. https://doi.org/10.1080/10402659.2025.2473410.

SINGER, MARGARET THALER, AND JANJA LALICH. *Cults in Our Midst: The Continuing Fight Against Their Hidden Menace.* Revised edition, Jossey-Bass, 2003. Original edition, Jossey-Bass, 1995.

SINGER, MARGARET, ET AL. *Margaret T. Singer Collection.* Edited by Carol Giambalvo and Rosanne Henry. Accessed July 20, 2025. https://www.prem-rawat-bio.org/academic/singer.html.

SKINNER-DORKENOO, ALLISON L., MEGHAN GEORGE, JAMES E. WAGES III, ET AL. "A Systemic Approach to the Psychology of Racial Bias Within Individuals and Society." *Nature Reviews Psychology* 2 (May 2023): 392–406. https://doi.org/10.1038/s44159-023-00190-z.

SLEEK, SCOTT. "Toxic Workplaces Leave Employees Sick, Scared, and Looking for an Exit." American Psychological Association, July 13, 2023. https://www.apa.org/topics/healthy-workplaces/toxic-workplace.

SLISCO, AILA. "Trump Unleashes Apocalyptic 'Final Battle' Fundraising Campaign." *Newsweek*, March 8, 2023. https://www.newsweek.com/trump-unleashes-apocalyptic -final-battle-fundraising-campaign-1786515.

SMITH, APRIL WILSON. "Deprogramming from AA—When a Fellowship Resembles a Cult." *Filter*, May 2, 2019. https://filtermag.org/deprogramming-from-aa-when-a -fellowship-resembles-a-cult.

SMITH, DANIEL, PHILIP SCHLAEPFER, KATIE MAJOR, ET AL. "Cooperation and the Evolution of Hunter-Gatherer Storytelling." *Nature Communications* 8 (2017): 1853. https://doi.org/10.1038/s41467-017-02036-8.

SMITH, DAVID. "Nearly One in Four Americans Believe Political Violence Justified to 'Save' US." *Guardian*, October 25, 2023. https://www.theguardian.com /us-news/2023/oct/25/us-political-violence-justified-survey.

SMITH, DAVID. "'She Got a Lot of Trouble for It': How Tammy Faye Bakker Went from Televangelist to Gay Icon." *Guardian*, September 18, 2021, accessed June 7, 2025, https://www.theguardian.com/film/2021/sep/18/tammy-faye-bakker-film-jessica -chastain.

SMITH, GREGORY A., ALAN COOPERMAN, BECKA A. ALPER, ET AL. "Religious Identity in the United States." In *Religious Landscape Study*. Pew Research Center, February 26, 2025. https://www.pewresearch.org/religion/2025/02/26/religious-landscape -study-religious-identity.

SMITHSONIAN INSTITUTION. "Human Characteristics: Social Life." Smithsonian Institution's Human Origins Program. Accessed July 10, 2025. https://humanorigins .si.edu/human-characteristics/social-life.

SMITHSONIAN WOMEN'S HISTORY MUSEUM. "Voices on Independence: Four Oral Histories About Building Women's Economic Power." October 25, 2024. https: //womenshistory.si.edu/blog/voices-independence-four-oral-histories-about -building-womens-economic-power.

SNOW, ROBERT L. *Deadly Cults: The Crimes of True Believers*. Praeger, 2003.

SOWERS, ALEXANDRIA RYAN. "Revolution Through Revelation: Jim Jones and the Peoples Temple in American Cultural History." Master's thesis, Eastern Kentucky University, January 2018. https://encompass.eku.edu/etd/492.

SRIVASTAVA, SANJAY, MAYA TAMIR, KELLY M. MCGONIGAL, ET AL. "The Social Costs of Emotional Suppression: A Prospective Study of the Transition to College." *Journal of Personality and Social Psychology* 96, no. 4 (April 2009): 883–97. https://doi .org/10.1037/a0014755.

STACK, PEGGY FLETCHER. "Does Tithing Requirement for Entry into LDS Temples Amount to Mormons Buying Their Way into Heaven?" *Salt Lake Tribune*, updated March 27, 2018. https://www.sltrib.com/religion/2018/03/26/does-tithing-requirement -for-entry-into-lds-temples-amount-to-mormons-buying-their-way-into-heaven.

STACK, PEGGY FLETCHER. "Teaching LDS Polygamy in Primary: Will the Kids Get It?" *Salt Lake Tribune*, December 27, 2024. https://www.sltrib.com/religion/2024/12/27/new-lds-church-cartoons-teach-kids.

STALLARD, KRISTA. "How Expensive Is a Divorce?" Standard & Bellof, January 24, 2024. https://stallardbelloflaw.com/how-expensive-is-a-divorce.

STANBOROUGH, REBECCA JOY. "How Black and White Thinking Hurts You (and What You Can Do to Change It)." Healthline, January 14, 2020. https://www.healthline.com/health/mental-health/black-and-white-thinking.

STARZ. "Seduced: Inside the NXIVM Cult | Q&A Moderated by Laura Dern." YouTube video, 1:10:47, February 24, 2021, https://www.youtube.com/watch?v=mqI6GV8e008.

STATISTA RESEARCH DEPARTMENT. "Countries with the Largest Number of Prisoners per 100,000 of the National Population February 2025." Statista, June 20, 2025. https://www.statista.com/statistics/262962/countries-with-the-most-prisoners-per-100-000-inhabitants.

STEIN, ALEXANDRA. "How Totalism Works." Aeon, June 20, 2017. https://aeon.co/essays/how-cult-leaders-brainwash-followers-for-total-control.

STEIN, ALEXANDRA. *Terror, Love and Brainwashing*. Routledge, 2021.

STELZNER, MARK, AND SVEN BECKERT. "The Contribution of Enslaved Workers to Output and Growth in the Antebellum United States." *Economic History Review* 77 (2024): 137–59. https://doi.org/10.1111/ehr.13255.

STEVER, GAYLE. "Parasocial and Social Interaction with Celebrities: Classification of Media Fans." *Journal of Media Psychology* 14 (2019).

STEYAERT, JAN. "1961 Erving Goffman: Total Institutions." History of Social Work. February 2011. https://historyofsocialwork.org/eng/details.php?cps=19&canon_id=161.

STOUT, MARTHA. *The Sociopath Next Door: The Ruthless Versus the Rest of Us*. Harmony, 2005.

STREEP, PEG. "5 Kinds of Blame-Shifting, and Why They Work." *Psychology Today*, February 14, 2023. https://www.psychologytoday.com/us/blog/tech-support/202302/verbal-abusers-and-the-fine-art-of-the-blame-shift.

STRINGS, SABRINA. *Fearing the Black Body: The Racial Origins of Fat Phobia*. NYU Press, 2019.

STRONG, KRYSTAL, SHARON WALKER, DERRON WALLACE, ET AL. "Learning from the Movement for Black Lives: Horizons of Racial Justice for Comparative and International Education." *Comparative Education Review* 67, no. S1 (February 2023). https://doi.org/10.1086/722487.

SUDAKOV, MONIKA. "'The Deep End': Why Teal Swan's Cult of Personality Is Dangerous to Trauma Survivors." The Mighty. Last updated September 6, 2024.

https://themighty.com/topic/post-traumatic-stress-disorder-ptsd/the-deep-end
-cult-teal-swan-trauma-ptsd.

SULS, JERRY. "Cognitive Dissonance of Leon Festinger." Britannica. Accessed July 20,
2025. https://www.britannica.com/biography/Leon-Festinger/Cognitive-dissonance.

SUTTLES, JASMINE. "Teacher Voices: Stress and Coping Mechanisms among the Teaching
Profession." Master's thesis, Dominican University of California, 2024. https://doi
.org/10.33015/dominican.edu/2024.EDU.03.

SYRACUSE UNIVERSITY. "Military Spouse Study Finds High Number of Female Spouses
Underemployed." February 11, 2014. https://news.syr.edu/blog/2014/02/11/military
-spouse-study-finds-high-number-of-female-spouses-underemployed-15198.

SZALAVITZ, MAIA. "The Cult That Spawned the Tough-Love Teen Industry." *Mother
Jones*, September/October 2007.

SZALAVITZ, MAIA. *Help at Any Cost: How the Troubled-Teen Industry Cons Parents and
Hurts Kids.* Riverhead, 2006.

TAMPA BAY TIMES. "Salvation Army Changes Rules for Married Officers." *Tampa Bay
Times*, updated September 27, 2005. https://www.tampabay.com/archive/2000/09/09
/salvation-army-changes-rules-for-married-officers.

TANASUGARN, ANNIE. "4 Common Patterns of Coercive Control in Relationships."
Psychology Today, June 8, 2022. https://www.psychologytoday.com/us/blog
/understanding-ptsd/202206/4-common-patterns-coercive-control-in-relationships.

TAYLOR, JON M. "Chapter 7: MLM's Abysmal Numbers," in The Case (for and) against
Multi-level Marketing: The Complete Guide to Understanding and Countering the
Effects of Endless Chain Selling and Product-based Pyramid Schemes. 1999. https:
//www.ftc.gov/sites/default/files/documents/public_comments/trade-regulation
-rule-disclosure-requirements-and-prohibitions-concerning-business-opportunities
-ftc.r511993-00008%C2%A0/00008-57281.pdf.

TAYLOR, SCOTT. "First Presidency Announces Increase in Monthly Missionary
Contribution." *Church News*, June 27, 2019. https://www.thechurchnews.com/2019
/6/27/23215166/first-presidency-lds-missionary-contribution.

TEMES, HANNAH, AND DAMIR KOVAČEVIĆ. "The Rise of QAnon: From Chatroom Board
to an International Movement." *ASTRA: The McNair Scholars' Journal*, University
of Wisconsin–Eau Claire, 2021. https://publicwebuploads.uwec.edu/documents
/Hannah-Temes.pdf.

TEMPERA, JACQUELINE, AND ALOIAN, ADDISON. "Here Are All the Rules FLDS
Church Members from Netflix's 'Keep Sweet' Documentary Have to Follow Every
Day." *Women's Health*, June 14, 2022. https://www.womenshealthmag.com/life
/a40221513/flds-rules-keep-sweet.

THEISEN, ANGELA. "Is Having a Sense of Belonging Important?" Mayo Clinic, December
8, 2021. https://www.mayoclinichealthsystem.org/hometown-health/speaking
-of-health/is-having-a-sense-of-belonging-important.

THIEL, PETER. *Zero to One: Notes on Startups, or How to Build the Future.* Crown Currency, 2014.

THIEL, PETER. "The Education of a Libertarian." *Cato Unbound*, April 13, 2009. https://www.cato-unbound.org/2009/04/13/peter-thiel/education-libertarian.

THOMAS JEFFERSON FOUNDATION. "Jefferson's Attitudes Toward Slavery." Monticello. https://www.monticello.org/thomas-jefferson/jefferson-slavery/jefferson-s-attitudes-toward-slavery/#footnote6_58z30m1.

THOMAS JEFFERSON FOUNDATION. "The Business of Slavery at Monticello." Monticello. Accessed June 22, 2025. https://www.monticello.org/slavery/jefferson-slavery/the-business-of-slavery-at-monticello.

THORNELY, JO. "'Flirty Fishing,' Incest and Child Abuse: Inside a Chilling Sex Cult." Yahoo! News, August 26, 2021. https://au.news.yahoo.com/flirty-fishing-incest-and-child-abuse-inside-a-chilling-sex-cult-075028223.html.

TIAYON, SHANNA B. "Do You Find Belonging in Groups or Communities?" Greater Good Magazine, July 16, 2024. https://greatergood.berkeley.edu/article/item/do_you_find_belonging_in_groups_or_communities.

TIKU, NITASHA. "Silicon Valley Goes to Therapy." New York Times, September 22, 2019. https://www.nytimes.com/2019/09/20/business/silicon-valley-therapy-anxiety.html.

TOBIN, THOMAS. "Judge Rules Court Can't Take On Couple's Dispute over Scientology Debt." *Tampa Bay Times*, March 8, 2012. https://www.tampabay.com/news/courts/judge-rules-court-cant-take-on-couples-dispute-over-scientology-debt/1219054.

TODAY'S MILITARY. "Boot Camp." Accessed July 20, 2025. https://www.todaysmilitary.com/joining-eligibility/boot-camp.

TOLIN, LISA. "Banned Books List 2025." Pen America. Accessed June 25, 2025. https://pen.org/banned-books-list-2025.

TORRES, MONICA. "4 Ways Elizabeth Holmes Manipulated Her Theranos Employees." HuffPost, updated November 18, 2022. https://www.huffpost.com/entry/elizabeth-holmes-office-employees_l_5c92abe3e4b01b140d351b6f.

TRAFTON, ANNE. "In the Blink of an Eye: MIT Neuroscientists Find the Brain Can Identify Images Seen for as Little as 13 Milliseconds." MIT News, January 16, 2014. https://news.mit.edu/2014/in-the-blink-of-an-eye-0116.

TRIANGLE SHIRTWAIST FACTORY FIRE MEMORIAL. "Triangle History." Accessed June 27, 2025. https://trianglememorial.org/triangle-history.

TRUTH IN ADVERTISING. "LuLaRoe Distributors in Bankruptcy as Founder Touts Financial Freedom." Updated June 10, 2019. https://truthinadvertising.org/articles/lularoe-distributors-face-bankruptcy-as-founder-touts-financial-freedom.

TUCKER, DARA STARR. "The Danger of Chick Tracts." YouTube video, 1:57. April 14, 2021. https://www.youtube.com/watch?v=7-S81-0XhTM.

UNITED STATES PATENT AND TRADEMARK OFFICE. Filing for "MAKE AMERICA GREAT AGAIN for applicant Donald J. Trump." Class 35, New York, 2015. https://trademarks.justia.com/857/83/make-america-great-85783371.html.

US ATTORNEY'S OFFICE, DISTRICT OF COLUMBIA. "Arkansas Man Sentenced for Assaulting Law Enforcement During Jan. 6 Capitol Breach." News release, July 24, 2023. US Department of Justice. https://www.justice.gov/usao-dc/pr/arkansas-man-sentenced-assaulting-law-enforcement-during-jan-6-capitol-breach.

US DEPARTMENT OF THE ARMY. "TRADOC Regulation 350-6: Enlisted Initial Entry Training Policies and Administration." United States Army Training and Doctrine Command, December 8, 2022. https://adminpubs.tradoc.army.mil/regulations/TR350-6.pdf.

US DEPARTMENT OF HEALTH AND HUMAN SERVICES. "U.S. Surgeon General Issues Advisory on the Mental Health and Well-Being of Parents." August 28, 2024. https://www.hhs.gov/about/news/2024/08/28/us-surgeon-general-issues-advisory-mental-health-well-being-parents.html.

US OFFICE OF PERSONNEL MANAGEMENT. Deferred Resignation Program "Original Email to Employees." January 28, 2025. https://www.opm.gov/about-us/fork/original-email-to-employees/.

US PAIN FOUNDATION. "No Pain, No Gain." October 20, 2020. https://uspainfoundation.org/blog/no-pain-no-gain.

VALESKA, TYLER, MICHAEL MILLS, MELISSA MUSE, ET AL. "Nondisclosure Agreements in the Trump White House." *NYU Journal of Legislation & Public Policy*, January 28, 2021. https://nyujlpp.org/quorum/nondisclosure-agreements-trump-white-house/.

VANDERGRIFF, DONALD E. *Adopting Mission Command: Developing Leaders for a Superior Command Culture.* Naval Institute Press, 2019.

VANDERGRIFF, DONALD E. "How the Germans Defined Auftragstaktik: What Mission Command Is—AND—Is Not." Small Wars Journal, June 21, 2018. https://archive.smallwarsjournal.com/index.php/jrnl/art/how-germans-defined-auftragstaktik-what-mission-command-and-not.

VAUGHAN-NICHOLS, STEVEN J. "Musk's Move Fast and Break Things Mantra Won't Work in US.gov." The Register, February 7, 2025. https://www.theregister.com/2025/02/07/opinion_column_musk.

VCU LIBRARIES SOCIAL WELFARE HISTORY PROJECT. "Oneida Community (1848-1880): A Utopian Community." Accessed July 20, 2025. https://socialwelfare.library.vcu.edu/religious/the-oneida-community-1848-1880-a-utopian-community.

VEERA. "Exploitation on the Menu: Labor Trafficking in the Restaurant Industry." Stop Modern Day Slavery, July 2021. https://stopmoderndayslavery.org/2021/07/exploitation-on-the-menu-labor-trafficking-in-the-restaurant-industry.

VENHAUS, JOHN M. *Why Youth Join al-Qaeda*. Special Report no. 236. Washington, DC: United States Institute of Peace, 2010. https://www.usip.org/sites/default/files /resources/SR236Venhaus.pdf.

VINE, DAVID. *The United States of War: A Global History of America's Endless Conflicts, from Columbus to the Islamic State*. University of California Press, 2020.

VINNEY, CYNTHIA. "The Psychology of Dehumanization." Verywell Mind, December 10, 2024. https://www.verywellmind.com/the-psychology-of-dehumanization-8723940.

VINNEY, CYNTHIA. "Why We Worship Celebrities and How It Impacts Our Mental Health." Verywell Mind, updated May 26, 2023. https://www.verywellmind.com /what-is-celebrity-worship-5219745.

VISIMEDIA. "What Makes People Hate MLM?" Warrior Forum. https://www.warriorforum .com/main-internet-marketing-discussion-forum/1354939-what-makes-people -hate-mlm.html.

WALCH, TAD. "Church Announces Cost Increase for Latter-day Saint Missions Beginning in 2020, the First Change in 16 Years." *Deseret News*, June 27, 2019. https://www .deseret.com/2019/6/27/20676566/church-announces-cost-increase-for-latter-day -saint-missions-beginning-in-2020-the-first-change-in-1.

WALKER, JASON. "Burnout: The Dirty Truth About How Employers Benefit From It." *Forbes*, February 5, 2025. https://www.forbes.com/sites/jasonwalker/2025/02/05 /burnout-by-design-the-dirty-truth-about-how-employers-benifit-from-it.

WALLIS, ROY, AND STEVE BRUCE. "Sex, Violence and Religion." In *Sociological Theory, Religion and Collective Action*, edited by R. Wallis and S. Bruce, 115–27. Queens University Belfast, 1986.

WALTER P. REUTHER LIBRARY. "African Americans and the UAW." Wayne State University. Accessed June 20, 2025. https://reuther.wayne.edu/node/10107.

WARNOCK, AMANDA. "The Dehumanization of Immigrants and Refugees." *Journal of Purdue Undergraduate Research* 9 (Fall 2019): 49–59. https://doi.org/https://doi .org/10.5703/1288284316932.

WARREN, ALAN R. *Doomsday Cults: The Devil's Hostages*. Independently published, 2020.

WATSON, ELEANOR, AND ROBERT LEGARE. "Over 80 of Those Charged in the January 6 Investigation Have Ties to the Military." CBS News, December 15, 2021. https://www .cbsnews.com/news/capitol-riot-january-6-military-ties.

WAXMAN, OLIVIA B. "HBO's The Synanon Fix Explores How a Rehab Program Became a Cult-Like Group." *Time*, April 1, 2024. https://time.com/6962417/synanon-fix-true -story-hbo.

WEBBER, DAVID, M. BABUSH, N. SCHORI-EYAL, ET AL. "The Road to Extremism: Field and Experimental Evidence That Significance Loss–Induced Need for Closure Fosters Radicalization." *Journal of Personality and Social Psychology* 114, no. 2 (2018): 270–85. https://doi.org/10.1037/pspi0000111.

WEBER, MAX. "The Nature of Charismatic Authority." In *Theory of Social and Economic Organization*, translated by A. R. Anderson and Talcott Parsons. Free Press, 2009.

WEBER, MAX. *The Protestant Ethic and the Spirit of Capitalism*, translated by Stephen Kalberg. Roxbury, 2003; first published 1905.

WHITE, L. MICHAEL. "Prophetic Belief in the United States: William Miller and the Second Great Awakening." Frontline. Accessed July 20, 2025. https://www.pbs.org/wgbh/pages/frontline/shows/apocalypse/explanation/amprophesy.html

WHITMAN, HOWE. "What the Puritans Can Teach Us About American Exceptionalism." Public Discourse, December 21, 2022. https://www.thepublicdiscourse.com/2022/12/86465.

WHITWORTH, DAMIAN. "Like Paris Hilton, I Was Sent to Brat Camp—It Was Horrifying." *The Times*, July 29, 2024. http://www.thetimes.com/life-style/parenting/article/paris-hilton-brat-camp-horrifying-c507mnphn.

WIEDEMAN, REEVES. "Adam Neumann and the Art of Failing Up." *New York*, June 10, 2019. https://nymag.com/intelligencer/2019/06/wework-adam-neumann.html.

WIENS, KANDI. "How Burnout Became Normal—and How to Push Back Against It." *Harvard Business Review*, April 23, 2024. https://hbr.org/2024/04/how-burnout-became-normal-and-how-to-push-back-against-it.

WILDING, MELODY. "How to Recover from a Toxic Job." *Harvard Business Review*, October 2022. https://hbr.org/2022/10/how-to-recover-from-a-toxic-job.

WILKERSON, ISABELLE. *Caste: The Origins of Our Discontents*. Random House, 2020.

WILLIAMS, C. M. *Active Engagement of Young Adults in the Church and a Sense of Belonging*. EdD thesis, Concordia University, St. Paul, 2019. https://digitalcommons.csp.edu/cup_commons_grad_edd/361.

WILLIAMS, COLLIN. "There Is No Place for a Cult Mentality in Startups—Here's How to Detect and Avoid This Type of Workplace." *Entrepreneur*, January 30, 2024. https://www.entrepreneur.com/leadership/how-to-detect-and-avoid-cult-like-workplaces-and-why-you/468052.

WILLIS, ROBIN EVAN. "The Final Bow: Finding Yourself After Artistic Career Loss." *Psychology Today*, October 28, 2024. https://www.psychologytoday.com/us/blog/road-weary/202410/the-final-bow-finding-yourself-after-artistic-career-loss.

WINELL, MARLENE. "Religious Trauma Syndrome: It's Time to Recognise It." CBT Today, May 2011. https://journeyfree.org/wp-content/uploads/RTS-article-in-CBT-Today.pdf.

WOLF, NAOMI. *The Beauty Myth: How Images of Beauty Are Used Against Women*. William Morrow and Company, 1991.

WONG, LEONARD, AND STEPHEN J. GERRAS. *Lying to Ourselves: Dishonesty in the Army Profession*. US Army War College Press, 2015.

WRIGHT, JAMIE. *The Very Worst Missionary: A Memoir*. Ten Speed, 2017.

WRIGHT, LAWRENCE. *Going Clear: Scientology, Hollywood, and the Prison of Belief.* Alfred A. Knopf, 2013.

WRIGHT, LINDSEYE. "The Jonestown Appeal: A Rhetorical Analysis of Jim Jones' 'The Death Tapes.'" Senior honors thesis, Liberty University, 2024. https://digitalcommons.liberty.edu/honors/1365.

YAKOWICZ, WILL. "Don't Tell Your Employees They're Family." *Inc.*, June 18, 2014. https://www.inc.com/will-yakowicz/dont-tell-your-employees-theyre-family.html.

YANG, JOHN, AND LAURIE SANTOS. "Why Americans Are Lonelier and Its Effects on Our Health." PBS NewsHour, January 8, 2023. https://www.pbs.org/newshour/show/why-americans-are-lonelier-and-its-effects-on-our-health.

YOUNG, DANIELLA MESTYANEK. *Uncultured: A Memoir.* St. Martin's Griffin, 2023.

YOUNGBLOOD, MASON. "Extremist Ideology as a Complex Contagion: The Spread of Far-Right Radicalization in the United States Between 2005 and 2017." *Humanities and Social Sciences Communications* 7 (2020): 49. https://doi.org/10.1057/s41599-020-00546-3.

ZHANG, SHELDON. "Understanding the Organization, Operation, and Victimization Process of Labor Trafficking in the United States." *Trends in Organized Crime* 18 (December 2015): 348–54. https://doi.org/10.1007/s12117-015-9257-9.

ZILBER, ARIEL. "Meta Keeps Secret 'Do Not Rehire' List of Ex-Employees—Despite Exceptional Performance Reviews: Report." *New York Post,* March 7, 2025. https://nypost.com/2025/03/07/business/meta-keeps-a-secret-do-not-rehire-list-of-ex-employees-report.

ZIMMER, BENJAMIN. Message to ADS-L mailing list in response to "figurative 'bootstraps' (1834)," August 11, 2005. The LINGUIST List. https://listserv.linguistlist.org/pipermail/ads-l/2005-August/052756.html.

Index

About the Authors

Daniella Mestyanek Young

Daniella Mestyanek Young is a cult survivor, US Army veteran, Harvard-trained organizational psychologist, and the author of two books about high-control groups—*Uncultured*, her critically acclaimed memoir, and *The Culting of America*, the book you've just heroically finished. (Nice work. That was a lot of cults.)

Born into the Children of God—the infamous sex cult known for weaponizing religion, sexuality, and isolation—Daniella escaped at fifteen, only to join another high-control institution: the United States Army. There, she became one of the first women in Army history to serve on an integrated ground combat team, all while working as an intelligence officer who studied terrorists for a living. Turns out, cults, terrorist groups, military units, and corporations have more in common than anyone wants to admit—and Daniella's been connecting those dots ever since.

Her work sits at the intersection of leadership, identity, group psychology, and coercive control. Whether she's writing, speaking onstage, or teaching you about everyday cults while knitting on TikTok, Daniella is driven by one big question: Why do we give ourselves over to groups—and how do we get our power back?

Amy Reed

Amy Reed is best known for writing critically acclaimed (and often banned) young adult novels, including *The Nowhere Girls*, *Beautiful*, *Clean*, and *Tell Me My Name*. She also serves as editorial director at Otterpine, an independent publishing services company based in Asheville, North Carolina. Amy was part of the writing team for *Uncultured*, the debut memoir by Daniella Mestyanek Young, and most recently co-authored *The Culting of America: What Makes a Cult and Why We Love Them* with her. She is currently working on her first novel for adults.

Ready to Go Deeper?

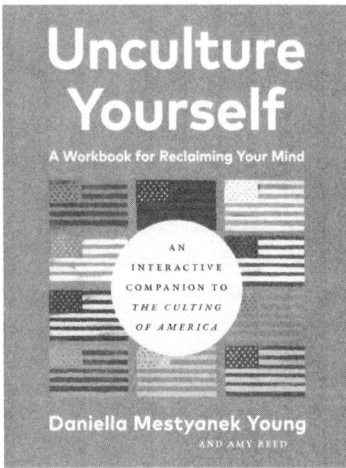

If *The Culting of America* opened your eyes to the invisible systems of control shaping our world, *Unculture Yourself: A Workbook for Reclaiming Your Mind* is your next step.

Designed as a practical companion to the book, this interactive guide will help you unpack how cultlike dynamics show up in your own life—from workplaces to religious communities to friend groups—and begin the process of reclaiming your autonomy.

This isn't your average workbook. No fluff, no toxic positivity. Just real, reflective prompts to help you unpack group dynamics, power, and belonging. With eleven deep-diving sections aligned with the book's chapters, *Unculture Yourself* is a space for honest journaling, self-assessment, and reclaiming your mind—on your terms.

Because it's not just about seeing the cults out there. It's about unculturing yourself, one insight at a time.